INTERMEDIATE MACROECONOMICS

Output, Inflation, and Growth

INTERMEDIATE

D. C. ROWAN

PROFESSOR OF ECONOMICS, UNIVERSITY OF SOUTHAMPTON, ENGLAND

THOMAS MAYER

PROFESSOR OF ECONOMICS, UNIVERSITY OF CALIFORNIA, DAVIS

MACROECONOMICS

Output, Inflation, and Growth

W · W · NORTON & COMPANY · INC ·
NEW YORK

Library of Congress Cataloging in Publication Data

Rowan, David Culloden.
    Intermediate macroeconomics.

    "Some of the material . . . was previously published
as Output, inflation, and growth . . . by D. C. Rowan."
    Includes bibliographies.
    1. Macroeconomics.   I. Mayer, Thomas, joint author.
II. Title.
HB171.5.777   339   72-665
ISBN 0-393-09391-3

1 2 3 4 5 6 7 8 9 0

TO OUR WIVES

Contents

Preface

THE APPROACH OF THIS BOOK emphasizes that economics is a social science which aims to develop testable predictions in terms of measurable concepts. Though it contains a good deal of theory, we have tried consistently to develop the view that theory is meant to be tested. To this end, each chapter is supplemented by questions and exercises, many of which require the use of data from published sources to make simple tests of economic predictions or hypotheses. *This means that the student is asked not only to read through the book but also to work through it.* It also gives the student the opportunity to learn economics in the best of all possible ways—by actually working out problems. By this approach, we hope not only to encourage an appropriate methodological outlook but also to discourage students from thinking, as many do, that economic theory is empty and arid and applied economics mainly unstructured description only loosely related to theory.

Many students are drawn to economics initially by an entirely natural and creditable concern with social problems. Unfortunately many courses, in their anxiety to give an adequate grounding in theory, devote little time to the application of theory to policy issues. The result is sometimes disenchantment. We have tried to avoid this problem by stressing the application of macroeconomic theory to policy problems. In doing so, we have examined issues at the center of the continuing debate between essentially Keynesian economists and the monetarist school.

Perhaps the most awkward problem facing the writer of an intermediate theory text is to decide what use to make of mathematics. The decision taken here is to assume no knowledge of mathematics beyond algebra and, in particular, no knowledge of the differential calculus. This point is important, for many people are discouraged from any systematic study of economics by the belief that the subject is now accessible only to well trained mathematicians. Obviously those who possess a grasp of mathematical methods of analysis, the most powerful tools for thinking yet developed, are in an advantageous position. Nevertheless, it remains true that a command of algebra is enough for the whole of this book.

Not infrequently, the fear of mathematics is misplaced. What looks like "mathematics" is simply the plentiful use of symbols (rather than words) and the frequent employment of the notion of a function. Few students would regard as unintelligible the proposition that "consumption depends upon income." Many, however, regard as "mathematics," and *therefore incomprehensible,* the statement $C = f(Y)$. We have attempted to eliminate this "pseudo-fear" or "symbol phobia" by two methods. The first is to devote a chapter to discussing and illustrating the use of symbols, functions, and identities. The second is to use symbols and functional notation wherever we can in the hope, which our experience suggests to be not entirely unjustified, that growing familiarity with this means of expression (which is becoming increasingly common in the literature and the texts) will breed confidence in its interpretation. To some readers, the result may seem excessively formal, pedantic, or even forbidding. We believe it represents a sensible way of meeting an awkward and unavoidable problem.

Structurally, the book is divided in the following way. Chapters 1–17 develop a predominantly static model of the macroeconomic system. Since most people who embark on economics think, instinctively, in dynamic terms, the static nature of the analysis is given continuous emphasis. Chapters 18–20 are explicitly dynamic. The first gives a short discussion of some aspects of economic growth, emphasizing the supply side of the problem and making use of the familiar, but to many objectionable, concept of the production function. The second gives a brief account of the cycle. The third discusses the problem of rising prices. Finally, Chapters 21–23 seek to relate the analysis of the earlier chapters directly to problems of policy, not in the sense of providing solutions or showing, with full benefit of hindsight, how much better things might have been managed than they were, but in order to show the very formidable difficulties of conducting macroeconomic policy in a dynamic world.

Analytically, the book is planned to follow what might be called "the principle of increasing difficulty." In the early chapters, basic ideas are spelled out in considerable detail; there are many illustrations and not a little repetition. As the book proceeds, the reader is assumed to acquire facility with economic analysis. Exposition becomes briefer and the demands placed upon the reader more severe but never, we hope, too severe.

Just as the exercises are an integral part of the book, so too are the reading lists which follow each chapter. Wherever possible, three types of references have been given: first, there are references which supplement the work of the text; second, there are references which provide an alternative approach to that presented in the text; third, there are references to more advanced treatments of problems discussed in the text.

Economics, though a difficult and, at present, regrettably imprecise subject, is nevertheless exciting and rewarding. We hope that we have communicated some of the excitement of economics to students, whether they intend to go beyond the intermediate course or to complete their study of macroeconomics at this level.

Foreword to the American Edition

WHEN DAVID ROWAN suggested that I prepare an American version of his *Output, Inflation and Growth,* I was very happy to comply because his book is a remarkably clear survey of macroeconomics.

In much of the book I have made only minor changes, changes usually necessitated by institutional differences between the United States and Britain. However, I have eliminated several chapters since the British edition is aimed at students taking their first university level economics course, whereas this version is aimed at students who have previously taken a Principles course. Moreover, due in part to this difference in the intended audience, and in part to differences in the structure of the two economies, I wrote several new chapters for this edition. The following chapters are completely, or in large part, new: Chapters 3 (National Income Measures), 5 (A Sketch of the American Experience), 9 (Theories of the Consumption Function), 11 (The Determinants of Investment), 15 (Prices, Wages, and Output), 17 (The Monetarist Challenge), 20 (Inflation), 21 (Economic Analysis and Economic Policy), 22 (Stabilization Policy: The Means), and 23 (Stabilization Policy: Problems and Difficulties). Professor Rowan made many penetrating comments on these chapters.

One characteristic of this book to which we attach great importance is the large number of problems and exercises at the end of each chapter. In some fields of study, such as history, for example, a student can learn the subject just by reading alone. But in some other fields, such as mathematics, this is impossible. Here one has to do a large number of exercises to grasp the material. Simply reading a text does not suffice. Economics is, in some ways, similar to both history and mathematics. It *is* possible to learn economic theory merely by reading, but this is not an efficient way of learning it. To make the material his own, the student has to apply it as well as read it. This is why we have included so many problems and exercises. We hope that they will involve the student in a more active—and hence more satisfying and efficient—way of learning than would be provided by a passive text.

In conclusion, I would like to express my gratitude to Professors Edmund S. Phelps of Columbia University and Thomas Sargent of the University of Minnesota for their numerous comments throughout the manuscript and to Professor David Fand of Wayne State University for his helpful comments on Chapter 17. My wife, Dorothy, provided help with the charts, and Mrs. Marguerite Crown valiantly typed a very messy manuscript. At W. W. Norton, Donald S. Lamm greatly facilitated my task throughout, Calvin Towle provided excellent copy editing, and Marjorie J. Flock undertook the designing. To all of these my sincere thanks.

THOMAS MAYER

University of California, Davis
February 1972

Foreword to the British Edition

THIS BOOK WAS BEGUN as long ago as 1955 when I held a lectureship at the University of Melbourne. Like most texts it developed from a lecture course—in this case an introduction to macroeconomics—which I then gave. In 1956 I moved to the University of New South Wales (then the New South Wales University of Technology) and by then the first draft was nearly two-thirds complete.

At New South Wales it was, for various reasons, impossible to complete the text. The finished chapters, however, were used as the basis for an introduction to macroeconomics which formed part of the first-year economics course for those reading for the Bachelor of Commerce degree.

In 1960 I returned to the U.K. and took up my present appointment at the University of Southampton. By 1964 it became possible to work on the book again and, by 1965, the basic draft was, at long last, complete. Since the end of 1965 I have undertaken considerable revisions.

In the task of revision I have been greatly helped by the constructive criticisms of those economists who have so generously read the book in whole or in part. So many economists have helped me in this way that I cannot thank each individually. I must, however, record particularly deep debts of gratitude to J. M. Fleming (University of Bristol); C. S. Soper (University of Melbourne); A. J. Hagger (University of Tasmania); E. B. Butler (University of Sheffield); and A. G. Ford (University of Warwick). Those defects which the book still retains must be attributed entirely to the shortcomings—and the obstinacy—of the author.

My thanks are also due to Dr. Shipra Dasgupta, Mr. D. Crossfield and Mrs. E. Rick, who prepared many of the tables and diagrams, and to

Mrs. P. Dunn, who has so painstakingly and patiently typed the many drafts and revisions.

I am also particularly grateful to Miss Diana Marshallsay, who was not only responsible for the Index but who also gave me immense help with the checking of proofs.

Finally I must record my debt to the many undergraduates of Melbourne, New South Wales and Southampton who, over the eleven years in which the book has been in preparation, have taught me so much about the way in which introductory courses should be taught.

D. C. ROWAN

University of Southampton
January 1968

INTERMEDIATE MACROECONOMICS

Output, Inflation, and Growth

1

The Process of Economic Analysis

THIS BOOK DEALS WITH the four main problems. They are:

1) what determines the level of output in any period;

2) what determines the rate at which "output" grows between any two periods;

3) what determines the general level of prices in any period;

4) what determines its rate and direction of change between any two periods.

We have thus selected particular aspects of the economic system for intensive study. How are we to set about analyzing these problems?

Since our aim is to develop a theory which explains the determination of output—that is, why output is what it is in any period and not some greater (or smaller) magnitude—our first task is that of economic description.

Since we hope to develop a theory which will explain the facts, we need to know what the facts are. The purpose of *economic description* is to give a systematic account of the facts which is, at one and the same time, sufficiently detailed for our purposes and sufficiently simple for us to comprehend it. Two processes are involved here: the definition, in operational terms, of a set of concepts with which a complex economic reality can conveniently be described; and the use of these concepts to provide a description.

All this no doubt sounds somewhat confusing. We shall now try to clarify it by an example.

What the economic system produces, in any period of time we may use for accounting purposes, is a flow of dissimilar goods and services. In principle it would be possible to make a detailed list of the quantity of each good and service produced in any given period. But such a list would contain several millions of dissimilar items many of which would need to be measured in different units. The result would be comprehensive but not readily comprehensible. Moreover there is no obvious way in which the quantities of the various heterogeneous goods and services could be added together to produce a single total. What, for example, is the sum of 1.2 million cars, 97 million cabbages, 7 million "books" (themselves not homogeneous), 3 new aircraft carriers, a new cathedral, and 2 new atomic warheads?

To deal with this difficulty we make use of an abstract concept of output. This has two characteristics:

1) it possesses the capacity to satisfy human wants[1];
2) it requires the use of scarce resources to produce it.

This definition it should be noted, is derived directly from the observation that all scarce goods—that is, goods which command a price—share the common property of being able in some degree to satisfy human wants.

Thus defined, output cannot be observed directly. All that can be observed is the flow of heterogeneous goods and services which are scarce (that is, command a price) and which are produced in any period. In addition to our definition we therefore need to write down a set of rules which will enable us to say that a given flow of heterogeneous goods and services is equal to a particular flow of output. Once this has been done, output is, in principle, *measurable*: that is, the abstract notion of "output" has been made operational. Provided we are prepared to undertake the work of measurement, or find someone to do it for us, we can then give a comprehensive, comprehensible, and numerical description of the facts in which we are interested.

In the next two chapters we shall discuss in some detail the concepts (of which "output" is only one) that we shall need to use to describe those facets of economic behavior which interest us. We shall also discuss how these concepts can be measured. At this stage, however, we anticipate some of our later results by introducing a graph on which three variables are plotted against time for 1929–1970. These three variables are

1) output;
2) industrial production;
3) the percentage of the labor force unemployed.

We shall not now comment on this set of observations of recent economic events. You are invited, however, to make a list of those problems in positive economics which Figure 1.1 suggests to you.

---

1. Wants may be satisfied directly or indirectly. Hence a shoe manufacturing machine indirectly, by aiding in the process of shoe production, satisfies wants.

Figure 1.1 / *Gross National Product, index of industrial production* (1967 = 100) *and unemployment.*

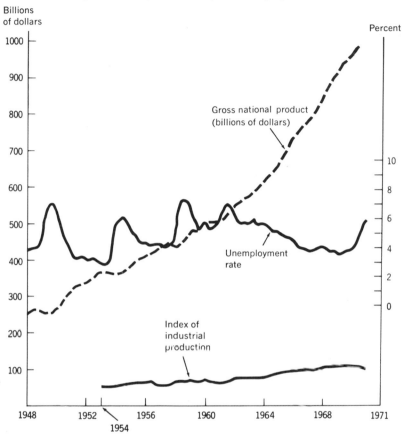

Source: U. S. Department of Commerce, *Business Conditions Digest*, March 1969, October 1971, August 1971; Executive Office of the President, *1971 Economic Report of the President.*

Economic description provides us with a systematic account of what we believe to be the relevant facts. Without some preliminary theory, that is without some notion of what it is we want to investigate, we have, of course, no idea what facts are relevant. Theory and fact in this sense are complementary, not opposed, concepts as the loose expression of everyday speech might lead us to suppose. Description, however, is not itself theory. For description can do no more than summarize for us, within the framework of a chosen conceptual scheme, what *has* happened. It does nothing directly to explain to us *why* whatever it was that happened actually did happen though it may suggest possible lines of inquiry to us. To explain events is the task of theory. What then is a theory?

Since economics is a social science, any economic theory must contain hypotheses concerning the way in which human beings behave. It is these hypotheses, which may obviously be correct or incorrect, which give economic theory its operational significance. These hypotheses must be expressed in terms of the conceptual framework in which the economic events are described. From these hypotheses by a process of logical deduction, we derive *predictions* in terms of the conceptual framework which we have used to describe events. These predictions can then be tested against actual observations. If our observations conform to our predictions, we may say that our theory is not refuted by events. We cannot say that it is "correct," for other observations may, and eventually will, be made which force us to modify or abandon it. On the other hand if our predictions are not in conformity with observations, our theory is refuted and must be abandoned or modified.

All this sounds very difficult and possibly rather dull. In some cases it is difficult though it is never dull. A simple example may aid in clarification. Suppose we are interested in explaining the monthly production of beer. We first define beer in such a way that the monthly production of it can be measured: that is, we provide an operational definition. This is not quite so simple as it sounds, for beer, like goods and services, is not homogeneous. Our definition must be in some degree arbitrary. Armed with our definition, we can measure "beer" production in each month and plot it on a graph.

Let us assume that the resultant curve looks like Figure 1.2. How are we to develop a theory to explain the fluctuations in production revealed by this graph?

From our discussion of the workings of a market economy we can argue that beer producers will try to adjust the quantity of beer produced in any month to the quantity consumed. For if they produce more than this, either stocks of unsold beer will accumulate (and deteriorate) or beer prices will fall. Either way producers will make less profit than they otherwise would. Equally if they produced less beer than the public wanted to consume, the producers would be forgoing profits. Since producers pursue profits and seek to avoid losses, we may assume that they aim to produce the quantity the public wants to purchase at the ruling market price. Accordingly we may adopt the hypothesis that beer producers will plan to produce in any month the quantity of beer they expect that the public will want to buy. How do they form their expectations?

The main guide we have to the future is what has happened in the past. We can thus think of brewers in general as adjusting their production of beer in each month to the consumption of beer in the previous month.

Figure 1.2 / *The quantity of beer produced over a period of 4 years (hypothetical data).*

Hence, we can write our first hypothesis about human behavior thus:

beer production in January = beer consumption in December.

We now need to formulate some hypothesis about the beer-drinking decisions of people in general in order to explain consumption. We should expect some systematic seasonal variation in monthly beer consumption due ultimately to variations in climatic conditions. It also seems reasonable to argue that, given the "weather" conditions, people drink more beer when they are more "prosperous." But surely, given the "weather" and the "degree of prosperity," people will drink more beer the "cheaper" it is in relation to other forms of alcohol. If whisky cost, per pint, the same as beer, would not people drink more whisky and less beer?

These considerations lead to a simple hypothesis about human behavior which states that

the quantity of beer consumed in any month depends upon
1) the "weather" in that month;
2) the general degree of "prosperity" in that month
3) the "cheapness" of beer in relation to other forms of alcohol in that month.

We now have to give operational meaning to our notions of "the weather," "the general degree of prosperity," and the relative "cheapness" of beer. This is not hard. In any month we can measure the weather by the average hours of sunlight or average daily temperature. Similarly since the "general level of prosperity" is likely to be inversely related to the percentage of the labor-force unemployed we can measure the "degree of prosperity" by the reciprocal of this percentage. To measure the "cheapness" of beer let us take the price of whisky as a proxy for the price of other forms of alcohol. Then the "cheapness" of beer is measured by: price of whisky (per bottle)/price of beer (per pint).

We now have three behavior hypotheses. These are:

1) beer producers (brewers) pursue profits and seek to avoid losses: hence they try to adjust production to expected consumption;

2) the rule they follow to do this is to make production in any month equal to consumption of the previous month;

3) consumption in any month depends upon:

    (*a*) average temperature;

    (*b*) the reciprocal of the percentage of the labor-force unemployed;

    (*c*) the ratio of the price of whisky to the price of beer.

We can now use our theory—in which every variable is operationally defined—to generate a number of predictions. Some typical predictions are as follows:

if, in any month, with no change in the "weather" (temperature) and no changes in the relative "cheapness" of beer (price of whisky in relation to price of beer) unemployment rises as a percentage of the labor force, then

1) beer consumption in the *same* month will fall; and

2) beer production in the *following* month will fall by an equivalent amount.

Predictions of this kind can be tested against observations of what actually occurs. If the observations conform with our predictions, we may continue to hold our theory. If they do not, we must abandon it.

The example is, of course, artificially simplified. As a result the process of deducing predictions logically from the behavior assumptions is extremely easy. It consists in saying:

$$
\text{if}
\left\{
\begin{array}{c}
A \\
\text{increase in the} \\
\text{percentage of the} \\
\text{labor-force unemployed}
\end{array}
\right\}
\begin{array}{c}
\text{occurs in} \\
\text{context}
\end{array}
\left\{
\begin{array}{c}
C \\
\text{no change in average} \\
\text{temperature} \\
\text{no change in the ratio} \\
\dfrac{\text{whisky prices}}{\text{beer prices}}
\end{array}
\right.
$$

$$
\text{then}
\left\{
\begin{array}{c}
B \\
\text{decrease in beer} \\
\text{consumption}
\end{array}
\right\}
\text{will occur.}
$$

$$\text{If } B \text{ occurs then } \left\{ \begin{array}{c} D \\ \text{fall in beer} \\ \text{production} \end{array} \right\} \text{ occurs one month later.}$$

An alternative way of putting the same thing is to say:
If, other things being equal (often written *ceteris paribus*), the percentage of the labor force unemployed in any month *rises, then,* in the same month beer consumption will fall, *and* in the next month beer production will fall by an equivalent amount.

In many economic theories the chain of reasoning, though ultimately reducible to this form, may be much more complicated. We may for example have to argue that, on our behavior hypotheses,

if *A* occurs in context *C*, then *Z* will occur	
if *Z* occurs	*Q* will occur
if *Q* occurs	*R* will occur
if *R* occurs	*S* will occur
if *S* occurs	*B* will occur.

Here again we can make the same predictions as before—*if A then B*—but only after a good deal more intellectual effort. But the greater complexity of the second example does not alter the fundamental nature of the process. This is the derivation of testable (or meaningful) predictions from hypotheses about human behavior. It is because positive economics seeks to develop testable predictions of this kind that it can lay claim to the adjective "scientific"—for the essential nature of scientific inquiry is precisely the development of predictions which can conceivably be tested by observation and experiment.

Two further points of great importance also emerge from this example. *Notice that the basic assumption of our method is that there is regularity in human behavior—in this case human beer drinking behavior and the production planning of brewers.* If there was no regularity, our behavior hypotheses would be false. Beer consumption would fluctuate capriciously from month to month and no systematic explanation would be possible. The assumption of regularity is, of course, familiar enough in the natural sciences. Is it a reasonable assumption in the social sciences?

To answer this question consider what would happen if there were no regularities in economic phenomena. Not only would beer consumption fluctuate capriciously—so would the consumption of all other commodities. Business planning, whatever producers tried to do, would be virtually impossible. Now as a matter of common observation business planning, though difficult, is not impossible. Hence we may argue that regularity is present in sufficient degree to make some prediction conceivable.

The second point to notice is that, in expressing our behavior assumption, we spoke deliberately of people in general. We are trying, in other words, to formulate hypotheses about group behavior—not individual behavior. Predicting individual behavior is notoriously difficult even if we choose individuals whom we have known intimately for most of our lives. Predicting group or average behavior is, however, far simpler. Why is this?

To see why, consider the case of an insurance company which proposes writing a life insurance policy for a man of 30. The policy is to mature at age 60. Medical examination shows no obvious physical defects. The man is, let us say, a librarian. Now the insurance company has no means of knowing at what age any particular man will die. Our librarian may be run over and killed ten minutes after the policy comes into force. Alternatively he may live to 90. On the other hand, from the statistics of deaths, the insurance company can easily calculate the percentage of "average healthy" adult male librarians who die at any given age. These percentages can be plotted on a graph like Figure 1.3.

Figure 1.3 / *The percentage (hypothetical data) of "average healthy" adult male librarians who die at any given age.*

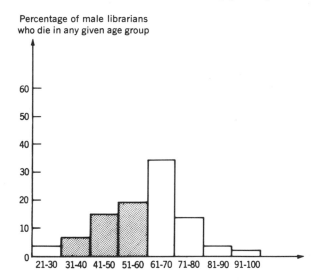

The next step is simply to interpret these percentages as "probabilities." The most probable age bracket in which death occurs is shown to be 61–70. Equally the probability of the average adult male librarian dying before the age of 31 is 0.03. The insurance company can now readily calculate the proportion of cases in which 30-year-old males will die before the age of 61. This is the sum of the probabilities in the shaded area. All it then has to do is (1) charge a premium sufficient to cover this risk and leave it a margin of profit and (2) write life policies for a sufficiently large number of librarians for the average behavior to be applicable. In short, life insurance, indeed all insurance, can be conducted profitably because though it is impossible to forecast what will happen in individual cases, it is possible to predict what will happen, on the average, in a large number of cases.

A similar situation exists in physics where the physicist, though he cannot predict the response of an individual electron to a given stimulus, can predict, with a useful degree of accuracy, the average response of a large group of electrons.

We may sum up what we have learned about the process of economic analysis so far as follows.

1) The first stage is to *select* a problem;
2) The second stage is *economic description* which consists in:
    (a) *defining* operational (or measurable) concepts in terms of which the problem is to be examined;
    (b) *measurement;*
3) The third stage is to formulate, in terms of these concepts, *hypotheses* (or *assumptions*) about human behavior;
4) The fourth stage is to derive, by logical processes, *conclusions* or *predictions* in terms of the concepts already defined.

These four stages are sometimes referred to as the development of a "model" of the economy (or a part of the economy).

5) The fifth stage is to test the predictions of the theory or model against observations.

If the predictions are shown to be in conformity with the observations, the theory is not shown to be correct. *It is merely shown not to be incorrect.* We can continue to hold it until its predictions cease to correspond with observation. When this happens we need to develop a new theory or model which generates predictions consistent not only with observations which the old model could explain, but also with observations which the old model could not explain. Our new theory (model) must therefore be more general in its scope than the old.

From this it is easy to see that the advance of knowledge, in all sciences, takes place through the continuous testing and reformulation of theories. Each new theory is more powerful, in the sense of being able to explain a greater range of observations, than the theory it replaces. Reformulation, in short, is a necessary part of the advancement of knowledge. From which it follows that, when we develop a theory or model, we should not simply look around for observations which support it. Even the least useful of theories can be supported by *some* observations. Rather we should seek to expose our model to the most stringent tests our ingenuity can devise. Indeed the golden rule for anyone studying positive economic theory is to ask himself continually the question: What *testable or falsifiable predic-*

tions does this theory generate? This, as we shall see in later chapters, is often a difficult question to answer.

We have now said enough about the process of economic analysis to make it clear that what we have called "positive economics" deals with issues which can be settled ultimately only by an appeal to the facts. This indeed is the characteristic of what we earlier called "how" or "why" questions.

By contrast, "normative economics" deals with questions which cannot be settled by an appeal to the facts. Consider for example the statement "The Government ought to raise taxes on cigarettes by 10 cents per pack of 20 in order to reduce lung cancer." This, on analysis, consists of three propositions:

1) if a tax of 10 cents per pack is imposed, then cigarette consumption per year will fall by a certain amount;

2) if cigarette consumption falls by this amount, then the incidence of lung cancer will decline;

3) it is desirable that the incidence of lung cancer should decline.

Proposition (1) is easily recognizable as a prediction about the way the economic system works. It is a proposition in *positive economics.* Proposition (2) is similarly a prediction in human biology. Both these propositions can, in principle, be tested by an appeal to observation.

Proposition (3) is, however, of an altogether different kind. It asserts that a reduction in the incidence of lung cancer is "good" or "desirable." We may agree with this. *But if we do not, the disagreement can never be settled by any appeal to the facts.* This is because Proposition (3) is what is called a "value judgment." It reflects the "value judgment" that one state of affairs is "better" than another. In general, though possibly not in this case, many people will disagree over judgments of this kind. Their disagreements however cannot be resolved by observation or research.

It follows that normative propositions in economics involve not only propositions in positive economics, which can be tested by an appeal to the facts, but also value judgments which cannot. This does not mean that normative propositions are unimportant. They are of very great importance, and we shall devote part of this book to the examination of some "normative" issues. What it does mean is that the student, particularly in his reading of the popular and semitechnical press, should be careful to distinguish positive economic statements from value judgments. For the former he should demand evidence. For the latter he can merely offer agreement or disagreement. In the same way, he should draw the same distinction in his own thinking and writing and, where his value judgments are inevitably involved, seek to make clear precisely what they are and where they enter the argument.

The terminology employed here seeks to distinguish between positive and normative economics because this distinction is useful pedagogically. The reader, however, must not fall into the trap of thinking that normative economics, as we have used the term, is in any sense inferior to positive economics. This view can all too easily be arrived at through excessive contemplation of the rather elementary examples used to illustrate what is meant by "normative." By definition normative propositions involve a value judgment and the value judgments involved are frequently unacceptable to the reader. At the same time the examples offered, in the interests of simplicity, often appear to require very little positive economic analysis. It is thus only too easy to assume that disputes over normative economic propositions are largely nontechnical disputes over value judgments. Any assumption of this kind is entirely unjustified. Indeed some of the most promising (and most technical) modern developments in economics, including linear and other programming techniques, are concerned precisely with the problem of how best to reach a given objective and are thus, in the general sense, normative.

Properly speaking, therefore, normative economics is concerned with economic problems in which some objective (or target) is either given explicitly or implied. Thus if a businessman's objective is to maximize profits, then given this target his problem is to discover how to do it. This is frequently a complicated programming problem.

By contrast, positive economics is concerned to describe, explain, and ultimately predict what actually occurs in the economic system.

SUMMARY

1. Positive economic analysis of a selected problem consists of
   a) economic description, which entails (1) the definition of measurable concepts; (2) measurement;
   b) formulation of behavior hypotheses in terms of these definitions;
   c) generation of testable or falsifiable predictions (in terms of the definitions) from the behavior assumptions;
   d) testing the predictions against observations.

2. Positive economics is thus concerned with issues which can, in principle, be settled by the examination of evidence.

3. The fundamental assumption of positive economics is that, on the average, the behavior of man in the everyday business of earning a living exhibits sufficient regularity to make possible a predictive science of economics.

4. That there are observable regularities in economic behavior is beyond dispute. What matters, however, is the degree of precision in pre-

diction these regularities permit and whether positive economics can attain a useful degree of precision.

     5. Normative economics consists of

          a) predictions derived from positive economics which are, in principle, testable coupled with

          b) value judgments which cannot be tested.

QUESTIONS AND EXERCISES

1. Using the theory of beer production outlined in the text, generate *ceteris paribus* predictions for the results of a "heat wave" in July; an additional ten percent tax on whisky in April; a survey showing that beer is the most popular drink of the elite published in March. In each case what is the precise meaning in terms of the theory of *ceteris paribus?*

2. What do we mean by saying that our predictions are in conformity with the facts? Plot on a graph the predicted values given by the table and compare them with the observed values. Plot also the difference between the predicted and observed values. Which is the "better" theory? Why? Give your reasons. What can you learn from examining the errors?

YEAR	ACTUAL VALUE	VALUE PREDICTED BY: THEORY 1	THEORY 2
1	100	100	101
2	51	51	50
3	43	44	42
4	43	44	41
5	47	49	49
6	62	64	61
7	81	83	82
8	111	113	112

3. Develop, on the general principles of our theory of beer production, an operational theory to explain the monthly production of automobiles in the United States. Use your theory to generate *ceteris paribus* predictions for the results of an increase in required down payments; a reduction in the excise tax; a reduction in U.S. tariffs on imported cars. Treat each case separately and, for each prediction, give a precise meaning, in terms of your theory, to *ceteris paribus.*

4. Can you develop an operational theory which would make it possible to test the proposition, "The root cause of juvenile delinquency is simply broken homes"?

5. "A tax on the magazine advertising of tobacco could not fail to bring immense social benefits." Analyze the propositions implied in this statement. Has it any meaning?

6. Is there any way of testing the following propositions?
   Honesty is, in the long-run, always the best policy.
   The higher the rate of tax on increments in income, the less professional men will be disposed to work.
   Virtue is always rewarded—in this world or the next.
   Women are inferior (superior) to men.

7. Suppose you are the son (or daughter) of a brewer who tells you that he neither seeks to maximize his profits nor plans his monthly beer production to be equal to the previous month's consumption. Does his statement invalidate the theory put forward in this chapter? If not, why not?

8. According to Fig. 1.2 beer production has a general tendency (trend) to rise from 1968 to 1971, for each successive seasonal peak (and trough) is higher than its predecessor. Can this be explained in terms of the model in the text? If so how? If not what additions would you make to the theory to explain it? Give your reasons.

9. What are the obvious objections to the beer model in the text? How would you seek to improve it? In what way do your modifications change its predictions?

10. Assume that brewers commonly hold stocks of beer. On the basis of the model in the text—and Fig. 1.2—graph the path of these stocks over time. Does this graph help you to answer Question 9?

11. "No theory predicts with complete accuracy: there is always some error." Do you agree? If so what is the difference between a "prediction" derived from a theory and a "guess"?

12. If the statement quoted in Question 11 is correct, how does science advance?

13. Meteorologists predict the weather. So do witch doctors. In what sense, if any, do they differ? If they do not, is it correct to regard a witch doctor as a scientist? And vice versa?

14. "That experience of privation in youth gives sound character in middle age is amply attested by research." Consider this statement. Do you think it reasonable? Can you think of the way in which research might have led to this conclusion?

15. "The essence of science consists in specifying the range of error of a prediction. The advance of science consists in reducing the error." Consider these statements carefully.

16. To many philosophers the distinction between positive and normative economics made in this chapter is unacceptable. Can you think of reasons why the distinction might break down?

17. "Corporal punishment should be used in place of prison sentences. It could be of a magnitude which would leave criminals no worse off than a prison sentence, and there is reason to think that those inflicting the punishment would enjoy it. Hence, it would increase welfare." Is this argument scientific?

SUGGESTED READING

J. Robinson, *Economic Philosophy* (New York: Anchor Books) Chap. 1.

F. Zeuthen, *Economic Theory and Method* (Cambridge: Harvard Univ. Press, 1955) Chaps. 1–5.

R. G. Lipsey, *An Introduction to Positive Economics,* 2nd ed. (London: Weidenfeld & Nicolson, 1967) introduction and Chap. 1.

M. Friedman, *Essays in Positive Economics* (Chicago: Univ. of Chicago Press, 1953) Chap. 1. *Advanced reference.*

T. W. Hutchinson, *The Significance and Basic Postulates of Economic Theory* (London: Macmillan, 1938). *Advanced reference.*

A. R. Louch, *Explanation and Human Action* (Berkeley: Univ. of California Press, 1969) Chaps. 4, 5. *Advanced reference.*

R. Rudner, *Philosophy of Social Science* (Englewood Cliffs, N.J.: Prentice-Hall, 1966).

C. Hempel, *Fundamentals of Concept Formation in Empirical Science, International Encyclopedia of Unified Science,* Vol. II, No. 7 (Chicago: Univ. of Chicago Press, 1952).

2

Definition of Concepts and Measurement of Output

IN THIS CHAPTER we define some of the concepts which we shall need to employ in describing how the economy operates and developing a theory to explain why the economy operates as it does.

Our picture of the economy, which is very much simplified, is this. Resources, which we shall call *factors of production,* are combined in various ways, by *firms* or *enterprises,* to produce an annual flow of *goods* and *services.* We define these terms as follows:

The *factors of production* are defined to be *land, labor,* and *capital.*

Land consists of natural resources provided free by nature: examples are mineral deposits, forests, and, surprisingly enough, water in the form of rivers and natural lakes.

Capital consists of all those aids to production which have been made by man. Examples are machinery, roads, houses, railways, tools, canals, and man-made lakes.

Labor consists of human resources. These are partly mental and partly physical. They are also partly inherited and partly acquired.

Production is the process of making goods and services which is organized by *enterprises.*

Enterprises are organizations (which may take various legal forms such as public companies, private companies, partnerships, nationalized corporations) which take economic decisions.

Those enterprises which take decisions relating to production we call *productive enterprises.*

This system of classification is set out schematically in Figure 2.1.

Here we see the factors of production, i.e., services of land, labor, and capital, being organized as *inputs* by enterprises so as to produce an *output* of goods and services.

Figure 2.1 / *The organization of production.*

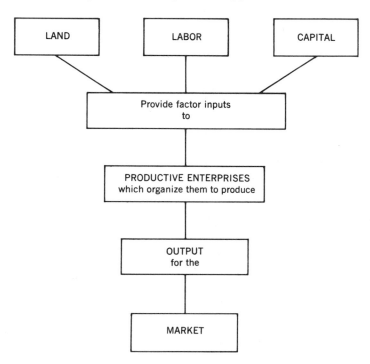

This flow of goods and services (or output) is available for the satisfaction of human wants. The process of using these goods and services for the satisfaction of immediate wants is called *consumption;* and goods that are used for this purpose we assume to be used up (or consumed) either at the moment of purchase or a very short while afterwards. Beer, for example, is an obvious type of consumption good and the purchase of beer an obvious form of *consumption expenditure*. In other cases such as expenditure on durable goods the distinction between *consumption* and *investment* is more difficult to draw.

Not all goods produced by the economy in any period are *consumed*. Some are added to the capital stock of the economy existing at the beginning of the period. *This process of adding to the capital stock is called investment.* Notice that this definition differs from popular usage.

Obviously, in any period, that part of output which is not *consumed* must be added to the capital stock existing at the beginning of the period.

This increment in capital is, by definition, *investment*. Hence the total flow of output becoming available to the community in any period is, again by definition, equal to the sum of the flows of *expenditure* on *consumption* and *investment*. This equality, which is illustrated in Figure 2.2, can be simply expressed as follows:

$$pO \equiv pC + pI,$$

where

pO is money value of the flow of goods and services in a given period;

pC is money value of the flow of consumption expenditure in that period;

pI is money value of the flow of investment expenditure in that period;

p is the price level, i.e., the price of a unit of output.

So that

O is the real flow of goods and services.

C is the real flow of consumption expenditure.

I is the real flow of investment expenditure.

This equality is written with three horizontal lines instead of the usual two to indicate that it is an *identity which is always true,* not an equation which is satisfied only for certain values of O, C and I.

The identity $pO \equiv pC + pI$ is illustrated in Figure 2.2, where we have introduced the new concept *households*. A household is defined as an individual (or group of individuals) that receives income from the sale of

Figure 2.2 / *National expenditure and national product.*

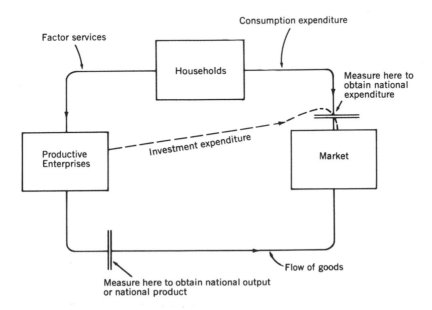

factor services and engages in consumption expenditures. Though in practice the household sector of the economy does engage in investment expenditure also, we have assumed here, and in general shall continue to assume, that (1) all consumption expenditure is made by *households;* (2) all investment expenditure is made by *productive enterprises.*

There is one difficulty here which needs to be faced if it is not to cause confusion. It relates to the meaning of investment expenditures.

As far as consumption expenditures are concerned, there is, in general, little difficulty in relating these expenditures to a money flow. By and large consumption goods are bought (by consumers) and sold (by enterprises) at identifiable market prices. As goods flow from enterprises to households, money flows from households to enterprises.

This analogy holds satisfactorily for investment where the investment of an enterprise consists in expenditure on some good (say a machine tool) which is produced and sold by some other enterprise. Again there is a money flow and an identifiable price.

Now consider the case (say of a farmer) where the investment by the farmer consists of the accumulation of inventories (stocks). Suppose, for example, the farmer grows a crop of which some part is sold to consumers. Again a money flow exists and there is an identifiable price. The remainder of the crop, that which is *unsold,* the farmer retains. It is thus an addition to his capital stock and, by definition, constitutes investment. But there is no money flow. The farmer does not purchase this part of the crop for himself. Moreover there is no identifiable market price.

To deal with this situation we assume an imputed expenditure by the farmer on the unsold part of his crop: that is, an investment in the form of inventory accumulation. Moreover we value this investment at the price at which the remainder of the crop was sold in the market. On this basis the value of output in any period is, by definition, equal to the value of expenditure on output though not all expenditures now can be identified with actual money flows. Some consist of imputed money flows.

Now $C + I$, if we measure it as a money flow, is simply the sum of the expenditures, valued at the prices ruling in the period, on output produced in the period and thus available for the satisfaction of human wants. Hence in any period the value of output, at the prices ruling in the period, is always by definition equal to the value of expenditure on that output. Thus for the economy of any country we may write:

the value of national output $\equiv$ the value of national expenditures $\equiv$ the value of consumption *plus* the value of investment.

The upshot of these simple considerations is that we have now developed a set of rules for measuring output. We add together the heterogeneous collection of goods and services becoming available in any period for the satisfaction of human wants by valuing each at its price. The resultant total is then expressible in terms of monetary units. It is simply the money value of national output or national product. For example suppose we picture a simple community which produces, in a given period, the following goods which become available for the satisfaction of human wants:

1000 loaves of bread
10 wheelbarrows
800 suits of clothes.

If the price of a loaf of bread is $0.50, that of a wheelbarrow $10, and that of a suit $100, then the value of national output, at these prices, is

$$\$[1000 \times 0.50 + 10 \times 10 + 800 \times 100] = \$80,600$$

We have thus established a method of adding together a heterogeneous collection of goods so as to produce a single readily comprehensible measure.

At this stage it is convenient to introduce four assumptions which are of considerable importance. In what follows we shall continue to assume (as we have in Figure 2.2) that

all *consumption* expenditure is made by *households;*
all *investment* expenditure is made by *enterprises;*
there is no government sector;
the economy does not engage in international trade.

On the basis of these assumptions we can now draw Figure 2.3. This shows a flow of *factor services* from *households* to *enterprises. Enterprises* use these services in *production.* The result is a flow of *goods* and *services* on to the *market.* The expenditure on goods and services is shown as a flow from *households* in the form of *consumption* plus a flow from *enterprises* in the form of *investment.*

If we measure the flow of goods and services from enterprises to the market, we obtain the value of *national output.* If we measure the flow of expenditure (including the imputed expenditure on stock accumulation) we obtain the value of *national expenditure.* These two totals are equal by definition. Or, as this proposition is usually stated and as we have stated it above,

national output ≡ national expenditure ≡ consumption + investment.

Figure 2.3 is considerably more satisfactory than Figure 2.2, for it shows where households obtain the incomes they spend on consumption and where enterprises obtain the resources they devote to investment. These two problems can now be explained more fully.

The factors of production used by enterprises are owned by the individuals who constitute households. In return for selling their factor services to enterprises these individuals receive rewards which constitute their

Figure 2.3 / *The circular flow of income, output, and expenditure.*

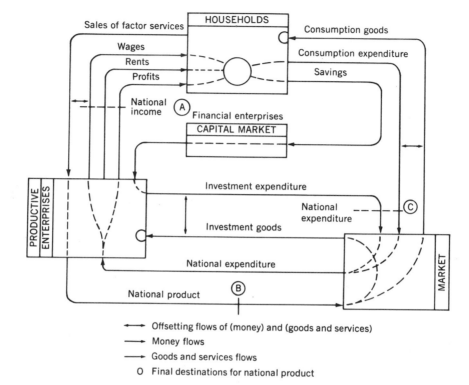

Offsetting flows of (money) and (goods and services)
Money flows
Goods and services flows
O   Final destinations for national product

incomes. For the sale of labor services, the reward is *wages;* for the sale of the services of land and buildings, the reward is *rent;* for the sale of the services of capital (other than buildings) the reward is interest, and for risk bearing it is profit. These are definitions of *factor incomes* or, to the enterprise, *factor costs.* What is cost to one is income to another.

Three of these costs, wages, rent, and interest, are contractual. The fourth, profit is a residual. Profit is now defined as the difference between the value of output and the sum of wages plus interest and rents, the contractual costs incurred in producing it. That is,

the value of output ≡ the values of wages + rent + profits + interest.

National income may now be defined as the *sum of factor incomes generated by the process of production.* Hence:

$$\begin{array}{l} \text{the value of} \\ \text{national output} \end{array} \equiv \text{wages} + \text{rent} + \text{interest} + \text{profits} \equiv \begin{array}{l} \text{national} \\ \text{income} \end{array}$$

Combining this identity with those on earlier pages we have:

$$\frac{\text{national}}{\text{output}} \equiv \frac{\text{national}}{\text{income}} \equiv \frac{\text{wages} + \text{rent}}{+ \text{interest}} \equiv \frac{\text{consumption}}{+ \text{investment}} \equiv \frac{\text{national}}{\text{expenditure}}\cdot$$

This is the fundamental identity of what is called national income accounting. It is always true because we have defined our terms so that it must be. In short, the three aggregates national income, national output and national expenditure are simply three ways of looking at the same thing.

The simple extension of our conceptual scheme shows where households obtain the income they spend, in part, upon consumption. How do they dispose of the whole of it?

Households do not invest. Hence their income must either be consumed or not consumed. The act of abstaining from consumption we define as *saving.* Hence, from the income disposal side,

$$\frac{\text{national}}{\text{income}} \equiv \frac{\text{sum of wages} + \text{rent}}{+ \text{interest} + \text{profits}} \equiv \text{consumption } \textit{plus} \text{ saving.}$$

However, we already know that national income is identically equal to national expenditure which is identically equal to consumption plus investment. Hence:

$$\frac{\text{national}}{\text{income}} \equiv \frac{\text{consumption}}{+ \text{saving}} \equiv \frac{\text{national}}{\text{expenditure}} \equiv \frac{\text{consumption}}{+ \text{investment}.}$$

So it is obvious that

$$\text{saving} \equiv \text{investment.}$$

We thus reach the conclusion that *as far as our national income accounting framework is concerned, saving and investment are always identically equal. That is, they are equal by definition.*

The commonsense of this result should be obvious. If in some period a part of the national product is not consumed, then, by definition, it is saved. It must therefore be added to the capital stock existing in the economy at the beginning of the period. But we have already defined the process of adding to the capital stock as investment. Hence saving and investment, *as we have here defined them,* are simply two different ways of looking at the same quantity of output.

Now this identity between the accounting concepts of savings and investment has, surprisingly enough, caused a lot of confusion. The student should remember that it is an identity which is true by definition; that it refers to the *results* of past decisions and does not tell us whether those results were expected or unexpected, wanted or unwanted. These are important points, for in the accounting sense, precisely the same identity holds between demand and supply. This can easily be seen as follows. The value of demand in any period can be defined as the value of purchases on the market, for all that is purchased must be demanded. That is:

value of demand ≡ value of purchases.

The value of supply on the other hand must be equal to the value of sales, for all that is sold must be supplied. Hence

value of supply ≡ value of sales.

Now since sales ≡ purchases (they are merely two aspects of the same set of transactions) demand must equal supply *by definition*. This means that, in accounting terms, demand and supply are always identically equal.

Though this last statement is correct, on these definitions, it does not prevent our arguing that demand and supply may be unequal, for when we do we are using the terms in different senses. Analogously there are, as we shall see, senses in which saving and investment can be unequal. In later chapters we shall refer to saving and investment in the accounting sense as actual saving and actual investment. Hence the identity above merely states that

actual or accounting saving ≡ actual or accounting investment

and does not preclude there being other important senses in which saving and investment need not be equal except in special circumstances.

We have now answered the question of where the enterprises obtain the real resources to devote to investment. The answer is, in our conceptual scheme, from the saving of households. The financial flows by which the saving of households is made available to enterprises does not at present concern us. We merely note that they usually occur through the medium of *financial enterprises*—such as banks,—which we define as constituting the *capital market*.

Thus Figure 2.3 sets out the full conceptual framework which we have elaborated. This diagram depicts what is often called the circular flow of income, expenditure, and output. If we enter the diagram at the point *A,* we measure the sum of wages *plus* profits *plus* rents—that is, national income. If we enter at *B* we measure the value of the flow of goods and services produced by enterprises—that is, national output or national product. If we enter at *C* we measure the value of consumption *plus* investment—that is, national expenditure. Whichever point of entry we choose, the total we arrive at will be the same for, as we have seen,

the value of   the value of   the value of
national output   ≡ national income ≡ national expenditure
(or national product)

QUESTIONS AND EXERCISES

1. "It is evident that everything produced in an economy during a period such as a year must have been used up by someone during the period or added to what someone possessed at the end of the period. Therefore national output must be equal to national expenditure." Explain.

2. What is the purpose of measuring national product and expenditure? How far do expenditure estimates represent money flows?

3. Can consumption exceed national income? If so what are the implications of such an excess for saving and investment? Illustrate your answer by reference to a situation in which

$$\text{national income} \equiv \$1,000 \text{ bil.}$$
$$\text{consumption} \quad\ \equiv \$1,100 \text{ bil.}$$

4. "Tests do not measure skill. They measure whatever qualities are necessary to pass tests. In the same way national income is whatever it is that the national income estimates measure." Discuss critically.

5. "The national income is a measure of the money value of goods and services becoming available to the nation from economic activity. It can be regarded in three ways: as a sum of incomes derived from economic activity . . . ; as a sum of expenditure . . . ; or as a sum of the products of the various industries of the nation." *National Income Statistics: Sources and Methods.* Explain.

6. From *The Economic Report of the President,* prepare a table showing quarterly estimates of gross national product cost for 1962–70 at current prices; at constant prices.

7. Express consumers' expenditure, fixed capital formation, and inventory investment as proportions of gross national product. Which item shows the "greater fluctuations"?

8. What is the meaning of the negative investment in inventories in 1954 and 1958? Can gross fixed capital formation ever be negative?

SUGGESTED READING

See the items listed at the end of the following chapter.

3

National Income Measures

IN MACROECONOMICS we try to determine the levels of income and employment. To do this properly we need a fairly precise definition of income. Moreover, if we are going to talk about the level of income in quantitative terms, our definition must be measurable. It is possible to define income in various ways; but some definitions, while useful for theoretical discussions, do not allow the statistician to measure income, and hence limit the extent to which we can test our theories or use them for predictive purposes.[1] Thus, in adopting a definition of income we shall have to give up theoretical elegance and use a definition which, while conceptually crude, allows us to measure what we are talking about. Moreover, as will become apparent in a moment, we need a whole set of definitions rather than just a single one.

PRELIMINARIES

Before going on to talk about the definition of income in some detail, we want to consider briefly why economists focus so much more on income than on employment. One reason is that money income, unlike employment, takes account of prices. A second reason is that we are concerned not only with problems of recession and unemployment, but also with the

1. A standard theoretical definition of income is that income is the amount one can consume within a period without reducing one's stock of capital. This definition is not useful for empirical work because we cannot measure capital precisely.

problem of the growth in productivity. Even if we achieve full employment, we would not be satisfied with our economic performance if per capita income in such a fully employed economy were not growing. In other words, employment is one of several inputs while income is the output. And output is a better measure of welfare than is input. Hence, while we will refer to employment and unemployment from time to time, we will focus primarily upon income. In the short run, the relation between income and employment in our economy is clear; if income declines there must be growing unemployment, and a significant short-run increase in income must be accompanied by rising employment.

We need more than a single definition of income, largely because we have to be clear whose income we are talking about; is it the income of the whole nation, or simply the income of consumers, for example? We therefore define income in several ways which are connected in a formal accounting framework. Like other accounting frameworks, the national income accounting system requires that terms which are often used loosely in other contexts be given precise technical meaning. These technical meanings are not intuitively obvious, and to master them requires memorization in the same way that the vocabulary of a foreign language does. This is unfortunate, but it cannot be helped.

The most obvious total one could start with is the total output of goods and services by each producer. Thus we could add up the output of coal, oil, shoes, leather, retail services, operatic arias, etc. But such a total would not be a meaningful measure of income. The reason for this becomes apparent when one looks at three of the items in the above list: leather, shoes, and retail services. Leather is manufactured into shoes, and then services of a retailer are added to these shoes to get a product the consumer can buy. Suppose the leather costs $5, the shoes, as sold by the factory, $20 and, as bought by the consumer, $30. If we add the value of the leather plus the factory value of the shoes plus the retail value, we get a total of $55. Obviously, something is wrong. And what is wrong is that we have added *gross* outputs and hence have double (or, rather, triple) counted. The shoes sold by the factory contain the leather which the shoe manufacturer bought. He bought the leather for $5 and added $15 of manufacturing services (and other materials) to them. Similarly, the retailer did not create $30 of value when he sold the shoes; before he applied his retail services the shoes were worth $20 already. In adding the leather plus the shoes at the factory plus the shoes at the retail level we have counted the leather three times and the manufactured shoes twice. Instead, we should only have counted the *value added* at each stage. If we do this we end up with a total of $30 rather than $55. It is the sum of these values added which gives us the income which has been produced. And this income, is, of course, equal to the final value of the product as bought by the consumer. All the $30 paid by the consumer for the shoes are income to someone, somewhere along the production chain. Hence, we can look upon income in two ways which must yield an identical total: the value added at each point of production or distribution, or as the value of the output sold to the final purchaser.

When we look at the sum of the values added or at the value of final output of all goods and services produced in the nation, we obtain what is called gross national product (GNP).[2] This is the broadest income total which enters the national income accounting system. It is therefore often used as a criterion of economic welfare—in fact, it is the only measure of national income most people are acquainted with. But, for several reasons, GNP is not a perfect measure of welfare.

One reason is that, though it is tempting to describe GNP as the value of all production during a period, this is not accurate. Many goods and services are produced which are not counted in GNP because GNP, with a few exceptions, counts only those goods and services which are exchanged in the market.[3] It does not count such nonmarket production as the work done by the do-it-yourself addict (a man cutting his own lawn, for example) or the services provided by the housewife. And the latter represent a substantial part of national production. Incidentally, this omission of housewife services creates an amusing paradox. If a man marries his housekeeper, who continues to do the same housework after her marriage, GNP is reduced. The reason why such nonmarket production is excluded from GNP is not that it differs in a fundamental way from market production. It is just that there is no adequate way of measuring it. Transactions which go through a market leave tracks the statistician can follow, but nonmarket transactions do not. Hence, true to the guiding principle that income consists only of things we can measure fairly accurately, the national income statistician excludes such nonmarket output.

A second problem is that the various goods and services entering GNP can only be added up by expressing their values in dollar terms. One relatively minor difficulty this creates is that to compare the GNP's of various years one has to express them in dollars of the same purchasing power—that is, one has to deflate money GNP to obtain real GNP.[4] If a nation's real output is constant and GNP in money terms rises by 20 percent only

2. The term "national" means that this is the output produced by residents of the country. United States GNP thus excludes income such as interest and dividends earned by foreign residents from U. S. sources, but it does include the foreign earnings of American residents.

3. The two most important exceptions are the *imputed* rent, i.e., the free services, which the homeowner received from the ownership of his house, and the free services (such as check clearing) obtained from financial institutions. These items are included in GNP because they can be measured relatively accurately.

4. To express the GNP of the current year in terms of prices ruling in a base year, one has to divide current GNP by the price index of the current year and multiply by the price index of the base year.

because prices have risen by 20 percent, it clearly does not follow that the country is 20 percent better off.

In addition, there is a more subtle difficulty. When valuing each item at its market price we justify this by saying that the market price expresses the utility of the item to the consumer. Hence, national income accounting is not value-free; instead it accepts the values the consumer puts in each item. Provided they cost the same, the religious tract, the pornographic magazine, the conservative pamphlet, and the SDS pamphlet are all equal in the eyes of the national income statistician.[5] And the prices which are established in the market do, of course, depend upon the distribution of income. The reader may consider this to be an undesirable practice; but what is the alternative? If the statistician were to evaluate goods and services on the basis of his own values, we would have almost as many different concepts of GNP as we have national income statisticians, and the resulting anarchy among the data would not be very helpful.

A third reason why GNP is not a good index of welfare is to be found in the *G* part of GNP. It is a gross measure of output—that is, it is calculated before depreciation. Some capital goods wear out in the process of production, while other capital goods lose part of their value with time. Thus a part of each year's production should be treated, not as income, but as offsetting the annual reduction in the value of the existing capital stock. GNP ignores this adjustment. However, there is a related concept, net national product (NNP), which avoids this difficulty. To obtain NNP the statisticians subtract from GNP their estimate of the amount of depreciation. Thus NNP is conceptually a better measure of the nation's income than GNP. However, while some economists do focus on NNP, most economists favor GNP on two grounds: (1) available estimates of depreciation are rather crude so that NNP is estimated less accurately than is GNP; and (2) GNP, by measuring total activity, is a better estimator of the demand for labor than is NNP. (The subtraction of depreciation from GNP is just a bookkeeping adjustment which does not affect the total economic activity taking place.)

One important type of depreciation which is not taken into account either in GNP or NNP is outside the market system. It is the type of damage which does not have to be paid for by the damager; in other words, much of the damage to the environment. Thus a company which does two million dollars of unrequited damage to the environment in the process of producing one million dollars worth of goods enters the national income accounts as a producer of a million dollars of output rather than as a net producer of minus one million dollars as, in principle, it should. The reason why pollution and other forms of environmental destruction

5. However, there is one way in which the statistician allows his value judgments to override those of the market: illegal activities are excluded from GNP.

are not subtracted in the process of going from GNP to NNP is again that, there being no market transactions, there are no adequate data on how much to subtract.

Still another weakness of GNP as a measure of welfare is that it makes no allowance for changes in factor inputs. For example, we could increase GNP substantially by raising the work week from forty hours to eighty hours. Yet most people would not consider this to be an increase in welfare. More realistically, a comparison of current per capita GNP with per capita GNP in, say, 1890 does not take into account the very substantial decrease in working hours since then and hence, *in this way,* understates the increase in welfare. (However, some of the reduction in working hours is offset by an increase in commuting time.)

Finally, there is the fact that GNP, even if it were to measure *economic* welfare accurately, would not be an adequate measure of *total* welfare. Economists are quite aware of the fact that economic welfare is just *one* of the dimensions of human welfare. For example, suppose our value system changed so that people became much more miserable about any lack of economic success. Presumably, they would work harder and GNP would increase. But would this increase total welfare and happiness? Similarly, if we want GNP to increase, one way we could do this would be to legalize certain activities which are now illegal so that they would be counted by the statistician. But playing such a game with economic statistics may not be sound policy.

Given all these problems with GNP and NNP, are these concepts of any use? The answer is yes. Although GNP relates only to one dimension of total welfare, economic welfare is an important *part* of total welfare. When presented with a proposal for increasing GNP, one simply has to ask whether this proposal, if acted upon, would have any unfavorable effects on some other aspect of welfare. If so, one has to make a judgment balancing the various aspects of welfare. Secondly, although GNP is not a complete measure, it does tell us *something* about economic welfare; by keeping in mind the other aspects of economic welfare discussed above, one can make allowances for the deficiencies of GNP as an indicator of economic welfare.

Thirdly, short-run changes in GNP are often used as indicators of the extent to which the economy is operating at full capacity. Thus, during a recession, an increase in real GNP is generally welcomed as an indication that the recession with its accompanying unemployment is over. Fortunately, it is just this sort of problem which we will be dealing with to a large extent in this book.[6]

6. Before leaving this topic it might be worth discussing briefly the question whether long-run GNP estimates actually overstate the rate of growth in economic welfare. There appears to be a fairly widespread opinion that the GNP growth rate greatly overstates the increase in

OTHER INCOME CONCEPTS

Gross national product and net national product are just two of several income concepts used in national income accounting. Another concept is *national income*. While this term is often used in a general way simply to mean the total income of the nation without specifying whether GNP, NNP, or some other measure is meant by it, it also has a technical meaning. This precise technical meaning makes "national income" a narrower concept than NNP. Specifically, it covers only the income received by the public as distinct from the income received, in the first instance, by both the public and the government jointly. Hence it is sometimes called "national income at factor costs." To obtain national income, one of the things we therefore have to do is to subtract indirect taxes, since they are not income to the factors. Consider, for example, a $10 item which is subject to a $1 retail sales tax. GNP and NNP record the transaction as the amount paid by the consumer, $11, because the amount paid by the consumer measures the value of the item to him. But how about the income generated for the producers of the item? Surely, this is $10 rather than $11. Thus national income measures the value of production not at its market cost, but at its "factor cost." And it is the factor cost rather than the market cost of production which the public (as distinct from the government) has available for its own expenditures.

But indirect taxes are not the only relevant item here. Any profit the government earns in selling its products to the public is, after all, very similar to a sales tax in that it does not represent income to the public. Hence, like sales taxes, it has to be subtracted from NNP to obtain national income. On the other hand, suppose the government sells goods and services at a loss, or subsidizes a private producer who does so. Such subsidies can be treated as negative indirect taxes. The public gets as factor payments not only the value of the output as sold in the market, but this value plus the subsidy. (In fact, the subsidy is nothing but the difference between the value of the output and its factor cost.) Hence, these losses and subsidies are added into national income. Conversely, surpluses

---

economic welfare because it deals with only some of the components of economic welfare. But this conclusion is questionable. One of the important aspects of economic welfare which is excluded from GNP is the reduction in the hours of work (and, perhaps one should add, in the unpleasantness of work, as "soft" office jobs replace hard manual labor). In this way the rise in GNP underestimates the growth of economic welfare, and this offsets some of the ways in which GNP overstates the rise. Incidentally, the common notion that industrialization has made the pollution problem much worse than it was in the past is also open to question as anyone who contemplates the amount of smoke created by wood fires should appreciate. In the eighteenth century it was said that travelers approaching London could smell the city before they could see it.

of government enterprises are subtracted. Finally, transfer payments by business are also subtracted, since they do not represent income earned by the factors of production, but merely a gift by one entity (business) to others (charitable institutions and persons).[7] After making these adjustments to NNP, we finally obtain national income.

The national income which is distributed to the factors of production is not the same thing as the income actually received by *persons*. This is so for several reasons. One is that the factors of production are not only individuals but also corporations. Hence, to obtain the next concept, *personal income,* one has to subtract from national income that part which becomes income to corporations but does not become income to persons *during the current accounting period*. All corporate net income is either (1) used to pay taxes, (2) withheld as saving by the corporation, or (3) distributed to stockholders. Only the last of these becomes part of *personal income* during the current accounting period. Obviously, taxes paid by corporations do not represent income received by persons. (To be sure, the government may pay these tax receipts to persons, but if and when this occurs, it is treated as personal income in its own right.) Corporate savings, also called *undistributed corporate earnings,* raise a more complex issue. While they may subsequently, in a later accounting period, be distributed as dividends to stockholders, for the time being they are not income to persons, and hence are not included in personal income. This does not mean that stockholders do not derive an immediate benefit from undistributed corporate profits. Saving by corporations raises their net worth, and this is reflected, at least in rough and ready fashion, in the price of their stock. Hence, corporate savings make the stockholder better off, but do so not via the stockholder's flow of income, but via the value of his wealth holdings. To what extent stockholders are aware of this and allow it to influence their consumption is another matter, a matter which is far from settled at present. (One final point may be worth noting. The procedure actually followed in national income statistics is to include in personal income only dividends paid rather than to include all corporate earnings and then to subtract corporate taxes and undistributed earnings.)

The adjustment for undistributed corporate earnings and corporate taxes is not the only adjustment one has to make to national income to obtain personal income. It is necessary to add an item which is income to persons but not to the whole nation (i.e., to persons, corporations, and government jointly). *Transfer payments* by government (such as unemploy-

---

7. Transfer payments are payments which do not require the recipient to furnish currently an equivalent amount of goods and services in return. Government transfer payments do not have to be subtracted because they are not included in NNP in the first case.

ment compensation, civil service pensions, or social security payments) and by business (such as scholarships for children of employees or the write-off of bad debts) are income to recipients.[8] A man receiving, say, $50 in unemployment compensation has $50 of income he can spend just as much as the man who obtains a $50 paycheck. Hence, we must include these transfer payments in personal income. And the same is true for the recipients of interest payments made by the government on the national debt or by consumers.[9]

On the other hand, there is an item which we have to subtract from national income in the process of getting personal income. This is the employer's part of social security taxes. These payments are not *current* income to the employee on whose behalf they are made, and hence they have to be excluded from personal income.

Only one more step remains to be taken now. Not all of a person's income is available for his own use for consumption or saving—some of it has to be paid in income and social security taxes. Suppose we want to determine a person's consumption. We would be able to do this better if we know his after-tax income than if we merely know his before-tax income. Hence, national income statisticians provide us not only with an estimate of personal income, but also with an estimate of *disposable personal income*—that is, personal income after personal taxes and social security contributions by the employee.

To summarize all of these adjustments, as well as to obtain an idea of the magnitudes involved, let us look at part of the actual national income accounts for 1970 shown in Table 3.1.

Most of the entries in this table have already been discussed, and all but one of the remainder are explained in the footnotes to the table. The exception is the item called "statistical discrepancy." It is just that. National income statistics are estimated from a wide variety of basic data, and the estimation techniques require such things as projecting on the basis of preliminary or partial data, or estimating on the basis of trends. Of necessity, the data are inaccurate. Hence, when one looks at the data on

8. The reader may recall that business transfer payments were taken out of NNP to get National Income because they do not represent income to the nation as a whole. But they have to be added back in now because they are income to persons. But if they are not income to the whole nation, how can we treat them as income to persons? The answer is that we adjust corporate saving accordingly. Suppose that a corporation makes a $1000 gift. This occasions two entries in the national income accounts. On the one hand, the income of persons goes up by $1000, but, on the other hand, undistributed corporate profits fall by $1000. Hence, the increase in personal income is offset by a decrease in an item we must add to personal income to get national income.

9. The treatment of interest on the national debt and on consumer debt is by no means a clear-cut matter. One *could* argue that they represent regular income earned in the provision of a service and hence should be included in GNP rather than just in personal income. In fact, interest paid by consumers was treated as part of GNP until 1966.when the national income accounts were revised.

Table 3.1 / *Relation of Gross National Product,
disposable personal income, and related concepts, 1970.*

	BILLINGS OF DOLLARS	PERCENT OF GNP	PERCENT OF PREVIOUS TOTAL
Gross National Product	974.1	100.0	—
Less: Capital consumption allowances[a]			
Equals: Net National Product	886.5	91.0	91.0
Less: Indirect business tax and nontax liability[b]			
Business transfer payments			
Statistical discrepancy			
Plus: Subsidies less current surplus of government enterprises			
Equals: National income	795.9	81.7	89.8
Less: Corporate profits and inventory valuation adjustment[c]			
Contributions for social insurance			
Wage accruals less disbursements[d]			
Plus: Government transfer payments to persons			
Interest paid by government (net) and by consumers			
Dividends			
Business transfer payments			
Equals: Personal income	803.6	82.5	101.0
Less: Personal tax and nontax payments[b]			
Personal contributions for social insurance			
Equals: Disposable personal income	687.8	70.6	85.6

Source: U. S. Department of Commerce, *Survey of Current Business*, July 1971, pp. 6 and 22.

    a. Capital consumption allowances include, in addition to depreciation in the narrow sense, accidental damage to fixed equipment.

    b. Nontax liabilities cover payments to the government such as tuition fees, hospital fees, fines, etc.

    c. The inventory valuation adjustment arises in the following way. As prices rise, the value of inventories held by firms rises too. But business accounting methods differ in the way they adjust for this, and for national income accounting it is necessary to put all corporate profits figures on the same accounting basis.

    d. Wage accruals less disbursements measures wages which have been earned but not yet paid out.

income receipts on the one hand, and at the data on output on the other hand, the two totals which are conceptually equal are not actually equal in the data. This clearly means that the data contain an error, and this is what causes the statistical discrepancy.[10]

    10. Unfortunately, the size of the statistical discrepancy does not tell us the magnitude of the total error in the national income statistics because there may be common errors on both sides of the accounts.

U.S. NATIONAL INCOME ACCOUNTS DATA

Having looked at the definitions of the national income accounts concepts, let us look at what these accounts show. There is little purpose in having the reader try to memorize the exact figures presented in the following tables, but it would be useful to get a general idea of some of the magnitudes involved. For example, in the subsequent discussion of the determinants of investment it might be useful to keep in mind that industrial equipment investment accounts for roughly half of fixed investment rather than for, say, 90 percent of it. For this reason we have added percentage distributions to the following tables. These tables are just a small sample of the numerous national income accounts tables published by the Department of Commerce each year.

Table 3.2 shows the components of GNP; that is, the way GNP is used. Not surprisingly, the greater part of GNP (63 percent for the years 1968–70) consists of consumption expenditures. They are divided into durables (10 percent), nondurables (27 percent), and services (26 percent). The next biggest component is government purchases of goods and

Table 3.2 / *Components of GNP.*

	1970 (BILLIONS OF DOLLARS)	PERCENT OF GNP 1968–70
GNP	974	100.0
Personal consumption expenditures	616	62.6
Durables	89	9.5
Nondurables	265	26.9
Services	262	26.2
Gross private domestic investment	135	14.4
Fixed investment	132	13.8
Nonresidential	102	10.5
Structures	37	3.7
Producers' durable equipment	65	6.8
Residential structures	30	3.3
Change in business inventories	3	0.6
Net exports of goods and services	4	0.3
Exports	63	6.1
Imports	59	5.8
Government purchases of goods and services	219	22.7
Federal	97	10.7
State and local	122	12.1

Source: U. S. Department of Commerce, *Survey of Current Business*, July 1971, p. 17.

services. (This item differs from total government expenditures because it excludes transfer payments). State and local government expenditures account for about half of the total. (Had transfer payments been included, they would account for only a bit more than one third of the total.)

The next item is gross private domestic investment. The term "gross" indicates that it is measured before depreciation, and the term "domestic" indicates that it excludes foreign investment. Gross private domestic investment is divided into two parts, inventory investment and fixed investment. Approximately half of fixed investment consists of producers' durable equipment (machinery, cars, trucks, aircraft, furniture, etc.) and the remainder is construction divided about equally between residential and nonresidential construction. The relative importance of producers' durable equipment reflects, in part, the shorter life of this item. If we had used net rather than gross investment, producers' durable equipment would have accounted for a much smaller proportion of fixed investment.

Changes in inventories, which consist of raw materials, goods in process, and finished goods, form the remainder of gross domestic investment. (Changes in inventories have to be classified as investment since they are output which has not been consumed, even though their owner might hold them only involuntarily because his sales have declined.) Inventory investment is a much more significant part of total investment than its relative size indicates because it is so highly volatile. Inventory investment is sometimes negative, while there is no year in which our official data going back to 1929 show fixed investment as negative.

The final component of GNP consists of net exports. Clearly one possible use of a nation's output is to export it, and exports are a part of GNP. On the other hand, imports have to be subtracted from GNP. If we did not exclude them, GNP would overstate output because a part of each of the other components of GNP (consumption, investment, and government) consists of imports rather than of domestically produced goods and services.

Table 3.2 looks at the national income accounts from the "use" side, which shows the disposition of output. Another way of considering the national income accounts is to look at the income side. Accordingly, Table 3.3 shows the allocation of national income among various claimants.

Finally, it may be useful to look at the sources of *gross* private saving. These are shown in Table 3.4. As this table shows, personal saving accounts for less than half of *gross* private saving, the biggest component of which is depreciation (strictly speaking, capital consumption allowances). However, when one considers *net* saving, which is equal to personal saving plus undistributed corporate profits, then personal saving becomes much more important, accounting for almost three quarters of the total.

Table 3.3 / *Composition of national income.*

	1970 (BILLIONS OF DOLLARS)	PERCENT DISTRIBUTION 1968–70
Compensation of employees	602	74.1
Proprietors' income	67	8.7
Rental income of persons	23	3.0
Corporate profits and inventory valuation adjustment	71	10.3
Net interest	33	4.0
National income	796	100.0

Source: U. S. Department of Commerce, *Survey of Current Business*, July 1971, p. 16.

Table 3.4 / *The sources of gross private saving.*

	1971 (BILLIONS OF DOLLARS)	PERCENT DISTRIBUTION 1968–70
Gross private saving	153	100.0
Personal saving	54	31.2
Undistributed corporate profits	16	14.3
Corporate inventory valuation adjustment	−4	−3.2
Corporate capital consumption allowances	56	36.6
Noncorporate capital consumption allowances	31	21.1

Source: U. S. Department of Commerce, *Survey of Current Business*, July 1971, p. 33.

NOTE ON SOURCES OF DATA

The U. S. National Income Accounts data are published each year by the Department of Commerce, usually in the July issue of its monthly *Survey of Current Business*. From time to time the Department of Commerce issues instead, during the summer months, a special National Income Supplement to the *Survey of Current Business* which gives all the data back to 1929.[11] And sometimes all of the data back to 1929 have been revised. Incidentally, each year the national income figures are given not only for

11. As of the current date (1971) the most recent *Supplement* was issued in 1966 and is entitled *National Income and Product Account of the United States 1929–1965 Statistical Tables.*
Although most of the government national income estimates go back only to 1929, Department of Commerce GNP estimates, as well as several private estimates of many national income

the previous year, but for the three previous years as well, and these figures contain many revisions. And such revisions need not be trivial. Hence anyone copying a time series from these sources should proceed as follows: If a National Income Supplement has just been published, he should, of course, use that. If not—as is the case in most years—he should take the figures from the latest national income issue of the *Survey of Current Business*. He should then go to the preceding year's issue and take the data only for the earliest year given there because the others may have been revised. He should then repeat this process until he comes either to an issue giving all the data back as far as he wants to go, or to a National Income Supplement. Only in this way can he be sure that he is using the latest revised data. This is, of course, a time-consuming nuisance. Fortunately, many of the data are also published in ready-to-use revised form (though rounded to the nearest hundred million) in the statistical appendix to the *Economic Report of the President* published each January or February. This source contains the earliest preliminary estimates available for the immediately preceding year.[12] In addition, national income figures are reprinted in many other sources too, such as the Department of Commerce's biennial volume *Business Statistics,* its monthly, *Business Conditions Digest,* or the *Federal Reserve Bulletin.*

National income statistics of varying quality are nowadays available for nearly all countries. They can be located in a United Nations Publication, *Yearbook of National Accounts Statistics.*

QUESTIONS AND EXERCISES

1. Suppose you were interested in the change in "economic welfare" in the United States between 1948 and the present. How would you seek to define it? Which aggregate or aggregates would you use to estimate it? Why?

2. Assume that the authorities replace *all* direct taxation by indirect taxes producing an equivalent yield. What would be the consequences for the estimates of gross national product, national income, and personal disposable income? Would your estimate of economic welfare be affected? If so, how and why?

3. "If a householder repairs his own leaking roof, national income is unaltered; if he hires a builder to do it, national income is increased." Is this so? If it

---

measures, are available for earlier years. Not surprisingly they are less reliable than the more recent data. They can be found, together with references to their sources, in a Department of Commerce publication, *Long Term Economic Growth.*

12. The statistical appendix of the *Economic Report* provides a compact but extremely well chosen statistical compendium. Anyone who plans to purchase only a single source of economic data should seriously consider this one.

is, does it imply any serious criticism of national income estimates? Can we increase economic welfare by doing each other's washing?

4. Suppose that an outbreak of lawlessness makes it necessary to put 25,000 additional men into the police force where they are paid (in total) precisely what they were paid in their previous occupations. What would happen to national income? What would be the effect on economic welfare? In the light of your answers discuss the limitations of the national income concept.

5. Suppose a new disease breaks out which can be cured by a certain weed grown on otherwise unused land. The rent on this land is now $1 billion. What has happened to GNP? Is the disease a "good thing"?

6. Give two criticisms of the way in which GNP is defined.

7. Interest on the national debt is treated as a transfer payment. Why is this? Where the expenditure financed by the government borrowing was used to build factories, is the procedure sensible?

8. Net investment is defined as gross investment *minus* depreciation. Explain the theoretical relationship between net investment and the community's stock of real capital. Can net investment be negative? If so in what periods of American history would you expect to find negative investment? Can gross investment ever be negative? Give your reasons.

9. In a particular period an economy consisting of two firms (*A* and *B*) and a public sector records the following data:

Firm *A*

ALLOCATIONS		RECEIPTS	
Purchases from		Sales to	
Firm *B*	6,000	Households	10,000
Foreigners (imports)	5,000	Firm *B*	21,000
Wages	20,000	Government	5,000
Rents	1,000	Foreigners (exports)	8,000
Indirect taxes	1,000	Additions to	
Taxes on profits	2,000	Fixed capital	6,000
Contributions for		Inventories	5,000
social insurance	1,000	Total	55,000
Depreciation	5,000		
Dividends	7,000		
Undistributed profits	7,000		
Total	55,000		

Firm *B*

Purchases from		Sales to	
Firm *A*	21,000	Households	47,000
Foreigners	19,000	Firm *A*	6,000
Wages	22,000	Foreigners	21,000
Rents	500	Additions to stocks	−1,000
Indirect taxes	1,500	Total	73,000
Taxes on profits	700		
Contributions for			
social insurance	1,500		

Firm B (*continued*)

ALLOCATIONS		RECEIPTS	
Depreciation	3,300		
Transfer payments	500		
Dividends	1,000		
Undistributed profits	2,000		
Total	73,000		

Government

Interest on national debt	1,000	Taxes: direct taxes	
Wages and salaries	6,000	on companies	5,700
Purchases from *A*	5,000	Direct taxes on persons	7,000
Subsidies	500	Indirect taxes	2,500
Transfer payments	2,500	Total	15,200
Net decrease in indebtedness	200		
Total	15,200		

a) Prepare estimates of gross national product.

b) From your results in (a) prepare estimates of national income, personal income, and personal disposable income.

c) Next prepare a capital account showing the saving and investment identity.

What is the saving of households, enterprises, and government? Has the government a surplus or deficit? What is the value of *net* investment?

10. Use the *Economic Report of the President* to provide data for GNP 1960–70. What are the *average* ratios over the period of the following subaggregates to gross national product?

a) Consumers' expenditure.

b) Government expenditure.

c) Investment (gross and net).

d) Exports.

e) Imports.

Do any of the ratios show fluctuations around their average? Can you suggest and defend a simple way of comparing the extent to which the different ratios fluctuate? Do you get a different picture if you distinguish between fixed capital formation and the increase in stocks? Which is the most "volatile" series?

11. Distinguish carefully between (a) the increase in the value of stocks; (b) the value of the increase in stocks. Write

P_1 for the price of a unit of stocks in year 1
P_2 for the price of a unit of stocks in year 2
Q_1 for the quantity of stocks in year 1
Q_2 for the quantity of stocks in year 2,

and formulate expressions for (a) and (b) above. Use your answer to explain the significance of the item "inventory valuation adjustment."

12. When we compare the value of output with the value of total income in our national income data, we find that the two are not equal. We therefore add an item called "statistical discrepancy" to make them equal. Does this amount to rejecting the facts because they don't fit the theory? Is this justified?

SUGGESTED READING

J. Powelson, *Economic Accounting* (New York: McGraw-Hill, 1955) Chaps. 7–20.

M. Yanovsky, *Social Accounting Systems* (Chicago: Aldine Publishing Co., 1965) Chaps. 1–2.

R. and N. Ruggles, *An Introduction to National Income and Income Analysis* (New York: McGraw-Hill, 1956).

G. Ackley, *Macroeconomic Theory* (New York: Macmillan, 1961) Chaps. 2–3.

E. Benison, "Welfare Measurement and GNP," *Survey of Current Business*, Vol. 51 (January 1971).

4

Output and Capacity

WE HAVE NOW DEFINED a set of accounting concepts in terms of which we can describe, in a systematic and unambiguous way, the behavior of the United States economy. To do this we had to spend some time and effort in looking at purely accounting problems. There is therefore a risk that in concentrating on the development of a conceptual framework we have lost sight of our main objective. Accordingly this is a good point at which, before looking at the behavior of the U. S. economy in Chapter 5, to take stock of what we have learned.

We began, in Chapter 2 by picturing the simplest possible economic system. In this there was no governmental economic activity and no international trade. Our sketch of the economy in operation was correspondingly simple. Households sold factor services to enterprises. Enterprises organized these services to produce a flow of goods and services. These passed, via the market, either to households (as consumption) or to enterprises (as investment). For convenience we reproduce Figure 2.3 describing this.

The whole of Chapters 2 and 3 were concerned to develop a consistent and unambiguous set of concepts in terms of which we could give a numerical description of economic activity in a model of this kind. Description, however, presupposes analysis. Our first aim was to measure the flow of goods and services becoming available, in any given period, to satisfy human wants while leaving the community as well off at the end of the period as it was in the beginning. Measurement of this flow—which we called real national income or real net national product—is obviously an important problem. For real national income is a measure of the potential economic welfare of society in any given period.

Our second aim, however, was rather more ambitious. We sought to answer the questions:

What determines the magnitude of real national income in any period?

What determines the rate at which real national income grows from one period to another?

Logically this second aim was prior to our first. It was *because* we wanted to explain the level of potential economic welfare in any period and its rate of growth between periods that we embarked on the tasks of defining national income and its associated aggregates and subaggregates and elaborating a set of rules for measuring them. Asking our two questions— that is posing our two problems for analysis—told us what facts were likely to be relevant to our enquiry. Now we have defined our facts—which we shall shortly need to explain—we can take a more systematic look at the analytical problem from which we started.

Obviously enough the level of real output produced in the economy in any accounting period depends upon the *capacity* of the economic system to produce output and the *extent* to which the capacity in existence is utilized. Equally clearly the growth in output between two accounting periods depends upon the growth in *capacity* between the two periods and the change between the two periods in the *extent* to which capacity is utilized.

It is therefore convenient to begin our inquiry into the determination of the level of output and its rate of growth by making these two notions— capacity and its degree of utilization—rather more precise.

THE DETERMINANTS OF CAPACITY

We have already spoken of the economy as possessing, at any given time, a given endowment of the factors of production which we shall call "labor" and "capital." It is also clear that, at any given time, the community will have a certain degree of technical knowledge about the way in which the services of these factors *may* be combined to produce a flow of output in any period. Accordingly we can think of the productive capacity of the system, in any short period such as a year or a quarter, as being determined by (1) the endowments of the two factors; and (2) the state of technology—and the actual output produced as being determined by the extent to which this capacity is utilized.

Output, in terms of commodities and services, is, as we know, multi-dimensional. To fix our ideas, however, we may think of output as consisting of only two commodities. These we can call "manufactures" and "agricultural produce." Approaching matters along these lines we can then construct a simple diagram showing the various combinations of these two outputs which the economy can produce with its "capacity" fully and optimally utilized. This is done in Figure 4.1.

Figure 4.1 / *Production possibility curve.*

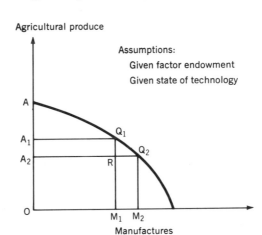

Interpreting this diagram is relatively straightforward. Suppose only agricultural produce is to be produced. If the whole of capacity is employed, output of agricultural produce is OA and output of manufactures is zero. Suppose now that the community's preferences change in favor of manufactures. Through the working of the market, enterprises redeploy factors so as to produce more manufactures and less agricultural produce. If this process continues we shall trace out a curve showing all the combinations of the two commodities which can be produced by the community on the assumptions that (1) both factors are fully employed; (2) the production of each commodity is optimally organized; (3) the state of technology is given. Of these three assumptions only (2) has a meaning which is not self-evident. What does "optimal" organization mean? The answer, which at this stage we ask the reader to take on trust, is that at all points on the curve AM (1) enterprises, in the search for profit, are using factors in such a way as to keep costs at a minimum and that, provided they do this, (2) at no point on AM is it possible to have more of either commodity without giving up a greater value of the other. The curve AM is thus not defined simply by the technical conditions of production and the factor endowment. It also depends on the implicit assumption that the market processes, which underlie the curve, produce an "optimal" allocation of resources in the sense defined above.

Given this assumption—which we shall continue to make—the shape and position of the curve *AM*, which we call *the production possibility curve*, depends upon the state of technology and the factor endowment. In formal terms it represents a first attempt at answering the question: What determines the capacity of the economy to produce output?

On this approach the *growth* of capacity over time takes the form of an outward shift in the curve. Clearly it can occur because the process of *net investment* increases the endowment of capital, because *technology is improving* or because the labor force is *growing*. To explain the rate of growth of capacity, economists need to develop a theory which explains the *rate* at which the factor endowments grow; the *rate* at which technology improves; and the way in which capacity output responds to these growth rates.

THE SLOPE OF THE PRODUCTION POSSIBILITY CURVE

Before we leave this production curve, can we say anything about the meaning of its slope? A little reflection shows that we can.

Consider the points Q_1 and Q_2 on the curve. If we move from Q_1 to Q_2 we obtain an additional output of manufactures of M_1M_2 at the *cost* of giving up A_1A_2 of "agricultural produce." We then say that the *opportunity cost* of M_1M_2 of "manufactures" is A_1A_2 of "agricultural produce." Their ratio, that is the "opportunity cost" of M_1M_2 in terms of A_1A_2, is given by the *slope* of Q_1Q_2. Clearly if the distance M_1M_2 is made smaller and smaller, then A_1A_2 is also made smaller and, by the same token the line Q_1Q_2 is shortened. As this process is continued, the slope of the line Q_1Q_2 becomes closer and closer to the slope of the production possibility curve. Where the distance Q_1 to Q_2 is indefinitely small, the "opportunity cost" of manufactures in terms of agricultural produce is simply the slope of the production possibility curve at the point under consideration.

This concept of "opportunity cost" is of considerable importance in economics. *It is a valid concept if, and only if, choice between alternatives is enforced by some limitation—in this case the capacity output of the system.* A precisely similar situation arises for a man who is acceptable in marriage to Joan and Jean and is strongly attracted to both. If it is not legally possible to marry both girls, Joan is the opportunity cost of Jean and Jean the opportunity cost of Joan. Where society permits polygamy the man can marry both and the concept of opportunity cost does not arise. The polygamous situation is depicted in economic terms by the point *R* in Figure 4.1. If the economic system is at a point like *R* *inside the production possibility curve* (as it was throughout the 1930s) capacity is *not* fully utilized. Here "agricultural produce" can be increased *without* reducing the output of manufactures. There is no opportunity cost of increasing either form of output simply because the whole of productive capacity is not being used.

In terms of Figure 4.1, we can now rephrase our questions, which become

1) What determines the position of the production possibility curve in any given period?

2) What determines whether the economy operates, in any given period, at a point (such as Q_1) *on* the production possibility curve or at a point (such as R) *inside* it?

3) What determines the rate at which, through time, the production *possibility curve* moves outward (to the right)?

4) What determines the rate at which, through time, actual output grows?

Finally one last point about the production possibility curve itself. We have seen that at any point on it, (say Q_1) the slope of the curve is the opportunity cost ratio. As the curve in Figure 4.1 is drawn, the opportunity cost of manufactures in terms of agricultural produce rises as the output of manufactures grows. Conversely, if we move *down* the curve the opportunity cost of agricultural produce in terms of manufactures also grows. Figure 4.1 thus depicts a situation of increasing opportunity cost.

Why should costs be increasing? In general this will follow even if the factors of production are homogeneous[1] and equally well adapted to the production of either agricultural produce or manufactures. A formal proof of this is a little complicated. But the following argument should serve to clarify the issue.

Suppose we are at some point (say Q) on the production possibility curve and we wish to give up a unit of agricultural produce to gain an extra unit of manufactures. Suppose also that, at Q, the factors labor and capital are used in the two forms of production as follows:

	UNIT OF AGRIC. PRODUCE	UNIT OF MANUFACTURES
Units of labor	1	1
Units of capital	4	10

If we give up a unit of agricultural produce we release 1 unit of labor and 4 of capital. But to produce a unit of manufactures we require 1 unit of labor and 10 of capital. Too little capital is therefore released to maintain the same cost of manufactures. In producing manufactures the ratio of labor to capital must rise above the ratio of 1 : 10. Since this was, *because businessmen choose the least cost combination in order to earn maximum*

---

1. Homogeneity simply means that one unit of any factor is indistinguishable (economically) from any other unit of the same factor.

profit, the cheapest method (optimal factor ratio) for producing manufactures, cost *must* rise. Hence there are increasing costs as we move *down*
the production possibility curve *AM* towards *M,* for what is true of point
Q is true of any point on *AM.*

Now move the other way from *Q*—that is, give up manufactures to
obtain *more* agricultural produce. Now inputs are *required* in the ratio
1 labor: 4 capital and *released* in the ratio 1 labor: 10 capital. Too little
labor is released. The ratio of labor to capital must *fall* in agricultural
produce. Hence, by the argument above, the cost of agricultural produce
must rise.

It follows that whichever direction we move from *Q,* we encounter
increasing costs; provided only that factors are not used in the same proportion in producing both types of output. This second condition will be
satisfied if both types of output do not possess the same production function
—a reasonable enough assumption.

Since we have not yet met the concept of a production function, a brief
explanation of this statement is necessary.

Consider the output of "agricultural produce." This depends upon
(1) the inputs of labor and capital; and (2) the state of technology. Given
(1) and (2) there will be a single value of output of "agricultural
produce." Thus we may write a *production function*[2] for agricultural
produce as:

$$Y_{ag} = f(N_{ag}, K_{ag}), \tag{4.1}$$

where

$Y_{ag} \equiv$ the output of agricultural produce;
$N_{ag} \equiv$ the labor input to the industry;
$K_{ag} \equiv$ the capital employed in the industry.

This equation may be read as follows:

$$
\begin{array}{ccc}
\text{output of} & & \left\{ \begin{array}{c} \text{a function of, i.e.,} \\ \text{systematically} \\ \text{dependent upon} \end{array} \right. & \left. \begin{array}{c} \text{the inputs of} \\ \text{labor} \\ \text{and capital} \end{array} \right\}
\end{array}
$$

output of agricultural produce — is — a function of, i.e., systematically dependent upon — the inputs of labor and capital

What about technology? We could have included a symbol (say *T*) in
this function to stand for the "state of technology." Indeed in later chapters
—as a pedagogic device—we adopt this procedure. In the above equation,
however, we simply regard the functional relation—denoted by the letter *f*
in front of the bracket—as reflecting a given state of technology. If technology changes, so does the function. For manufacturing there will be a
function of a similar type written formally:

$$Y_{man} = f(N_{man}, K_{man}) \tag{4.2}$$

2. The notion of a "production function" is more fully explained in Chapter 6.

For our earlier argument to hold we simply require these two functions (systematic relationships) to be different in the sense that, given the prices of the factor inputs, the *ratios* in which they are employed in order to minimize costs differ in the two uses. As the reader will see, this is not a strong assumption since agricultural output is likely, in general, to require very different factor inputs, at any given set of factor prices, from manufactured goods.

At this stage some readers may find this argument hard to follow. They should take courage for, in the Questions and Exercises which follow Chapter 6, they will find themselves proving, with great ease, most of the propositions which we have here asserted.

Figure 4.2 / *Production possibility curves. Increasing, constant, and decreasing cost.*

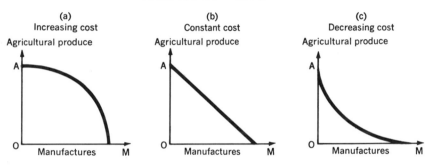

From this argument in terms of ratios it is easy to see that if, given the price of factor inputs, the ratios in which factors are employed in order to minimize costs *are the same in each use,* then the opportunity cost curve will be a straight line and costs will be constant. This is illustrated in Figure 4.2 (b).

How can we have decreasing costs? At first sight our two ratio arguments seem to exclude this possibility. But suppose the production function for manufacturing is of the particular form:

$$Y_{man} = AN_{man}K_{man},$$

where A is some constant. To fix ideas put $A = 1, N = 100, K = 1000$. Then

$$Y_{man} = 1 \times 100 \times 1000$$
$$= 100,000.$$

Now suppose both N_{man} and K_{man} to double. We have:

$$Y_{man} = 1 \times 200 \times 2000$$
$$= 1 \times 100 \times 1000 \times 2 \times 2$$
$$= 4[1 \times 100 \times 1000]$$
$$= 400,000.$$

Doubling factor inputs has *more* than doubled output—it has in fact quadrupled it. When this occurs, or more generally when a doubling of factor inputs lead to *more* than doubling output, we say that there are *economies of scale* or *increasing returns to scale*. Conversely when a doubling of inputs leads to *less* than doubling output we say that there are *decreasing returns to scale* or *diseconomies of scale*.

Our earlier arguments assumed, implicitly, that both production functions were of a form which insured *constant returns to scale*: that is, a doubling of inputs exactly doubled output. They are valid on that assumption. If, however, manufacturing has a production function which exhibits increasing returns to scale then, even if input ratios differ (the case we assumed to argue increasing costs of one output in terms of another), the effect of these ratios in raising costs as resources are transferred into manufacturing will be offset in whole or in part, *or even more than offset,* by the influence of the *economies of scale*. Increasing returns to scale thus make it *possible* for the production possibility curve to be concave to the origin. They are a necessary but not a sufficient condition for Figure 4.2 (c) to be the appropriate one.

Thus each of the production possibility curves we have drawn is logically permissible. Which is appropriate is a question of fact. In general we shall proceed on the assumption that the production functions in our economy (1) exhibit constant returns to scale; and (2) differ in the sense explained on pp. 44–45.

It thus follows that the reader may picture the production possibility curve—or, as it is sometimes called, "the transformation curve"—as it is drawn in Figure 4.1.

THE THREE PROBLEMS

Now that we have restated our three problems concerning determination of output in terms of the production possibility curve, we can develop a convenient method of approach to them. We shall begin by examining the question, "What determines whether the economy operates *on* the production possibility curve (i.e., at full capacity) or at some point *R* inside it (i.e., at less than full capacity)?"

In considering this problem we shall take the position of the production possibility curve as given and invariant. Since the position of this curve depends upon

1) the real capital stock—which we know is increasing as the result of net investment;

2) the labor force—which we know is also growing as the result of population growth and the increasing proportion of the population which seeks employment;

3) the state of technology—which is also improving—

we are taking as constant and unchanged variables which we know in practice to be changing. To do this is obviously convenient, for it enables us to leave the problem of the growth of capacity for later examination. But is it justified? Provided we restrict the time period involved, it is a reasonable procedure, for though capacity does grow over time, in any period of (say) a year it grows relatively little—probably by about 4 percent or even less. We proceed, in other words, like a man buying a new suit. He knows that, in fact, his measurements *are* changing. He is getting heavier. His stomach muscles are weakening. Nevertheless he proceeds on the assumption (sometimes shown to be unjustified) that over the expected life of the suit these changes can be ignored. In economic terms the man buying the suit undertakes a *short-run* analysis. That is, he obtains a garment which fits his existing contours on the assumption that in the short-run they are constant even though he knows that, in practice, they are changing.

Our analysis will be a *short-run* analysis in this sense. For we shall take, as given and invariant, the determinants of *the position of the production possibility curve* even though we know that, over time, these are changing: that is, *economic growth* in capacity is proceeding. This device simplifies matters but requires the reader to make the proper intellectual allowances for its limitations and the artificiality it inevitably introduces.

In much of what follows we shall make a further simplification in that we shall not in general explicitly introduce time into our analysis. To see what this means consider Figure 4.3.

Figure 4.3 / *Capacity and its utilization.*

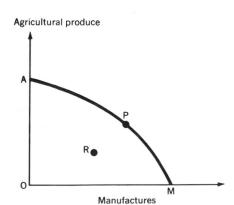

Agricultural produce

Suppose we succeed in developing a theory which explains why the economy operates at the point R. Let us suppose that this theory tells us that if some variable (let us call it x) takes the value x_1 we shall be at R while if it takes the value x_2 we shall be at P. On the basis of this theory we can work out that if x changes from x_1 to x_2 the economy will move from R to P. This information is obviously useful. But it is equally obviously incomplete, for it does not tell us (1) how long the system takes to get from R to P; (2) by what path it gets from R to P; (3) whether, once at P, the system will stay there. Economic theories that only compare positions such as R and P we call *static* theories. Theories which also explain the path the system takes from R to P—and how long it takes to get there—we call *dynamic* theories since they involve time in an *explicit* way.

Dynamic theories, since they tell us more, are obviously likely to be (and in practice are) more complicated than static theories. For simplicity therefore we begin by developing a static theory. Once again the reader, who intuitively thinks in dynamic terms, must make the necessary intellectual adjustment. Above all he must avoid mixing statics with dynamics. Since static analysis is artificial, this requires a continuous intellectual effort.

These warnings do not imply that this book contains no discussion of dynamic problems. It does. Those chapters, however, which develop a short-run macroeconomic theory of the determination of output are largely *static* while those which discuss economic growth, economic fluctuations, and rising prices respectively are explicitly *dynamic*.

We are now almost ready to embark upon the development of our *short-run* and *static* theory of the determination of output. Before we do so, however, we shall first examine the record of the United States economy (in Chapter 5) and then (in Chapter 6) say something about the analytical and expository techniques employed by economists and, in particular, about the use of mathematics.

QUESTIONS AND EXERCISES

1. Why do we describe real national income as a measure of "potential economic welfare" rather than "economic welfare"? What limitations are there to the validity of either description?

2. Construct a figure similar to 4.3. Show, geometrically, how you would seek to measure the proportion of capacity employed at the point R. With what observable phenomena, for which statistical data are usually available, would you expect your measure to be related? Give your reasons.

3. From the following data plot the production possibility curves. Do they describe increasing, decreasing, or constant costs?

Three production possibility curves: Numerical data.

1		2		3	
OUTPUT OF		OUTPUT OF		OUTPUT OF	
AGRI-CULTURAL PRODUCTS (1)	MANU-FACTURED PRODUCTS (2)	AGRI-CULTURAL PRODUCTS (3)	MANU-FACTURED PRODUCTS (4)	AGRI-CULTURAL PRODUCTS (5)	MANU-FACTURED PRODUCTS (6)
1000	nil	1000	nil	1000	nil
950	24.5	950	34	950	15
900	49.0	900	67	900	31
850	73.5	850	99	850	48
800	98.0	800	130	800	66
750	122.5	750	160	750	85
700	147.0	700	189	700	105
650	171.5	650	217	650	126
600	196.0	600	244	600	148
550	220.5	550	270	550	171
500	245.0	500	295	500	195
450	269.5	450	319	450	220
400	294.0	400	342	400	246
350	318.5	350	364	350	273
300	343.0	300	385	300	301
250	367.5	250	405	250	330
200	392.0	200	424	200	360
150	416.5	150	442	150	391
100	441.0	100	459	100	423
50	465.5	50	475	50	456
nil	490.0	nil	490	nil	490

4. "As a nation we spend far too little on education. We should increase our expenditure on it by at least $10 billion a year." Discuss this statement in the light of the concept of "opportunity cost."

5. "In the short run, by definition, some variable or variables which are known to be changing over time are assumed to be constant. How misleading short-run analysis is, is therefore a question of fact." Elucidate.

6. A tank is connected to a hose through a valve controlled by a ball cock. Initially the water in the tank is at a level of 3 inches. The hose is turned on at 11 A.M. Give (a) a static and (b) a dynamic analysis of the operation of this system. What is the new equilibrium level?

7. Construct hypothetical production possibility curves, in terms of agricultural produce and manufactures for the United States and Brazil. Would you expect their shapes to differ? If so in what way? Justify your hypothetical curves.

8. Suppose the community, with a production possibility curve defined by cols. (1) and (2) of the data in Question 2 is in equilibrium at the following point:

OUTPUT OF	
AGRICULTURAL PRODUCTS	MANUFACTURED PRODUCTS
550	220.5

What is the price of agricultural output in terms of manufactures? Why? Interpret your answer in the light of the earlier discussion of the working of a market economy.

9. What statistical data would be relevant to any attempt to test your answer to Question 7? Why?

SUGGESTED READING

E. Dennison, *The Sources of Economic Growth and the Alternatives before Us.* (Washington: Committee for Economic Development, 1962).

5

A Sketch of American
Economic Experience

IN CHAPTER 4, in making use of the concept of the production possibility curve, we distinguished between two macroeconomic problems. The first of these, which we called a short-run problem, was to find an answer to the question, "Given the capacity of the economic system to produce output, what determines the extent to which the given capacity is utilized?" The second, which we called the long-run problem, was to find an answer to the question, "What determines the rate at which the capacity to produce output grows over time?"

These problems were clearly distinguishable in terms of the production possibility curve. But this is simply a geometric device: We now need to inquire whether they are real problems capable in principle of investigation by positive economic analysis. If, for example, examination of the record of the American economy showed that the economy always operated at full capacity, our first problem would lose much of its interest. If alternatively there was no evidence that capacity ever grew, so would the second. Moreover, if the record shows them to be real problems, its examination may also suggest particular aspects of them which call for analysis.

The function of this chapter is, therefore, to sketch the economic experience of the U. S. economy in terms of macroeconomic concepts we have already met (and some of those we shall soon meet) in order to see what are the facts which our theory needs to explain.

OUTPUT, CAPACITY, AND UNEMPLOYMENT

Our first step is to examine what has happened to annual output—the flow of goods and services produced by the economy in each year. To do this we make use of a series for real GNP, as well as per capita real GNP and disposable income shown in Figure 5.1.[1] This figure is semi-logarithmic so that a straight line denotes a constant *percentage* rate of growth. The most obvious thing Figure 5.1 shows is the great increase in GNP both in absolute and in per capita terms. For example, in the period 1910–70, aggregate GNP rose sixfold, while per capita real GNP rose by 171 percent. A second thing shown by Figure 5.1 is that the growth rate has been quite uneven. There are numerous years in which output actually fell.

The factors determining the actual growth of GNP can be classified into two types. In the first place, there are the determinants of capacity growth: the growth rate of the labor force, of the capital stock, of land, and the development of new techniques of production. These factors determine capacity (or potential) output. But capacity output is not the same thing as actual output; it merely sets a limit to it. There exists a second set of factors which determine how close to capacity output the economy is actually operating. Accordingly, Figure 5.1 shows, in addition to actual GNP potential GNP, that is an estimate of how much GNP would have been had the economy operated at full capacity.[2] As becomes clear by comparing actual and potential GNP, the economy generally does not work at full capacity, but usually operates with some slack, a slack whose most obvious manifestation is unemployment.[3]

Looking at the full capacity growth rate, Figure 5.1 shows it growing at a relatively steady rate. There is no evidence that the future will bring either stagnation or an explosive (percentage) growth rate. Actual GNP has grown along with potential GNP. As a rough generalization one can say that actual GNP has tended to equal or slightly exceed potential GNP

1. Two different estimates of real GNP are shown in the figure. Estimating GNP is a very difficult task, particularly for the earlier years for which fewer data are available. Hence, different investigators obtain different results. This may be unfortunate, but a student of economics has to accept this; our data are quite imperfect.

2. The notion of full capacity (or potential) GNP is not a simple one. Obviously, it is not to be taken in the literal sense of what GNP would be if the nation bent all its efforts towards increasing GNP, for example, by greatly lengthening the workday. Rather it corresponds to a state of full employment output under normal conditions.

3. But occasionally—for example, during wartime—actual GNP exceeds full capacity GNP. At such times the work week is above its normal level, the employer's desperate search for labor brings additional workers into the force, and stand-by plant and equipment come into production. A less dramatic example occurs in peacetime years of full employment and high capacity growth when output may be somewhat above the long-run trend we use to measure potential GNP.

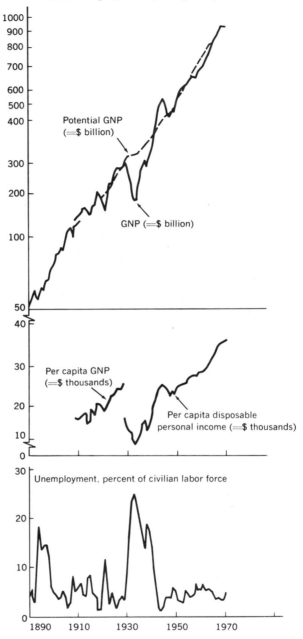

Figure 5.1 / *GNP, disposable personal income, and unemployment (1958 prices).*

Sources: U. S. Department of Commerce, *Long Term Economic Growth:* Executive Office of the President, *1971 Economic Report of the President;* Stanley Lebergott, *Manpower in Economic Growth.*

during cyclical peaks, but in most other years has been significantly below it.[4] Again, no tendency for either stagnation or for rapid acceleration is evident in the data, though the postwar growth rate does exceed the pre-World War II growth rate.

One way of measuring the discrepancy between potential and actual GNP is by the unemployment rate. This is not to say that the unemployment rate is a perfect measure of the shortfall of GNP. One reason is that labor, while the most important of the factors of production, is only one of them. A second reason is that fluctuations in output are greater than fluctuations in employment. An empirical rule of thumb known as "Okun's Law" after its developer, Arthur Okun of the Brookings Institution, is that the difference between actual GNP and potential GNP is 3.2 times as great as the difference between the actual unemployment rate and the 4 percent unemployment rate that most economists regard as "full employment." Third, our unemployment data do not take account of part-time unemployment, that is, employees involuntarily on a short work week. Fourth, the data do not include people, such as secondary earners and the retired, who would like to work but left the labor force because they have given up even trying to find jobs.

Nonetheless, unemployment is one measure, albeit an imperfect one, of the slack in the economy. And since the federal government publishes unemployment figures each month while data on capacity operations are available only quarterly, the unemployment data are often used as *the* measure of slack in the economy. Quite apart from problems about the availability of data, the use of unemployment figures is also justified by the fact that unemployment is a measure of one type of human suffering.

Hence, Figure 5.1 shows the unemployment rate in addition to GNP. It shows that unemployment has been a feature of our economy for a long time. If we rather arbitrarily define full employment as 4 percent or less of the labor force being unemployed, then we have had only 20 peacetime years of full employment in the period 1890–1970. It is simply not correct to say that prior to the Great Depression of the 1930s the demand for labor always exceeded the supply (which incidentally would hardly be an equilibrium condition) and that the American economy had very little unemployment before 1929.

Still, with the exception of the Great Depression, unemployment has usually not been very great. Excluding the decade of the 1930s, unemployment has exceeded 6 percent in only seventeen years from 1890 to 1970.

4. For the reasons why actual GNP can exceed potential GNP, see the preceding footnote. A warning is in order here. The potential GNP data were developed, in part, from actual GNP data which differ to some extent from the actual GNP data in Figure 5.1. Hence, the actual and potential GNP figures are not strictly comparable.

(The years 1893–99 accounted for seven out of these seventeen cases.) It is clear that there exists some mechanism which raises actual output along with the growth of potential output.

One obvious question which arises at this point is whether, nowadays, when we have available policies to counter recessions the average unemployment rate is less than it used to be. The answer to this question is *no*. The average rate of unemployment in the past 25 years has been 4.6 percent, while in the 25 years ending in 1929 it was 4.7 percent. To be sure, in the 25 years ending in 1940 it was 10.9 percent, but this is so only because this period includes the abnormal year of the Great Depression. We have not in the postwar period ever had a year with as high unemployment peaks as we had prior to 1929. So, while we have not succeeded in reducing average unemployment, we have *perhaps* learned to avoid periods of particularly high unemployment. But, as is so often the case, these facts do not tell us what we really want to know: the extent, if any, to which our stabilization policies have reduced unemployment. This is the case, because we do not know what unemployment would have been in the absence of stabilization policies.

We can now list the questions suggested by Figure 5.1 for which we may reasonably require our theory to suggest explanations. These are:

1) What explains the rate at which capacity grows?
2) What explains how close to capacity the economy is operating?
3) Why does output show wavelike fluctuations?
4) How effective has stabilization policy been?
5) What has kept actual output growing roughly in line with potential output?

PRICES AND MONEY WAGES

Output and employment are not the only two macroeconomic variables of interest to economists. Macroeconomics is also concerned with such variables as the general level of prices and money wages. Accordingly, Figure 5.2 brings together series for prices and money wages, while Figure 5.3 plots derived series for the annual percentage rate of changes of prices money wages, and real wages.

The term "price level" as used in economic analysis is a theoretical term rather than a term relating directly to something which can be observed empirically, but it can be approximated in several ways. One such approximation is the *GNP deflator*. This price index measures the prices of all goods and services entering GNP weighted in accordance with their importance in GNP. It therefore includes capital goods as well as the price of government services.[5] Another measure of the price level is the wholesale price index (which measures the price of consumer and capital goods, but not private or governmental services, the first time they enter

Figure 5.2 / *Prices, money wages, and unemployment, 1890–1970.*

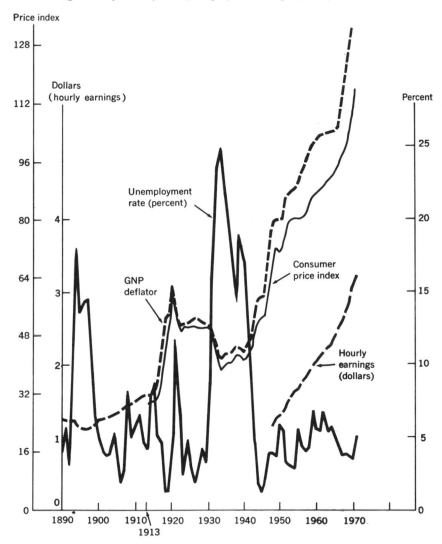

Note: Hourly earnings are dollars per hour in private nonagricultural industries and in agriculture.

Sources: Same as for Figure 5.1. Price indices 1958 = 100.

5. However, due to the difficulty of measuring the output of government, we measure the price of government output by wages and materials costs paid by governments. This is a very crude approximation which reduces the meaningfulness of the GNP deflator.

organized markets) and the consumer price index (sometimes misleadingly called "the cost of living index"). Unlike the wholesale price index, the latter excludes capital goods but includes private services and weights all items in proportion to their consumption by urban low- and middle-income families.

The GNP deflator depicted in Figure 5.2 and in rate of change form in Figure 5.3, shows considerable instability. If stability is defined, rather arbitrarily, as a change of less than 2 percent per year, then it has been stable in less than half of the years from 1890 to 1970. Although we might now be accustomed to thinking of prices as rising every year, this is not in accordance with longer run historical experience. From 1890 to 1941, the GNP deflator fell in about one-third of the years, reflecting, in part, the effects of the Great Depression. Moreover, the GNP deflator fell in the last third of the 19th century and did not surpass its average for the 1869–78 decade until 1916. And while it has generally risen in the postwar period, in about half the years since 1948 the increase was less than 2 percent. But since prices generally rise more in years of inflation than they fall in years of deflation, the trend of prices has been upward.

One would expect to find that the years of increase and of decrease are not randomly distributed over the economic landscape. And this is indeed the case. The years of rapid increase were all either war years or years following a war (such as 1920 and 1946–47). Every significant inflation we have had has occurred either during a war or shortly thereafter. By contrast, the years of sharp deflation, 1894, 1921–22, 1931–32 have been years of high unemployment. However, this correlation of falling prices and high unemployment may not have applied to all earlier historical periods or to periods when prices fell only slowly as in the 1880s.

In the postwar period the GNP deflator has risen in every year, except one. However, except for the war years the increase has, in every case, been less than 4 percent, and in half the cases (1948–70) it has been less than 2 percent. The difference between the prewar and postwar periods is not that in the postwar period annual price increases have been larger than they were in the prewar period, but that in the prewar period rising prices in some years were, in considerable part, offset by prices falling in other years.

Turning to the consumer price index, we find that Figures 5.2 and 5.3 show this index rising sharply during World War I and then declining sharply in the early 1920s as well as the 1930s. It did not reach its 1920 peak again until 1947. Since 1948 it has risen in all but two years, but in close to half of these years the increase was less than 1.5 percent. And such an increase in the index *may perhaps* be the result of a bias in the index rather than of genuine inflation (see p. 357). Whether this bias is large enough to account for a 1½ percent increase in the index is still an un-

Figure 5.3 / *Percentage changes in prices and money wages, 1891–1970.*

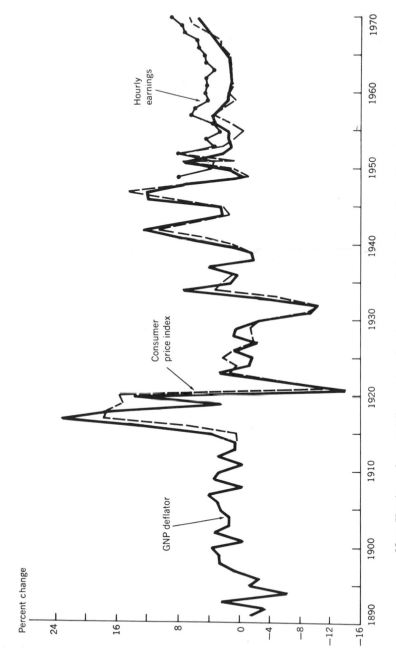

Note: Hourly earnings are dollars per hour in private nonagricultural industries and in agriculture.
Sources: Same as for Figure 5.1.

settled question. The only two postwar periods of greater than 5 percent price increases were war periods.

Since 1947, as Figures 5.2 and 5.3 show, money wages have risen every year by more than the consumer price index. This means, of course, that real wages have been increasing every year. When one compares the money wage curve with the unemployment and price curves, there appears to be a not very surprising relationship between them. In years of relatively large price increases money wages have tended to rise by relatively large amounts. In years of high unemployment, on the other hand, money wages have tended to rise less than in other years.

Thus Figures 5.2 and 5.3 suggest that we shall need our macroeconomic theory to be able to explain (1) the *level* of prices and money wages; (2) the *rate* and *direction* of changes in both.

Since the rate of change of money wages seems to be related to the percentage of unemployment and to price changes, it is clear that any theory we put forward to explain price/wage phenomena will need to be an integral part of our theory of output and its fluctuations.

MONEY AND INTEREST RATES

Now let us look at two financial variables, money and interest rates. These are shown in Figure 5.4. As is so common in economics, there are some definitional and measurement problems. While the most widespread definition of money is currency plus demand deposits held by the public, there is an alternative broader definition which makes the money supply equal to currency *and demand plus time* deposits in commercial banks. These two definitions are sometimes referred to as narrow money and broad money.[6] Both are shown in Figure 5.4.

A variable to which attention will frequently be directed as we develop our theory is "the rate of interest." There is, of course, no single interest rate any more than there is a single "price" of output. To measure the general price level we make use of an index number which calculates the price of a defined basket of goods or the implicit GNP deflator. We could follow the same procedure in measuring "the" interest rate. Instead, economists often use the interest rate on government bonds, i.e., on virtually risk-free bonds, as a measure of "the" interest rate. However, since there were no government bonds outstanding in the earlier years shown in Figure 5.4, we have used instead the highest grade corporate bonds (bonds graded

6. They are also called M_1 and M_2. But these abbreviations are sometimes used to denote something quite different: the transactions and precautionary demand for money on the one hand, and the speculative demand on the other. These concepts will be explained in Chapter 12.

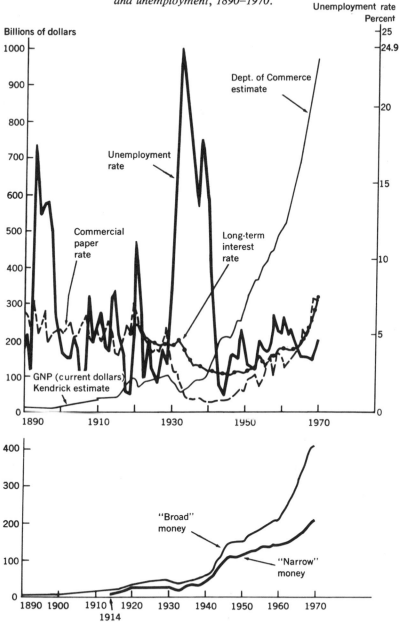

Figure 5.4 / *Money supply, interest rates, money GNP, and unemployment, 1890–1970.*

Note: Narrow money is defined as currency held by the public and adjusted demand deposits. Broad money includes in addition time deposits in commercial banks. The commercial paper rate relates to prime 4–6 months commercial paper and the long-term interest rate is Moody's Aaa bond rate.

Sources: U. S. Department of Commerce, *Historical Statistics of the U. S.* and *Long Term Economic Growth;* Executive Office of the President, *1971 Economic Report of the President;* Federal Reserve *Bulletin*, December 1970; Milton Friedman and Anna Schwartz, *Monetary Statistics of the United States.*

as Aaa by Moody's Rating Service).[7] In addition, we have charted in Figure 5.4 one short-term interest rate, the rate on 4–6 months prime commercial paper (promissory notes issued by the soundest corporations).

Figure 5.4 also includes money GNP. This nominal GNP series and the two money supply series show a fairly close relationship. Whether this reflects a causal rather than just coincidental relationship, and if so, which is cause and which is effect, is something we will take up later. The quantity theory of money (to be discussed in Chapter 17) argues that the correlation between the two money series and nominal GNP exists because changes in the money supply bring about most of the change in money income. But this proposition is disputed by Keynesian theory, which we shall study at length in the subsequent chapters. Here the reader should just note that there *is* a correlation, leaving open, for the time being, the question of which, if either, is cause and which is effect.

The two interest rate series shown in Figure 5.4 differ from most of the other series we have presented in all the previous figures by not having a pronounced secular (that is, long-run) trend for the whole period. They showed little trend prior to the 1930s and then they, particularly the short-term rate, fell during the Great Depression. In the postwar period, however, they have shown an upward trend. In part, this reflects the abnormally low level of the 1930s and 1940s. As of the time of writing (1971) interest rates are abnormally high and have been so for the last few years. This, for reasons explained below (see p. 198), probably is the result of inflation.

Two of the other series shown in Figure 5.4 show some correlation with the interest rate series. The money stock series appear to be positively correlated with interest rates. As will be discussed later, one explanation for this (but not the only one) is that a rise in the money stock, after some time, raises interest rates. On the other hand, the unemployment rate, also shown in Figure 5.4, is negatively correlated with interest rates, suggesting that as economic activity falls, the demand for funds declines, and hence the price of borrowing funds (i.e., the rate of interest) falls too.

THE ALLOCATION OF OUTPUT

In developing our national income accounting concepts we saw that GNP is allocated among the following major uses: consumption, fixed investment, inventory investment, federal government expenditures on

7. Another problem with using the interest rate on government bonds is that these bond issues were tax exempt at one time but are no longer. Hence, time series of their yields really measure different things at different times.

goods and services, and state and local government expenditures on goods and services. In Figure 5.5 we have divided GNP among these uses.

Consumption shows an uninterrupted trend. Only in a severe depression will consumption actually fall, and we have not had such a severe depression in the postwar period. However, this relative steadiness in consumption expenditures relates only to nondurables and services. Purchases of durables, which may be looked upon as "consumer investment," show much less steadiness and did register several declines in the postwar period.

Fixed investment is more erratic than total consumption expenditures; and, like consumer durables, it too declined in some postwar years. Inven-

Figure 5.5 / *Components of GNP in 1958.*

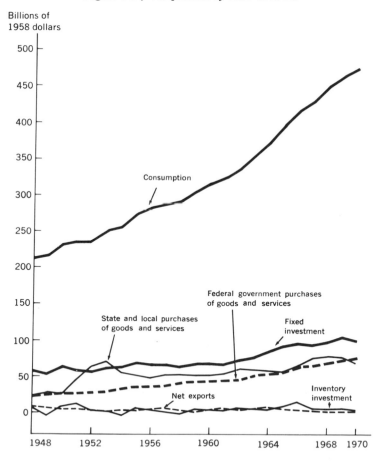

Source: Executive Office of the President, *1971 Economic Report of the President.*

tory investment is much more erratic than fixed investment, and is sometimes even negative. Net exports also exhibit substantial fluctuations. This is not surprising since *net* exports are a small residual obtained by subtracting imports from exports. Hence, relatively small dollar changes in either series tend to show up as large *percentage* changes in net exports.

Federal government purchases of goods and services have, of course, been rising, but there have been interruptions in this upward trend. The peaks in this series can be explained by the effects of U.S. involvement in wars in Korea (1950–53) and Vietnam (1964–71). A strong, uninterrupted upward trend is apparent in the figure showing state and local government expenditures on goods and services.

Finally, a word of warning is in order. Though fluctuations in each of the series are important, the effect of a given percentage change in any one depends upon its relative importance in GNP. For example:

1 PERCENT CHANGE IN	VALUE FOR 1970 (MILLIONS OF DOLLARS)
Consumer expenditures	6,158
Fixed investment	1,353
Inventory investment	28
Federal government expenditures on goods and services	972
State and local government expenditures on goods and services	1,222

Source: U. S. Department of Commerce, *Survey of Current Business*, July 1971, p. 5.

These calculations are simply illustrative. The point they illustrate, however, is important.

OBSERVATIONS AND THEORY

In this chapter we have sought to give a sketch of the behavior of the principal macroeconomic variables. In the following chapters—after a brief digression to discuss some analytical techniques—we seek to develop a macroeconomic theory which will (1) provide a systematic explanation of the observations we have described, and (2) provide us with the means of assessing policy recommendations designed to influence their behavior in the future.

Though the description of these sections has been brief, it is clear that the phenomena we have to explain are diverse. Moreover, there are reasons, even at this stage, for believing them to be interrelated. The theory which follows is, for pedagogic reasons, presented in parts and has been somewhat simplified. It forms, however, a single integrated whole. The reader should, therefore, at the conclusion of Chapter 20, return to this chapter and ask himself: How far can the theory of later chapters explain the observations recorded in this one?

All that can be asked from a text of this kind is that the theory it presents shall do four things: throw some light on the observations and give the reader some understanding of the analytical problems involved; make the reader constructively skeptical of popular dogma and insistent on systematic evidence in support of arguments; make clear where the theory needs extension or modification; and whet the reader's intellectual appetite for more advanced studies.

QUESTIONS AND EXERCISES

1. What do you expect to happen to the capacity growth rate in the near future? How about the far future?

2. What do you think were the effects of (a) the Great Depression, and (b) World War II on the capacity growth rate?

3. What circumstances could result in a negative capacity growth rate?

4. We talk about recessions primarily in terms of unemployment rather than in terms of unemployed capital. Can you think of some reasons for this?

5. What do you expect to happen to the unemployment rate in the future? How about prices?

6. Actual output has grown more or less in line with capacity output. What factors could account for this?

7. Unlike most of the series presented in this chapter, the interest rate does not have a secular trend. Why?

8. Add a series that you think relevant to one of the figures in this chapter and describe its relationship to the other series in that figure.

9. Take the latest issue of the *Economic Report of the President* and bring the figures of this chapter up to date.

10. Prices rose from 1934 to 1937. They also rose from 1948 to 1970. It is common nowadays to speak of the price increase in the second period as constituting "inflation." Did we have "inflation" from 1934 to 1937? If not, why not? What does your view imply for the definition of inflation?

11. Between 1942 and 1965 real GNP grew at an average rate of 3.2 percent. Did economic welfare grow faster or slower than this? How would you seek to define economic welfare and measure its growth rate?

12. It is sometimes said that the rate of change of prices is explained by the percent of the labor force unemployed. Do the data of this chapter support this hypothesis?

13. Why have we never had a year, at least since 1890, with unemployment as low as 1 percent?

SUGGESTED READING

E. Dennison, *The Sources of Economic Growth* (Washington: Committee for Economic Development, 1962).

Economic Report of the President (Washington, D.C., issued every year).

R. A. Gordon, *Business Fluctuations* (New York: Harper and Row, 1961) Chap. 8.

A. G. Hart, P. Kenan, and A. Entine, *Money, Debt and Economic Activity* (Englewood Cliffs, N.J.: Prentice Hall, 1969) Chaps. 14 and 15.

E. Lundberg, *Economic Instability and Economic Growth,* (New Haven: Yale University Press, 1968).

G. Orwell, *The Road to Wigan Pier* (New York: Harcourt, Brace, 1958).

U.S. Department of Commerce, *Long Term Economic Growth* (Washington: U.S. Government Printing Office, 1966).

6

Analytical and Expository Techniques

MANY STUDENTS of economics find the analytical and expository techniques used by economists forbidding or even frightening. This is particularly the case where the techniques employ—or look as if they employ—mathematical modes of expression and mathematical methods of reasoning.

Those who read this book are therefore reassured at this stage that, in the pages which follow, no mathematical knowledge of manipulatory skill above high school algebra is assumed. If you resolutely refuse to be upset by the use of symbols—however terrifying they look—you have nothing to worry about at all. If you have taken college level mathematics so much the better.[1] But a little determination is all that is required.

After this reassurance you are now asked to study carefully the following short notes on particular concepts and techniques and to work through the Questions and Exercises at the end of the chapter.

THE CONCEPT OF A FUNCTION

In later chapters we shall frequently have to make assumptions about human behavior which imply that some variable (call it X) depends systematically upon some other variable (call it Y). In this case we shall say that

X is a function of Y

1. The advantage of mathematical knowledge in studying economics is immense. The fact that such knowledge is not necessary for this book should not obscure from the reader the gains to be derived from access to the principal technique of analytical thinking developed by man.

and write this:

$$X = f(Y) \tag{6.1}$$

where the notation f can be translated "is a function of" or "depends systematically upon."

The notation $X = f(Y)$ is used because of its convenience. It is obviously nothing to worry about since it merely states a general dependence of X (the *dependent* variable) on Y (the *independent* variable) and this is not of itself a very difficult idea.

Now $X = f(Y)$ is a general statement. It tells us nothing about the way X depends upon Y. If we want to know this, we must know the *form* of the function. Three simple forms are as follows:

$$\left. \begin{aligned} X &= A + bY \\ X &= F + cY^2 \\ X &= H + dY^{-2} \end{aligned} \right\} \tag{6.2} \qquad\qquad \left. \begin{aligned} X &= 100 + 0.8Y \\ X &= 80 + 2Y^2 \\ X &= 50 + 11Y^{-2} \end{aligned} \right\} \tag{6.2n}$$

where A, F, and H are constants independent of Y and thus give the value of X where Y is zero.

All of these are special cases of the general statement $X = f(Y)$. They tell us *generally* that a particular value of Y implies a particular value of X and *specifically* how to calculate X given Y, the constant term (A, F, H) and the coefficient (b, c, d).

Obviously it is possible for one variable (X) to depend systematically upon (be a function of) more than one variable. Thus we could write;

$$X = f(Y, Z, Q, L, M) \tag{6.3}$$

which is simply translated as:

X depends systematically upon the variables Y, Z, Q, L, and M.

A particular and simple example is:

$$X = A + aY + bZ + cQ + dL + eM \tag{6.4}$$

or, to give a numerical version:

$$X = 0.79 + 0.2Y + 4.7Z + 6.23Q + 8L + 0.0001M \tag{6.4n}$$

This tells us that, to calculate X, we now need to know the values of the constant A and of the five independent variables Y, Z, Q, L, and M. Once we know these, and the values of the coefficients a, b, c, d, e, it is a simple matter to calculate X.

In Chapter 1 we developed a rather crude behavior hypothesis to explain the monthly consumption of beer. This was to the effect that the monthly consumption of beer (the dependent variable) depended systematically upon, or was a function of,

1) the weather (defined as the average monthly temperature);

2) the level of general prosperity (defined as the reciprocal of the percentage of unemployment); and

3) the ratio of the price of whisky to the price of beer.

Written in general functional form this would appear:

$$B_c = f(T, U, P_w/P_B) \tag{6.5}$$

where

$B_c \equiv$ monthly beer consumption

$T \equiv$ average monthly temperature

$U \equiv$ average percentage of the work force unemployed in each month

$P_w \equiv$ average price of whisky in each month

$P_B \equiv$ average price of beer in each month.

Let us take the "beer" example a little further. In Chapter 1 we argued that if, with U and P_w/P_B constant, T increased, then B_c would increase.

We now define a symbol to indicate this *marginal response* of the *dependent* variable (beer consumption) to a change in *one* of the *independent* variables, *the remaining independent variables being held constant:*

$\dfrac{\partial B_c}{\partial T} \equiv$ marginal response of beer consumption to a change in

T (temperature) $-$ U and $\dfrac{P_w}{P_B}$ constant

$\dfrac{\partial B_c}{\partial U} \equiv$ marginal response of beer consumption to a change in

U (unemployment) $-$ T and $\dfrac{P_w}{P_B}$ constant

$\dfrac{\partial B_c}{\partial(P_w/P_B)} \equiv$ marginal response of beer consumption to a change in $\dfrac{P_w}{P_B}$

(the ratio of the price of whisky to the price of beer) $-$ T and U constant.

Our behavior hypothesis did not specify numerical values for these *marginal response coefficients*. That is, it did not set out either the *form* of the function or the *numerical value* of the *marginal response coefficient* as, for example, we did at (6.2n). It did, however, specify the *sign* of the coefficients, as the reader can easily see by looking back. We argued that

$$\frac{\partial B_c}{\partial T} > 0 \quad \frac{\partial B_c}{\partial U} < 0 \quad \text{and} \quad \frac{\partial B_c}{\partial(P_w/P_B)} > 0.$$

To fix our ideas let us now give an (assumed) *form* and *set of numerical values* to (6.5) and write:

$$B_c = aT + b\frac{1}{U} + c\left(\frac{P_w}{P_B}\right); \tag{6.6}$$

$$B_c = 0.7T + 6.71\frac{1}{U} + 32\left(\frac{P_w}{P_B}\right) \tag{6.6n}$$

If we now assume values for T, U and (P_w/P_B) we can calculate the resulting values for B_c by (fairly) simple arithmetic. A few such calculations are given in Table 6.1.

Table 6.1 / *The monthly consumption of beer
varying with the weather, the level of general prosperity,
and the price-ratio of whisky and beer.*

$$\left(\text{Hypothetical values of } T, U, \frac{P_w}{P_B}\right)$$

MONTH	$\dfrac{\partial B_c}{\partial T}$	T	$\dfrac{\partial B_c}{\partial(1/U)}$	$\dfrac{1}{U}$	$\dfrac{\partial B_c}{\partial(P_w/P_B)}$	$\dfrac{P_w}{P_B}$		B_c
1	0.7	(40)	+6.71	$(\frac{1}{3})$	+32	(1.2)	=	68.6
2	0.7	(44)	+6.71	$(\frac{1}{3})$	+32	(1.2)	=	71.4
3	0.7	(48)	+6.71	(1/3.2)	+32	(1.5)	=	83.7
4	0.7	(52)	+6.71	(1/3.2)	+32	(1.5)	=	86.5
5	0.7	(56)	+6.71	$(\frac{1}{3})$	+32	(1.9)	=	102.2
6	0.7	(60)	+6.71	$(\frac{1}{3})$	+32	(1.9)	=	105.0
7	0.7	(64)	+6.71	$(\frac{1}{3})$	+32	(2.0)	=	111.0
8	0.7	(70)	+6.71	$(\frac{1}{3})$	+32	(1.9)	=	112.0
9	0.7	(64)	+6.71	$(\frac{1}{3})$	+32	(1.9)	=	
10	0.7	(55)	+6.71	(1/3.4)	+32	(1.3)	=	
11	0.7	(45)	+6.71	(1/3.4)	+32	(1.3)	=	
12	0.7	(40)	+6.71	(1/3.2)	+32	(1.3)	=	

In this table a number of values of B_c have been left blank. These you should calculate for yourself.

A lot can be learned from this table. For example, between months 4 and 5 all three independent variables changed. What was the resultant *change* in beer consumption? If we look carefully we see that it was:

$$15.7 = 0.7 \times (4.0) + 6.71 \times (0.021) + 32 \times (0.4), \tag{6.7n}$$

or, to forget our numbers for a moment,

$$\Delta B_c = \frac{\partial B_c}{\partial T} \times \Delta T + \frac{\partial B_c}{\partial(1/U)} \times \Delta\left(\frac{1}{U}\right) + \frac{\partial B_c}{\partial(P_w/P_B)} \times \Delta\left(\frac{P_w}{P_B}\right) \tag{6.7n}^2$$

where the notation Δ indicates "the change in" the variable to which it is applied. It all looks very complicated at first sight but a little patience—and a little practice—will soon convince you that it is not complicated at all.

2. Those readers familiar with the calculus will be aware of the special nature of this case.

Let us now take one more example of the use of functions. In Chapter 4 we argued that real output depended upon (or was a function of) (1) the quantity of capital employed; (2) the input of labor services; and (3) the state of technology. This hypothesis can be, and often is, written in the form of a *production function* which would appear thus:

$$Y = f(K, N, T)$$

where

$Y \equiv$ real output
$K \equiv$ real capital stock employed in production
$N \equiv$ labor employed
$T \equiv$ state of technology.

For this function we would expect $\partial Y/\partial K > 0$, $\partial Y/\partial N > 0$, $\partial Y/\partial T > 0$, since it is reasonable to suppose that an increase in any input (the quantity of the other input(s) and the state of technology remaining constant) would raise output as would an improvement in technology (with both inputs constant).

A particular production function, commonly met in macroeconomics, is

$$Y = TK^{\alpha}N^{1-\alpha}.$$

This too is an awkward looking expression at first sight, but again there is really nothing to be afraid of. Suppose $\alpha = 0.5$ so that $1 - \alpha$ also is 0.5. For simplicity assume $T = 10$. Then since any number raised to the power of 0.5 is merely the square root of the number, we can calculate Y from the values of the two independent variables K and N either by using logarithms or, simpler still, by employing a table of square roots. This is done for assumed values of K and N in Table 6.2. As before, you should complete the table for yourself.

If we read *down* any column of Table 6.2 we find what happens to output when the input of labor increases with capital and technology constant. If we read *across* any row we find what happens to output when the input of capital increases with labor input and technology constant. If we read down a *diagonal* we discover what happens to output when both labor and capital inputs experience *equiproportional* increases.

We now give the names to the *marginal coefficients* of the *production function* employed by economists. These are:

$\dfrac{\partial Y}{\partial K} \equiv \begin{matrix}\text{marginal product}\\ \text{of capital}\end{matrix} \equiv$ the increase in output produced by a unit increase in K with N, T constant.

$\dfrac{\partial Y}{\partial N} \equiv \begin{matrix}\text{marginal product}\\ \text{of labor}\end{matrix} \equiv$ the increase in output produced by a unit increase in N with K, T constant.

Table 6.2 / *Production function relating output to varying combinations of inputs.*

NUMBER OF UNITS OF LABOR	NUMBER OF UNITS OF CAPITAL										
	25	50	75	100	125	150	175	200	225	250	275
5	**112**	158	194		250	274	296	317	336	354	371
10	158	**224**	274	316	353		418	447	474	500	524
15	194	274	**336**	387	432	474	512	547	581	612	642
20	224	316	387	**448**	500	548	592	632	671	707	
25		353	432	500	**560**	613	662	707		791	829
30	274	387	474	548	613	**672**	725		822	866	909
35	296	418		592	662	725	**784**	836	888	936	982
40	317		547	632	707	775		**896**	948	1,000	1,049
45	336	474	581	671		822	888	949	**1,008**	1,060	1,113
50	354	500	612	707	791	866	936	1,000	1,060	**1,120**	1,173
55	371	524	642	742	829	909	982	1,049	1,113	1,173	**1,232**

$$Y = TK\alpha N1^{-\alpha} \quad \text{where } \alpha = 0.5 \text{ and } T = 10.$$

You should now check, from the table, that the following propositions are correct for this particular production function:

1) doubling (trebling) both capital and labor always doubles (trebles) output;

2) the marginal product of both factors is always positive;

3) the marginal product of either factor tends to fall as more of it is employed with the other factor constant;

4) the marginal product of either factor is greater the smaller is the ratio of the quantity of it employed to the quantity employed of the other factor.

This particular function has a number of other important and interesting properties which we shall have to discuss in detail when we turn to consider economic growth. At this stage, however, they do not concern us, for our aims are merely

1) to explain what is meant by a function;

2) to show that the functional notation is nothing to worry about; and

3) to explain what is meant by *marginal response coefficients*.

GRAPHS

Economists make considerable use of graphs (or diagrams) to represent functional relations. A graph expresses a relationship between two variables, one of which is the dependent variable and the other the independent variable. Graphs are useful but, since we are limited to drawing them in a two-dimensional plane, less powerful than the analytical methods discussed under the heading of *marginal response coefficients* which, obviously enough, can handle any number of "systematic dependencies" we care to postulate. To illustrate we can draw a graph derived from our production function:

$$Y = f(K, N, T) \tag{6.8}$$

This graph measures Y on the vertical axis and N on the horizontal. To construct the graph we then take K and T to be constant. The resulting relationship gives Y as a function of N (output as a function of labor input) with both the stock of capital (K) and the state of technology (T) given. It is thus a *short-run production function*. The slope of this curve relating Y and N is easily seen to be the *marginal response coefficient* $\partial Y/\partial N$—that is, the marginal product of labor—or the increment in output brought about by a unit increase in labor (N) with both capital (K) and technology (T) constant.

We have drawn the curve to illustrate the propositions that
1) the marginal product of labor is always positive;
2) the marginal product of labor diminishes as labor input increases.
If K and/or T changes, the curve itself will shift. Suppose, for example, we were to draw a second curve on the basis of a greater capital stock. This curve would lie above the old.

Figure 6.1(a) / *The relationship between total product and varying units of labor output.*

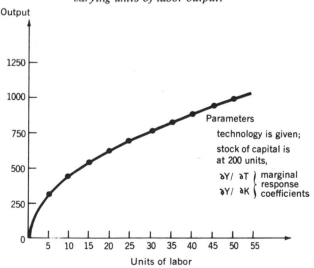

Figure 6.1(b) / *The relationship between total product and*
varying units of capital input.

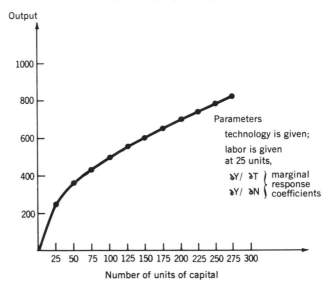

The points to notice about graphs are:

1) a graph shows only the relationship between a dependent variable and *one* independent variable of which the former is a function; given

2) the values of any other independent variables on which the dependent variable systematically depends (i.e., of which it is a function);

3) the slope of the graph is the *marginal response coefficient* relating the dependent variable to the independent variable.

The independent variables not measured on either axis and their marginal response coefficients, taken as given in drawing a graph (i.e., in our example *K, ∂F/∂K, T,* and *∂Y/∂T*) are termed the *parameters* of the curve. Hence whenever the student is confronted with a curve relating two variables he should *always* ask himself two questions:

1) What are the parameters of this curve?

2) Which way would the curve shift if one of the parameters changed?

THE CONCEPT OF ELASTICITY

So far we have discussed the response of one (dependent) variable to a change in another (independent) variable in terms of the concept of a marginal response coefficient. Thus the marginal response of beer consumption to a change in temperature was defined as $\partial B_c / \partial T$ and given, in equation (6.7n) the hypothetical value of 0.7.

The marginal response coefficient is an important concept. Nevertheless it is not free from ambiguity, for it depends crucially upon the units in which the dependent and independent variables are measured. To see this, assume beer to be measured in thousands of barrels (of standard size) and temperature in degrees Fahrenheit. Then:

$$\frac{\partial B_c}{\partial T} \frac{\text{(in thousands of barrels)}}{\text{(in degrees Fahrenheit)}} = 0.7.$$

So a one-degree rise in temperature increases beer consumption by 700 barrels; for, holding all other variables in equation (6.7) constant,

$$\Delta B_c = \frac{\partial B_c}{\partial T} \times \Delta T$$
$$= 0.7 \text{ thousand barrels per degree} \times 1.0$$
$$= 700 \text{ barrels.}$$

If we now measured beer in units of 100 barrels, we should have $\partial B_c / \partial = 7.0$ and, if we measured in single barrels, $\partial B_c / \partial T = 700$. Behavioristically speaking nothing has changed: only the units of measurement have altered and with them $\partial B_c / \partial T$.

This dependence of marginal response coefficients, the constants of human behavior in linear functions like (6.6), on the units in which the variables are measured is awkward for it makes it hard to estimate their importance—and thus compare two or more marginal response coefficients. Hence economists tend to use a measure which is independent of the units in which the variables are measured. This measure is known as *elasticity* and defined as:

the proportionate change in the dependent variable $\equiv \dfrac{\Delta B_c}{B_c}$

divided by

the proportionate change in the independent variable $\equiv \dfrac{\Delta T}{T}$.

bringing it about.

So that the elasticity of beer consumption with respect to temperature alone is:

$$\frac{\Delta B_c}{B_c} \div \frac{\Delta T}{T} \equiv \frac{\Delta B_c}{\Delta T} \times \frac{T}{B_c}$$

$$\equiv \frac{\dfrac{\partial B_c}{\partial T} \times \Delta T}{\Delta T} \times \frac{T}{B_c}$$

$$\equiv \frac{\partial B_c}{\partial T} \times \frac{T}{B_c} \equiv \frac{\partial B_c}{\partial T} \div \frac{B_c}{T}.$$

In short, the elasticity is the marginal response coefficient relating B_c to T divided by the ratio B_c/T. Since the latter expression is measured in the same units as the former, the choice of units has no influence on the elasticity, which is a pure number. For example, using equation (6.7n) and taking two hypothetical values of T, we have:

$$B_c = 0.7 \times (40) + 6.71(\tfrac{1}{3}) + 32(1.2) = 68.6 \qquad (6.9n(a))$$
$$B_c = 0.7 \times (44) + 6.71(\tfrac{1}{3}) + 32(1.2) = 71.4 \qquad (6.9n(b))$$
$$\therefore \Delta B = 0.7 \Delta T$$
$$= 0.7 \times 4.0$$
$$= 2.8.$$

and the elasticity is:

$$\text{elasticity}_{(1)} \equiv \frac{\partial B_c}{\partial T} \div \frac{B_c}{T} \simeq 0.7 \div \frac{68.6}{40} = 0.7 \div 1.715 = 0.408$$

Why do we use the sign $\simeq$ signifying *approximate* equality? Simply because we *could* have written, by using (6.9n(b)) to give the values of B_c and T,

$$\text{elasticity}_{(2)} \equiv \frac{\partial B_c}{\partial T} \div \frac{B_c}{T} \simeq 0.7 \div \frac{71.4}{44.0} = 0.7 \div 1.623 = 0.431.$$

Hence the numerical value of the elasticity over a *range* of change in the independent variable is not unambiguous. If we began with (6.9n(a)) and moved to (6.9n(b)) we estimated the elasticity as 0.408. Reversing the procedure, we found a different value. A diagram may make the point clearer.

Figure 6.2 / *Beer consumption function.*

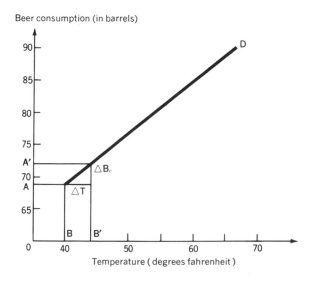

At 40° F the ratio
$$\frac{B_c}{T} = \frac{OA}{OB} = \frac{68.6}{40.0}$$

At 44° F the ratio
$$\frac{B_c}{T} = \frac{OA'}{OB'} = \frac{71.4}{44.0}.$$

The marginal response coefficient

$$= \frac{\partial B_c}{\partial T} = \frac{\frac{\partial B_c}{\partial T} \times \Delta T}{\Delta T} = \frac{\Delta B_c}{\Delta T}.$$

Suppose now we make the temperature change not four degrees but 0.004 degrees: that is, one-thousandth part of our first example. We have for our two measures:

$$\text{elasticity}_{(1)} \simeq 0.7 \div 1.715 = 0.408163$$

and
$$\text{elasticity}_{(2)} \simeq 0.7 \div 1.71505 = 0.408151.$$

Clearly the smaller we make the temperature change (and thus the resultant beer consumption change) the nearer our two elasticity measures approach. As the temperature change tends to zero—that is, becomes smaller and smaller—the elasticity becomes closer to $0.7 \div 68.6/40.0$. In the limit—that is, when ΔT is indefinitely small—we can say that the elasticity *at temperature 40* is given by:

$$\text{elasticity (at } T = 40) = 0.7 \div \frac{68.6}{40.0}.$$

This last concept, the elasticity of a schedule (in this case the beer consumption schedule) *at a particular point upon it*—is the concept usually employed in economics. It is safe to use it only when the change in the independent variable is small. Where this is not the case, we generally need to use the concept of elasticity over a range—in our example over the range of 40–44 degrees of temperature.

The reader should notice that the elasticity depends upon two factors:

1) the slope of the schedule (the marginal response coefficient) at the point at which elasticity is being measured; and

2) the *ratio* of the values of the dependent and independent variables at the same point.

For the special case of a straight line schedule the slope is constant, as the figure makes clear. But the ratio between the values of the variables is not (in general) constant. Hence the elasticity will vary along the curve. The reader should make sure that he understands this point by working a few examples in addition to those given in the Questions and Exercises at the end of this chapter.

Though in general straight line curves do not exhibit constant elasticity, some straight line curves exhibit this property.

There are in fact two special straight line curves commonly used to illustrate elasticity. They are shown in Figure 6.3.

The first of these curves has zero elasticity of demand for butter over the price range $p_A - p_B$. The second has infinite elasticity at the price p_x. The reader should satisfy himself that these statements are consistent with our earlier discussion of elasticity.

Apart from its freedom from the problem of units, the concept of elasticity has other uses. Suppose that the community's demand for peanuts

Figure 6.3 / *Hypothetical demand curves for butter.*

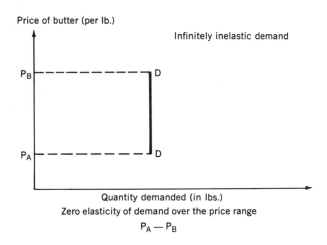

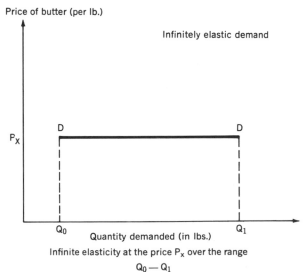

(X) depends only on their price (p). Suppose now that producers lower price by (say) 1 percent. If the elasticity of demand is -1, then the proportionate change in quantity will be equal (in absolute value) but opposite in sign to the price change. The quantity sold will increase by 1 percent. Hence the value of total sales will be constant. If the elasticity is algebraically less than -1 (say -3) a 1 percent cut in prices will be associated with a 3 percent increase in sales. Conversely, if the price elasticity were algebraically greater than -1 (say equal to zero) the quantity sold would not change. Hence the effect of a price cut on total revenue ($\equiv$ price $\times$ quantity sold) depends upon the elasticity of demand, which is for peanuts in this case.

The term "elasticity" is frequently used with reference to the absolute value of the elasticity rather than its algebraic value. The sign of the elasticity is usually clear from the context. Adopting this convention we may summarize the peanut example by saying that if the price of peanuts is reduced by a small percentage then the value of sales will

    1) *increase*   if the elasticity of demand > 1;
    2) *decrease*   if the elasticity of demand < 1;
    3) *remain unchanged* if the elasticity of demand = 1.

We call case (1) elastic demand and case (2) inelastic demand. Why do we say a *small* percentage? To see this denote

$$p \equiv \text{price of peanuts}$$

$$\Delta p \equiv \text{change in price of peanuts}$$

$$X \equiv \text{quantity purchased}$$

$$\Delta X \equiv \text{change in quantity purchased.}$$

Then before the price change, total revenue $= pX$. After the price change we have:

$$\text{total revenue} = (p + \Delta p)(X + \Delta X)$$
$$= pX + p \times \Delta X + X \times \Delta p + \Delta p \times \Delta X.$$

Hence the change in revenue is given by:

$$\Delta \text{ (total revenue)} = pX + p \times \Delta X + X \times \Delta p + \Delta X \times \Delta p - pX$$
$$= p\Delta X + X \times \Delta p + \Delta X \times \Delta p.$$

Now this expression can be rewritten as:

$$\Delta \text{ (total revenue)} = pX \left\{ \frac{\Delta X}{X} + \frac{\Delta p}{p} + \frac{\Delta X}{X} \times \frac{\Delta p}{p} \right\}$$

$$= pX \left\{ \begin{array}{c} \text{prop.} \\ \text{change} \\ \text{in} \\ \text{quantity} \end{array} + \begin{array}{c} \text{prop.} \\ \text{change} \\ \text{in} \\ \text{price} \end{array} + \begin{array}{c} \text{prop.} \\ \text{change} \\ \text{in} \\ \text{quantity} \end{array} \times \begin{array}{c} \text{prop.} \\ \text{change} \\ \text{in} \\ \text{price} \end{array} \right\}.$$

Suppose the last term is sufficiently small to be neglected. Then:

$$\Delta \text{ (total revenue)} \gtrless 0 \qquad pX \left\{ \begin{array}{c} \text{prop.} \\ \text{change} \\ \text{in} \\ \text{quantity} \end{array} + \begin{array}{c} \text{prop.} \\ \text{change} \\ \text{in} \\ \text{price} \end{array} \right\} \gtrless 0.$$

Clearly, since the proportionate change in price is *negative,* the right-hand inequality can be written:

$$pX \left\{ \frac{\text{prop. change in quantity}}{\text{prop. change in price}} + 1 \right\} \lessgtr 0.$$

i.e. $pX\{\text{elasticity of demand} + 1\} \lessgtr 0.$

Hence revenue will increase if the elasticity is < -1; which is the result which we reached verbally above. To reach this result we have, however, had to set $\Delta p/p \times \Delta X/X$ (the product of the proportionate changes) to zero. This is permissible if Δp is close to zero. Hence our elasticity result, not very surprisingly in view of our definition of point elasticity, holds strictly only where Δp is indefinitely small. *In all other cases it is an approximation which involves an error dependent on $\Delta p/p \times \Delta X/X$.* The reader should calculate for himself how good this approximation is by assuming a variety of values for $\Delta p/p$ and $\Delta X/X$.

FUNCTIONS AND SCHEDULES

In our beer consumption example we wrote quite generally

$$B_c = f\left(T, U, \frac{P_w}{P_B}\right),$$ (6.5)

and specifically:

$$B_c = aT + b\left(\frac{1}{U}\right) + c\left(\frac{P_w}{P_B}\right)$$ (6.6)

This specific function (6.6) is said to be *linear* in the independent variables because it involves no powers of these variables other than unity. Had we written

$$B_c = a_1 T + aT^2 + b\left(\frac{1}{U}\right) + c\left(\frac{P_w}{P_B}\right)^2 + d\left(\frac{P_w}{P_B}\right)$$

the function would have been *quadratic* in T and (P_w/P_B) and *linear* in $(1/U)$.

In general, in economics, we must expect nonlinear relationships to occur. Nevertheless, in most of this book, we shall only use functions which are linear—that is, of the form:

$$Y = a + b \times x + c \times z + d \times w$$

or logarithmically linear—that is, of the form:

$$\log Y = \log a' + b' \log x + c' \log z$$

The latter function, since multiplying the logarithm of a variable means raising the variable to the power of its multiplier, can be written:

$$Y = a' x^{b'} z^{c'}$$

a form we have already met in the production function discussed earlier.

The justification for restricting ourselves to linear or log linear functions is two-fold. The first point is that these functions are algebraically convenient. Thus the linear function (6.6) has the constant marginal response coefficients $\partial B_c / \partial T = a$, $\partial B_c / \partial (1/U) = b$ and $\partial B_c / \partial (P_w / P_B) = c$ while the log linear function also has the constant marginal response coefficients $\partial \log y / \partial \log x = b'$ and $\partial \log y / \partial \log z = c'$.

There is also the second point that any function, *over a sufficiently small range of values of the independent variable, can be approximated by a linear function*. This is illustrated in Figure 6.4, which shows how two functions which are certainly not linear can be approximated in this way.

Thus in Figure 6.4 (a) for values of the independent variable close to x_1 we can approximate the function by the line aa', for values around x_2 by the line bb' and so on. In the same way the function in Figure 6.4 (b) can be approximated reasonably well by the four straight lines aa', bb', cc' and dd' each of which is applicable only over a range of values (or a particular value) of the independent variable.

To visualize the properties of the logarithmic function (6.7) consider some variable Y which is growing through time as follows:

Time	0	1	2	3	4
Value of Y	10	15	22.5	33.75	50.625.

It is easy to see that the law of growth in this case is a 50 percent increase in Y per period of time. If we graph this function using a logarithmic scale for Y and a natural scale for time, we have the values:

Time	0	1	2	3	4
Log Y	1.0	1.1761	1.3522	1.5281	1.7042
Y	10.0	15	22.5	33.57	50.625.

Figure 6.4 / *Linear approximations to nonlinear relations.*

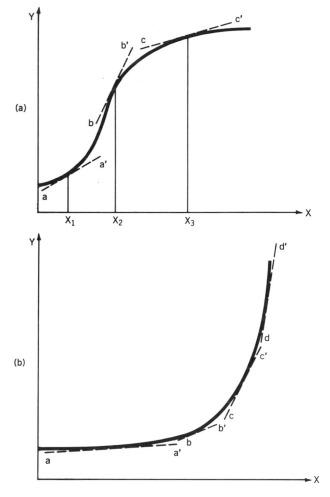

From this table it is easy to see that constant *absolute* differences in the logarithm of a variable imply constant percentage increases in the variable itself. The graph of log Y against time will thus be a straight line the slope of which is the percentage rate of growth in Y per period. This function is plotted in Figure 6.5.

Now consider the function (6.7) which is:

$$\log Y = \log a' + b' \log X + c' \log Z$$

If we use this relationship to plot log Y against log X holding log Z constant at some fixed value log $\bar{Z}$ and using a log scale for both the x and y

Figure 6.5 / *Constant percentage rates of growth.*

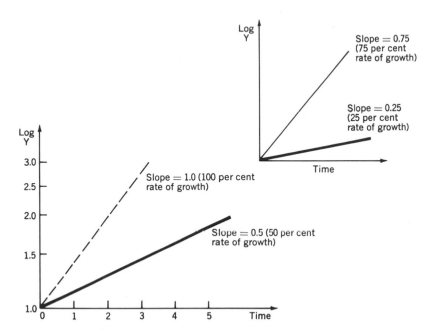

axes, we shall get a straight line function relating log X and log Y. The slope of this function will be the marginal response coefficient $\partial \log Y / \partial \log X = b'$. The constant will define the origin of the curve at the point log $X = 0$ and log $Z = \log \overline{Z}$. This curve is plotted in Figure 6.6.

Suppose now that log X increases from x_1 to x_2. This distance defines a percentage increase in X. The resultant change in log Y from y_1 to y_2 defines a percentage increase in Y. The slope of the function is thus:

$$\frac{\Delta Y}{Y} \div \frac{\Delta X}{X} \equiv \text{elasticity of } Y \text{ with respect to } X.$$

Hence functions of the form of (6.7) have constant marginal response coefficients which are elasticities (slopes of straight lines in the logarithms). Thus the properties of (6.7) are:

$$\frac{\Delta Y}{Y} \div \frac{\Delta X}{X} \equiv \text{elasticity of } Y \text{ with respect to } X$$

$$\equiv \frac{\frac{\partial Y}{\partial X} \times \Delta X}{Y} \div \frac{\Delta X}{X} \equiv b$$

$$\frac{\Delta Y}{Y} \div \frac{\Delta Z}{Z} \equiv \text{elasticity of } Y \text{ with respect to } Z$$

$$\equiv \frac{\dfrac{\partial Y}{\partial Z} \times \Delta Z}{Y} \div \frac{\Delta Z}{Z} \equiv c$$

These relationships are useful to remember when interpreting graphs and functions.

Figure 6.6 / *Elasticities and logarithmic relationships.*
Three different marginal response coefficients.

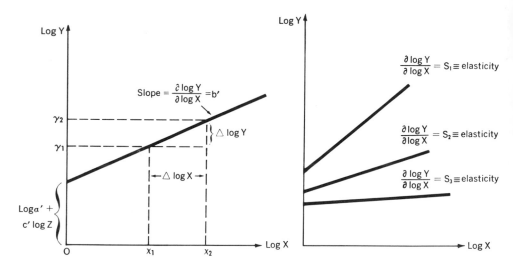

EQUATIONS AND IDENTITIES

In Chapters 2 and 3 we set out the framework of definitions which we use in national income accounting. In these chapters we always wrote equality with this sign $\equiv$ rather than the more familiar $=$. Thus we wrote:

$$Y \equiv C + S$$
$$Y \equiv C + I$$
$$\therefore \quad S \equiv I.$$

This was done to emphasize the point that these expressions were identities which held by definition of the concepts employed whatever the values of Y and C.

By contrast, in writing our "beer-drinking function" and production function we used the more familiar two-bar sign for equality. *This is a convention which we shall consistently employ throughout this book.* We use it to distinguish between hypotheses about economic behavior—which can be true or false—and definitions which cannot. Our convention, which does not correspond precisely with mathematical usage, is this:

1) *Definitions* and equalities arising from them we shall express with a three-bar sign for equality, e.g.

$$Y \equiv C + I.$$

These will be referred to as *identities*.

2) *Hypotheses* about economic behavior, including, of course, equilibrium conditions, we shall express with the two-bar sign for equality; e.g., our "beer-drinking hypothesis," which we write:

$$B_c = f\left(T, U, \frac{P_w}{P_B}\right).$$

These we shall speak of as *equations*.

In short, meaningful (because conceivably testable) propositions will always be expressed as *equations* simply because they may or may not be found to hold in the real world. Such relations are often called *behavior equations*. Definitional relationships, which *always* hold irrespective of the values of the variables, we shall always express as *identities*.

This distinction we employ between identities and equations is of great importance and is commonly found in economic writing. The significant point is that identities, which hold whatever the values of the variables, tell us nothing about economic behavior and cannot be tested by empirical observation. Equations, on the other hand, embody propositions about economic behavior which can be tested by empirical observation either directly or via predictions derived from them.

STOCKS AND FLOWS

Economic variables fall into two groups which we shall call *stocks* and *flows*: a *stock* variable is one which has no time dimension but is described at a moment of time: a *flow* variable necessarily involves a time dimension.

To give an example of a flow variable we may take income. To say that a man's income is $1000 is meaningless *unless* we know the *time period of measurement*. An income of $1000 *per year* is very different from an income of $1000 *per decade* or $1000 *per week*. All flow variables are thus rates (of flow) over some defined time period. This applies, as a little reflection will make clear, to all the national income accounting concepts we discussed in Chapters 2 and 3.

Stock variables, on the other hand, do not require a time dimension to have meaning. It makes sense to say that on January 1, 1971 a man's height is 5 feet 11 inches or his wealth $10,027 without specifying a period of time. We may conclude that

1) *flow* variables are necessarily defined with reference to a period of time, i.e., a year, month, decade, or quarter, and can be measured and given meaning only in terms of this (or some other) period;

2) *stock* variables are measured at a moment of time and have meaning independently of any period.

It should also be clear that many flow variables are simply the change in some stock variable *over a given period*. For example, if at the end of December 1969 real capital (a stock variable) is $10 million and at the end of December 1970 it is $14 million, then the increment in real capital *over the year* is $4 million. We have already defined the increase in real capital as real net *investment*. Hence the *rate* of real *net* investment (a flow variable) is $4 million *a year* for the year 1970.

Much confusion arises from a failure to distinguish between *stocks* and *flows*. You are strongly recommended to ask yourself, on meeting any economic variable for the first time, is this a *stock* variable or is it a *flow?*

THE CONCEPT OF EQUILIBRIUM

Economists constantly speak of the "economic system" or the "market for some commodity" as being in "equilibrium." By this they imply no more than that the system or market has reached a position from which it has no tendency to depart—in short, a position of rest. Such a position will occur only if the forces making for movement in one direction are exactly counterbalanced by the forces making for movement in the opposite direction. The *equilibrium* value of any variable is thus simply the value of the variable which, if reached, will tend to persist unchanged.

Since, as we have seen, economics is a social science and thus concerned with human behavior, we may now ask what this concept of equilibrium implies *in terms of human behavior*. To see this let us take an example and inquire what is meant by, let us say, the market for peanuts being in equilibrium at a price of 10 cents per bag and a monthly volume of sales of 2 million bags. Clearly the market will only be in equilibrium if both buyers and sellers are "satisfied" with the ruling price and quantity sold. If they are not, one group or the other will, in future periods, modify its behavior, which will change the price and quantity sold. Thus we may enunciate the general proposition that, for equilibrium to exist in any period, people must be "satisfied" with the actual price ruling in the market and the actual quantities sold in any period. When they are not satisfied, *disequilibrium* exists, *and some persons will modify their behavior.*

What is meant by being satisfied? All we mean by this expression is that what people plan to do is in conformity with what actually occurs. For where this is not so, those people whose plans are not satisfied, will, in the next period of time, modify their plans. Equilibrium thus requires all plans to be satisfied, which again requires all *plans to be consistent.*

Table 6.3 depicting hypothetical situations in the market for peanuts will serve to illustrate the point.

Table 6.3 / *Equilibrium and the peanut market.*

POSITION	PRICE (PER BAG IN CENTS)	PLANNED SALES OF PRODUCERS (M)	PLANNED PURCHASES OF CONSUMERS (M)	REMARKS
1	10	2.0	2.0	Consistent plans— equilibrium
2	10	2.0	1.5	Inconsistent plans— disequilibrium
3	9	1.75	1.75	Consistent plans— equilibrium

Suppose that, in some period producers plan to make and sell 2 million bags of peanuts at a price of 10 cents per bag and that, in the same month, consumers plan to purchase 2 million bags at 10 cents per bag. In this case

1) all plans are consistent; and

2) the actual price and quantity sold (and purchased) will correspond with the plans of both groups; hence

3) the market is in equilibrium.

Suppose now that, in period two, producers' plans are the same as period one but, because of a change in consumers' tastes, consumers now plan to purchase only 1.5 million bags at a price of 10 cents.

In this case

1) all plans are not consistent;

2) the actual price and/or quantity sold (and purchased) can not and hence will not correspond with the plans of both groups; hence

3) the market is in *disequilibrium* and, in the next period, producers will obviously wish to modify their plans.

We may sum up the discussion so far by the following statements:

1) to say that a system is in equilibrium means that it has reached a position of rest from which it has no tendency to depart;

2) where an economic system is in equilibrium then:
   (a) the actual values of the variables it contains must correspond with
   (b) the values of the same variables which people planned or expected;
3) this can only occur when all plans are consistent;
4) where plans are not consistent disequilibrium exists;
5) the sign of the existence of disequilibrium is that, for some persons or groups, planned and actual values of variables do not coincide;
6) the outcome of disequilibrium is a change in plans by the persons or groups for whom actual and planned variables do not coincide.

It is obviously a simple matter to extend this argument one stage further. Suppose our peanut market reaches position 2—a position of disequilibrium. Then producers will modify their plans until a new position (say position 3) is reached. At this position we have once again a situation in which

1) all plans are consistent
2) the actual price and quantity sold (and purchased) corresponds with the plans of both producers and consumers so that
3) neither group has any need to modify its behavior and
4) the peanut market is in equilibrium once again.

STATICS AND DYNAMICS

In Chapter 4 we drew a distinction between *static* and *dynamic* analysis. This distinction can now be illustrated in terms of our "peanut" example.

In *static* analysis—commonly called *comparative statics*—we compare only positions of equilibrium: that is, we compare positions 1 and 3 and note that, as a consequence of a change in consumers' tastes both the *equilibrium price* of a bag of peanuts and the *equilibrium quantity* sold (and purchased) are lower than in the initial equilibrium position.

We do not, however, seek to explain either how long (i.e. how many months) it takes to get from position 1 to position 3 or the path by which price and quantity adjust to the new equilibrium position, for these questions, though important, form part of *dynamic* analysis.

Comparative statics thus simplifies reality by ignoring the *process* of change. Hence in comparative statics the rates at which variables change are ignored. At one period we are at position 1. At another we are at position 3. Our sole aim is to compare these two positions. Perhaps the simplest way of moving in this somewhat unreal world is to regard all changes as taking place instantaneously.

QUESTIONS AND EXERCISES

1. The "beer-consumption" hypothesis of (6.6n) is:

$$B_c = 0.7T + 6.71 \frac{1}{U} + 32 \left(\frac{P_w}{P_B}\right).$$

Assume U to be constant at 2 percent (i.e. $U = \frac{1}{2}$)

$\frac{P_w}{P_B}$ to be constant at 1.5 per cent.

Then calculate the values of B_c for the following values of T

$$T = 40, 45, 50, 55, 60, 65, 70, 75, 80.$$

Draw a graph with B_c on the vertical axis and T on the horizontal. From this curve identify the marginal response coefficient $\partial B_c / \partial T$ and the quantity $6.71(\frac{1}{2}) + 32(1.5)$.

On what does the position of the curve depend? In what way would the curve shift if the public's taste for beer suddenly increased?

What is the (theoretical) value of beer consumption when T is zero?

2. From the following data, again using (6.6n) plot a graph with B_c on the vertical axis and T on the horizontal.

T	U	P_w/P_B
40	2	1.5
45	2	1.5
50	3	1.8
55	3	1.8
60	2	1.8
65	4	2.0
70	1	1.1

a) What meaning, if any, can be given to the *slope* of this curve?

b) What is the relation between the slope of this curve and the slope of the curve constructed in Question 1?

c) In what circumstances, if any, could the slope of a curve which simply plots observed values of a dependent variable (in this case B_c) and one independent variable (in this case T) give a good estimate of the marginal response coefficient $\partial B_c / \partial T$?

3. Plot the following graphs putting X on the vertical axis and Y on the horizontal.

$$X = A + bY \quad \text{where } A = 100; \ b = 0.8$$
$$X = F + cY^2 \quad \text{where } F = 100; \ c = 0.2$$

and Y takes the following values:

$$Y = 0, 2, 10, 12, 20, 40, 50.$$

In each case find the value of $\partial X/\partial Y$ (the marginal response coefficient) when $Y = 2$ and $Y = 10$. What difficulties arise with the second function?

Show that, for one curve, $\partial X/\partial Y$ is a constant while for the other $\partial X/\partial Y$ depends upon (is a function of) Y.

At what value of Y do the two curves cut? What is the corresponding value of X?

4. In economics the elasticity of any dependent variable (X) with respect to some other independent variable (Y), of which it is a function, is defined as follows:

$$\text{elasticity} \equiv \frac{\text{proportionate change}}{\text{in } X} \div \frac{\text{proportionate change}}{\text{in } Y}$$

$$\equiv \frac{\Delta X}{X} \bigg/ \frac{\Delta Y}{Y} = \frac{\frac{\partial X}{\partial Y} \times \Delta Y}{X} \bigg/ \frac{\Delta Y}{Y}$$

Using this formula find the approximate elasticity of both curves in Question 3 when Y changes from 50 to 51 and 100 to 101.

Can you find the elasticity of output (Y) with respect to labor (N) from the production function $Y = TK^\alpha N^{1-\alpha}$? Put $T = 10$, $K = 10{,}000$, $N = 100$, $\alpha = 0.5$. Is there a relationship between this elasticity and $1 - \alpha$? [Hint: use the logarithmic formulation].

5. Fig. 6.1(a) is drawn on the assumption that the production function is:

$$Y = TK^\alpha N^{1-\alpha} \quad \text{where } T = 10, \ K = 200, \text{ and } \alpha = 0.5.$$

What would happen to the curve if K became 100? Would the slope of the curve $\partial Y/\partial N$ be greater, less or the same at any given value of N? What does your answer mean in terms of economics? Suppose alternatively that with $K = 200$, T became 20. Plot the new curve and explain your result.

6. Using the same production function $Y = TK^\alpha N^{1-\alpha}$ put $T = 1$ and $\alpha = 0.5$ and show that the following table gives numerical values of K and N which produce a given constant output.

K CAPITAL STOCK UNITS	N LABOR INPUT UNITS
8	1,250
10	1,000
20	500
25	400
40	250
50	200
100	100

a) What is the constant value of Y?

b) What is the cheapest method of those shown of producing the given output when
1) labor costs $1 per unit per year; capital $25 per unit per year?
2) labor costs $1 per unit per year; capital $4 per unit per year?
3) labor costs $2 per unit per year; capital $50 per unit per year?
c) What can you learn by comparing (1) and (3)?
d) What can you learn by comparing (2) and (1)?
Explain your results and the lessons you draw from them.

7. Using the same function as Question 6, the marginal physical products of labor and capital respectively are:[3]

$$\frac{\partial Y}{\partial K} \equiv \frac{\text{marginal physical}}{\text{product of capital}} = T\alpha \left(\frac{N}{K}\right)^{1-\alpha} = 0.5 \left(\frac{N}{K}\right)^{1/2}$$

$$\frac{\partial Y}{\partial N} \equiv \frac{\text{marginal physical}}{\text{product of labor}} = T(1-\alpha) \left(\frac{K}{N}\right)^{\alpha} = 0.5 \left(\frac{K}{N}\right)^{1/2}.$$

Find numerical values for these marginal physical products for your answer to Question 6 (b) (1). What do you notice about the relationships of marginal physical products to factor prices? Can you find a simple formula expressing minimum cost conditions?

8. Reread and reformulate in the light of your answers to these two questions the discussion of the shape of the production possibility curve in Chapter 5. What kinds of production possibility curve would you expect to derive from the following pairs of production functions? Give your reasons.

Situation *A*.

$$\text{agricultural output} = T_A K_A^{\alpha_A} N_A^{1-\alpha_A} \qquad \text{where } \alpha_A = \alpha_M$$

$$\text{manufacturing output} = T_M K_M^{\alpha_M} N_M^{1-\alpha_M} \text{ where } T_M \gtrless T_A.$$

Situation *B*.

$$\text{agricultural output} = T_A K_A^{\alpha_A} N_A^{1-\alpha_A} \text{ where } \alpha_A \neq \alpha_M$$

$$\text{manufacturing output} = T_M K_M^{\alpha_M} N_M^{1-\alpha_M} \text{ where } T_A \gtrless T_M.$$

9. Suppose the production function is:

$$Y = TK_\alpha N^{1-\alpha} \quad \text{where } T = 1; \ \alpha = \tfrac{1}{3}.$$

Show (as in Question 6) that the following table gives numerical values of K and N which produce a given constant output.

K CAPITAL STOCK	N LABOR INPUT
1	1,000
4	500
6.25	400
16	250
25	200
100	100

3. Readers familiar with the calculus will readily accept these results. Those not so familiar are asked to take them on trust.

Show that, of the possibilities depicted in this table, the combination $K = 25$, $N = 200$ is the cheapest when labor costs \$1 per unit per year and capital costs \$4 per unit per year. Compare this result with that of Question 6. What is its relationship to the argument by which we justified the increasing cost production possibility curve of Chapter 4?

10. The elasticity of output with respect to labor asked for in Question 4 is given by:

$$\frac{\Delta Y}{Y} \Big/ \frac{\Delta N}{N} \equiv \frac{\frac{\partial Y}{\partial N} \times \Delta N}{Y} \Big/ \frac{\Delta N}{N} \equiv \frac{\frac{\partial Y}{\partial N} \times \Delta N}{Y} \times \frac{Y}{N} \equiv \frac{\partial H}{\partial N} \times \frac{Y}{N}$$

Using the information given in Question 7, express this in terms of α.

11. Suppose labor is paid its marginal product. Then

$$\frac{\text{wage bill}}{\text{output}} \equiv \text{share of wages}$$

$$\equiv \frac{\text{no. of workers} \times \text{marginal product of labor}}{\text{output}}$$

Calculate this for the production function of Question 4 using the information given in Question 7. What is its relation to α? What is the share of capital? Is capital paid its marginal product?

12. The production function $Y = TK^{\alpha}N^{B}$ has constant returns to scale if $B = 1 - \alpha$. Show that it has increasing returns if $\alpha + B > 1$ by two arithmetic examples. If either α or B are < 0 the function does not make economic sense. Why?

13. Suppose the production function is $Y = TK^{\alpha}N^{B}$ when $\alpha = 0.5$; $B = 0.6$. Find the share of labor. If labor receives this, can capital also receive its marginal product? If not, why not? Can you give an economic interpretation to your results?

14. The demand for peanuts is a function of the price of peanuts (P_p) in relation to the price of potato chips (P_c); and consumer money income (Y). Such that

$$QD \equiv \text{no. of bags of peanuts demanded (in thousands)}$$

$$= a\left(\frac{P_c}{P_p}\right) + bY = aP_c + aP_p^{-1} + bY.$$

Would you expect the marginal response coefficients to be positive or negative?

Putting $a = 2$; $b = 1$ construct a demand curve plotting Q^D (on the horizontal axis) and P_p on the vertical axis for all integral values of P_p from 1 to 20. To do this take $P_c = 1$ and $Y = 100$.

Suppose that suppliers offer peanuts in accordance with the functions (supply schedule).

$$Q_s \equiv \text{no. of bags of peanuts supplied (in thousands)}.$$

$$= A + cP_c + dP_p.$$

What signs would you expect for the marginal response coefficients c and d? Why?

If $A = 0$; $c = -7.8$; $d = 11.0$, what are the equilibrium price and quantity (bags)?

Plot both the demand and supply schedules on the same graph and interpret your result.

15. The elasticity of any dependent variable (X) with respect to any independent variable (Y) of which it is a function is given by:

$$\frac{\Delta X}{X} \bigg/ \frac{\Delta Y}{Y} \equiv \frac{\frac{\partial X}{\partial Y} \times \Delta Y}{X} \bigg/ \frac{\Delta Y}{Y} \equiv \frac{\frac{\partial X}{\partial Y} \times \Delta Y}{\Delta Y} \times \frac{Y}{X} \equiv \frac{\partial X}{\partial Y} \times \frac{Y}{X}.$$

If $X = A + bY$, show that the elasticity is not in general a constant; and that it will be constant if $A = 0$.

Illustrate your conclusions by a graph identifying both $\partial X/\partial Y$ and Y/X. What general conclusion can you reach regarding the relationship between constant marginal response coefficients and constant elasticities? Show, by a numerical example of your own choice, that while the elasticity is independent of the *units* in which X and Y are measured, the marginal response coefficient is not.

16. Suppose the *observed* change in some dependent variable (X) is ΔX and the *observed* change in some independent variable (Y) on which X depends is ΔY. In what circumstances will the observed ratios $\dfrac{\Delta X}{X} \bigg/ \dfrac{\Delta Y}{Y}$ be a good measure of the elasticity $\dfrac{\partial X}{\partial Y} \times \dfrac{Y}{X}$? Check your answer with the data at Question 7.

SUGGESTED READING

R. G. D. Allen, *Mathematical Analysis for Economists,* rev. ed. (New York: St. Martin's, 1962) Chaps. 1, 3, 9.

F. Zeuthen, *Economic Theory and Method* (Cambridge: Harvard Univ. Press, 1955) Chaps. 6–9.

Those who wish to proceed further with mathematics should continue with:

R. G. D. Allen, *Mathematical Analysis for Economists.*

W. J. Baumol, *Economic Dynamics* (New York: Collier-Macmillan, 1959).

B. Roberts and D. Schulze, *Modern Mathematics and Economic Analysis* (New York: Norton, 1972).

7

The Determination of
Equilibrium Output

IN THIS CHAPTER we begin our main job of constructing an economic theory which can be used to explain *why* the economic system behaves as we saw it did in Chapter 5. We approach this task by developing *a model* of the economic system. Since the economic system is complicated, the model, to be useful, must necessarily also be complicated. We shall begin, however, by constructing a model of extreme simplicity and introduce complexities later only when the properties of the simple model have been thoroughly understood. Accordingly we start with a system in which (1) there is no government (i.e., no public sector) economic activity; and (2) there is no international trade. We also make one additional assumption, namely that the price of a unit of output is constant. This enables us to identify changes in the money values of variables with changes in their "real" values and postpone discussion of the determination of prices. Each of these assumptions is removed later.

OUTPUT, EMPLOYMENT, AND BUSINESS DECISIONS

In any period of time it is enterprises which determine how much output shall be produced. Since our theory is a short-run theory which takes as given both the real stock of capital (K) and the state of technology (T) then our production function tells us that $Y = f(N)$ with K and T given, or that the level of output (Y) per period depends only on the input of labor (N). Assuming hours per period per worker to be unchanged, this tells us that a given level of output determines a given level of employment in terms of workers. Hence if we can explain the level of output which enterprises produce, we can also explain, in the short run, the level of employment.

The full study of the behavior of enterprises belongs to micro-economics. We can, however, make considerable progress by assuming, as a first approximation, that *the behavior of enterprises* is, in general, *governed by the aim of maximizing profits.* Since profits can only be earned by the sale of products, we can argue that (1) what enterprises will plan to produce in any period is what they think they can sell in that period; (2) what they think they can sell depends upon their expectations regarding demands. We can indeed go a little further than this by arguing that the planned level of output not only depends upon *expected* demand but will adjust itself to *actual* demand so that, if actual demand in any period is less than expected, output will tend to be reduced, in later periods, to the level of actual demand. Only when expected and actual demand, and so planned and actual sales, coincide will the enterprise be in equilibrium.

The following arithmetical example should make the point clear:

EXAMPLE	PRICE PER UNIT OF OUTPUT	PLANNED OUTPUT – ACTUAL OUTPUT	PLANNED VALUE OF OUTPUT	WAGE COST	PLANNED PROFIT	ACTUAL SALES	UNSOLD OUTPUT ADDED TO STOCKS	REALIZED DISTRIBUTABLE PROFIT	RESULT
(1)	(2)	(3)	(4)	(5)	(6)	(7)	(8)	(9)	(10)
1	$1	$15,000	$15,000	$12,000	$3,000	$10,000	$5,000	$2,000	Contraction
2	1	15,000	15,000	12,000	3,000	17,000	−2,000	3,400	Expansion
3	1	15,000	15,000	12,000	3,000	15,000	nil	3,000	Equilibrium

This statement tells us that, in some period, which we have called 1, the XYZ Co. expected demand for its products to be, at given prices, equal to $15,000. It therefore planned to produce, and did produce[1] this value of output. At the ruling level of money wages this involved a wage bill of $12,000. To this wage cost the firm added a 25 percent "mark-up" which gave it an *expected* profit of $3000. In the event, however, actual sales were only $10,000 as against the planned value of $15,000. As a result the XYZ Co. would certainly contract output (and employment) in future periods.

The position depicted is clearly one of disequilibrium in that we have:

planned sales $\neq$ actual sales, *but* planned sales $>$ actual sales

planned profits $\neq$ actual profits, *but* planned profits $>$ actual profits

1. We shall assume that producers' plans are always realized in that planned output = actual output.

and our argument tells us that, in a disequilibrium of this particular kind, the result would be *contraction* in output and employment.

How are the figures in this table to be interpreted? The first eight columns give no trouble. The ninth, however, requires a word of explanation.

The realized distributable profit of an enterprise will be estimated by an accountant as:

sales *plus* value of increase in stocks − costs ≡ realized distributable profit.

Accountants, however, will value the increase in stocks not at the price at which the enterprise would *sell* from stocks but at the cost it incurs in increasing its stocks. That is, the profit element is not included in the valuation of stock increases. Now in our example the planned profit margin is $\dfrac{\$3000}{\$15,000}$ which, in percentage terms, is 20 percent. We thus have, in the first case:

realized distributable profit

$$\equiv \text{sales} + \text{increase in stocks (valued at cost)} - \text{total costs}$$
$$\equiv \$10,000 + \$5000[1 - \tfrac{20}{100}] - \$12,000$$
$$\equiv \$10,000 + \$4000 - \$12,000$$
$$\equiv \$2000.$$

This is the figure shown in the ninth column of the table.

Now take the second case. We have, since inventories *fall*:

realized distributable profit

$$\equiv \text{sales} + \text{increase in stocks (valued at cost)} - \text{total costs}$$
$$\equiv \$17,000 + (-\$2000[1 - \tfrac{20}{100}]) - \$12,000$$
$$\equiv \$17,000 - \$1600 - \$12,000$$
$$\equiv \$3400.$$

Finally in case three we have:

realized distributable profit

$$\equiv \text{sales} + \text{increase in stocks (value at cost)} - \text{total costs}$$
$$\equiv \$15,000 + \text{nil} - \$12,000$$
$$\equiv \$3000.$$

Obviously, as the table shows,

in case 1   planned profit > realized distributable profit.
      2   planned profit < realized distributable profit.
      3   planned profit = realized distributable profit.

Notice that in cases 1 and 2—the disequilibrium situations—the XYZ Co. experienced *unplanned* stock changes. Only in case 3—the equilibrium situation—is there *no unplanned* change in stocks.

It follows from this example that only if actual sales turn out to be exactly $15,000—as the XYZ Co. planned, is there equilibrium, for then planned sales = actual sales; planned profits = realized distributable profits, and the firm has no reason to change its plans.

Let us now generalize this example to all firms and define

total value of planned output ≡ aggregate supply.

We may, on the demand side, also write:

total value of planned expenditure ≡ aggregate demand.

Then utilizing the assumption that

total value of planned expenditure = total value of actual expenditure,

that is, the assumption that consumers' plans are always realized, we can argue that

1) for *output* to be in equilibrium we required aggregate demand = aggregate supply
and predict that if

2) aggregate demand > aggregate supply, output will expand,
while if

3) aggregate demand < aggregate supply, output will contract.

These three possibilities are depicted in the table below.

Table 7.1 / *Aggregate demand and supply (billions of dollars).*

| SITUA-TION | VALUE OF PLANNED AND ACTUAL OUTPUT | | | VALUE OF AGGRE-GATE SUPPLY | AGGREGATE DEMAND | | | UNSOLD OUTPUT ADDED TO STOCKS | RESULT |
	WAGES	RENTS	PLANNED PROFIT		PLANNED EXPENDI-TURE	ACTUAL EXPENDI-TURE	REALIZED PROFITS		
1	100	50	50	200	200	200	50	nil	Equilibrium
2	100	50	50	200	220	220	55	−20	Expansion
3	100	50	50	200	180	180	45	20	Contraction

In each situation enterprises pay out $150 billion in wages and rents. They *plan* a profit of $50 billion. Aggregate supply is therefore $200 billion.

In situation 3, planned expenditure (and hence by assumption actual expenditure) equals $180 billion. The result is: planned profits > realized distributable profits and output *contracts*.

We thus have the following propositions:

1) If aggregate demand > aggregate supply, planned profits will be less than realized distributable profits. Result: expansion of output.

2) If aggregate demand < aggregate supply, planned profits will be greater than realized distributable profits. Result: contraction of output.

3) If aggregate demand = aggregate supply, planned profits will equal realized distributable profits. Result: equilibrium.

We can now take our analysis a little further and show its relationship to our national income accounting concepts.

It will be remembered that we have assumed prices to be constant throughout the discussion. Hence planned output (which we have assumed to be actually produced) is equal in value to the national product. This, in each situation, is equal to $200 billion.

In situation 1 of Table 7.2 only $180 billion is sold on the market to consumers. It follows that the remaining $20 billion of output must be added to stocks. But this, by definition, *is investment whether firms planned to make the addition or not.* Accordingly we can rearrange the data of Table 7.1 as shown.

Table 7.2 / *Aggregate demand and supply (billions of dollars).*

| | | | | EXPENDITURE SIDE | | | EARNINGS SIDE | | | |
| | | | | | | | | | PROFITS | |
SITUA-TION	VALUE OF OUTPUT	WAGES	RENTS	PLANNED DISTRIBU-TABLE PROFITS	CON-SUMP-TION	INVEST-MENT IN INVEN-TORIES	WAGES	RENTS	REALIZED DISTRIBU-TABLE PROFIT	UN-REALIZED PROFIT
	(1)	(2)	(3)	(4)	(5)	(6)	(7)	(8)	(9)	(10)
1	200	100	50	50	180	20	100	50	45	5
2	200	100	50	50	200	nil	100	50	50	nil
3	200	100	50	50	220	−20	100	50	55	−5

On looking at this table we have:

national product ≡ sum of cols. (2), (3), and (4) ≡ $200 bil.

On the expenditure side we have:

national expenditure ≡ consumption + investment
≡ $180 bil. + $20 bil.
≡ $200 bil.

On the earnings side, matters are a little more complicated. We know that

national income ≡ wages + rents + profits
≡ $100 bil. + $50 bil. + $50 bil.
≡ $200 bil.

This, however, appears to show that, at $50 billion actual profit equals planned profit—a situation we have learned to think of as one of equilibrium. This is awkward since we know that the situation we are depicting is one of disequilibrium. How do we reconcile this apparent contradiction?

We have:

national income
  $\equiv$ wages + rents + profits
  $\equiv$ wages + rents + realized distributable profits + unrealized profits
  $\equiv$ $100 bil. + $50 bil. + $45 bil. + $5 bil.
  $\equiv$ $200 bil.

Disequilibrium manifests itself in the discrepancy between actual profits, as measured by the national income statistician ($50 billion) and the realized distributable profits accruing to the enterprise ($45 billion). The difference arises from the mark-up hypothesis.

In situation 2 we have:

national product $\equiv$ $200 bil.
national expenditure $\equiv$ consumption + investment
                     $\equiv$ $200 bil. + nil
                     $\equiv$ $200 bil.
national income $\equiv$ wages + rents + profits
                     $\equiv$ wages + rents + realized distributable profits
                       + unrealized profits
                     $\equiv$ $100 bil. + $50 bil. + $50 bil. + nil
                     $\equiv$ $200 bil.

In situation 3:

national product $\equiv$ $200 bil.
national expenditure = consumption + investment
                     $\equiv$ $220 bil. $-$ $20 bil.
                     $\equiv$ $200 bil.
national income $\equiv$ wages + rents + profits
                     $\equiv$ $100 bil. + $50 bil.
                       + realized distributable profits
                       + unrealized profits
                     $\equiv$ $100 bil. + $50 bil. + $55 bil. $-$ $5 bil.
                     $\equiv$ $200 bil.

In short, we can say that unless the situation is one of equilibrium then (1) there will be *unplanned* increases/decreases in stocks; (2) realized distributable profits will *not* be equal to planned profits. Only in equilibrium will there be *no unplanned* increase/decrease in stocks and no discrepancy between planned profits and realized distributable profits.

Notice that though in each situation we have our familiar identity of

national product $\equiv$ national expenditure $\equiv$ national income,

each situation is, *from the point of view of behavior,* a very different one.

To say that disequilibrium manifests itself in a discrepancy between actual profits as measured by the national income statisticians and realized distributable profits is, on our definitions and assumptions, correct. Some explanation of what this implies is nevertheless necessary.

In our table we have taken the value of output, as measured by the statistician, to be $200 billion. Of this sum wages are $100 billion, rents $50 billion; and profits $50 billion. If the national income statistician adopts this definition, he must value the increase in stocks at $20 billion to preserve the definitional relationship: output $\equiv$ consumption *plus* investment. This means that he values the increase in stocks *inclusive* of the profit element. On this basis the income accruing to households in the form of wages, rents, and profits is $200 billion but the statistician is including, in the profits of the current period, an element which will not be *realized* until the goods added to inventory are actually sold.

As we have seen, in situation 1, the realized distributable profit of firms, as calculated by their accountants, will be $45 billion and not the $50 billion taken (on this contention) by the national income statistician. If the whole of this $45 billion is paid out to households, the income received by households, $195 billion, will be *less* than the income which the statisticians attribute to them. Conversely in situation 3 it will be more.

If, on the other hand, the statistician adopts the accountants definition of realized profit, he must value the change in stocks at cost. In which case each of our hypothetical situations yields a different total for national income thus:

Situation 1:

$$\text{national income} \equiv \text{wages} + \text{rents} + \text{realized distributable profits}$$
$$\equiv \$100 \text{ bil.} + \$50 \text{ bil.} + \$45 \text{ bil.}$$
$$\equiv \$195 \text{ bil.}$$

Situation 2:

$$\text{national income} \equiv \$100 \text{ bil.} + \$50 \text{ bil.} + \$50 \text{ bil.}$$
$$\equiv \$200 \text{ bil.}$$

Situation 3:

$$\text{national income} \equiv \text{wages} + \text{rents} + \text{realized distributable profits}$$
$$\equiv \$100 \text{ bil.} + \$50 \text{ bil.} + \$55 \text{ bil.}$$
$$\equiv \$205 \text{ bil.}$$

In each case, by assumption, the flow of output is the same. The second way of defining profit therefore leads to a contradiction worse than the first for the main purpose of national income accounting is to measure the flow of goods and services produced in the current period. A system of definitions which describes an identical flow by three different totals is obviously awkward. Accordingly the first definition of profit—arrived at by valuing the increase in stocks at market prices—seems preferable.

Notice that, in all this, there is no dispute as to what has occurred. This was assumed at the start. What matters is to find a consistent and convenient way of *describing what has occurred.*

The fundamental lessons of this example are, however, clear enough:

1) Though actual expenditure and actual output as defined in national income accounting are always identically equal, it makes sense to speak of planned expenditure being equal to, greater or less than, planned output.

2) The national income accounting concepts can tell us nothing about economic behavior for though each of our three situations is, from the behavior aspect, entirely different, from the national income accounting point of view they exhibit no essential differences.

The general point is a simple one:

1) national income accounting is concerned with actual magnitudes;

2) economic behavior is determined by the relationship between planned magnitudes about which national income accounting, of itself, has nothing whatsoever to say.

This reflects the important points we made in discussing the concept of equilibrium in Chapter 5. *Plans to purchase, sell, and produce may not be realized.* They will, in fact, only be realized when they are consistent: that is when equilibrium exists. In this situation, and only in this situation, will all actual magnitudes correspond with planned magnitudes.

Of course, in any given period there will only be one set of actual magnitudes in terms of national accounting definitions and these are what the statisticians will record. But in disequilibrium situations these actual magnitudes result from the interaction of inconsistent plans. The statisticians' estimates do not record the existence of inconsistent plans although, as we have shown, plans may well be inconsistent. They merely record what happens whether it is planned or unplanned. This is why they are identities and not equations and, by the same token, why they can tell us nothing about economic behavior except its results. It is, indeed, precisely because they give a measure of these results that the statistician's estimates are important.

This section contains propositions of such fundamental importance that a summary of them is essential. The propositions are as follows:

1) Output and employment are only in equilibrium when aggregate (planned) demand = aggregate (planned) supply.

2) Where aggregate demand > aggregate supply the resultant disequilibrium will manifest itself as

    (a) an unintended decumulation in inventories: i.e. unplanned disinvestment in stocks;

(b) an excess of realized distributable profits over planned profits. The result will be an expansion in output and employment.

3) These propositions are simply reversed for the situation where aggregate demand < aggregate supply.

4) Despite the fact that, in national income accounting,

$$\text{actual expenditure} \equiv \text{actual output}$$

it is perfectly possible, provided plans are inconsistent, for

$$\text{aggregate demand} \neq \text{aggregate supply.}$$

5) Without additional assumptions relating planned to actual magnitudes, national income concepts can tell us nothing about plans and therefore do not register any inconsistency in them.

THE SAVING AND INVESTMENT ANALYSIS

We now know that output is in equilibrium only when aggregate demand = aggregate supply. In our present simple model we can divide aggregate demand into two components thus:

aggregate demand = planned consumption plus planned net investment.

If we assume, as we have so far, that producers' plans for output are always realized, then

$$\text{aggregate supply} \equiv \text{planned value of output} \equiv \text{national product}$$
$$\equiv \text{aggregate income.}$$

Hence our equilibrium condition can be rewritten:

national income = planned consumption + planned net investment,

or, using the notation which is now fashionable,

$$Y = C_p + I_p, \tag{7.1}$$

where the suffix p denotes planned magnitudes and Y denotes national income. Planned net saving is now defined as income minus planned consumption, i.e.

$$S_p \equiv Y - C_p. \tag{7.2}$$

Hence, combining (7.1) and (7.2), our equilibrium condition becomes:

$$S_p \qquad = \qquad I_p \tag{7.3}$$
$$\text{planned saving} \quad \text{planned investment}$$

Thus the propositions:

$$\text{aggregate demand} \gtreqless \text{aggregate supply}$$

and

$$\text{planned investment} \gtreqless \text{planned saving}$$

are simply alternative ways of saying the same thing.

We have already shown that, despite the fact that, by definition, national expenditure is always equal to national product, it makes sense to speak of aggregate demand being equal to, greater, or less than aggregate supply. We now show that despite the fact that, by definition, actual saving is always identically equal with actual investment, it makes sense to speak of planned saving being equal to, greater, or less than, planned investment.

Obviously when we write:

$$S_p \gtreqless I_p$$
$$S \equiv I$$

we are using the terms in different senses. This is the crucial point and must be understood. It looks and is simple. But in the past failure to understand the distinction has caused great trouble not only to students but also to professional economists.

The former equation refers to planned saving and investment and the expression is a genuine equation which may or may not be satisfied: the latter identity refers to actual saving and investment which by definition are always equal since they are, in fact, alternative ways of describing the same thing.

Since economic terminology is not uniform, you may meet in your reading many expressions which are, broadly speaking, synonyms for our terms "planned" and "actual." For convenience they may be tabulated as follows:

$$S_p \gtreqless I_p$$

$$\left.\begin{array}{l}\text{planned}\\ \textit{ex ante}\\ \text{scheduled}\\ \text{intended}\end{array}\right\} \text{saving} \gtreqless \left.\begin{array}{l}\text{planned}\\ \textit{ex ante}\\ \text{scheduled}\\ \text{intended}\end{array}\right\} \text{investment}$$

while,

$$S \equiv I$$

$$\left.\begin{array}{l}\text{actual}\\ \textit{ex post}\\ \text{observable}\\ \text{realized}\end{array}\right\} \text{saving} \equiv \left.\begin{array}{l}\text{actual}\\ \textit{ex post}\\ \text{observable}\\ \text{realized}\end{array}\right\} \text{investment}$$

Although we may now be satisfied that, since we are using the terms "saving" and "investment" in two senses, we are not involved in a logical contradiction, it is nevertheless interesting to inquire how it is that actual saving and investment can be equal when planned saving and investment are not equal; that is, when the system is in disequilibrium. This may be made clear by taking a further look at our earlier examples.

Table 7.3 / *Saving-investment relation (billions of dollars).*

CASE	AGGRE-GATE SUPPLY	PLANNED CON-SUMP-TION	ACTUAL CON-SUMP-TION	PLANNED SAVING	ACTUAL SAVING	PLANNED INVEST-MENT	ACTUAL INVEST-MENT	UNPLANNED INVEST-MENT	OVERALL SITUA-TION
	Y_p	C_p	C	S_p	S	I_p	I	I_u	
1	200	180	180	20	20	zero	20	20	$S_p > I_p$
2	200	220	220	−20	−20	zero	−20	−20	$I_p > S_p$
3	200	200	200	nil	nil	zero	zero	zero	$S_p = I_p$

Consider case 1. The value of output is $200 billion. But aggregate demand $(C_p + I_p)$ is equal to only $180 billion. It follows therefore that output unsold during this period will be $200 billion − $180 billion = $20 billion. This unsold output (saving) must be added to stocks existing at the beginning of the period. It therefore constitutes actual investment. But it does not constitute planned investment which, by assumption, is zero. In case 1, therefore, actual saving (output which is not consumed) is, as it must be, equal to actual investment. Actual investment, however, exceeds planned investment by an amount we shall speak of as unplanned invest-ment. It follows therefore that when planned saving exceeds planned invest-ment, actual investment also exceeds planned investment by the value of unplanned investment. This unplanned investment, taking the form of an unexpected (and unwelcome) accumulation of stocks, is a signal to firms to contract output. Nevertheless, despite the assumed discrepancy between planned saving and investment and the resultant disequilibrium, it is clear that actual saving and investment, as measured by the national income statistician, are necessarily equal.

Case 2 illustrates the alternative form of disequilibrium. In that case planned investment exceeds planned saving, which means that aggregate demand $(C_p + I_p)$ exceeds aggregate supply. Clearly this is so, for the table shows aggregate demand of $220 billion and the aggregate supply of $200 billion. To meet this excess demand of $20 billion producers must decumulate stocks. Now the decumulation of stocks constitutes *dis-investment*. Hence actual investment, which we know to be equal to planned investment plus unplanned investment, is given by:

$$I \equiv I_p + I_u$$
$$\equiv \text{nil} - \$20 \text{ bil.}$$
$$\equiv -\$20 \text{ bil.}$$

In this case an unexpected decumulation of stocks is a signal to producers to expand production and thus employment and incomes.

In case 3 we have assumed equilibrium. In this situation planned and actual investment coincide at zero. Unplanned investment is therefore also zero. Hence producers' expectations are realized. They therefore have no incentive to expand or contract production, employment, and incomes.

From this account of matters we may draw the following conclusions:

1) there is no contradiction in the statements

    (a) planned saving and investment are equal only when incomes are in equilibrium; and

    (b) actual (accounting) saving and investment are always equal by definition:

2) where planned saving is not equal to planned investment the resulting disequilibrium will show itself in the form of a discrepancy between planned and actual investment;

3) we define:

unplanned investment		actual investment		planned investment
I_u	$\equiv$	I	$-$	I_p

4) where $S_p > I_p$ then $I_u > 0$, i.e. there is unintended inventory accumulation;

    where $I_p > S_p$ then $I_u < 0$, i.e. there is unintended inventory decumulation;

    where $I_p > S_p$ then $I_u = 0$, i.e. no unintended change in inventories;

5) it is the presence of unintended investment (positive or negative) which provides the signal to firms to contract or expand output. This is merely another aspect of the discrepancy between planned and actual (sales) and planned and realized distributable profits illustrated earlier.

THE BASIC POSTULATE OF THE SAVING AND INVESTMENT ANALYSIS

The analysis of the earlier sections of this chapter has made it plain that

1) any inconsistency between the rates at which the community plans to invest and to save will involve discrepancies between:

    (a) firms' expected and realized distributable profits; and

    (b) firms' planned and actual investment;

2) such discrepancies will cause firms to modify their production plans in the light of experience, thus bringing about changes in output (income) and employment;

3) there is no contradiction between speaking about the possible inequality of planned saving and planned investment while at the same time

insisting upon the definitional identity of actual savings and investment as measured in national income accounts.

So far so good. But this analysis, though logically consistent, would be of little interest if, as a matter of experience, planned saving and investment tended automatically (in the sense of without any need for changes in the level of output) to achieve and maintain equality. In that case the saving and investment analysis and the theory of income determination which we develop in later chapters would be a theoretical curiosity of no empirical significance whatsoever. Clearly, if a theory based upon the saving/investment analysis is to have any practical importance it can only be because, as a matter of fact, there is no mechanism tending to insure that any plan to save (or invest) will automatically be matched by a corresponding plan to invest (or save).

Now there are two important facts concerning saving and investment decisions in the modern developed "mixed economy" which make it reasonable to accept the view that there is no "automatic" correspondence between the amount per period that the community plans to save and invest. They are that (1) saving and investment plans tend to be made by different groups in the community; i.e. broadly speaking households save, firms invest; and (2) decisions to save and invest are undertaken for very different reasons. Admittedly enterprises (firms) do undertake saving in the form of depreciation allowances and undistributed profits. But a considerable part of saving is still performed by persons. Again it is true that households and persons do undertake investment expenditure such as house purchases.[2]

Nevertheless the overwhelming share of private investment is undertaken by firms. It is thus in accordance with experience and acceptable to common sense to admit that saving and investment decisions are carried out to a significant extent by different groups. As a first approximation we might assume that only households save and only enterprises invest. This indeed will be a convenient assumption on which to build the model from Chapter 8 onwards. You should remember its limited correspondence with facts.

The second assertion, that saving and investment decisions are undertaken for different reasons, is also in accordance with common observation once the precise economic meaning of the term investment is recalled. Men save, after all, for a bewildering variety of reasons. The more obvious are: to provide for old age; to provide a contingency fund against any sudden loss in earning power; because they were brought up to believe that to save was a "proper" mode of behavior; because they were in the past unable to resist the appeals of life insurance salesmen; because they are

2. See John Lansing and E. S. Maynes, "Inflation and Saving by Consumers," *Journal of Political Economy*, Vol. LX (October 1952), pp. 383–91.

compelled to do so through a legal obligation to join a pension plan; or merely because of habit. None of these have much (if anything) to do with the wish to undertake investment which, as we know, is defined as making an addition to the real stock of capital. Most of the things savers do with their saving, and therefore which presumably provide much of the motive for saving do not constitute investment. Many savers for example buy government bonds. If Brown buys a bond and Smith sells it, Brown's "investment" is cancelled by Smith's "disinvestment." In any case the transaction does not directly increase the real capital stock and so, by definition, is not investment. This argument can be extended to cover nearly all the transactions undertaken by persons who save, most of whom use their saving to carry out what economists call capital transfers. Once it is realized that purchases of bonds, shares, life policies, mortgages, debentures, old houses and so on through commonly called investment do not constitute investment as economists define the term but are merely transfers, the very remote relation between personal planned saving and planned investment becomes clear.

If we accept that plans to save and plans to invest are made independently of each other, then the economic system must contain some mechanism to bring the different plans into equality. The central tenet of modern macroeconomics, derived from the work of John Maynard Keynes, is that the price mechanism does not effectively perform this task and in particular that the rate of interest does not do so. Consequently adjustment requires a change in the level of income (output). To put the same point rather differently we can, given the independence of the plans to save and invest, develop a model of the economy which uses the saving and investment analysis to explain the determination of output (income) and employment.

It is important, however, for the student to notice that, while it is reasonable to accept the postulated dichotomy between savers and investors in a modern developed "mixed economy," it is not a reasonable assumption in all economies or in the same economy at all times. This is obvious even if we neglect the special case so thoughtfully provided by Daniel Defoe. Robinson Crusoe clearly saved (refrained from consumption) only in order to invest (add to his real capital stock). Neglecting Robinson, however, broadly similar conditions prevail in the subsistence economies of some underdeveloped territories in which peasant farmers, in general, save only in order to invest: indeed, to put the matter more concisely, a plan to save *is* a plan to invest. Hence, though the dichotomy certainly holds with respect to the United States today, it would probably not have held in the U.S. during the eighteenth century and it may not hold during the twenty-first.

This is an important point. A theory which seeks to explain the level of output by requiring it to adjust in order to bring the community's plans to save and invest into equality will always be logically consistent. It may not, however, be a useful theory in the sense that the community may have another mechanism for adjusting saving and investment plans or, alternatively, may be organized institutionally in such a way that automatic correspondence between saving and investment plans is assured. The importance of Keynes' theory arises because under modern social conditions and institutional arrangements it is both logically consistent and useful.

SUMMARY

This is an important chapter outlining a number of ideas fundamental to the whole theory of income determination. The basic ideas underlying the theory and sketched in the earlier sections are summarized below.

1) A firm will adjust output in accordance with its experience of demand. This proposition, which is, of course, empirical and not logical in nature, may be regarded as either

(a) derived from the study of business behavior or
(b) deduced from the assumption that firms seek to maximize profits—which is itself an assumption derived from observing business behavior. This assumption about business behavior, when generalized for all firms, enables us to derive the equilibrium condition for output as a whole $(S_p = I_p)$ and the conditions in which output will tend to expand $(I_p > S_p)$ or contract $(S_p > I_p)$.

2) In a modern "mixed" capitalist economy saving and investment decisions are taken by different groups for dissimilar reasons. This fact enables us to argue that the consequences which must logically follow if, in any period, $S_p \neq I_p$ are of great practical interest since there is no reason to suppose that S_p will automatically tend to equal I_p.

3) In the short run, the quantity of employment is uniquely related to the quantity of output firms plan to produce.

These three propositions form the basis for the whole of the analysis contained in the rest of this part of the book. The remaining assumptions, namely the absence of government activity, the absence of international trade, and the constancy of the price level are made for expositional convenience only and are relaxed later. Beyond stating and examining the implications of the ideas listed above, the chapter is also concerned to explain and emphasize the distinction between planned saving (investment) on the one hand and actual saving (investment) on the other. The comprehension of this distinction is fundamental. The student is advised to read the section on saving and investment analysis very carefully and to work out some arithmetic examples for himself.

QUESTIONS AND EXERCISES

1. "The aim of the Government's policy is to equate saving and investment at a level of output corresponding to full employment. Their success is demonstrated by this year's national income estimates which show saving equal to investment." Discuss.

2. "If saving increases then, since saving equals investment, investment increases. It follows that aggregate demand and supply always increase together and are always equal." Discuss.

3. Assuming

$$C_P = C_A = \$1000 \text{ bil. per period;}$$

$$I_P = \$500 \text{ bil. per period,}$$

what is the *equilibrium* level of output?

If planned output is $1700 billion per period and planned output = actual output find gross national product; gross national expenditure; actual investment; unintended investment.

In future periods would you expect output to expand or contract? Why? In what forms does the disequilibrium in the system show itself?

4. "People spend with that part of their income that they save just as surely as with that part of their income they consume." Do you agree? If so, why? If not, why not? What, in terms of this chapter, is the assumption implicit in the statement?

5. The national income estimates of a hypothetical economy reveal the following data for the first half of 1970:

GNP	$1000 bil.
Consumption	750 bil.
Gross investment in:	
fixed capital	225 bil.
inventories	25 bil.

Do these figures throw any light upon whether the economy was in equilibrium or not? If so, how?

6. Suppose that, contrary to our assumptions, an act of saving was undertaken only in order to make investment. How would the level of output in an economy of this kind be determined? Would "full capacity" output be automatic? If so where would the equilibrium of the economy appear on the "production possibility curve"?

7. Assume

$$C_p = C_A = \$600 \text{ bil. per period};$$

$$I_p \equiv I_{fp} + I_{sp}$$

   planned investment planned investment
$$\equiv \quad \text{in fixed capital} \quad + \quad \text{in inventories.}$$

If $I_{fp} = \$150$ bil. per period; $I_{sp} = \$50$ bil. per period;

What is the equilibrium level of output?
If planned output = actual output is \$900 bil. then
 a) how much is actual investment in inventories?
 b) how much is unplanned investment in inventories?
 c) how much are actual saving and investment?

8. Reconstruct the example of Table 7.1 and the subsequent discussion on the assumption that the "mark-up" of firms is 50 percent, not 25 percent. Show that the basic analysis is unaffected by this change.

9. Reformulate the discussion of Table 7.1 *et seq* on the assumption that firms adjust their "mark-up" percentage to the level of output. Assume that planned profit $\equiv P^*$ is given by: $P^* = A + bY$ where $b = 0.1$ and $Y \equiv$ actual = planned output. What is the value of A assumed in Table 7.1? Does the new assumption *significantly* affect the analysis? What do you mean by *significantly*?

10. "The function of what is called the capital market—that is, the Stock Exchange and related financial institutions—is to facilitate capital transfers." Discuss.

SUGGESTED READING

F. Brooman and H. Jacoby, *Macroeconomics* (Chicago: Aldine, 1970) Chap. 1.
P. Davidson and E. Smolensky, *Aggregate Supply and Demand Analysis* (New York: Harper & Row, 1964) Chap. 1.

8

The Consumption Function and the Multiplier

IN THE LAST CHAPTER we argued that enterprises would adjust their output per period until planned sales and actual sales were equal. At this level of output enterprises would be in equilibrium: that is, have no reason to adjust their output plans in any way.

Examining this condition a little further, we discovered that output (income) would be in equilibrium when aggregate supply = aggregate demand, or, what is the same thing, $S_p = I_p$. Where this condition prevailed all planned and actual magnitudes would coincide: both sectors of the economy—that is enterprises and households—would then have no reason to modify their behavior.

Retaining our assumption that production plans are always realized so that actual and planned production coincide, and the notation of Chapter 7, we can write our equilibrium condition as:

$$Y \quad = \quad C_p + I_p$$
aggregate supply = aggregate demand.

Hence, to explain the equilibrium value of Y, we need to develop theories which explain the determination of C_p and I_p. These theories will, obviously enough, contain hypotheses about human behavior, for what we are trying to explain is the rate at which households (in general) will plan to spend upon consumption and the rate at which enterprises (in general) will plan to spend upon investment.

In this chapter we concentrate on the first problem and seek to develop a theory of consumption. Accordingly we shall assume, without either explanation or justification, that enterprises plan to spend upon investment at some fixed rate. This assumption, which is obviously artificial and made merely for convenience, will be relaxed in the next chapter. It amounts to treating planned investment expenditure as an *exogenous* variable—that is, one determined (like the weather) outside our model. Formally it may be expressed as follows:

$$I_p = \bar{I} \tag{8.1}$$

$$I_p = \$200 \text{ bil. per year} \tag{8.1n}$$

This leaves us free to concentrate on the determination of planned consumption.

THE AGGREGATE CONSUMPTION FUNCTION

The aim of our consumption hypothesis is to explain the determination of "real" *aggregate* planned consumption expenditure—that is the total "real" expenditure of all households together. On what variables is it reasonable to argue that aggregate "real" planned consumption would depend?

The first (and most important variable) is clearly *the level of real income.* Statistical studies of household expenditure confirm that the simple hypothesis that the real expenditure of households is related to their real income levels is well grounded. Moreover the same studies show that households with "high" real incomes (say those in the top 10 percent) save more, proportionately to income as well as absolutely, than those in "low" real income groups (say the bottom 10 percent). Since any given total of household incomes may be distributed more (or less) equally and since the more equally any given total household income is distributed the greater will be the level of planned consumption associated with it, we know, from these studies, two variables that influence real planned consumption. They are: (1) the level of real income: (Y) and (2) the distribution of real income (α).[1] Of these the first, the level of real income, is of primary importance in the sense that variations in planned consumption are due largely to changes in income.

It also seems plausible to argue, and there is empirical evidence to support the hypothesis, that in general any individual with a given real income

1. We use the term α to describe the distribution of income so that the greater is α the more equally income is distributed. The parameter α thus refers to income distribution in this sense and not to the functional distribution between wages and profits.

The proposition that the more equal the distribution of income the greater is consumption has been challenged by the permanent income theory and the life cycle hypothesis. We will discuss these theories in the following chapter. For the time being we will ignore these theories and assume that consumption is a positive function of the equality of the income distribution.

will plan to consume *more* the greater is his real *wealth*. We thus have a third variable to consider: the real value of assets.

The real value of assets is a *stock* concept which relates to the capital account or balance sheet of the household and not its income account. Our hypothesis states that, in general, if we look at two households which are otherwise identical and which each enjoy an income of (say) $20,000 per year, one of which holds (say) bank deposits, government bonds, equity shares, and real property to the value of $10,000 and the other which holds only bank deposits to the value of $100, the former type of household will in general plan the higher rate of consumption. Extending this hypothesis to the community as a whole gives us a third variable influencing the value of real planned consumption: the real value of household asset holdings (A).

A fourth variable which may influence consumption expenditure is the rate of interest which we now define as the rate of return (percent per annum) obtainable in the market on long-term government securities.

As everyone knows, the act of saving—that is, of abstaining from consumption—does not, of itself, entitle the saver to receive interest. If, for example, accumulated savings (wealth) are held in the form of bank notes, no interest accrues. Nevertheless accumulated savings (wealth) can be held in a form which provides their owner with an income in the form of interest (for example, as bonds or savings and loan deposits). Hence it is reasonable to believe that some people would plan to save more out of their incomes if the rate of interest were (say) 20 percent rather than 5 percent. Moreover, some people who now tend to consume more than their incomes (that is, to dis-save) by making use of consumer credit, would probably be less willing to do so if the rate charged by sales finance companies (which is related to the rate of interest) was 40 rather than 16 percent.

In short there are some reasons to suppose that, the *higher* the rate of interest, the *more* willing some people will be to save and the *less* willing some other people will be to dis-save.

As against this some people save, in the main, to provide an income on retirement. The higher the rate of interest, the smaller the accumulated savings necessary to provide any given income on retirement. Those who save primarily to provide for retirement and who aim at a fixed income at a certain age (say 60) may thus save *less* if the rate of interest is (say) 20 percent than they would if it were (say) 5 percent. It follows that though there are some reasons for thinking that the rate of interest is a variable which influences consumption out of any given income, we cannot, on *a priori* grounds, be any too confident about either the direction or magnitude of its influence. Nevertheless it is clearly a variable which needs to be included in any hypothesis designed to explain aggregate consumption. Hence our fourth variable is the rate of interest (r).

A fifth variable is the psychological attitude of members of households (consumers) as conditioned by the "accepted" behavior of the society in which they live and have their upbringing. Some people are brought up to believe that to save is a virtue which, if not rewarded in this world, will be in the next. Others believe that income is for spending. Hence these psychological attitudes—which we shall call preferences—are an important determinant of aggregate consumption.

There are a whole host of other variables which have some claim to be considered as factors influencing consumption plans. The age composition of society, for example, might well be an influence. So might expectations with regard to future incomes and expectations with regard to future prices. The problem in economics is not, however, to find the *longest* possible list of independent variables which might, in general, be thought to exert some influence on the dependent variable, aggregate consumption, but to find the *smallest* number of variables which permits us to make useful predictions of the dependent variable. *Which these variables are is a question of fact.* It is thus always wise to begin with a simple hypothesis and modify it only when tests show it to be inadequate. Accordingly we shall put forward the following hypothesis to explain real aggregate planned consumption:

$$\text{aggregate real planned consumption depends upon} \begin{cases} \text{real income} \\ \text{real value of assets} \\ \text{rate of interest} \\ \text{distribution of income} \\ \text{preferences.} \end{cases}$$

In our functional notation this may be conveniently written as a *consumption function* thus:

$$C_p = f(Y, A, r, \alpha) \tag{8.2}$$

where the last influence, households' preferences, is expressed in the form of the functional relationship (systematic dependence) between C_p (the dependent variable) and $Y, A, r,$ and α (the independent variables).

At this point the reader should notice the obvious analogy between the *consumption function* of (8.2) and our "beer-drinking" function of earlier chapters. This new function, like the earlier one, expresses a hypothesis about economic behavior which may be true or false. Moreover since $Y,$ $A, r, \alpha,$ and (assuming that consumption plans are always realized) C_p are all conceptually measurable, our consumption function hypothesis is meaningful: that is, it can be tested.

What properties is this consumption function likely to have? If we refer to Chapter 6, we see that this question first requires us to say what signs we expect the marginal response coefficients to possess. Our discussion has already given us expectations about these, so we can immediately write down the signs of the marginal response coefficients as follows:

$$\frac{\partial C_p}{\partial Y} \equiv \begin{array}{l} \text{the increase in real planned consumption resulting from} \\ \text{a unit increase in real income } alone \end{array} > 0$$

$$\frac{\partial C_p}{\partial A} \equiv \begin{array}{l} \text{the increase in real planned consumption resulting from} \\ \text{a unit increase in the real value of assets alone} \end{array} > 0$$

$$\frac{\partial C_p}{\partial \alpha} \equiv \begin{array}{l} \text{the increase in real planned consumption resulting from a} \\ \text{unit increase in the equality of income distribution } alone \end{array} > 0$$

$$\frac{\partial C_p}{\partial r} \equiv \begin{array}{l} \text{the increase in real planned consumption resulting from} \\ \text{a unit increase in the rate of interest } alone \end{array} ?$$

(8.3)

Notice that these marginal response coefficients are descriptive of human behavior.

This information, which simply restates the results of our earlier discussion, tells us something about the consumption function. We now ask what is the *form* of the function?

On empirical grounds there are good reasons for writing the function in the following form:

$$C_p = Q + cY + dA + e\alpha + fr, \qquad (8.4)$$

which is the form illustrated in Chapter 6. In this notation Q is *autonomous* consumption—that is, consumption which is independent of Y, A, α, and r.[2] The form chosen in addition to being plausible on empirical grounds is also convenient, for with it each of the marginal response coefficients is a constant. Thus:

$$\frac{\partial C_p}{\partial Y} \equiv c > 0, \qquad \frac{\partial C_p}{\partial A} \equiv d > 0, \qquad \frac{\partial C_p}{\partial \alpha} \equiv e > 0, \qquad \frac{\partial C_p}{\partial r} \equiv f \gtrless 0.$$

These are the properties which, in what follows, we shall assume our consumption function to possess. We·now proceed to illustrate by means of a numerical example.

2. This autonomous consumption represented by the constant term of the consumption function can be interpreted in two ways. One is to say that it represents what the household would consume even if its income were zero. This interpretation suffers from the fact that the amount a household consumes if its current income is zero obviously depends upon its assets, and would therefore decrease from year to year if income remains at zero. The other alternative is to say that when fitting a consumption function statistically (by using least squares regression) the use of a constant term allows a straight-line function to fit the data more accurately. Looked at in this way, the magnitude of the constant term should really not be interpreted as consumption out of zero income, but as a statistical artifact which allows the fitted function to give a better representation of consumption at those income levels which predominate in our data. For most purposes we are interested in obtaining a good representation of consumption at fairly normal income levels rather than in determining consumption at zero income.

*THE PROPENSITY TO CONSUME AND
ITS FORMAL PROPERTIES*

Our consumption hypothesis is that real planned consumption is a function of four variables. Of these real income Y is by far the most important. Hence, if we take the values of Q, A, α, and r as given together with the values of their marginal response coefficients, we can draw, on a graph, the relation between C_p and the remaining independent variable Y. This is done in Figure 8.1 using data set out in the table. The resultant curve or schedule is called the *propensity to consume schedule*. It shows (for given values of Q, A, α, r, d, e, and f) the rate of real planned consumption at each real income level. Since real planned saving is equal, by definition, to real income minus real planned consumption, the same information can be used to draw a schedule relating real planned saving to real income. This too is done in the diagram. The resultant curve is called the *propensity to save schedule*.

Table 8.1 / *Determination of real planned consumption
(annual rates).*

AGGREGATE REAL PLANNED CONSUMPTION	AUTONOMOUS REAL PLANNED CONSUMPTION	$\dfrac{\partial C_p}{\partial Y}$	REAL INCOME	$\dfrac{\partial C;}{\partial A}$	REAL VALUE OF ASSETS	$\dfrac{\partial C_p}{\partial \alpha}$	INCOME DISTRI- BUTION	$\dfrac{\partial C_p}{\partial r}$	RATE OF INTEREST	REAL PLANNED SAVING $Y_s - C_p$
p	0	c		d	A	c	α		r	p
$bil.	$bil.		$bil.		$bil.		Index		%	
40	28	0.8	0	0.01	1,000	1.0	50	3.0	4.0	−40
200	28	0.8	200	0.01	1,000	1.0	50	3.0	4.0	0
360	28	0.8	400	0.01	1,000	1.0	50	3.0	4.0	40
440	28	0.8	500	0.01	1,000	1.0	50	3.0	4.0	60
520	28	0.8	600	0.01	1,000	1.0	50	3.0	4.0	80
600	28	0.8	700	0.01	1,000	1.0	50	3.0	4.0	100

Table based on the hypothesis that

$$C_p = Q + cY + dA + c\alpha + fr \tag{8.4}$$
$$C_p = 28 + 0.8Y + 0.01A + 1.0\alpha + 3.0r \tag{8.4n}$$

The position of the propensity to consume (save) schedule depends upon households' preferences, the values of $A, \alpha r$, and their marginal response coefficients, and the value of Q. Hence, the two curves, given these values, can be written:

$$C_p = H + cY \tag{8.5}$$
$$C_p = 100 + 0.8Y \tag{8.5n}$$
$$S_p = -H + (1 - c)Y \tag{8.6}$$
$$S_p = -100 + 0.2Y \tag{8.6n}$$

Figure 8.1 / *Propensity to consume and save schedules.*

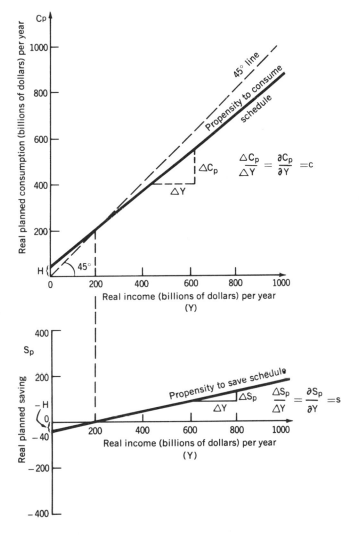

The *slope* of the propensity to consume schedule is $\partial C_p/\partial Y \equiv c$: the marginal response of real planned consumption to real income. This has a special name in economics, the *marginal propensity to consume*. It is the increment in real planned consumption resulting from a unit increase in real income alone. Analogously the *slope* of the propensity to save schedule is known as the *marginal propensity to save* $\partial S_p/\partial Y \equiv s$. Since, by definition, households must plan to save (or consume) the whole of any increase in income, then:

$$\frac{\partial C_p}{\partial Y} + \frac{\partial S_p}{\partial Y} \equiv 1 \quad \text{or} \quad c + s \equiv 1$$

so that

$$\frac{\partial S_p}{\partial Y} \equiv 1 - \frac{\partial C_p}{\partial Y} \quad \text{or} \quad s = 1 - c.$$

The consumption schedule, as plotted, shows that, when real income is zero, real planned consumption is H or, in numerical terms, $40 billion per annum. *This is the value of consumption which is autonomous with respect to income.* Notice that it depends on Q, A, α, r as well as d, e, and f. Analogously autonomous saving is $-\$40$ billion—which, of course, is simply *dis-saving,* for when Y = zero,

$$S_p \equiv Y - C_p \equiv 0 - \$40 \text{ bil.} \equiv -\$40 \text{ bil.}$$

Finally we define the *average propensity to consume* as:

$$\frac{C_p}{Y} \equiv \frac{\text{real planned consumption}}{\text{real income}}$$

and the *average propensity to save* as S_p/Y. Clearly since all income must be consumed or saved we have:

$$C_p + S_p \equiv Y$$

or

$$\frac{C_p}{Y} + \frac{S_p}{Y} \equiv 1$$

that is, the average propensities to save and consume add to unity. Notice that, if autonomous consumption (H) is positive, the average propensity to consume exceeds the marginal. If autonomous consumption is zero, the two are equal. If autonomous consumption is negative, the marginal propensity exceeds the average.

This is easily established from (8.5) where we wrote:

$$C_p = H + cY$$

so:

$$\frac{C_p}{Y} = \frac{H}{Y} + c,$$

which tells us that the average propensity to consume C_p/Y is equal to the marginal propensity (c) *plus* the term H/Y. Clearly if H is negative $c > C_p/Y$ and conversely if H is positive.

We have now listed the formal properties of the propensity to consume schedule. But formal properties are not of themselves economics. We now look at the economics.

The *position* of the schedule depends upon
  1) households' preferences;
  2) the values of Q, and A, α, r—the three independent variables not shown in the figure;

3) the marginal response coefficients *d, e,* and *f.*
A change in any one of these will shift the whole schedule—upward or downward—leaving its slope unaltered. Suppose, for example, α increases (income becomes more equally distributed). The schedule shifts upwards and we say that the propensity to consume has increased, for now, at *each* level of real income, real planned consumption is greater.

The *slope* of the schedule—the marginal propensity to consume—describes the reaction of real planned consumption to an increase in real income, *everything else held constant. It is an important proposition of economics that, when real income increases real consumption also increases but by less than the increase in real income.* That is, the marginal propensity to consume $\partial C_p / \partial Y$ is greater than zero but less than unity—a proposition which also applies to the marginal propensity to save. Thus we have the hypothesis:

$$0 < c \equiv \frac{\partial C_p}{\partial Y} < 1$$

$$0 < s \equiv \frac{\partial S_p}{\partial Y} < 1.$$

An increase in the propensity to consume must be sharply distinguished from an increase in consumption. The former, as we have seen, means an upward shift of the whole schedule indicating that, *because of a change in one of the parameters of the schedule,* households now plan a higher rate of real consumption at *each* level of real income. This is called an autonomous increase in consumption, since it is autonomous with respect to income.

By contrast an increase in real planned consumption may occur simply because real income rises and, as a result, we move *along* an *unchanged* propensity to consume schedule. Consumption then rises because, as we have already seen, the marginal propensity to consume is positive. This is called an *induced* increase in consumption, because it is brought about (induced) by an increase in real income.

It is extremely important to bear these distinctions clearly in mind. Words are often used loosely in the belief that their precise meaning can be distinguished in the context. Thus "an increase in consumption" is a potentially misleading phrase since, of itself, it does not make it clear whether there has been a *shift* in the consumption function (propensity to consume schedule), or movement along it, or some combination of the two. The same confusion can occur with the phrase "an increase in demand" referred to some commodity—say peanuts. Does this mean a shift in the demand schedule, a movement along it or some combination of the two?

In practice, though for pedagogic reasons we discuss shifts in the consumption function (and hence the propensity to consume schedule), this function is believed to be relatively stable: that is, to shift rather rarely. Hence most increases in consumption which are observed are probably induced: that is, due to movements along an unchanged function.

THE DETERMINATION OF THE EQUILIBRIUM LEVEL OF OUTPUT

At the beginning of this chapter we wrote our equilibrium condition in two equivalent ways: $Y = C_p + I_p$, and $S_p = I_p$. We also assumed that $I_p = I$ and took, as a numerical illustration, the value of I to be $200 billion a year. This value we treated as *exogenous*—that is, determined outside our model—and hence independent of income (output). We shall continue to treat r, A, and α also as *exogenous* and assume them to take the special values $\bar{r}$, $\bar{A}$, $\bar{\alpha}$, shown in Table 8.1. Obviously from Table 8.1, simply by adding the rate of planned investment (I_p) to the rate of planned consumption, we can draw up a new table showing aggregate demand ($C_p + I_p$) *at each level of real income*. This is done in Table 8.2. Plainly the equilibrium level of income, defined by the condition $Y = C_p + I_p$, is $1,200 billion.

Table 8.2 / *Aggregate demand at each level of real income*
(billions of dollars.)

REAL INCOME (AGGREGATE SUPPLY)	REAL PLANNED CONSUMPTION	REAL PLANNED INVESTMENT	REAL AGGREGATE DEMAND
	C_p	I_p	$(C_p + I_p)$
0	40	200	240
200	200	200	400
400	360	200	560
500	440	200	640
600	520	200	720
700	600	200	800
800	680	200	880
1000	840	200	1040
1200	1000	200	1200
1400	1160	200	1360
1600	1320	200	1520
1800	?	200	?
2000	?	200	?
2200	?	200	?
2400	?	200	2160

Assumptions:

(1) $I = I = $200 bil.

(2) $C = Q + cY + dA + c\alpha + fr$ with the value of the parameters as in Table 8.1.

By the same token we can use Table 8.1 to give the rates of real planned saving at each level of real income. Our second version of the equilibrium condition tells us that income will be in equilibrium when real planned saving is $200 billion—i.e., equal to the fixed rate of real planned investment. The reader can easily verify that this gives the same result.

Precisely the same result can be arrived at by elementary algebra. We have, in fact a simple problem which can be set out and solved as follows: First we write the equilibrium condition:

$$Y = C_p + I_p$$

Our consumption hypothesis tells us that:

$$C_p = Q + cY + d\bar{A} + c\bar{\alpha} + f\bar{r} \tag{8.7}$$

$$C_p = 28 + 0.8Y + 0.01\bar{A} + 1.0\bar{\alpha} + 3.0\bar{r} \tag{8.7n}$$

Our investment assumption gives:

$$I_p = \bar{I} \tag{8.8}$$

$$I_p = \$200 \text{ bil.} \tag{8.8n}$$

If we now substitute (8.7) and (8.8) into the equilibrium condition, we obtain a single equation in Y—which is equilibrium income—which can easily be solved in terms of $\bar{I}$, the given rate of investment, and the parameters of the consumption function. The manipulation is extremely simple. We have, on substitution,

$$Y = Q + cY + d\bar{A} + c\bar{\alpha} + f\bar{r} + \bar{I} \tag{8.9}$$

$$Y = 28 + 0.8Y + [0.01 \times 1000] + [1.0 \times 50] + [3.0 \times 4] + 200 \tag{8.9n}$$

therefore:

$$Y - cY = Q + d\bar{A} + c\bar{\alpha} + f\bar{r} + \bar{I}$$

$$Y - 0.8Y = 28 + [0.01 \times 1000] + [1.0 \times 50] + [3.0 \times 4] + 200$$

so that

$$Y = [\{Q + d\bar{A} + c\bar{\alpha} + f\bar{r}\} + \bar{I}]\frac{1}{1 - c} \tag{8.10}$$

$$Y = [\{28 + 10 + 50 + 12\} + 200]\frac{1}{1 - 0.8} \tag{8.10n}$$

The elementary algebra yields, as it must, the same result as elementary arithmetic. Equilibrium real income is $1,200 billion per year. The algebraic formulation of (8.10) however, brings out explicitly three points which the arithmetic formulation obscures.

First, the expression in the braces ({}) is that rate of consumption which is independent of (autonomous with respect to) income. It is, in fact, the constant (H) of equation (8.5). Equation (8.10) therefore confirms *ex-*

plicitly that H depends on the values of A, α, r, and their marginal response coefficients as well as on Q. It, in short, depends on *all* the parameters of the propensity to consume schedule—a point which we earlier stated without full demonstration. Second, the result for equilibrium Y takes the form of one expression (in the brackets) *multiplied* by a second expression which is $1/1 - c$. What is the expression in the brackets? A moment's thought shows that it is the sum of all those planned expenditures—whether consumption or investment—which are independent of income. This tells us that the equilibrium level of income is given by the sum of those expenditures which are independent of income multiplied by the expression $1/1 - c$. Third, what can we say about the expression $1/1$ c? This is simply $1/1$ —marginal propensity to consume. Since the marginal propensity to consume is positive—but less than unity—the denominator of this expression must be less than 1. Hence $1/1 - c$ must be greater than 1. Indeed in our example it is 5. We should also remind ourselves that, since $1 - c \equiv s$, this "multiplier" can also be written as $1/s$. The precise significance of this "multiplier" will be explained later. It is, however, obvious that the "multiplier" will be greater the greater is c—that is, the more nearly c approaches unity.

We have now shown that either via arithmetic or algebra we can, if we are given (1) the consumption function and (2) the rate of planned investment, determine the equilibrium level of income (output) and hence the equilibrium level of employment.

This is the crucial result of the modern theory of the short-run determination of output and employment. Its meaning is simply that, given the rate of planned investment, income will adjust (upward or downward) until it reaches a level at which households will plan to save at the same rate at which enterprises plan to invest. In short, income (and hence employment) is the variable which moves to equate the saving and investment plans of the community.

These are important results which we have reached by arithmetic and algebra are commonly presented geometrically. Since arithmetic is tedious and some people dislike algebra, we now perform the same exercise, using the same data, geometrically.

On the vertical axis of Figure 8.2(a) we measure real planned expenditures (C_p and I_p); on the horizontal axis, real income. The line marked C_p is thus the propensity to consume schedule of Figure 8.1. Its *slope*, as before, is the marginal propensity to consume. Its *position* is determined by OA—the rate of planned consumption, which is independent of income. The distance OA is therefore given by:

$$OA \equiv Q + d\bar{A} + c\bar{\alpha} + f\bar{r} \equiv H$$

$$\equiv \$40 \text{ bil. per year.}$$

Figure 8.2(a) / *Income determined by the aggregate demand schedule.*

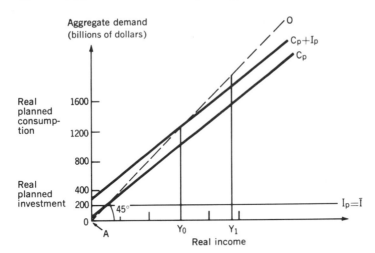

From the origin of the diagram we draw a line *00* at an angle of 45°. Geometrically this line has the property that any point on it subtends equal distances along the horizontal and vertical axes. It follows that at any point on *00*

aggregate real planned expenditure = aggregate real income (output)

that is $$C_p + I_p = Y$$

or $$I_p = S_p$$

The line 00 thus defines all possible positions of equilibrium.

To this diagram we now add a third line showing the rate of real planned investment (I_p). Since this is independent of income ($I_p = \bar{I}$) the line is horizontal and drawn showing a rate of $200 billion per year. We now add this rate of planned investment to the rates of consumption shown by the consumption schedule. This gives us the $C_p + I_p$ schedule or *the schedule of aggregate demand*. The schedule cuts *00* at the point *X*. At *X* income is Y_0. Y_0 is the equilibrium level of income, for since *X* lies on *00* it is a point at which aggregate demand is equal to aggregate supply (income). It is indeed the only point at which, with our given consumption and investment schedules, aggregate demand does equal aggregate supply.

The same result is depicted on Figure 8.2(b) where we have drawn, instead of the consumption schedule, the saving schedule. On this we have superimposed the investment schedule. Where these two curves cut —that is, where $I_p = S_p$—determines the equilibrium level of income. Again this is $Y_0 = \$1,200$ billion per year.

Both diagrams thus depict the determination of equilibrium output (income) either (as in Figure 8.2(a)) by the condition that $Y = C_p + I_p$ or (as in Figure 8.2(b)) by the equivalent condition that $S_p = I_p$.

Figure 8.2(b) / *Income determined by saving and investment schedules.*

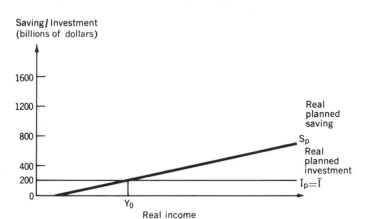

Suppose income is not at Y_0 but at some higher level Y_1. Will it tend to move toward Y_0? At Y_1 we can see from Figure 8.2(a) that $C_p + I_p$ (aggregate demand) is less than Y (aggregate supply). Hence some part of output will be unsold so that there will be unintended investment in inventories. In short, actual investment $(Y_1 - C_p)$ will exceed planned investment (I_p). In this situation, as we have already shown, enterprises will reduce output and employment. Hence income will move *toward* Y_0. This argument is readily reversible for income levels less than that of Y_0. It follows that Y_0 is not only the equilibrium level of income but is a *stable*[3] equilibrium in the sense that, if income departs from it, forces will be set up which tend to compel it to return to Y_0.

We have now shown, by arithmetic, algebra and geometry, that if we know (1) the consumption function; and (2) the rate of planned investment, we can determine the equilibrium level of income (output) and employment. We have also shown that, provided the marginal propensity to consume is less than unity, the equilibrium level of income is *stable*.

The meaning of this analysis can be summed up as follows: Assuming (1) constant prices; and (2) a given level of the interest rate; then, (a) the variable which adjusts to equate aggregate demand with aggregate supply—that is, to reconcile the saving plans of households with the investment plans of enterprises—is income; and (b) the equilibrium level

---

3. Strictly, stability is a dynamic concept.

of income which reconciles these plans need not be—and in general will not be—a level of income corresponding to full employment.

THE MULTIPLIER AND THE MARGINAL PROPENSITY TO CONSUME

Our analysis so far tells us that, given the rate of real planned consumption, which is independent of income (H in equation 8.5) and the rate of real planned investment, we can determine the equilibrium level of real income. It follows that if either of these determinants changes, so will the equilibrium level of income. What determines the extent of the change?

Originally we assumed I_p to be $200 billion per year. Suppose this rises to $300 billion. What will be the new equilibrium level of income?

A glance back at Table 8.1 tells us that, to generate a rate of planned saving of $300 billion a year, incomes will need to be $1700 billion. Hence:

$$\Delta Y \equiv \text{the change in equilibrium real income}$$
$$= \$1700 \text{ bil.} - \$1200 \text{ bil.} = \$500 \text{ bil.}$$

while
$$\Delta I_p \equiv \text{the change in real planned investment}$$
$$\$300 \text{ bil.} - \$200 \text{ bil.} = \$100 \text{ bil.}$$

Hence

$$\frac{\Delta Y}{\Delta I_p} = \frac{\$500 \text{ bil.}}{\$100 \text{ bil.}} = 5$$

We now define $\Delta Y / \Delta I_p$ as the "multiplier": that is, *the coefficient relating the change in real income to the change in real autonomous expenditure bringing it about*. We use "real autonomous expenditure" rather than "real investment" because *the same multiplier applies to changes in autonomous consumption*. If we refer to equation 8.10 or Figure 8.2(a), this is obvious enough. Using this equation we have, for the initial equilibrium level which we now call Y_0:

$$Y_0 = [H + \bar{I}] \frac{1}{1 - c} \quad \text{where } H = Q + d\bar{A} + c\bar{a} + f\bar{r} \quad (8.11)$$

If $\bar{I}$ increases by $\Delta\bar{I}$ the new equilibrium level Y_1 is given by:

$$Y_1 = [H + \bar{I} + \Delta\bar{I}] \frac{1}{1 - c} \quad (8.12)$$

so that

$$\Delta Y = Y_1 - Y_0 = \Delta I \frac{1}{1 - c} \quad \text{and} \quad \frac{\Delta Y}{\Delta I} = \frac{1}{1 - c} = \frac{1}{1 - 0.8} = 5.$$

Obviously had the change been in the propensity to consume so that H increased by ΔH we should have had:

$$\frac{\Delta Y}{\Delta H} = \frac{1}{1 - c} = \frac{1}{1 - 0.8} = 5† \tag{8.13}$$

In the short run, therefore, *any* change in autonomous real expenditure has a multiplied effect on income whether (in terms of Figure 8.2(a)) it shifts the consumption schedule upwards or the investment schedule.

The multiplier is given by the formula:

$$\frac{1}{1 - c} \equiv \frac{1}{s} \quad \text{where } c \equiv \text{marginal propensity to consume};$$

$$\text{and } s \equiv 1 - c \equiv \text{marginal propensity to save.}$$

So far this, though obvious enough, is merely algebra. What does it mean in economic terms?

Suppose autonomous consumption increases by \$10 billion each year, i.e., $\Delta H = \$10$ billion. Additional income is thus created for those who produce the additional output. From this income they spend \$10 billion. This generates further output and incomes which cause a further induced increase in consumption. This in turn generates further income for those who produce the additional consumption goods and so the process continues.

We have, indeed, the following series for the increase in income:

$$\Delta Y = \$10 \text{ bil.} + c\$10 \text{ bil.} + c^2\$10 \text{ bil.} + c^3\$10 \text{ bil.}$$
$$+ \cdots + c^n\$10 \text{ bil.}$$

or $\Delta Y = \$10$ bil. $+ 0.8\ \$10$ bil. $+ (0.8)^2\ \$10$ bil. $+ (0.8)^3\ \$10$ bil.
$+ \cdots + (0.8)^n\ \$10$ bil.

This series is easily added to give:

$$\Delta Y = \$10 \text{ bil.} \times \frac{1 - c^{n+1}}{1 - c} = \$10 \text{ bil.} \times \frac{1 - (0.8)^{n+1}}{1 - 0.8} \tag{8.14}$$

As n, the number of income "rounds," approaches infinity, c^{n+1}, since c is less than unity, approaches zero. Hence the *limit* of 8.14 as $n \to$ infinity is:

$$\Delta Y = \$10 \text{ bil.} \frac{1}{1 - c}$$

which is, clearly enough, our formula at (8.13), for we have simply taken ΔH to be \$10 billion.

† In this example the multiplier is 5 because the marginal propensity to consume is 0.80. It is this high because the only leakage out of the income stream taken into account here is saving. In a more realistic model part of the household's earnings is not currently received by it, but is saved by corporations, part goes to pay taxes, and part is spent on imported goods. As a result the "real world" multiplier is around 2 to 3, not 5.

In other words the new equilibrium level of income, reached after an infinitely large number of income "rounds," is greater than the original level by:

$$\Delta Y = \$10 \text{ bil.} \frac{1}{1-c}$$
$$= \$10 \text{ bil.} \times 5$$
$$= \$50 \text{ bil.}$$

The change in come is greater than the change in autonomous expenditure which causes it because, as long as $c > 0$ the multiplier, $1/1 - c$ must be > 1. Notice that if $c = 0$ the multiplier is unity. This, however, is economically quite implausible.

The common-sense proposition underlying this result is that one man's income is another man's expenditure—which is obviously correct—and, as a result, the more the latter spends the more the former will receive and spend in his turn.

The multiplier is thus a *leverage coefficient* and, as such, works in either direction. To see this suppose ΔH to be negative and equal to $- \$10$ billion. We should then have:

$$\Delta Y = -\$10 \text{ bil.} \frac{1}{1-c}$$
$$= -\$50 \text{ bil.}$$

so that, in this case, equilibrium income would *fall* by \$50 billion.

To know that, after an infinite passage of time ($n \to$ infinity) equilibrium income will rise (or fall) by an amount determined by the multiplier and the increase (decrease) in the rate of autonomous expenditure is interesting. We are, however, not primarily concerned with what will *eventually* occur but only with *what will occur after the lapse of a finite period of time*. To see this we must engage in some elementary dynamics. Accordingly in the table which follows we (1) *express* all flows at quarterly and *not* annual rates; (2) *divide* time into periods of 3 calendar months' duration; (3) *assume* that output takes one period (3 months) to adjust to a change in demand. On these assumptions, making use of the consumption function specified in Table 8.1—that is, holding the variables A, α, and r constant—we can set out the following multiplier process.

We begin in period 0 with income in equilibrium at \$450 billion. In period 1, I_p increases to \$100 billion. Output however does not increase until period 2, since, by assumption, it takes one period to adjust. Hence in period 1 aggregate demand ($C_p + I_p$) exceeds aggregate supply and there is involuntary decumulation of stocks to the extent of \$50 billion.

In period 2 output adjusts upwards by \$50 billion. Since the marginal propensity to consume is 0.8, this raises consumption by \$40 billion. Again aggregate demand exceeds supply, this time by $40 billion, and there is a second involuntary decumulation of stocks.

Table 8.3 / *The Multiplier Process* (*billions of dollars at quarterly rates*).

PERIOD	IN-COME	PLANNED CONSUMP-TION	ACTUAL = CONSUMP-TION	PLANNED SAVING	= ACTUAL SAVING	PLANNED INVEST-MENT	ACTUAL INVEST-MENT	UNINTENDED INVEST-MENT
	(1)	(2)	(3)	(4)	(5)	(6)	(7)	(8)
0	450	400	400	50	50	50	50	nil
1	450	400	400	50	50	100	50	−50
2	500	440	440	60	60	100	60	−40
3	540	472	472	68	68	100	68	−32
4	572	497.6	497.6	74.4	74.4	100	74.4	−25.6
5						100		
6						100		
.								
.								
n	700	600	600	100	100	100	100	nil

(1) Based on the consumption function of Table 8.1.

In period 3 output expands again—this time by $40 billion. Hence consumption rises by $(0.8) \times \$40$ billion $= \$32$ billion, and in this way the process continues with enterprises always adjusting output upward in an attempt to catch up with expanding aggregate demand.

This table, which gives a somewhat oversimpled account of a dynamic multiplier process, conveys some interesting information. This can be summarized as follows:

1) The *ultimate* change in the *quarterly* rate of income is given by:

$$\Delta Y = \Delta I_p \times \frac{1}{1 - c}$$
$$= \$50 \text{ bil.}$$
$$= \$250 \text{ bil.}$$

By the fourth period—that is, after one year—48.8 percent of this change has occurred.

2) From period 1 to period $(n - 1)$ the system is in disequilibrium. Hence:

$$Y < C_p + I_p$$

and

$$I_p > I$$

and so periods 1 to $(n - 1)$ are characterized by unintended disinvestment in stocks which diminishes as the system moves towards its new equilibrium.

3) In *all* periods—that is, whether equilibrium exists or not,

$$S \equiv I$$

and

$$Y \equiv C + I$$

where S, I, and C denote saving, investment, and consumption in their national accounting sense.

These points the reader should check for himself. He should also calculate the values for columns (1) (2) (3) (4) (5) (7) and (8) for periods 5 and 6.

QUESTIONS AND EXERCISES

1. Suppose relief payments are increased, the increased expenditure being financed by an increase in direct taxes on those with incomes in excess of $8000 per year. What would be the effect on (a) the propensity to consume schedule and (b) the equilibrium level of output?

2. The following observations are generated by a consumption function of the form: $C_p = Q + cY + dA + e\alpha + fr$.

YEAR	C_p	Y	A	α	r
1	662.4	1000	1000	0.5	4
2	762.4	1200	1000	0.5	4
3	767.4	1200	1500	0.5	4
4	817.4	1200	1500	1.0	4
5	766.2	1200	1500	0.5	2

Calculate the numerical values of the marginal response coefficients c, d, e, f and the constant Q. Next, taking $A = 1000$, $\alpha = 0.5$ and $r = 4.0$ percent, plot the propensity to consume schedule. What is the value of consumption when income is zero? Draw a second schedule for the value $A = 1000$; $\alpha = 1.0$; $r = 4$ percent.

3. The elasticity of consumption with respect to income is defined as:

$$\frac{\Delta C_p}{C_p} \bigg/ \frac{\Delta Y}{Y},$$

when Y is the only independent variable to change. This can be rewritten:

$$\frac{\Delta C_p}{\Delta Y} \times \frac{Y}{C_p}.$$

Since $\Delta C_p = (\partial C_p/\partial Y) \times \Delta Y$ calculate from *both* the propensity to consume schedules the elasticity of consumption with respect to income. Show that the elasticity will be unity only if autonomous consumption is zero. Why is this? What general relationship does it reflect between the average and marginal propensities and the elasticity? In what circumstances will the elasticity be independent of the level of income?

4. Use the U. S. national income estimates to obtain figures for real consumption and real income on a quarterly basis for the years 1967–71. Draw (freehand) a straight line through these observations when plotted on a graph. Measure consumption on the vertical axis and income on the horizontal axis.

    a) Explain and justify your choice of data.

    b) What is the slope of your straight line?

    c) In what circumstances, if any, would the slope of your line be a "reasonable" estimate of the marginal propensity to consume?

    d) Assuming that it is a "reasonable" estimate, what is the value of the multiplier?

    e) What do you think is meant by "reasonable"?

5. Assume that the propensity to consume is described by:

$$C_p = 100 + 0.5\,Y; \quad c = \frac{\partial C_p}{\partial H} = 0.5.$$

    a) Write down the values of C_p for the following values of income: $Y = 100$; $Y = 200$; $Y = 300$; $Y = 400$; $Y = 500$; $Y = 600$; $Y = 1000$.

    b) From these values construct the propensity to save schedule.

    c) What are the equilibrium values of income if (a) $I_p =$ zero; (b) $I_p = 100$.

    d) What would be the change in the equilibrium level of output if autonomous consumption rose from 100 to 110? What is the multiplier? What is the *induced* increase in consumption?

6. Using the data of Question 2, plot C_p and Y as for Question 4. Again draw (freehand) a straight line through the observed points. Why is the slope of this line not a good estimate of $\partial C_p / \partial Y$?

7. *Ceteris paribus* according to Table 8.1 a 10-unit increase in income "induces" an 8-unit increase in consumption. Give a precise statement of what is meant by *ceteris paribus*. Explain the meaning of "induced."

8. Write down the assumptions of the dynamic multiplier of Table 8.3. Which assumptions do you consider particularly unrealistic and why?

9. For the multiplier of Table 8.3 what proportion of the ultimate change in income is completed after (a) two quarters; (b) four quarters; (c) eight quarters.

10. Discuss critically the assumptions about human behavior underlying the consumption function of Question 2. Are all the variables measurable (a) in principle (b) in practice? How would you attempt to measure A, α, and r?

11. The multiplier model of Table 8.3 can be written formally as follows:

$$C_p(t) = H + cY(t) \qquad \text{with } H = 40, \ c = 0.8$$
$$I_p(t) = \bar{I} \qquad\qquad\qquad\quad \bar{I} = 50,$$
$$Y(t) = C_p(t-1) + I_p(t-1)$$

where the suffixes in parentheses indicate the period $(t, t-1,$ etc.$)$ of the variable and the last equation indicates that it takes one period for output to adjust to demand.

An alternative model can be written:

$$C_p(t) = H + cY(t-1)$$
$$I_p(t) = \bar{I}$$
$$Y(t) = C_p(t) + I_p(t),$$

where the lag of output behind demand no longer exists and, in its place, we have put the hypothesis that this period's consumption depends upon last period's income.

Construct a table similar to 8.3 showing the multiplier process for this model. How does disequilibrium manifest itself? Why are there no unplanned stock changes? Is the equilibrium result of the two processes the same? Which model do you consider the more realistic?

12. Plot the following data on an appropriate graph:

PERCENT OF INCOME RECIPIENTS	PERCENT OF INCOME RECEIVED
10	3
20	7
30	11
40	16
50	22
60	29
70	36
80	47
90	59
100	100

What would a graph showing equal distribution of income look like? Construct one and compare it with the graph of the data. From your comparison suggest a way of measuring α (the parameter of income distribution). What would graphs of $\alpha = 0$ (perfect inequality of income distribution) and $\alpha = 1$ look like?

13. The capital account of the household of A. Snodgrass on December 31, 1970, was as follows:

LIABILITIES		ASSETS	
Credit card liabilities	$ 250	Notes and coin	$ 128
Mortgage	12,500	Bank deposits	332
		House	46,500
Net worth	41,550	Shares (market price)	2,100
		Car (valuation)	1,240
		Government bonds	4,000
Total	$54,300	Total	$54,300

On the basis of this statement what are Snodgrass' (a) gross assets; (b) net assets? Use your answer to determine how you would define, and seek to measure, the real assets of households (A) in the consumption function hypothesis. Justify your procedure.

14. The multiplier process of Table 8.3 can be written as follows:

PERIOD	CHANGE IN INCOME
2	ΔI_p
3	$c\Delta I_p$
4	$c^2\Delta I_p$
5	$c^3\Delta I_p$
.	
.	
.	
$n + 2$	$c^n\Delta I_p$

So the total change in income is:

$$\Delta H = \Delta I_p[1 + c + c^2 + \cdots + c^n]$$
$$= \Delta I_p\left[\frac{1 - c^{n+1}}{1 - c}\right].$$

Use this formula to calculate the proportion of the total change which will have occurred by the end of (a) period 2; (b) period 4; (c) period 10. Would your results have been different if c had been 0.5 and not 0.8? Do your results imply that the greater the multiplier the greater the number of periods required to achieve any given proportion (say 50 percent) of its equilibrium result?

15. How would you characterize the business behavior assumed in Table 8.3?

16. From the Economic Report of the President obtain figures for the quarterly expenditure on (a) consumption of non-durables; (b) consumption of durables, for the years 1968–70. Graph them against income. Compare these graphs with that you prepared for Question 4. What does the comparison suggest to you? What additional variables (if any) would you introduce into the consumption function hypothesis to obtain a better explanation of expenditure on durables? How would you seek to measure them?

SUGGESTED READING

J. M. Keynes, *The General Theory of Employment, Interest, and Money* (New York: Harcourt Brace, 1936) Chaps. 8–10.
G. Ackley, *Macroeconomic Theory* (New York: Macmillan, 1961) Chaps. 10–11.

M. Evans, *Macroeconomic Activity* (New York: Harper and Row, 1959) Chaps. 2 and 6. *Advanced reference.*

W. Salant, "Taxes, Income Determination and the Balanced Budget Theorem," *Review of Economics and Statistics,* Vol. 39 (May 1957), pp. 152–61. *Advanced reference.*

9

Theories of the Consumption Function

IN THE PREVIOUS CHAPTER we described the mechanics of the consumption function. Let us now pursue this subject further by looking briefly at various theories which try to explain what determines the propensity to consume. To be useful such a theory must be confirmed by empirical tests. It is relatively easy to list factors that are likely to influence consumption and saving behavior, but this type of "theorizing" is only a preliminary step. To see whether any factor has an important effect on consumption or whether its influence is so trivial that it can be ignored is an empirical question. In other words, to see whether a particular variable should be included in a theory of the consumption function, one must see how well it can predict or explain the observable consumption behavior of households. By far the greater part of the economist's work on consumption functions has therefore dealt, not with formulating theories, but with testing them. However, since this book deals primarily with economic *theory,* we will pay little attention to the empirical tests. The reader interested in the empirical tests can find them in the books and articles listed as "Suggested Reading" at the end of this chapter.

Although we want our consumption function theory to be consistent with the empirical evidence, we do not want it to provide a detailed *description* of the way households make their consumption decisions. A detailed description would have to include so many factors that our theory would become too complicated and clumsy. Theory should abstract from reality, and that means suppressing many details. Some of these details may be very important for many purposes—for example, they may be vital for a market researcher—but they would not form a useful part of a macroeconomic theory.

THE ABSOLUTE INCOME THEORY

The original consumption function theory presented by Keynes in 1936 in his *General Theory of Employment, Interest and Money* is nowadays referred to as the *absolute income* theory. This theory asserts three propositions. First, consumption is a fairly stable function of income. Second,[1]

the fundamental psychological law upon which we are entitled to depend with great confidence both *a priori* from our knowledge of human nature and from the detailed facts of experience, is that men are disposed, as a rule and on the average, to increase their consumption as their income increases, but not by as much as the increase in their income. . . .

Third,

apart from short period *changes* in the level of income, it is also obvious that a higher absolute level of income will tend, as a rule, to widen the gap between income and consumption. For the satisfaction of the immediate primary needs of a man and his family is usually a stronger motive than the motives towards accumulation which only acquire effective sway when a margin of comfort has been attained. These reasons will lead, as a rule, to a greater *proportion* of income being saved as real income increases.

In the debate following the publication of the *General Theory* these conclusions, which Keynes had based primarily on intuition and casual observation, were subjected to statistical tests and seemed to be vindicated by them. Thus annual data on national income and consumption show a very close correlation, and a comparison of household budgets demonstrates that the higher a household's income, the smaller the percent of income it consumes.

This theory has a very important implication. As full employment income rises over time, the proportion of income consumed falls, so that, to maintain full employment, a greater and greater volume of investment relative to income is needed each year if full employment is actually to be attained.

But this absolute income theory, for all its intuitive attraction, ran into two serious difficulties. One was that data became available on the percent of income consumed going back into the last third of the nineteenth cen-

---

1. J. M. Keynes, *The General Theory of Employment, Interest and Money* (New York: Harcourt Brace, 1936), pp. 96–97.

tury. These data showed that the percent of income consumed was no greater then than it is now. This historical stability in the average propensity to consume creates a problem for the absolute income theory; given the great increase in per capita income which has occurred, this theory predicts (incorrectly) that the percent of income consumed would have fallen substantially.[2]

The second problem for the absolute income theory was that it failed dramatically when used during World War II to predict consumption after the war. Predictions which were based on the absolute income theory greatly underestimated postwar consumption, and, not surprisingly, this fact served to discredit the theory.

THE RELATIVE INCOME THEORY

Fortunately, another theory of the consumption function, the relative income theory, was developed (mainly by Professors James Duesenberry and Franco Modigliani) just around the time when it became apparent that the absolute income theory was predicting badly. This theory can best be understood by looking at it as an attempt to resolve a rather confusing paradox. This paradox is that the relationship of income and consumption seems to be quite different when one looks at historical data on national income and consumption (time series data), and if one looks at household budgets at any one point of time (cross-section data). The latter show very clearly that the higher a household's income, the smaller the proportion of income it consumes, and thus seems to confirm the absolute income theory. But time series data tell a very different story: the great increase in income since 1870 has not been accompanied by a decline in the proportion of income consumed. The solution which the relative income theory offers is the following: A household's consumption depends not on its absolute income, but on its *relative* income; relative that is to (1) the income of other households and (2) its own previous income. The reason consumption depends on a household's income relative to the income of other households was explained by Duesenberry in terms reminiscent of Veblen's notion of conspicuous consumption.[3]

A family in given circumstances manages to achieve a *modus operandi*

2. These historical data do not *necessarily* contradict the absolute income theory. One can reconcile the two by arguing that the rise in income has indeed lowered the average propensity to consume, but that this movement along the function has been offset by other factors which have shifted the whole function upward, such as urbanization, the declining importance of individual entrepreneurship and of agriculture, the introduction of new goods, etc. However, it is hard to believe that these factors have had just the right strength to account for the continued failure of the average propensity to consume to fall with rising income.

3. James Duesenberry, *Income, Saving, and the Theory of Consumer Behavior* (Cambridge, Massachusetts: Harvard Univ. Press, 1949), pp. 26–27.

between its desires for increased consumption and its desires for saving. The solution, whatever it is, is a compromise. The family knows of the existence of higher quality goods and would prefer them to the ones now in use. But it could only attain these by giving up saving. Once a compromise is reached the habit formation provides a protective wall against desires for higher quality goods. In given circumstances, the individuals in question come into contact with goods superior to the ones they use with a certain frequency. Each such contact is a demonstration of the superiority of these goods and is a threat to the existence of the current consumption pattern. It is a threat because it makes active the latent preference for these goods. A certain effort is required to resist the impulse to give up saving in favor of higher quality goods. (This resistance need not, of course, be entirely conscious, but psychic effort is required all the same.)

Suppose the consumption patterns of other people are given. Consumption expenditures of a particular consumer will have to rise until the frequency of contact with superior goods is reduced to a certain level. This level of frequency has to be sufficiently low to permit resistance to all impulses to increase expenditures. The strength of the resistance will depend on the strength of desires for saving.

It now becomes clear how the habit pattern can be broken without a change in income or prices. For any particular family the frequency of contact with superior goods will increase primarily as the consumption expenditures of others increase. When that occurs, impulses to increase expenditure will increase in frequency, and strength and resistance to them will be inadequate. The result will be an increase in expenditure at the expense of saving.

Apart from its own current income and other people's incomes, a household's consumption also depends on its own past income. The reason for this is that a household acquires consumption habits, i.e., an accepted standard of living, which it is reluctant to give up. In the face of a decline in income it will therefore cut its saving or even dis-save. This accustomed standard of living can be approximated statistically by taking income at the last cyclical peak. Explaining consumption in this way by both past and current income is, of course, entirely consistent with Keynes' statement cited above.

The way the relative income theory differs from the absolute income theory is twofold. First, it introduces other people's income into the determination of a household's consumption; and second, it does not claim, as does the absolute income theory, that, *apart from this "demonstration effect"* of other people's consumption, there is any reason for thinking that a household with high current and peak income will consume a smaller proportion of its income than a household with a lower current and peak income.

Let us see how this theory can resolve the paradox. Looking at long-run data, as income rises over time, the incomes of other households rise along with the income of any one household. Hence, the typical household's *relative* income is constant, and so is its contact with superior goods. Its average propensity to consume is therefore constant too. Now consider a cross-section of households at any one moment in time. High-income households have relatively little contact with goods superior to their own while low income households have much more such contact. Low-income households therefore have more of an incentive to consume a larger proportion of their income, and hence we find that, when comparing households with different incomes, the low-income households consume a larger proportion of their income. In other words, we observe what appears to be the usual Keynesian consumption function. Thus, the theory is able to explain why in cross-section data the marginal propensity to consume is less than the average propensity, while in time series data the average and the marginal propensities to consume are similar. Moreover, the relative income theory also explains why in a cyclical trough a greater proportion of income is consumed than at a peak. The reason is that during the recession the effect of consumption habits acquired during the past income peak keeps consumption up relative to income.

MORE COMPLEX CONSUMPTION FUNCTIONS

Both the absolute income theory and the relative income theory place nearly all their stress on one determinant of consumption: income. But neither of these theories would deny that other variables too may affect consumption. And, in fact, a substantial amount of research effort has gone into determining what these other variables are.

Some variables which have been introduced are demographic ones, family size and age. The data show that the larger the family, the greater is its propensity to consume. Similarly, age differences account for differences in the propensity to consume of various households. Both young households and old households have a high propensity to consume, while middle-aged households save a larger proportion of their income. This can readily be explained by the fact that typically incomes peak in the middle years. Hence, households tend to do much of their saving in these years and to save little, or even to dis-save, at other stages of their life cycle.

Another set of relevant factors are financial variables such as wealth, liquid assets, credit availability, and interest rates. Since the purpose of saving is to accumulate wealth, given constant tastes, the greater a household's existing stock of wealth, the less is its incentive to save. Hence, an increase in wealth raises the propensity to consume, unless the holding of wealth somehow increases the household's taste for wealth.

Not only the total stock of wealth, but its composition *may* be relevant. It has been argued that it is liquid assets (such as money, saving and loan shares, government securities, etc.) more than illiquid wealth which stimulate consumption, because the possession of liquid assets allows a household to dis-save easily. For similar reasons, the availability of consumer credit *may* be important.

In addition to the above, there are many other variables which have been introduced into consumption function analysis with varying degrees of success. One, for example is income distribution, which along with wealth and the interest rate we used in the consumption function of the previous chapter. Then there is home-ownership. The data suggest that home owners tend to save more than renters, other factors being equal. This could be due to their need to repay their mortgages. Other variables which have been suggested are the existence of government and private pension systems, price level changes, and changes in the degree of optimism or pessimism felt by the public.

THE "NEW" THEORIES OF THE CONSUMPTION FUNCTION

The most recent breakthrough in consumption function theory has been the development of an approach which gets away from relating consumption only to current income or to current income plus past peak income. Instead it stresses the long run.

The most widely discussed of these theories is the "permanent income theory" of Professor Milton Friedman. To understand this theory let us go back to the work of Irving Fisher.[4] Irving Fisher gave three reasons why households save. One was to even out the income stream—that is, to transfer resources from years of high earnings to years of low or zero earnings. The second is to take care of an increase in needs anticipated in the future, and the third is to earn interest. The first of these reasons suggests that households in deciding on consumption look not only at current income but at the expected income over their life span. Given constant needs, and ignoring the possibility of earning interest, a rational household will maximize utility by consuming throughout its life at a steady rate— that is, by saving any income which is above its average and dis-saving it in those years when its income is below its lifetime average. In other words, consumption depends upon "permanent" income; "transitory" income is

4. Irving Fisher, who was probably the greatest American economist, was born in 1867 and died in 1947.

saved.[5] The saving of transitory income may strike the reader as contrary to everyday experience. We find that people frequently use transitory income to buy a consumer durable such as a car. But this problem can be handled readily by treating the purchase of a durable not as consumption but as saving; in other words, as an "investment" by the household. And this is what the permanent income theory does. It defines consumption as the *use* of consumer goods, not as their purchase. Hence, it treats as consumption only the depreciation (and interest cost) and not the original purchase of a consumer durable. (This means that we need a separate theory to explain the purchase of durables.)

What does the permanent income theory tell us about the relation of the average and the marginal propensities to consume *permanent* income? In other words, if a household with a $10,000 permanent income saves 10 percent of its income, would one expect a household with a $20,000 permanent income to save a larger, a smaller, or the same percent of its income? The answer given by the *absolute* income theory is that it would save a larger percent, but the permanent income theory denies this. It claims that there is no valid *a priori* reason for assuming this, that saving is like any other commodity in that its income elasticity should be determined from the empirical data rather than on an *a priori* basis. And the permanent income theory claims that the empirical evidence shows that the income elasticity of saving is about unity, i.e., that households with high and low *permanent* incomes save, on the average, the same proportion of their permanent incomes. While this hypothesis explains why the average propensity to consume has been constant over time, it seems, at first glance, to be clearly contradicted by the cross-section data. Household budgets very definitely show that high-income households save a larger proportion of their income than do low income households. But, according to the permanent income theory, this merely reflects the fact that these data classify households by the income of a single year (so-called "measured income") rather than by permanent income. In any one year many of the households in the high-income brackets are there due to some temporary factor, such as an extraordinary bonus, and their permanent incomes are below their current measured incomes. Hence, the high savings of the top measured income classes reflects merely the saving of transitory income. Similarly, many households in the lowest income classes are likely to have negative transitory income due to some factor such as unemployment or sickness. Their permanent incomes exceed their current measured incomes. Since households tend to even out their consumption stream, these house-

5. Permanent income can be defined in several ways. One way is to call it the income the household takes as permanent over the length of time it looks ahead. Another is to say that it is equal to the household's total productive assets, including human earning power, times the yield on these assets. Empirically, it can be approximated by looking at the past income of previous years and at their trend.

holds tend to dis-save; and this is what accounts for the low, or even negative, savings of the low-income households.[6]

In brief, the permanent income theory asserts the following three propositions:

1) Consumption is a function of permanent income rather than of current income.

2) Transitory income is all saved if positive and dis-saved if negative.

3) The proportion of permanent income consumed is independent of the level of permanent income.

These propositions are, of course, controversial, and have been the subject of much research and debate in recent years. It is worth noting that even if they are not fully correct, they need not be completely false either. It is possible to take an intermediate position, to argue that (1) consumption depends on the income of several years, but that current income predominates; (2) that while some transitory income is consumed, the propensity to consume is less for transitory income than for permanent income; and (3) that while the proportion of permanent income consumed does decrease as one goes up the income scale, this decrease is substantially less for permanent income than it is for measured income.

The permanent income theory is not the only theory which stresses long-run considerations. The "life cycle hypothesis" developed by Professor Franco Modigliani and associates is similar in many respects to the permanent income theory. In this theory

. . . there need not be any close and simple relation between consumption in a given short period and income in the same period. The rate of consumption in any given period is a facet of a plan which extends over the balance of an individual's life, while the income accruing within the same period is but one element which contributes to the shaping of such a plan.[7]

Instead of stressing current income it is better to start with the assumption that an individual maximizes his utility function

. . . subject to the resources available to him, his resources being the sum of current and discounted future earnings over his lifetime and his current net worth. As a result of this maximization the current consumption of the indi-

6. To be sure, *some* low-income households will have positive transitory incomes, and *some* high-income households will have negative transitory incomes, but on the average, transitory income will tend to be negative in the low-income brackets and positive in the high-income brackets. If we classify households by permanent *plus* transitory income, i.e., by measured income, we must expect that high-income households tend to have positive transitory income because the very fact that they have positive transitory income works to make us classify them as high-income households. Similarly, households with negative transitory incomes tend to have low permanent plus transitory incomes.

7. Franco Modigliani and Richard Brumberg, "Utility Analysis and the Aggregate Consumption Function: An Interpretation of Cross Section Data," in Kenneth Kurihara (ed.) *Post–Keynesian Economics* (Brunswick, N.J.: Rutgers University Press, 1954), pp. 391–92.

vidual can be expressed as a function of his resources and the rate of return on capital with parameters depending upon age.[8]

In other words, consumption is a function of the following variables: (1) current and expected labor income, (2) net worth, and, for reasons to be explained in a moment, (3) age.

This life cycle hypothesis differs from the permanent income theory in several ways.[9] One is its use of (human plus nonhuman) wealth rather than permanent income as its leading variable. But this is a difference of expression rather than of content. As pointed out above, permanent income can be defined as human plus nonhuman wealth times its yield. A more substantial difference between the two is that in the permanent income theory the household passes on its assets to its heirs, while in the life cycle hypothesis the household does not do this; instead it saves during its active years only to consume all these savings after retirement. Hence, if a household expecting to live another ten years receives a $10,000 unexpected gain, it will consume approximately $1,000 out of this gain each year. Its consumption out of an unexpected gain therefore depends, in part, on its age. On the other hand, the permanent income theory household will save the whole $10,000 and consume only out of the interest it earns on this investment.

While the permanent income theory and the life cycle hypothesis are the main protagonists of the "new" consumption theories, they are not the only ones. Another theory, for example, makes consumption a function of a household's normal income, its transitory income, and the difference between its actual and desired stock of wealth. Other theories just introduce a wealth term in addition to the measured income term into the consumption function. The rise in wealth can explain why the propensity to consume has not fallen over time, and it is also entirely consistent with the cross-section data.

In conclusion it may be worth pointing out briefly the implications of the relative income theory and the permanent income theory for the value of the multiplier. As pointed out in the previous chapter, the value of the multiplier depends upon the marginal propensity to consume, and these theories have something to say about that. The relative income theory implies that the marginal propensity to consume is less for income decreases than it is for increases in income above its previous peak. In the former case the household's memory of its previous higher consumption limits the extent to which it cuts its current consumption as its current

8. Albert Ando and Franco Modigliani, "The 'Life Cycle' Hypothesis of Saving," *American Economic Review*, Vol. LIII (March 1963), p. 56.

9. The use of the terms "permanent income *theory*" and "life cycle *hypothesis*" should not be read as denoting a difference in the validity or generality of the two; it merely results from different authors choosing different words to describe their work.

income falls. But since households are always ready to improve their living standards, no such factor operates to reduce the marginal propensity to consume when income rises above its previous peak. Hence, the value of the multiplier differs in these two cases.

The permanent income theory has a somewhat similar implication for the value of the multiplier. For a change in permanent income the marginal propensity to consume is high, and hence the value of the multiplier is large. However, transitory income is saved to the extent that it is not spent on durables. Hence, for transitory income increases the multiplier is relatively small. Since income declines are usually only short-term and transitory, the permanent income theory suggests that the multiplier tends to be smaller for income declines than for income increases.

QUESTIONS AND EXERCISES

1. How would you evaluate consumption function theories? Are there considerations apart from their "truth" or accuracy you would consider?

2. Can you think of some way of testing the relative and absolute income theories empirically? Do you think the necessary data could be obtained?

3. How would you expect the average propensity to consume to be affected by: (a) the development of a widespread pension system, (b) an increase in prices, or (c) a more equal distribution of income?

4. Apart from the variables discussed in this chapter, can you think of any others which may affect consumption? How would you test their significance?

5. "An increase in the interest rate may either raise or lower the average propensity to consume." Explain in your own words.

6. Explain carefully why a rational household with constant needs and tastes would, in the absence of interest, consume the same amount each year.

7. Can you think of some factors why households may not actually behave this way?

8. Write a paragraph or two (a) defending the proposition that a household's propensity to consume permanent income is independent of the level of permanent income, and (b) criticizing this idea.

SUGGESTED READING

J. M. Keynes, *The General Theory of Employment, Interest and Money* (New York: Harcourt Brace, 1936) Chaps. 8–9.

J. Duesenberry, *Income, Saving, and the Theory of Consumer Behavior* (Cambridge: Harvard University Press, 1949) Chaps. 3–4.

G. Ackley, *Macroeconomic Theory* (New York: Macmillan, 1961) Chaps. 10–12.

M. Evans, *Macroeconomic Activity* (New York: Harper and Row, 1969) Chaps. 2–3.

M. Friedman, *A Theory of the Consumption Function* (Princeton, N.J.: Princeton University Press, 1957) Chaps. 2–3, 9.

F. Modigliani and R. Brumberg, "Utility Analysis and the Consumption Function: An Interpretation of Cross-Section Data," in Kenneth Kurihara (ed.), *Post-Keynesian Economics* (New Brunswick, N.J.: Rutgers University Press, 1954), pp. 388–436.

F. Modigliani, "The Life Cycle Hypothesis of Saving, the Demand for Wealth and the Supply of Capital," *Social Research* (Summer 1966), pp. 160–217.

D. Suits, "The Determinants of Consumer Expenditure: A Review of Present Knowledge," in Commission on Money and Credit, *Impacts of Monetary Policy* (Englewood Cliffs, N.J.: Prentice-Hall, 1963), pp. 1–57.

R. Ferber, "Research on Household Behavior," *American Economic Review,* Vol. LII (March 1962), pp. 19–63.

M. Farrell, "The 'New' Theories of the Consumption Function," *Economic Journal,* Vol. LXIX (December 1959), pp. 678–96.

T. Mayer, *Permanent Income, Wealth and Consumption* (Berkeley: University of California Press, forthcoming) Chaps. 1, 2, 16.

10

The Theory of Investment

IN CHAPTER 9 we showed that if we knew (1) the propensity to consume schedule and (2) the rate of real planned investment, we could determined the equilibrium level of output and hence, via the production function, the equilibrium level of employment. We also demonstrated that the equilibrium level of output (= income) was stable.[1]

These are important conditions. We established them, however, on the pedagogically convenient assumption that the rate of real planned investment was exogenously determined by, say, some hypothetical "planning authority." In a market economy there is no such authority. It follows that, to develop our theory, we must now put forward an explanation of how real planned investment gets determined. The purpose of this chapter is therefore to develop a theory of how investment gets determined—or, as we shall call it, by analogy with the consumption function already discussed, the theory of the investment function.

At this stage you should recall our definition of the term "investment." This must be carefully distinguished from colloquial usage in which it is common to speak of "investment" in financial assets such as bonds, shares, or deposits. There are three fundamental points:

1) Real net investment is the process of increasing the real capital stock of the community.

2) An investment decision is a decision to bring about such an increase.

3) Real gross investment is defined as real net investment *plus* real depreciation.

---

1. We return to this issue—in a dynamic context—in Chapter 19.

In practice, net investment expenditure by the private sector takes three forms which it is useful to distinguish:

$$I_f \equiv \text{real planned net investment in fixed capital}$$
$$\text{(other than dwellings)};$$

$$I_d \equiv \text{real planned net investment in dwellings};$$

$$I_s \equiv \text{real planned net investment in inventories}$$

so that

$$I_p \equiv \text{real planned net investment} \equiv I_f + I_d + I_s.$$

Discussion of I_s is postponed until the next chapter. Hence the theory of this chapter should be regarded as applicable primarily to investment in fixed capital and dwellings.

We begin by asking: Who makes investment decisions and why?

INVESTMENT DECISIONS

In our simple model, by assumption, all investment decisions are taken by enterprises or, more strictly, by the businessmen who run them. We have assumed that the aim of businessmen is to maximize profits; our problem is therefore to explain in what circumstances a profit-maximizing businessman will plan to invest.

The easiest approach to this problem is to consider a simple hypothetical example. Let us assume, therefore, that some businessman is considering whether or not to invest by adding a new machine costing $10,000 to his shoe manufacturing factory. He *knows* the cost of the machine. Is it worth his while to purchase it?

In buying the machine the businessman can be thought of as purchasing the right to the net returns produced by the machine over its *useful economic life*. Since these returns lie in the future, he cannot *know* them. He must *forecast* them. Equally he cannot know the economic life of the machine, since this too depends on future events—for example, the development of economically superior machines. This too must be forecast. However, making such forecasts and making decisions under uncertainty is precisely the job of the creative businessman. How, then, does he go about it?

His first step is to forecast the economic life of the machine. This is *not* the same as its technical life. The machine may be operating efficiently, from a technical point of view, long after it has become economically inefficient because of the development of superior machines. This is one consideration. A second is that, since he cannot know the future, he may feel unable to make forecasts for more than a few years ahead simply because the future is economically, and perhaps politically, uncertain. Let us suppose that after weighing what (he believes) are the relevant factors, he forecasts the economic life of the machine as five years.

We shall assume that no second-hand market in capital assets exists. The machine, once purchased, must be held for five years and then sold as scrap. Our businessman forecasts the scrap value as $1,900. This gives him the following data:

1) he *knows* the cost of the machine to be $10,000;
2) he *estimates* its useful economic life at five years;
3) he *estimates* its scrap value at $1,900.

He must now make further estimates of the net returns from the asset in each year of its useful life. This is not simple, for to obtain estimates he must calculate:

1) the output of shoes in each year and the prices in each year at which the output can be sold;
2) the raw materials required in each year and their prices in each year;
3) the labor required to work the machine in each year and its wage cost in each year.

To do this he has information on the technical capacity of the machine to produce shoes, its technical requirement for raw materials, the present and past costs of raw materials and labor, and present and past shoe prices. He can only do the best he can with the information he has. Let us suppose that he does this and produces the following *estimates* of returns net of raw material and labor costs:

Year 1	$2,500	Year 4	$2,000
2	$2,500	5	$2,000
3	$2,500		

Given these (obviously uncertain) estimates, how can the businessman decide whether to invest or not? There are two possible methods of proceeding.

In the first method he asks: What is the *present value* of this stream of prospective returns—that is, what sum, if held in a form which yielded the current interest rate, would provide an equivalent income stream? If this calculated present value *exceeds* $10,000—the known cost of the capital asset—the investment is worthwhile; if the value is less, it is not worthwhile.

An elementary example may make this clearer. Suppose a man is asked: What sum would you pay *today* for $105 receivable in *one year's time?* He can answer this question by asking himself: What sum accumulated for one year at the existing rate of interest would provide $105 in one year's time? This sum is the *present value* of $105 in one year's time.

If we call the present value ($\equiv$ PV) z, we have the equation

$$z(1 + r) = \$105$$

where r is the market rate of interest. Obviously if $r = 5$ percent (that is 0.05) we have

$$z(1.05) = \$105$$

so that

$$z = \$100.$$

That is, the PV of $105 in one year's time is $100 if $r = 5$ percent.

Suppose instead the man had been offered $105 in *two* years' time. Interest would then have accumulated twice, and the expression for the PV would be

$$z(1.05)^2 = \$105$$

which gives

$$z = \$95.45.$$

In general, the PV of a stream of prospective returns over the life of an asset can be written:

$$PV = \frac{Q_1}{1+r} + \frac{Q_2}{(1+r)^2} + \cdots + \frac{Q_n}{(1+r)^n} \qquad (10.1)$$

where $Q_1 \ldots Q_n$ are the returns expected in each year; n is the number of years; r is, as before, the rate of interest. Notice that this formula somewhat simplifies matters by assuming a constant value of r over the life of the asset.

Applying this formula to an example, we have:

$$PV = \frac{\$2,500}{(1+r)} + \frac{\$2,500}{(1+r)^2} + \frac{\$2,500}{(1+r)^3} + \frac{\$2,000}{(1+r)^4}$$
$$+ \frac{\$2,000 + \$1,900}{(1+r)^5} \qquad (10.2)$$

which for three assumed values of r ($r = 0.05$; $r = 0.10$; $r = 0.15$) yields, to a close approximation: PV = $10,000.

Notice that if $r < 0.10$ (10 percent), the present value exceeds the cost; conversely if $r > 0.10$, the cost exceeds the present value. In the former case the investment is profitable; in the latter it is not.

An alternative approach is to calculate not the present value, but the rate of return which the businessman obtains by purchasing the asset. In this case we replace PV (the unknown) in equation (10.2) by the *known* cost of the asset ($10,000). The unknown is now the rate of return, which we shall call x. We thus obtain:

$$\$10,000 = \frac{\$2,500}{(1+x)} + \frac{\$2,500}{(1+x)^2} + \frac{\$2,500}{(1+x)^3} + \frac{\$2,000}{(1+x)^4}$$
$$+ \frac{\$2,000 + \$1,900}{(1+x)^5} \qquad (10.3)$$

which we solve for x.

Clearly x is the rate of return which makes the present value of the stream of prospective returns expected over the life of the asset exactly equal to its supply price (cost). This rate is known as the *marginal efficiency of the capital asset.*[2] As our PV calculation has already shown, it is equal to 0.10 (10 percent). The decision rule is now: if $x > r$, the project is worth-while; if $x < r$, it is not.   *rate of return in greater than interest rate*

THE DEMAND FOR CAPITAL AND THE MARGINAL EFFICIENCY OF INVESTMENT SCHEDULES

We have now seen how our hypothetical businessman can calculate the marginal efficiency of a particular capital asset and, by comparing the esti-mated MEC with the rate of interest, make a rational (profit-maximizing) decision to purchase the asset or not.

At any time the typical businessman will be faced with a number of possible capital asset purchases. Since the estimation of the MEC can be applied to any type of capital asset, the MEC can be calculated for each and the projects ranked in descending order. This is done in Figure 10.1 with K, defined as the real quantity of *additional* capital, measured along the horizontal axis, and the marginal efficiency of capital (x) and the in-terest rate (r) are measured on the vertical axis. Because of our ranking, the resultant schedule is downward sloping from left to right.

If we now superimpose the rate of interest (assumed to be constant) on the diagram, it is easy to see that this determines an optimum value of K—meaning that value of K which the businessman estimates will maxi-

Figure 10.1 / *The marginal efficiency of capital schedule.*

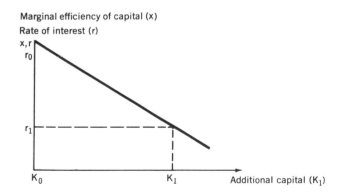

2. This is substantially identical to one definition given by Keynes in *The General Theory of Employment, Interest and Money*, pages 135–6.

mize his profits at the given value of r. For example, if $r = r_1$ then $K = K_1$, and so on. We see at once that the value of K will be greater as r is lower.

Suppose $r = r_0$. Then, according to our figure, $K - K_0 = $ zero. Does this mean that the optimal capital stock is zero? Certainly not. It simply means that at r_0 it is not worth the businessman's while to purchase any of the *additional* capital assets he has in mind. But if this is so then, at r_0, the the capital he actually possesses, which we denote by K, must coincide with the optimal value. This enables us to relabel the horizontal axis of Figure 10.1 in a way which makes clear precisely what we meant when we defined it earlier as additional capital. We now define:

$$\hat{K} \equiv \text{optimal real capital stock};$$

$$\overline{K} \equiv \text{the existing real capital stock}.$$

Hence the horizontal axis of Figure 10.1 can now be labeled: $\hat{K} - \overline{K}$ where we earlier used the notation K.

Figure 10.2 / *Determination of the rate of real planned investment.*

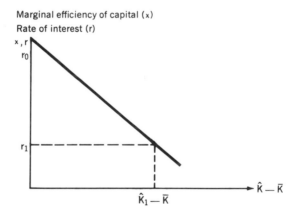

We now see that, given this schedule, (1) any value of r determines a value of $\hat{K} - \overline{K}$; (2) this value will be greater as r is lower; (3) $\hat{K} - \overline{K} = 0$ for $r = r_0$. These conditions may be written formally.

$$\left. \begin{array}{c} \hat{K} - \overline{K} = f(r) \\[2ex] \dfrac{\partial(\hat{K} - \overline{K})}{\partial r} < 0 \\[2ex] \hat{K} - \overline{K} = 0 \text{ for } r = r_0. \end{array} \right\} \tag{10.4}$$

What would happen if $r > r_0$? Theoretically we should have $\hat{K} - \overline{K} < 0$ —which simply states that, if $r > r_0$, our businessman's optimal capital stock is *less* than he presently possesses. Hence it would be optimal to *decumulate* capital, whereas if $\hat{K} - \overline{K} > 0$, it is optimal to *accumulate* capital. We shall confine ourselves to situations in which $\hat{K} - \overline{K} \geq 0$: that is, situations depicted in the diagram.

What determines the position of this schedule? Clearly all the elements which we have already found to enter into the estimation of the marginal efficiency of capital. In particular these are: the cost of capital assets; the wage rate; the state of technology; the existing capital stock $(\overline{K})$; the state of expectations; the degree of uncertainty attaching to the state of expectations.

How changes in these parameters of the schedule will shift it to the left or right should be clear from our earlier calculations. In the long run, of course, all are variables. It seems likely, however, that, over relatively short periods of time, shifts in the position of the schedule, if they occur, will be due mainly to changes in expectations and the uncertainty attaching to them. An increase in business optimism will shift the curve to the right; a leftward shift would occur if optimism declined. You should work out further possibilities for yourself.

Conceptually, we can construct such a curve for each and every businessman and, by adding the individual values for $\hat{K} - \overline{K}$ for any given interest rate, obtain an aggregate curve for the private sector as a whole. The resultant curve we define as the Marginal Efficiency of Investment Schedule. For formal completeness we redefine the marginal efficiency of capital as the marginal efficiency of investment (MEI). Why do we do this? Simply because the quantity of $\hat{K} - \overline{K}$ is the optimal amount of capital accumulation at any given interest rate. Since additions to the real capital stock are, by definition, real net investment, $\hat{K} - \overline{K}$ defines the optimum *quantity* of real net investment at any given value of r. For this reason the aggregate schedule, depicted in Figure 10.3 can properly be called the Marginal Efficiency of Investment Schedule.

In the opening section of this chapter we were careful to define $I_p \equiv$ real planned investment as a rate per period of time. The quantity $\hat{K} - \overline{K}$ does not enable us to determine the *rate* of real planned investment, for this depends on how *quickly* businessmen undertake expenditure to eliminate the gap between $\hat{K}$ and $\overline{K}$. For example, if they planned to eliminate it within one quarter, the quarterly rate of net investment would be $\hat{K} - \overline{K}$. Alternatively, if they planned to eliminate it within a year, the (average) quarterly rate would be $\dfrac{\hat{K} - \overline{K}}{4}$.

In short, additional analysis is required to move from (1) the existence of a positive value of $\hat{K} - \overline{K}$ to (2) a *rate* of real planned net investment (I_p). All we can say at this moment is that I_p is likely to be functionally

Figure 10.3 / *The marginal efficiency of investment schedule.*

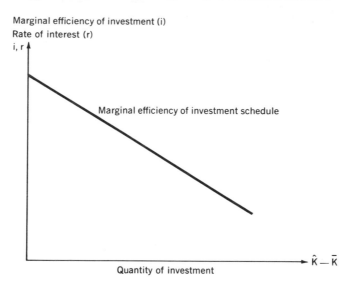

Marginal efficiency of investment (i)
Rate of interest (r)

i, r

Marginal efficiency of investment schedule

Quantity of investment

$\hat{K} - \bar{K}$

related to $\hat{K} - \bar{K}$ and thus to r. We now seek, by analysis of the problems involved, to develop a relationship between I_p and r, given the values of certain other variables. The resultant schedule we shall call the Investment Demand Schedule.

INVESTMENT DEMAND SCHEDULE

Simply to fix our problem precisely, let us begin by supposing that businessmen always undertake real net investment at a rate proportional to $\hat{K} - \bar{K}$. We should then have a theory which stated:

$$I_p = \lambda[\hat{K} - \bar{K}] \qquad 0 < \lambda \leq 1 \tag{10.5}$$

which, since, given a number of other variables, $\hat{K} - \bar{K}$ is a function of r, could be written:

$$I_p = \lambda f(r) \tag{10.5a}$$

where λ is the constant proportionality factor which is always positive but cannot exceed unity.[3] We can now gain a better understanding of the problem by examining why λ is, in practice, unlikely to be constant.

3. In looking at the relation of investment to the interest rate you should keep in mind that we are taking r_0 as fixed. Once the capital stock adjusts to the new interest rate, net investment will again be zero.

In the first place, undertaking net investment involves the typical firm in internal costs which are likely to rise as the rate of investment increases. For example, the higher the rate of investment, the more time the firm's executives will have to devote to the organization and planning connected with it. To do this they have to be diverted from more and more important work connected with the firm's existing operations—a process which is certain to result in rising internal costs. Hence, unless $\hat{K} - \bar{K}$ is very small, we may reasonably expect λ to be less than one. Moreover, as $\hat{K} - \bar{K}$ increases, we may, on this account, expect λ to decline.

So far, we have assumed that, whatever the rate at which net investment is undertaken—that is, whatever the rate at which the capital goods industries are required to produce—the price of such goods (in terms of the output they will generate) is constant. This assumption, though convenient, is unrealistic. As the rate of net investment increases, we must expect the supply price of capital goods (relative to the price of their output) to rise. Hence, if we refer back to our formula for calculating the marginal efficiency of capital, we must expect the estimated rate of return per dollar of investment to decline. Hence the return per dollar on investment will tend to fall as the rate of investment increases for reasons which are external to the firm.

If we now incorporate these modifications into our Marginal Efficiency of Investment Schedule and (recalling that profit maximization implies that businessmen will equate the MEI with r) plot r on the vertical axis and I_p on the horizontal, we obtain a curve we shall call the Investment Demand Schedule.

Note that because of the internal and external cost factors, this curve is more steeply sloped than our original MEI Schedule. Note also that it expresses the rate of real net investment (I_p) as a function of r and suggests that the slope of the schedule becomes steeper as r declines.

Figure 10.4 / *Investment demand schedule.*

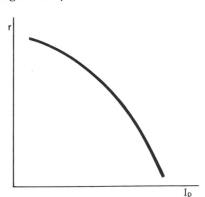

As we have constructed it, the curve reflects the following hypotheses:

1) $\hat{K} - \bar{K}$ is a function of r with $\dfrac{\partial(K - \bar{K})}{\partial r} < 0$.

2) At r_0, $\hat{K} - \bar{K} = 0$; hence, at r_0, I_p will be zero.

3) The supply price of capital assets (in terms of the prices of their output) rises as I_p increases.

4) The internal costs associated with I_p rise with I_p so that λ will be unity only if $\hat{K} - \bar{K}$ is small and will decline after $\hat{K} - \bar{K}$ reaches some critical value.

Given this Investment Demand Schedule, we can now determine I_p for any given value of r. For example, at r_1, the rate of net investment is I_{p1}.

It may now be helpful if we bring together the elements of our theory. These are as follows:

The optimum capital *stock* ($\bar{K}$) is determined by the condition that the rate of interest is equal to the marginal efficiency of capital.

2) The optimum *quantity* of real net investment is determined by $\bar{K}$ and the existing quantity of real capital (K).

3) The *rate* at which businessmen will plan to undertake net investment—eliminate the gap between $\hat{K}$ and $\bar{K}$—depends upon (a) the internal costs of net investment; (b) the supply conditions of capital goods.

It follows that if we take as given items 3(a) and 3(b) *and* the parameters of our Marginal Efficiency of Investment Schedule, we may write:

$$I_p = f(r) \qquad \text{with } \frac{\partial I_p}{\partial r} < 0. \tag{10.6}$$

This theory is commonly simplified by saying that the rate of real planned net investment is determined by the rate of interest and the Marginal Efficiency of Investment Schedule.

Since the Investment Demand Schedule depends upon all the parameters of the Marginal Efficiency of Investment, it clearly incorporates the assumption of a given capital stock ($\bar{K}$). But net investment is simply the rate of increase of the capital stock. It appears therefore that we are seeking to determine the rate of increase in K on the assumption that K is constant at $\bar{K}$. This looks like an internal contradiction. Can we rationalize it?

There are two ways of doing this. The first, which is imprecise, consists in saying that, in the period of time in which we are interested, the rate of net investment makes so small an addition to the capital stock that we can neglect it—at least as a first approximation.

The second, which is precise, is to relate our procedure to that of the differential calculus. Suppose, for example, we describe K, the real capital stock, as a function of time as depicted in Figure 10.5, which plots $K = f(t)$ where t is time.

Figure 10.5 / *Real capital and time.*

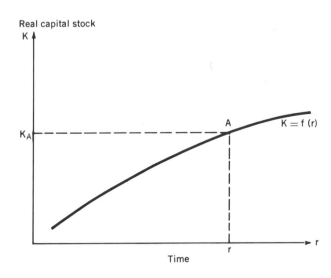

Now, by definition, $\dfrac{dk}{dt}$ is the rate of increase of the capital stock—that is, the rate of net investment. Graphically, it is also the slope of the curve. If we evaluate this slope at a point on the curve, say point A, we obtain the rate of net investment at a particular point in time (r_A) or, alternatively, at a particular value of $K = K_A$. Thus, for those who are familiar with the differential calculus—which is generally not necessary for comprehension of this book—I_p need only be identified with $\dfrac{dK}{dt}$ for a rationalization of our assumption that K is held constant at $\overline{K}$.

A final difficulty relates to the objection that, given r, sooner or later continuing net investment must eliminate the gap $\check{K} - \overline{K}$. When this occurs, provided r is unaltered, net investment must cease. As a matter of observation, however, net investment is typically positive. Is there, then, some contradiction between our theory and observation?

There is no contradiction once we recall that, in the dynamic real world, the MEI Schedule will typically be moving to the right because of expected increases in the demand for output and technical innovations. Thus, though our theory is essentially a capital *stock* adjustment theory, there is no presumption that we shall ever observe a situation in which, for all firms, $\hat{K} = \overline{K}$ and hence I_p is zero: that is, a situation in which the actual capital stock is precisely adjusted to the optimal capital stock for all firms in the economy.

THE INVESTMENT FUNCTION

Our investment demand schedule is essentially a *two*-dimensional representation of a function which involves *more* independent variables than *r*. These variables are treated as parameters in constructing the MEI Schedule. Can we now develop, from our earlier analysis, an investment function analogous to our consumption function?

An important parameter of the MEI Schedule (and thus the Investment Demand Schedule) was the state of business expectations. Essentially, this refers to the demand for output which businessmen expect in the future. Since demand depends upon income, we might make our notion of expectations more precise by relating it to the income expected when the new capital goods begin to produce output. Let us call this Y^*.

Clearly a wide variety of factors will influence Y^*. Perhaps the most important, however, will be the present level of income (Y). On this assumption we might write our investment function provisionally as:

$$I_p = f_1[r, Y^*, u_{y^*}, K] \tag{10.7}$$

where u_{y^*} is an index of the uncertainty attaching to the expectation Y^*.

Then, introducing the assumption that Y^* is a function of Y, we obtain:

$$I_p = f_2[r, Y, u_{y^*}, K] \tag{10.8}$$

with

$$\frac{\partial I_p}{\partial r} < 0, \qquad \frac{\partial I_p}{\partial Y} > 0, \qquad \frac{\partial I_p}{\partial u_{y^*}} < 0, \qquad \frac{\partial I_p}{\partial K} < 0.$$

In this relation the state of technology, the supply conditions for capital goods, and the internal investment cost schedules of the individual firms are subsumed in the function itself.

The expression in (10.8) relates only to the rate of net investment. If we wish—as we usually do—to explain the rate of gross investment, we recall:

$$I_{pg} \equiv \text{rate of real planned gross investment}$$
$$\equiv I_p + D = f_2(r, Y, u_{y^*}, \overline{K}) + D \tag{10.9}$$

where D is real depreciation.

What explains depreciation? A simple hypothesis is that $D = \delta \overline{K}$ with $0 < \delta < 1$: that is, depreciation is a constant proportion of the existing capital stock. Since (10.7) already contains $\overline{K}$, we may now write:

$$I_{pg} = f_3[r, Y, \overline{K}, u_{y^*}] \tag{10.10}$$

Unfortunately, we can now say nothing definite regarding the sign of $\frac{\partial I_{pg}}{\partial K}$ since it consists of two elements: the negative marginal response coefficient $\frac{\partial I_p}{\partial K}$ and the positive marginal response coefficient $\frac{\partial D}{\partial K}$ $(= \delta)$. Clearly, their sum could be positive, negative, or zero.

If we now set out a linear version of (10.8)—which in view of an earlier analysis of the Investment Demand Schedule is not very plausible—we obtain:

$$I_{pg} = a_1 r + a_2 Y + (a_3 + \partial)\bar{K} + a_4 u_y^* \qquad (10.11)$$

with the expectation that a_1, a_3, a_4, < 0 and a_2, $\partial > 0$.

This is a simple formal representation of our basic theory of the rate of real planned gross investment.

THE RATE OF INTEREST AND THE COST OF FUNDS

Thus far we have identified the cost of borrowed funds to the firm with the rate of interest, which we have already defined as the rate of return on government bonds. This approximation obviously requires reconsideration since typically firms cannot borrow as cheaply as the U. S. Government.

In addition, we have implicitly assumed that each firm can borrow as much as it likes at the going rate of interest: that is, that the cost of funds to the firm does *not* rise as the amount borrowed increases. If this is not correct, then the marginal cost of funds will exceed the average cost, and this fact needs to be allowed for in our formulation.

Lending to the U. S. Government is riskless in the sense that the nominal capital and interest are fully secured. Lending to any business, however, involves *some* risk. Any business may fail—through incompetence, dishonesty, or the occurrence of events which no reasonable degree of competence could have foreseen. Hence lenders will typically require from firms a premium over the interest rate to compensate them for assuming these risks. We may call this the lenders' risk premium. Thus the cost of borrowing may be thought of as

rate of interest *plus* a lenders' risk premium.

In general, it is also likely to be the case that individual firms cannot borrow as much as they like at a constant cost. As firms borrow—and the Debt/Equity ratio rises—bond holders tend to feel increasingly vulnerable in the face of any short-fall in profits. Hence they will supply additional funds only at higher rates. Thus the marginal cost of borrowing to the firm will differ from the average cost and must be regarded as the relevant concept in determining I_p.

Accordingly, in so far as firms invest with borrowed funds, the rising average cost of borrowing will consist of the rate of interest (as defined) plus a rising lenders' risk premium.

In practice, of course, much net investment is undertaken from firms' own savings in the form of undistributed profits. If the alternative to employing this net cash flow to finance net investment is for the firm to hold government bonds, then for the rate of net investment which this flow could finance, the rate of interest is in the opportunity cost and is constant over the relevant range.

Taking all these considerations into account, the determination of real planned net investment is shown in Figure 10.6, which superimposes the Investment Demand Schedule on a schedule showing the marginal cost of borrowing.

On this slightly more complete formulation, the rate of real planned investment is now determined by the condition:

marginal efficiency of investment = marginal borrowing cost

Figure 10.6 / *Real net investment and cost of borrowing.*

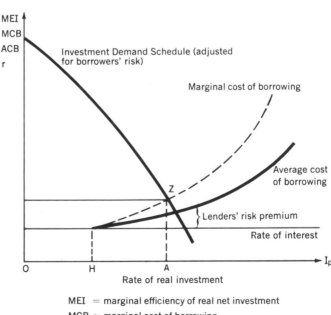

MEI = marginal efficiency of real net investment
MCB = marginal cost of borrowing
ACB = average cost of borrowing
r   = interest rate
OH = imputed rate on undistributed profits

where the marginal cost of borrowing is equal to the rate of interest *plus* a lenders' risk premium. That is, the rate of investment is *OA* determined by the intersection of the IDS and MCB schedules at *Z*.

Since borrowers also assume risks while we have made no mention of a borrowers' risk premium (which clearly reduces the MEI associated with any given value of I_p) we have in Fig. 10.6 emphasized that the Investment Demand Schedule, as we have defined it, already allows for the risk arising from uncertainty of expectations. In our formal presentation in (10.8) we symbolized this adjustment by the inclusion of the variable u_{y*}—defined as an index of uncertainty.

SOME FINAL PROBLEMS

We can now summarize our rather simple theory of the determination of the rate of real planned investment. It consists of the following propositions:

1) The equilibrium rate of real planned investment is determined where the Investment Demand Schedule (incorporating an allowance for borrowers' risk) cuts the schedule of the Marginal Cost of Borrowing.

2) The average cost of borrowing is the rate of interest *plus* an allowance for lenders' risk, which probably rises with the rate of borrowing.

3) The higher the Marginal Cost of Borrowing, the lower, given the Investment Demand Schedule, will be the equilibrium rate of real planned investment.

This theory can be expressed in functional form (for net investment) as:

$$I_p = f_2[Y, \tilde{r}, u_{y*}, \overline{K}] \tag{10.8a}$$

where $\tilde{r}$ is now defined as the Marginal Cost of Borrowing.

Is this function likely to be stable in the sense in which we have referred to the consumption function as stable? This is a difficult question to answer despite the fact that, since expectations have obviously a crucial role in it, the scope for instability seems greater. Unfortunately, there is no generally accepted test by which we could assert the relative instability of an investment function of this form. We thus leave this question unanswered; thus, though we would expect investment functions to be typically less stable, we cannot, in the present state of knowledge, assert this to be so for the U. S. since World War II.

On the other hand, if the function does shift, say in response to a change in the expectational relation connecting Y^* with Y, it is unlikely that any such shifts would be offset by changes in *r*. Hence shifts in the function would generate sharp changes in the rate of real planned investment, which, as we know from our previous examination of the consumption function, bring about "multiplied" changes in real income.

Moreover, as we shall see, dynamic versions of the same rather general investment hypothesis—that is, versions which explicitly involve dating the variables entering the function—are compatible with considerable fluctuations in real net investment even if the dynamic function is relatively stable.

Can we make our investment function operational in the way we made our earlier consumption hypothesis operational? In its linear version, for gross investment, we wrote:

$$I_{pg} = a_1 r + a_2 Y + (a_3 + \partial)\bar{K} + a_4 u_{y*}. \tag{10.11}$$

Y is directly observable and we can use estimates of K (which exist) at the beginning of any period as a measure of $\bar{K}$. Difficulty arises, however, with u_{y*} and with $\tilde{r}$, which we now know should replace r. No obvious measure of u_{y*} can be defined or approximated. We therefore truncate our theory, replace r by $\tilde{r}$, and concentrate upon:

$$I_{pg} = a_1 \tilde{r} + a_2 Y + (a_3 + \partial)K_{-1}$$

where $K_{-1} \equiv$ the real capital stock at the end of the previous period. In particular, we concentrate upon the meaning of $\tilde{r}$.

Strictly $\tilde{r}$ is the marginal cost of borrowing. Typically, we have no means of measuring this so we are generally content to use the average cost of borrowing and measure this by (say) the corporate Aaa rate.

This use of the average rate as a proxy for the marginal rate will involve an error; but a more important source of error may arise from the use of a *nominal* rate rather than a *real* rate. To see the distinction—and its importance—consider the following example:

Suppose today (at time t) we lend $100 for one year on the promise of $106 at the end of the period. The nominal rate of interest (r) is 6 percent. In real terms, however, the gain from the transaction appears thus:

$$\frac{\$106}{p(t+1)} - \frac{\$100}{p(t)} = \$100\left[\frac{1+r}{p(t+1)} - \frac{1}{p(t)}\right]$$

where

$p(t) \equiv$ price level ruling now; and

$p(t + 1) \equiv$ price level expected to rule at the time of repayment.

Assume:

$p(t + 1) = p(t)[1 + \alpha]$ where $\alpha \equiv$ *expected* percentage price change.

Therefore the expected real rate of return (r_r) is—putting $p(t) = 1$—given by:

$$r_r = \frac{1+r}{1+\alpha} - 1 = \frac{r - \alpha}{1 + \alpha}$$

Hence:

$$r_r - r = \frac{r - \alpha}{1 + \alpha} - r = \frac{-\alpha - \alpha r}{1 + \alpha}$$

which is a measure of the difference between the real rate (r_r) and the nominal rate (r) valued at the prices of period $t + 1$. Revaluing in terms of prices at times t gives:

$$r_r - r = -\alpha - \alpha r$$

whence

$$r_r = r - \alpha - \alpha r.$$

Typically, the term in αr is neglected since for plausible values of α and r it is small compared with either. Hence the usual approximation is:

$$r_r \approx r - \alpha \quad \text{where } \alpha \equiv \text{expected percentage change in prices.}$$

The obvious conclusion is that we must distinguish between nominal and real rates whenever, as is currently the case, there is a general expectation of price changes.

We have no theory to explain satisfactorily how people form their expectations concerning $\frac{1}{p}\frac{dp}{dt}$ —that is, select α. This being so, we cannot exclude the possibility that r and r_r may not always move together in the relatively short run. Hence it may matter very much whether we interpret r in equation (10.11) as appropriately measured by the corporate Aaa rate (a nominal rate); the dividend yield on common stocks (a rough proxy for r_r); a weighted average of the two (which is an increasingly common proceeding); or the corporate Aaa rate minus an estimate derived from past rates of price change.

Though we would expect the real rather than the nominal rate to be relevant (we shall return to this problem later) most empirical work until recently has employed a nominal rate: in the U. S., usually the corporate Aaa rate. But clearly this is an important issue requiring further investigation.

Given a definition of r, equation (10.11) is now operational and we may, by appropriate econometric means, hope to estimate a_1, a_2, and $(a_3 + \alpha)$. From our estimate of a_2 ($\equiv \frac{\partial I_p}{\partial r}$) we can obtain an estimate of:

$$\frac{\partial I_p}{\partial \tilde{r}} \frac{\tilde{r}}{I_p} \equiv \text{the Borrowing Cost Elasticity of Gross Investment.}$$

Considerable controversy—which we will discuss briefly in the following chapter—has been waged over this partial elasticity, and much early work yielded very low estimates. Some more recent studies suggest, however, a value in the neighborhood of -0.4. This is certainly not a negligible elasticity and clearly has important implications, if it is correct, regarding the possibility of influencing I_p through variations in the cost of borrowing.

Finally, a word of warning to the reader. In some formal expositions later in this book we shall continue, in the interests of pedagogic simplicity, to make use of investment functions written

$$I_p = f[r]$$

or, in more explicit linear form,

$$I_p = Z + hr$$

where r denotes the cost of borrowing. Since our original function, in linear form, would have been written

$$I_p = a_1 r + a_2 Y^* + a_3 \bar{K} + a_4 u_{y^*}$$

we must have

$$Z = a_2 Y^* + a_3 \bar{K} + a_4 u_{y^*}$$

$$h = a_1$$

Hence, for simplicity, treating Z as constant involves treating Y^* as constant. This means, in models in which we seek to determine Y, that we are ignoring the (empirically plausible) link between Y and Y^*; otherwise changes in Y, by changing Y^*, would change Z.

This procedure is followed *only* to simplify exposition. It would readily be possible to work with

$$I_p = Z + a_1 r + a_2 Y$$

with

$$Z \equiv a_3 \bar{K} + a_4 u_{y^*}$$

but the gain in generality does not seem sufficient compensation, in elementary comparative statics, to justify the resulting complication.

QUESTIONS AND EXERCISES

1. If the market rate of interest is 5 percent, what is the present value of the following two prospects?

PROSPECT	RETURN AT END OF YEAR 1	RETURN AT END OF YEAR 2
1	$105	$110.25
2	110.25	105

which would you prefer? Would you purchase either at $200? Give your reasons. Why are the present values not identical?

2. Would you invest if the market rate of interest (= cost of borrowing) was 7 percent?

YEAR	CAPITAL COST	ESTIMATED RETURN
1	$10,000	$2800
2		2800
3		2800
4		2800

At the end of Year 4 the asset is expected to have a disposal value of $990.

3. What do you think would happen to the Marginal Efficiency of Investment schedule if a threat of war arose in Europe? Why?

4. You are asked to construct an investment hypothesis which gives the rate of real planned investment in fixed capital as a function of observable quantities. What function would you propose and why? What variables, other than those discussed in the text, would you include in the function?

5. From the national income estimates of the U. S. obtain quarterly figures for real gross private investment in manufacturing for the years 1958–70 and plot them on a graph measuring (1) the quarterly rate of investment on the vertical axis; (2) time on the horizontal axis.

   Do these observations tend to support our judgment that the Marginal Efficiency of Investment schedule is likely to be volatile? How would you explain the observed fluctuations in investment in fixed capital?

6. Perform the same exercise for investment in stocks. Are there any special theoretical difficulties in interpreting this series?

7. Using the data of Question 2 assume that a 20 percent corporate income tax is levied on the net annual return *after* charging depreciation. Recalculate the marginal efficiency of capital. Is the investment still worthwhile if the cost of borrowing is 7 percent? Use your answer to show the effect on the Marginal Efficiency of Capital schedule of (1) raising the corporate income tax, and (2) increasing the tax allowance for depreciation.

8. Suppose the corporate income tax, the relationship between planned investment and the rate of interest is given by:

$$I_p = Z - g.r. \quad \text{where } Z = 1000 \text{ and } -g = \frac{\partial I_p}{\partial r} = -10.$$

Plot the resulting investment function for all integral values of r up to 20 percent.

$$C_p = A + bY \quad \text{where } A = 100 \text{ and } b \equiv \frac{\partial C_p}{\partial Y} = 0.8$$

then

$$\text{aggregate demand} \equiv C_p + I_p = A + bY + Z - g.r.$$

In equilibrium we require, assuming planned and actual output to be equal,

$$Y = A + bY + Z - g.r.$$

Find

    a) all the pairs of values of Y, r which satisfy this equation:

    b) plot the resulting values on a graph with r on the vertical axis and Y on the horizontal;

    c) interpret the curve traced out by these pairs of values.

Show

    d) which way the curve would move if

        (1) business expectations became more optimistic;

        (2) incomes were redistributed from "rich" to "poor"; and

    e) interpret these changes in terms of the equations describing the investment and consumption hypotheses.

9. Using the investment function of Question 8, find the *interest elasticity of investment* defined thus:

$$\frac{\Delta I_p}{I_p} \Big/ \frac{\Delta r}{r} \equiv \frac{\Delta I_p}{\Delta r} \times \frac{r}{I_p}$$

$$\equiv \frac{(\partial I_p/\partial r)\,\Delta r}{\Delta r} \times \frac{r}{I_p},$$

when

$$r = 10 \text{ percent}, \quad r = 5 \text{ percent}.$$

At what rate of interest will the elasticity be -1?

Why is the elasticity not a constant? Is the marginal response coefficient $\partial I_p/\partial r$ a constant? What can you infer about the elasticity of any straight line schedule?

10. In the text we proceed on the assumption of constant prices. What sense (if any) do you therefore find in the explanation of the downward slope of the MEI schedule? What is meant by "rise in the price of capital goods"?

11. Superimpose on your graph for Question 5 a second graph plotting quarterly values for the rate of interest (represented by the rate of return on corporate bonds (Aaa). Can you reconcile your observations with the theory of this Chapter? What are your difficulties?

12. Consider the view that the theory of investment put forward in this chapter fails because its central hypothesis is that businessmen's investment behavior is rational—that is, dictated by the aim to maximize profits.

13. Using the theory of equation 9.5, put:

$$g \equiv \frac{\partial I_p}{\partial \pi} = 100$$

$$h \equiv \frac{\partial I_p}{\partial \mu} = -200.$$

Then (a) complete the following table; and (b) explain the behavior of I_p. How much of the behavior of I_p is explained by shifts in the function and how much by movements along it? Is the theory of expectations implicit in 9.5 compatible with the data?

PERIOD	I_p	OBSERVED VALUES π	μ
1	1000	12	4
2	1000	12	4
3	1200	14	5
4	1400	16	8
5	1900	20	8
6	1500	18	8
7	1100	15	8
8	1100	12	6
9	1100	12	6
10	1200	10	4

14. Following Question 9 would you, in practice, expect the interest elasticity of investment to be significant? Give your reasons.

15. "We do not need a downward sloping MEC Schedule to explain a downward sloping Marginal Efficiency of Investment Schedule." Do you agree? If not, why not?

16. According to equation (10.6) replacement investment depends upon the existing capital stock and a constant δ. Is it plausible to regard δ as a constant? What reasons can you give for thinking that δ might vary? How would variation in δ affect the analysis?

17. "The explanation of the downward sloping Marginal Efficiency of Investment Schedule implicitly introduces the relative prices of capital and consumption goods." Is this so? If it is, what difficulties does it involve for our earlier analysis? In particular does it raise problems for the definition of real income and the price level?

18. "The linear investment hypothesis of (10.5) clearly misrepresents the Investment Demand Schedule of Figure 10.4" Do you agree? What implications of Figure 10.4 are obscured by the use of equation (10.5)?

19. In what circumstances would the Marginal Efficiency of Investment Schedule be vertical over at least a part of its length?

20. In the light of our earlier analysis, can you interpret the following theory of real planned net investment?

$$K_t - K_{t-1} = \lambda[\hat{K}_t - K_{t-1}]$$
$$\hat{K}_t = a_0 + a_1 Y_t + a_2 r_t$$
$$I_{pt} \equiv K_t - K_{t-1}$$

so that:

$$I_{pt} = \alpha a_0 + \alpha a_1 Y_t + \alpha a_2 r_t - \lambda K_{t-1}$$

where:

$$K_t \equiv \text{capital stock at end of period } t$$
$$K_{t-1} \equiv \text{capital stock at end of period } t - 1$$
$$Y_t \equiv \text{real output in period } t$$
$$r_t \equiv \text{debenture rate in period } t$$
$$I_{pt} \equiv \text{real planned net investment in period } t$$

21. Show, using Equation (10.8a) and the earlier analysis, that the stability of the Investment Demand Schedule relating I_p to $\tilde{r}$ is *not* implied by the stability of the investment function.

SUGGESTED READING

F. Brooman and H. Jacoby, *Macroeconomics* (Chicago: Aldine Publishing Co., 1970) Chap. 7.

J. M. Keynes, *The General Theory of Employment, Interest and Money* (New York: Harcourt, Brace, 1936) Chaps. 11–12.

11

The Determinants of Investment

LET US NOW LOOK AT some of the theories which have been proposed as explanations of investment. Again, as in the case of the consumption function, we will deal here only with the theories themselves. Some articles involving empirical tests appear in the "Suggested Reading." We will discuss only three investment theories: the accelerator theory, the finance (or liquidity) theory, and the profits theory.[1] To do so we will have to step for some time outside the strict static framework in which we had stayed so far and to take up some simple dynamics.

THE ACCELERATOR

Since the function of investment is to increase the capital stock, and since the function of the capital stock, in turn, is to generate additional output, one way of explaining the level of investment is to look at changes in desired output. This is what the accelerator theory does. There are two versions of this theory, the rather simple (and older) rigid accelerator, and the more modern "capital stock adjustment" accelerator.

To start with the former, consider the example of a businessman who

1. Another important theory is the neoclassical theory, which combines elements of the accelerator theory and the finance theory, as well as consideration of the cost of capital goods into a strict profit-maximizing framework. Since this theory is rather complex, we will not discuss it here. For an exposition of this theory, see Dale Jorgenson, "Anticipations and Investment Behavior," in James Duesenberry, Gary Fromm, Lawrence Klein, and Edwin Kuh (eds.), *The Brookings Quarterly Econometric Model of the United States* (Chicago: Rand McNally, 1965), pp. 35–92.

produces, and has produced for many years, 10,000 pairs of shoes. To produce these shoes he requires 10 machines. One machine wears out each year and each year is replaced by an identical machine. In tabular form we have

YEAR	TOTAL OUTPUT (PAIRS OF SHOES)	TOTAL NUMBER OF MACHINES REQUIRED	ANNUAL CAPITAL DEPRECIATION (IN TERMS OF MACHINES)	NET INVESTMENT (IN TERMS OF MACHINES)	GROSS INVESTMENT (IN TERMS OF MACHINES)
I	10,000	10	1	0	1
II	10,000	10	1	0	1
III	11,000	11	1	1	2
IV	11,000	11	1	0	1
V	22,000	22	2	11	13
VI	44,000	44	4	22	26

Suppose now that in year III the demand for shoes rises to 11,000 pairs. In the very short run the businessman may satisfy this demand by using his existing 10 machines more intensively—say by working double shifts. By assumption, however, to maximize profits at an output of 10,000 pairs he requires 10 machines. Hence to maximize profits with an output of 11,000 pairs he requires 11 machines.

If he adds the new machine, he undertakes *net investment* of one machine. As a result we have (1) doubling of *gross* investment; and (2) an increase in *net* investment from zero to one machine. Suppose now demand remains at 11,000. The businessman has adjusted his stock of machines completely to this output. He has no need for further machines. Hence net investment falls to zero: gross investment falls to the one machine required for replacement. It follows from this simple example that the level of net investment depends upon the *change* in output. Net investment is positive only when output is rising. When output is constant net investment is zero. The dependence of the *level* of investment on the *rate of change* of output can readily be explained. Net investment is nothing but another word for the rate of change of the capital stock. And since the desired level of the capital stock depends upon the level of output, the rate of change of the capital stock (i.e., investment) depends upon the rate of change of output. Hence when output is constant (i.e., its rate of change is zero) net investment is zero too.

The above example also shows that the percentage increase in investment sometimes exceeds the percentage increase in output. This is generally referred to as "magnification." Thus in year III desired output increases by 10 percent, but, as a result, gross investment increases by 100 percent. In year V output doubles and gross investment increases twelvefold. But now consider year VI. Here output doubles too, but there is no magnification. The reason for this is that magnification only occurs if the rate of change of output is itself increasing (i.e., if the second derivative of output is positive). This is the case in year III (when the rate of change of output goes from zero in the previous period to 10 percent in the current period) and in year V (when the rate of change of output goes again from zero in the previous year to 100 percent). But in year VI, although output itself doubles, the increase in the rate of change is zero since output doubled in the previous period too. Hence, there is no magnification. The reason for this is not far to seek. Magnification refers to the rate of change of investment, and as we saw before the level of investment relates to the rate of change of output. Hence the *rate of change* of investment relates to the rate of change of the rate of change (i.e., the second derivative called "acceleration") of net output. Only if the rate of change of output is itself increasing will the demand for capital increase proportionately more than the increase in output.

The fact that investment depends upon the rate of change of output rather than upon the level of output has an implication for the timing of investment. It means that investment will reach its peak, not when output is at a maximum, but when the *rate of increase* of output reaches its peak. Since the rate of change of output reaches its peak ahead of the level of output, one would expect that investment reaches its peak ahead of output.

This rigid accelerator theory just described is open to a number of criticisms. The idea that businessmen always react to an increase in demand by installing new capacity is often wide of the mark. If demand is expected to fall again, existing equipment will simply be used more intensively and no new investment will take place. Moreover, even if the businessman wanted to buy additional machines, it is by no means clear that he will do so all at once; he may spread this investment out over time. Then there is the fact that the wish to invest, and actual investment, are not the same thing. If the funds are not available, if interest rates or machinery prices are too high, the firm may simply have to make do with its existing stock of capital. Finally, it is worth noting that the accelerator works only one way. Since the market in used capital equipment is very imperfect, a firm is usually limited in its disinvestment to the amount of its depreciation. Thus, if in the above example output were to drop back to 10,000 units in year VII, the firm's capital in year VII will consist of 40 machines (the 44 it started with minus the 4 which depreciated) rather than the 10 machines that would be required to produce 10,000 units. If demand were then to increase again to, say, 20,000 units in period VIII, there would be sufficient machines on hand, and investment would not take place.

Fortunately, many of these weaknesses of the rigid accelerator can be avoided by using the so-called "flexible" or "capital stock adjustment" accelerator. This version of the accelerator assumes that firms do not immediately adjust their capital stock fully to a change in demand.[2] Rather in each period they adjust their existing capital stock only part of the way toward that capital stock which would minimize costs for the current level of demand, in other words the variable λ that we introduced in the previous chapter is less than unity. This partial adjustment takes account not only of the fact that investment costs rise as the firm undertakes more investment, but also that when demand increases, the businessman may treat only part of this increase as permanent and part as due to transitory factors. Moreover, it also takes into account that new machines take time to order and install, and that a shortage of available funds may force the firm to spread its investment out over several years.

Symbolically, we begin with the assumption that the desired (because most profitable) stock of fixed capital bears a fixed relation to output and that the current capital stock is already adjusted to current output. Formally:

$$K = K^* = \alpha Y, \tag{11.1}$$

where

K is the actual capital stock;

K^* is the desired stock of fixed capital;

Y is annual output;

α is the (average) ratio of K^* to Y and the marginal ratio of $\Delta K^*/\Delta Y$.

Now let Y_t and Y_{t-1} stand for output in years t and $t-1$ and K_t^* and K_{t-1}^* stand for desired capital at the end of years t and $t-1$. We have:

$$K_{t-1}^* = \alpha Y_{t-1} \tag{11.2}$$

$$K_t^* = \alpha Y_t \tag{11.2a}$$

whence

$$K_t^* - K_{t-1}^* = \alpha(Y_t - Y_{t-1}) \tag{11.2b}$$

We assume (as we did in our numerical example) that the capital stock actually in existence at the end of year $t-1$ which we call K_{t-1}) was optimally adjusted to the output of that period. It follows that

$$K_{t-1} = K_{t-1}^* \tag{11.2c}$$

and

$$K_t^* - K_{t-1} = \alpha(Y_t - Y_{t-1}) \tag{11.2d}$$

This tells us that the desired capital stock for year t will exceed the capital stock in existence at the end of the previous year by an amount which

---

2. Adjustment models such as this are nowadays used very widely in economic analysis, and have proved able to explain many phenomena better than models which assume immediate adjustment.

depends upon (1) the capital/output ratio (α); and (2) the change in output between the two years.

Now to bring the actual capital stock to the desired level—raise K_{t-1} to K_t^*—businessmen will undertake net investment. How much will they undertake in the year? As we saw in the previous chapter this depends upon the *speed* at which they adjust the capital stock. Hence we can write, more generally,

$$I_t = \lambda\alpha(Y_t - Y_{t-1}), \qquad (11.2e)$$

where

$I_t \equiv$ net investment in year t

$\lambda \equiv$ a coefficient measuring the *speed of response* with $0 < \lambda \leq 1$

and $\lambda\alpha \equiv$ the accelerator coefficient which we shall call V.

In our numerical example $K_{t-1} = 10$ and $K_t^* = 11$ for $Y_t = 11,000$,

$$Y_{t-1} = 10,000 \text{ and } \alpha \equiv \frac{K}{Y} = \frac{1}{1000} \text{ so that}$$

$$I_t = \lambda\frac{1}{1000}(11,000 - 10,000) \qquad (11.2en)$$
$$= \lambda.$$

Since we argued that net investment would be *one* machine, we made, in our numerical example, the special assumption that λ was unity: that is, that the shoe manufacturer's speed of response was such that he adjusted his capital stock *completely* during a single year. This may or may not be the case. It is commonly assumed,[3] with the result that the accelerator theory is often written:

$$I_t = \alpha(Y_t - Y_{t-1})$$

which gives it a rather narrow technical interpretation and obscures the element of time response completely. We shall write it

$$I_t = V(Y_t - Y_{t-1}), \qquad (11.2f)$$

where

$$V \equiv \lambda\alpha$$

so that V, our accelerator coefficient, depends upon two elements:

$\alpha \equiv$ the optimum (most profitable) capital/annual output ratio;

$\lambda \equiv$ the speed with which businessmen seek to adjust actual capital to the optimum.

The implications of this version of the *capacity* theory of investment are important. First, net investment determined by the accelerator will be positive if, and only if, output is rising. Second, net investment will fall if

---

3. For ease of exposition we shall adopt this assumption in our formal examples.

the rate at which output is rising declines. Third, net investment (due to the accelerator) will be zero if output is constant. Fourth, net investment will be negative if output is falling. However, as a result of using an adjustment coefficient, the capital stock adjustment version of the accelerator theory no longer implies that there has to be magnification if the rate of output accelerates, and that the time path of capital will lead output.

So far we have interpreted this *accelerator* theory only in relation to investment in fixed capital. It can, however, readily be adapted to the task of explaining investment in inventories or, for that matter, in housing, consumer durables, or even human capital. But we will develop the argument only for inventories. To do this we introduce the assumption that businessmen seek to maintain stocks in a fixed ratio to output. Thus we have:

$$S_t^* = \alpha'(Y) \tag{11.2g}$$

where

$S_t^* \equiv$ the desired (optimal) level of stocks

$\alpha' \equiv$ the desired (optimal) ratio of stocks to output

$Y \equiv$ output.

The formal structure of the argument is then identical with that already put forward. It yields:

$$I_{st} = V'[Y_t - Y_{t-1}] \tag{11.2h}$$

where

$I_{st} \equiv$ net investment in inventories

$V' \equiv$ the (inventory) accelerator coefficient.

THE LIQUIDITY THEORY

The rigid accelerator theory explains investment by focusing on the need for capital as determined by changes in demand. It treats the supply of funds for investment as readily available. An alternative approach, the "liquidity theory" or "finance theory," proceeds in just the opposite way. It looks upon demand for output as being sufficient to justify new investment *if* the cost and availability of investment funds are right.[4] According to the liquidity theory, it is not changes in demand as much as changes in the interest rate and the availability of investment funds which determine

4. If the interest rate falls, the firm will have an incentive to invest because it can produce its output at lower cost by using more capital and less labor. Moreover, this tendency to use more capital at a lower rate of interest is reinforced by the shifts of demand between products. If interest rates fall the relative prices of capital intensive items fall. Hence, consumer demand will shift to a more capital intensive product mix, and thus the economy will be using more capital per unit of output.

investment. The interest rate is the price of capital, and just as, other things being equal, the quantity of apples demanded depends upon the price of apples, the quantity of investment undertaken depends, other things being equal, on the price of capital—i.e., on the real rate of interest.

The firm has two sources of finance available to it. One consists of internal funds. Internal finance takes two forms, retained profits and depreciation reserves. Retained profits or corporate saving are simply total profits after payment of dividends, and the firm can, to some extent, adjust its dividends to obtain funds for investment. Depreciation reserves are a bookkeeping item which is subtracted from total receipts to reflect the wear and tear and obsolescence of the firm's capital. Since depreciation reserves are just a book entry rather than actual expenditures made by the firm, they provide the firm with investable funds just as much as corporate savings do. Both of these items jointly are sometimes called "cash flow."

In addition to these internal funds a firm can also obtain external funds by borrowing from banks, by floating bonds, etc. But the firm is not able to obtain unlimited funds in this way. The capital market does not function as does, say, the market for apples, where you can buy as much as you want at the market price. Instead, as we pointed out in the previous chapter, lenders, such as, banks, frequently ration credit; that is, they limit the amount they will lend to the firm. In part they do this because they feel that a loan which is large relative to the firm's own equity capital is too risky.[5] Hence, there are frequently many firms that would like to borrow more at prevailing real interest rates, but are unable to do so, at least without raising the interest rate they would have to pay on all their loans. If the central bank now adopts an easy money policy and makes more reserves available to banks, banks and other lenders will be looking for additional borrowers to absorb the additional loans they can make. At such times firms formerly unable to borrow now find that loans are available. Hence they go ahead and borrow and use these funds for new investment. This is one way in which an increase in bank reserves results in additional investment.

In addition, an increase in bank reserves lowers, temporarily, the rate of interest as banks find themselves with an excess of loanable funds at the prevailing interest rate. And, as was explained in the previous chapter, at a lower rate of interest investment projects which were previously not profitable are now undertaken.

While it is obvious that, in principle, lower interest rates stimulate

---

5. The larger the firm's debt relative to its equity capital, the smaller is the percentage loss in its capital which suffices to make it insolvent. Suppose, for example, that a firm has a capital stock of $1,000,000 and debts of only $500,000. The firm can lose up to half its assets without losses to its creditors. But if instead the firm had debts of $900,000, then any loss of more than 10 percent would make it insolvent. And, in this way, an increase in the debt-equity ratio raises the risk to the firm's creditors and stockholders.

investment, there has been much controversy about the magnitude of this effect. It is certainly conceivable that a very large change in interest rates would change investment by only a trivial amount; that the interest rate is not a significant variable affecting investment. Basically, this is an empirical issue which has to be settled by a recourse to data, but nonetheless some theoretical arguments can be adduced.

Several of these arguments suggest that the interest elasticity of investment is likely to be rather low. One is that for short-run investment interest costs amount to only a small fraction of total costs. Hence, a cut in the interest rate is not likely to stimulate much investment. For long-term investment, interest costs account for a larger proportion of total costs, but long-run investment involves so much risk, the argument runs, that a cut in the interest rate is not likely to induce much investment. However, more recent analysis has shown that the riskiness of long term investment need not necessarily reduce its interest elasticity.[6]

Still another argument is that there are other costs of borrowing apart from interest rates. One is borrower's risk, discussed in the previous chapter; another is the fact that the loan agreement may give the lender some control over the borrower's business. Moreover, the more a firm borrows now, the greater is the risk that if it has to borrow in the future it will be refused credit. If these other costs of borrowing are constant when interest rates change, then this fact will tend to lower the interest elasticity of investment. (This is an example of the fact that derived demand tends to be less elastic than final demand.)

On the other hand, there are some reasons for thinking that the interest elasticity of investment may be substantial. One is that it is capital rather than investment which enters the firm's production function. Suppose, for example, that the interest elasticity of *capital* is—let us assume quite arbitrarily—only 0.01. If the annual rate of investment is equal to one twentieth of the capital stock, then the increase in the capital stock expressed as a percentage, not of the capital stock, but of *investment* is 0.01 × 20 = 0.2, times the percentage change in the interest rate. Suppose that this investment is spread over a two-year period. The *short-run* interest elasticity of *investment* is then 0.1, a by no means insubstantial figure. A second reason for taking the interest rate seriously is that the real interest rate is a variable which frequently shows substantial changes, and one of the things which makes a variable important is that it varies a great deal.

In any case, as already mentioned, whether or not the interest rate has

6. See Lorie Tarshis, "The Elasticity of the Marginal Efficiency Function," *American Economic Review*, Vol. LI (December 1961), pp. 958–85; Oliver Williamson, "The Elasticity of the Marginal Efficiency Function: Comment," *American Economic Review*, Vol. LII (December 1962), pp. 1099–1103.

a significant effect on investment is really an empirical issue, and recent empirical studies have, on the whole, tended to find that it is significant.

Apart from internal finance and borrowing, there is still another way in which a firm can obtain finance. This is to float stock. The cost of floating stock is the dilution of earnings: that is, that the new stockholders will now share in the future earnings of the firm. Whether or not a stock flotation is good for the existing stockholders depends on (1) the price at which this stock can be sold, (2) the earnings it expects to obtain from new capital and from its previous capital, (3) the amount of new borrowing the firm can undertake now that it has more equity capital, (4) the effect of this new capital on the interest rate paid by the firm and on the riskiness of the firm for its stockholders, and (5) the cost of alternative ways of financing investment—that is, by borrowing or by reducing dividends. This means that expectations are very important. They affect not only the firm's estimate of how much it can earn on new capital, but also the price at which the firm can sell its stock. The purchaser of stock obtains a right to share in the firm's earnings, and the greater his estimate of what these earnings will be, the more will he pay for the stock. Another factor influencing stock prices is the rate of interest. It determines the *present value* of expected earnings. Put another way, the prospective customer of the firm's stock can buy either stock or interest-yielding securities, and his choice between these alternatives will depend on the expected earnings on these assets as well as their riskiness and illiquidity.

THE PROFITS THEORY

The most obvious theory of investment is the profits theory. Investment is undertaken to earn profit, and hence, by looking at the net profit to be obtained from prospective investment one should be able to determine the amount of investment. But, standing by itself, this principle does not give us an *empirical* theory of investment because it does not tell us how to determine the expected rate of profit on potential investment. And unless we know this, we cannot say how much investment will be undertaken. What the profits theory therefore does is to give us a rule for estimating the rate of expected profit on prospective investment. It takes this rate as being, in rough and ready fashion, equal to the rate of profit the firm is currently earning. This procedure is, of course, open to challenge. To start with, the firm's profit rate is an average rate on its existing capital stock, and what is relevant for investment is the profit rate on additional capital—i.e., the marginal, not the average rate. Second, past earnings need not be at all a good guide to the earnings the firm expects in the future. Again, it is basically an empirical issue. The only way to tell whether the firm's current average rate of profit is an adequate estimate of its expected marginal rate of profit is to see whether such a theory allows one to predict investment. Unfortunately, this is not easy to determine. Changes in output and changes in profits are closely correlated so that it is difficult to separate the predictions of the profits theory from the predictions of the accelerator theory.

But, in addition to the argument running from current average profit to prospective marginal profit, the profits theory has another aspect. Even if current profits are not a good guide to expected marginal profits, an increase in current profits still tends to raise investment because it provides the firm with funds which are available for investment. But since undistributed profits are only one part of the internal liquidity available to the firm, this aspect of the profits theory is less general than the previously discussed liquidity theory.

QUESTIONS AND EXERCISES

1. Describe how the government could use tax policy to stimulate investment.

2. Can you think of several ways one could estimate expected profits apart from just saying that they are equal to current profits?

3. From the *Economic Report of the President* chart annual data for investment, GNP, and corporate profits for 1950–1970. What does this chart suggest to you?

4. Use the accelerator to explain the demand for economists.

5. Discuss how the accelerator applies to residential construction. Judging from the accelerator theory, how would you expect residential construction to behave? Now look at the data on residential construction given in the *Economic Report of the President*. Do they show this behavior? If not, what reasons would you suggest?

6. Compare the operation of the accelerator in two industries. In one, depreciation is very high and half the capital stock has to be replaced each year; in the other, only 10 percent of the capital stock is replaced each year. What does this comparison suggest about the accelerator?

7. Prepare an example of the workings of the accelerator as given in this chapter, using different numbers.

8. It is possible that different industries require different theories of investment. Under what conditions would (1) the accelerator theory, (2) the

liquidity theory, and (3) the profits theory perform well? Under what conditions would they do poorly?

9. Select one theory of investment and write a brief statement why you prefer it to the other theories. Now select another theory and state why you think it is inferior.

10. Suppose you are planning to undertake an empirical test of investment theories. How would you go about it?

SUGGESTED READING

G. Ackley, *Macroeconomic Theory* (New York: Macmillan, 1961) Chap. 17.

M. Evans, *Macroeconomic Activity* (New York: Harper and Row, 1969) Chaps. 4 and 5.

J. M. Keynes, *The General Theory of Employment, Interest and Money* (New York: Harcourt Brace, 1936) Chap. 12.

J. M. Keynes, "The General Theory of Employment," *Quarterly Journal of Economics,* Vol. LI (February 1937).

J. Hirschleifer, "On the Theory of Optimal Investment Decisions," *Journal of Political Economy,* Vol. LXVI (August 1958). *Advanced reference.*

R. Matthews, *The Business Cycle* (Cambridge, England: Cambridge University Press, 1959), pp. 33–48.

R. Eisner, "A Permanent Income Theory of Investment," *American Economic Review,* Vol. LVII (June 1967). *Advanced reference.*

D. Jorgenson and C. Siebert, "Theories of Corporate Investment Behavior," *American Economic Review,* Vol. LVIII (September 1968). *Advanced reference.*

R. Eisner and R. Strotz, "Determinants of Business Investment," in Commission on Money and Credit, *Impacts of Monetary Policy* (Englewood Cliffs, N.J.: Prentice-Hall, 1963), pp. 60–233.

L. Grebler and S. Maisel, "Determinants of Residential Construction: A Review of Present Knowledge," in Commission on Money and Credit, *Impacts of Monetary Policy* (Englewood Cliffs, N.J.: Prentice-Hall, 1963), pp. 475–620. *Advanced reference.*

D. Jorgenson, "Econometric Study of Investment Behavior: A Survey," *Journal of Economic Literature,* Vol. IX (December 1971), pp. 111–47. *Advanced reference.*

P. Lund, *Investment: The Study of an Economic Aggregate* (San Francisco: Holden Day, 1971). *Advanced reference.*

12

Liquidity Preference and the Theory of Interest

IN CHAPTER 10 we developed a theory of investment and found that, given (1) the Marginal Efficiency of Investment schedule adjusted for borrowers' risk; and (2) the cost of borrowing, we could determine the equilibrium rate of real planned investment. Given the rate of real planned investment (determined in this way) we could then, from the schedule of the propensity to consume (itself derived from the consumption function) determine the equilibrium level of output and employment from the condition that, in equilibrium, planned saving must be equal to planned investment.

Moreover our analysis of the determinants of investment—in particular of the Marginal Efficiency of Investment schedule—showed that the rate of real planned investment depended crucially upon (1) business expectations; and (2) business uncertainty. Hence, even in the short run, investment seemed likely to fluctuate sharply (thus bringing about fluctuations in the equilibrium levels of output and employment) since both business expectations and uncertainty were liable to change in response to the "state of the news."

Our theory has thus come closer to completion, for we are now able to abandon the artificial assumption that the rate of real planned investment is determined by some hypothetical (and mythical) planning authority.

In formal terms our theory now stands as follows:

$$Y = C_p + I_p \tag{12.1}$$

$$C_p = f(Y, r) \tag{12.2}$$

$$I_p = f(r) \tag{12.3}$$

We thus have three equations to determine the four unknown variables Y, C_p, I_p and r. Such a system cannot give us a solution. This reflects the fact that, so far, we have no theory to explain the determination of the rate of interest. To provide a theory of interest determination is the task of this chapter.

ASSUMPTIONS AND DEFINITIONS

To simplify our exposition we need to speak of "the rate of interest." A glance at the financial page of any newspaper, however, makes it clear that there is not one rate of interest but many. Accordingly our first assumption is that

all rates of interest in the market move together, so that any one can stand as an index of all rates.

On this assumption we then continue to define *the* rate of interest as

the percentage rate of return per year obtainable in the market on long-term government securities.

Defined in this way the rate of interest must be carefully distinguished from the *coupon rate* on long-term government securities. An example should make this distinction clear.

Today, looking in the *Wall Street Journal,* we find the following information:

$3\frac{1}{2}$ percent Treasury bonds 1984	Price $80	Rate of interest percent 5.45

This tells us that

1) the market price of $1000 nominal value of $3\frac{1}{2}$ percent Treasury bonds is $800; and
2) at this price the rate of interest obtainable until 1984—when the government will repay $1000 is 5.45 percent;
3) the *coupon rate* is $3\frac{1}{2}$ percent.

The method of calculation is essentially the same as that we have already employed to find the "marginal efficiency of investment." Each year that we hold $1000 *nominal* of this security we receive as income the *coupon rate* on the *nominal* value of the security:

$$3\tfrac{1}{2}\% \times \$1000 = \$35.$$

In 1984 we shall be repaid in full: that is, the government will redeem its bond by paying us $1000 in cash. We thus have (in 1984) an asset with

1) a price of $1000;
2) a life of 12 years;
3) twelve annual returns of $35;
4) one return (the last) of $1000.

We find the rate of interest r from the formula[1]

$$S = \frac{Q_1}{(1 + r)} + \frac{Q_2}{(1 + r)^2} + \cdots + \frac{Q_n}{(1 + r)^n}$$

where S is the price of the bond. Or:

$$\$1000 = \frac{\$35}{(1 + r)} + \frac{\$35}{(1 + r)^2} + \cdots + \frac{\$35}{(1 + r)^{12}} + \frac{\$1000}{(1 + r)^{12}}$$

We do not need to go to the trouble of calculating r since the *Wall Street Journal* has already done so. The formula reminds us, however, that (1) the *coupon rate* ($3\frac{1}{2}$ percent) is *not* the rate of interest; and (2) the rate of interest (on any bond) is *lower* the *higher* is the *market price* of the bond.

In short, the rate of interest depends upon three factors: the price of the bond; the coupon yield; the length of time which must elapse before the bond is redeemed. And the rate of interest will be *lower* the *higher* is the price of bonds.

In the discussion which follows we shall take the last two factors as given. Hence the rate of interest will be determined simply by the price of bonds and is inversely related to it.

We now know not only what we mean by the rate of interest but also how to calculate it. In the theory we shall shortly develop to explain the determination of the rate of interest (i.e., bond prices) we need to make use of a second concept. This is the *quantity* of *money*. We define this to be

> the quantity of currency and coin and demand deposits in the pos-
> session of the non-bank public.[2]

Throughout this chapter we shall assume, for simplicity, that the quantity of money—which is often called the *money supply*—is fixed and invariant with respect to all other variables in the system. Notice that, unlike consumption, saving, and investment, the money supply is a *stock* variable. On our present assumption it is also an *exogenous* variable independent of every other variable in the system.

AN OUTLINE OF THE LIQUIDITY PREFERENCE
THEORY OF INTEREST

The first problem which arises in developing any interest theory is why is interest paid at all? At first sight it seems natural to answer that interest is the reward for saving. A moment's reflection shows that this view is

---

1. In practice, since interest is paid half-yearly, this formula is only an approximation.
2. You should note carefully that money, as defined in economics is not, as in colloquial speech, a synonym for income. Failure to draw this distinction can cause a great deal of confusion.

untenable. Saving is the act of refraining from consumption, and this is not a sufficient condition for interest. If an individual saves (i.e., refrains from consumption) *and holds his accumulated savings in the form of money* (say as notes and coin) he receives no interest. Interest is received only if the saver is prepared *to hold his accumulated savings in the form of bonds.*[3] This tells us two things: first, interest is paid to induce wealth owners to hold their accumulated wealth in the form of bonds rather than money; hence, second, the determination of the rate of interest is intimately connected with the decisions of wealth owners as to how to hold their wealth: or, more precisely, how they should allocate their wealth between money (which provides no interest) and bonds (which do).

Why is an inducement necessary to persuade wealth owners to hold their assets in the form of bonds rather than money?

As an asset money has a number of obvious attractions. These are:

1) it is *perfectly liquid* in the sense that it can readily be converted into anything (good or service) which is sold on a market;

2) it can be held, either as legal tender or better still as demand deposits, without incurring either

    (a) significant storage costs *or*

    (b) risks of loss;

3) *if the price level is constant* (as we are at present assuming) money is an asset which does not deteriorate over time.

Hence to hold accumulated wealth in the form of money is to obtain a subjective *convenience yield* (due to 1 and 3 above) at virtually zero costs (due to 2).

To sacrifice this convenience yield, wealth owners must be offered an inducement. This inducement is the rate of interest.

Approaching the problem in this way, we can think of the rate of interest as the price of holding money: for interest is what wealth owners must *forgo* if they wish to hold wealth in the form of money rather than bonds; and interest is what an individual who wishes to hold money must pay to some other individual to induce him to part with it.

If the rate of interest is the price of holding money, how is it determined? Economists are accustomed to argue that equilibrium prices are determined by the equality of demand and supply. There is a simple analogy here with our theory of income determination. In this we argued that the equilibrium level of income was determined by the equality of aggregate demand and aggregate supply. In a commodity market we argue that the equilibrium price is determined by the equality of planned purchases (demand) and planned sales (supply). Putting the interest problem in these terms we may say that

3. Bonds stand here for all interest bearing financial assets.

the rate of interest is the price which equates the community's planned money holdings (demand for money) with the quantity of money (supply of money) in existence.

To illustrate this argument consider the following example.

Suppose we construct a schedule showing the quantity of money the community will plan to hold at any given real rate of interest. We assume (what we shall later defend and elaborate) that the quantity of planned money holdings *is less the higher is the rate of interest*. Formally we have the general proposition:

$$M_p^D = f(r) \quad \text{and} \quad \frac{\partial M_p^D}{\partial r} < 0 \qquad (12.4)$$

and the specific proposition:

$$M_p^D = R + q \times r \qquad M_p^D = \$900 \text{ bil.} - \$100 \text{ bil. } r, \qquad (12.5)$$

where

$$M_p^D \equiv \text{planned money holdings}$$

$$r \equiv \text{rate of interest}$$

$$q \equiv \frac{\partial M_p^D}{\partial r} \equiv -\$100 \text{ bil.}$$

We plot the curve defined by (12.5) as the *LL* schedule of Figure 12.1.

Figure 12.1 / *The rate of interest and the demand for and supply of money.*

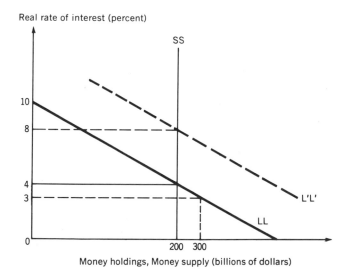

Real rate of interest (percent)

Money holdings, Money supply (billions of dollars)

For equilibrium in the money market—that is, for the rate of interest to be in equilibrium—we require:

$$M_p^D = M_p^S \qquad (12.6)$$

which is simply the statement that planned holdings must equal planned supplies.

We assume that actual supplies $(M_A^S) = M_p^S$. That is, whoever (which we have yet to explain) plans the supply of money always carries out his plans. Since we have already assumed that the quantity supplied is fixed (say equal to M^0) we have:

$$M_p^S = M_A^S \qquad (12.7)$$

$$M_A^S = M_0 \qquad M_0 = \$200 \text{ bil.} \qquad (12.8)$$

Hence equilibrium requires:

$$M_p^D = M_0.$$

To illustrate this we construct a line (SS) on Figure 12.1 at a distance along the horizontal axis equal to $200 billion. This line is vertical, reflecting the assumption that M_p^S is independent of r.

Equilibrium is determined where the LL curve cuts the SS curve. At this point the rate of interest is 4 percent and the planned money holdings are $200 billion, exactly equal to actual money supplies. All actual and planned magnitudes coincide.

Suppose the rate of interest was not 4 percent but 3 percent. Then, from (12.1) we should have:

$$M_p^D = \$300 \text{ bil.}$$

This is greater than M_p^S. Planned holdings in short *exceed* planned supplies. Hence some persons, *who hold less money than they plan,* offer bonds for sale. Hence, bond prices fall and the interest rate rises. The rise in the interest rate reduces M_p^D until, when it has reached 4 percent, the demand for money equals the supply.

This example can easily be reversed for an initial interest rate greater than 4 percent.

Taken together the two examples show that, as we have drawn Figure 12.1, the money market is *stable* and that there is a simple explanation of how the rate of interest reaches its equilibrium level.

Suppose the *LL* curve shifts so that planned money holdings *are greater at each real interest rate* (i.e., the demand for money increases). We have a new curve $L'L'$ and a new equilibrium rate of interest, 8 percent. How do we get it? An increased demand for money means that some persons who at 4 percent were happy to hold bonds now wish to hold money. They offer bonds for sale. Bond prices *fall*. The real rate of interest *rises* until, at the new rate of 8 percent, we have once again:

$$M_p^D = M_A^S$$

planned money holdings = actual (= planned) money supplies.

Notice that, unless M_A^S *changes,* the community cannot hold more (or less) money than $200 billion. *All that it can determine is the price at which it will hold the given supply.*

The demand for money (represented by LL and $L'L'$) depends, among other things, on wealth owners' preferences for holding accumulated wealth in the form of money. This, for reasons which should be obvious, we call "liquidity preference." Hence the essentials of what is called the liquidity preference theory of interest can be summarized as follows:

1) interest is paid to induce persons to sacrifice the convenience of holding wealth in liquid form: i.e., to overcome liquidity preference;

2) the determination of the rate of interest is thus bound up with decisions of wealth owners as to how to distribute their assets between money and bonds;

3) the rate of interest is the price or opportunity cost of holding money;

4) it is determined by the relationship between the demand for money (planned money holdings) and the supply of money (planned quantity of money supplied);

5) the greater (smaller) is the demand for money then, with a given money supply, the higher (lower) is the equilibrium rate of interest;

6) the greater (smaller) is the money supply then, with any given demand for money, the lower (higher) is the rate of interest;

7) the higher (lower) is the price of bonds the lower (higher) is the rate of interest.

These propositions should be carefully studied. We now seek to develop this skeletal interest theory by examining, in greater detail, the determinants of the demand for money—that is, the LL curve of Figure 12.1.

THE FOUR DEMANDS FOR MONEY

To analyze the demand for money we break it down into four components: the transactions demand; the precautionary demand; the asset demand; the speculative demand. Aggregated together these constitute the total demand for money. We begin with the *transactions demand.*

Transactions Demand / Households and enterprises are continually receiving money and making money payments. A certain money holding is, on average, required over any period of time, to avoid the difficulties which can arise from running completely out of money and thus being unable to make necessary payments. How much is required depends upon (1) the value of receipts and payments in the period; (2) the time correspondence between receipts and payments. To see this, picture an individual whose annual income is $3650 and who spends it all at the regular rate of $10 per day.

If this income is received at the rate of $10 per day, his average balance over the year would be $5. If, alternatively, his income was received as a single payment on January 1 his average balance would be $1825. In practice some incomes are received daily, some weekly, some monthly, some quarterly, some half-yearly, and some at varying intervals throughout the year. However, in modern financially developed communities the ways in which most people receive their incomes change very slowly. *There is, in short, an institutional pattern of income receipts which, though it does change, can in a short-run analysis such as ours, be taken as given and invariant.*

In the same way conventions exist regarding a whole host of payments from rent, mortgage payments and automobile license fees to wages.

We may thus argue that where the time correspondence pattern of receipts and expenditures is determined by a developed institutional environment, households and enterprises will need a certain minimum average amount of transaction balances to finance any given level of *foreseeable* expenditures.

The value of these expenditures depends upon two quantities. The first is the planned level of *real* expenditure. The second is the price level. Since real expenditure depends upon real income, it follows that the demand for transactions balances depends upon real income and the price level. Formally:

$$M_{p(\text{transactions})}^{D} = f(Y, p) \tag{12.9}$$

where

$M_p^D \equiv$ planned holdings of transactions balances

$Y \equiv$ real income (= output)

$p \equiv$ price of a unit of output,

and both marginal response coefficients are positive; that is,

$$\frac{\partial M^D}{\partial Y} \text{ and } \frac{\partial M^D}{\partial p} > 0.$$

What form is this function likely to take? If money income is zero it is reasonable, as a first approximation, to expect the transactions demand to be zero. In addition we have, at this stage, developed no theory to suggest that as income increases, the transactions demand will increase other than proportionately. A plausible first approximation would thus be a linear and proportional relationship between transactions demand and money income of the form:

$$M^D_{p(\text{transactions})} = KYp \tag{12.10}$$

or, in numerical form,

$$M^D_{p(\text{transactions})} = 0.15\,Yp \tag{12.10n}$$

with $K = 0.15$.

At the moment we are taking the price level p as given and invariant. Hence any change in Y will bring about an equal proportionate change in Yp—which is money income. Moreover, since p is constant, money income can change only if Y—real income—changes. Hence we can, for the time being, simplify (12.10) by writing:

$$M^D_{p(\text{transactions})} = KY \text{ (with } p \text{ given and taken equal to unity)} \tag{12.10*}$$

where K is the planned ratio of transactions balances to real income at the given constant price level $p = 1$. To give a numerical illustration we write:

$$M^D_{p(\text{transactions})} = 0.15\,Y \text{ (with } p = 1) \tag{12.10n*}$$

The demand curve for transactions balances is now depicted in Figure 12.2 as the L_T function.
Its parameters are:
1) institutional arrangements regarding receipts and payments;
2) the given level of prices.

Figure 12.2 / *The transactions demand for money holdings.*

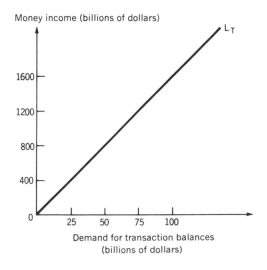

Precautionary Demands / Not all income receipts or payments can be *foreseen with certainty*. Hence, in practice, households and enterprises will need to hold rather more than the minimum amount of transaction balances to guard against the risks arising out of the uncertainty of future receipts and payments. Consider for example a businessman setting out to drive from New York to Philadelphia to negotiate an important contract. He calculates his expenditure in gas, food, drink, and accommodation and, in accordance with (10.10), sets off with the minimum amount of transaction balances necessary to finance these foreseeable expenditures. En route his car breaks down and he has to pay a garage $100 for repairs. He must now either go without food, drink, or accommodation and/or incur the expense and delay of telephoning his New York bank for funds. If he selects the first alternative, he will suffer discomfort. If he takes the second, he may lose his contract and suffer serious loss. Had he started on his journey with sufficient *precautionary* balances over and above his *minimum transaction* requirements, he could have avoided both.

It is easy to see that this illustration applies with particular force to enterprises that may suffer severe losses due to an unforeseen shortage of money holdings arising from the need to make an unforeseen payment or the unforeseen postponement of an expected receipt.

The demand for precautionary balances is thus readily explicable in terms of uncertainty about the timing of future expenditures and receipts and their expected values. We thus regard this demand as a function of real income, the price level and uncertainty of this particular type. Formally, again taking p as given:

$$M_p^D {}_{(\text{precautionary})} = f(Y, u_y) \tag{12.11}$$

where u_y is an index of uncertainty regarding future receipts and payments.

This demand is now added to the transaction demand to get what is called the *demand for active balances*. Thus:

$$M_{p(\text{active})}^D \equiv M_{p(\text{trans.})}^D + M_{p(\text{precautionary})}^D = f(Y, u_y) \tag{12.12}$$

which, *for a given value of* u_y, we can assume to take the specific form:

$$M_{p(\text{active})}^D = k'Y \quad or \quad M_{p(\text{active})}^D = 0.20\,Y \tag{12.13}$$

again taking $p \equiv$ price level $= 1$, and to be represented diagrammatically as in Figure 12.3 as the L_1 function.

This curve, the demand curve for active balances, we call the L_1 function. Its position depends upon (1) institutional arrangements for receiving income and making payments; (2) uncertainty regarding future income payments and receipts; (3) the given level of prices; and (4) the rate of interest. The interest rate is relevant because if interest rates are high, money holders look for ways to economize on transactions balances and,

Figure 12.3 / *The demand curve for active balances.*

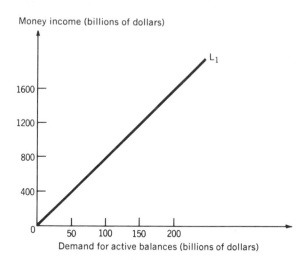

in addition, are willing to take greater risks and operate with smaller precautionary balances.

The Demand for Idle Balances: Asset Demand / Some households and enterprises will plan to hold money in excess of their planned holdings of active balances. These additional balances we call *idle*. Hence in addition to the demand for active balances (analyzed above) there is a demand for idle balances which requires analysis. To facilitate this analysis we divide idle balances into two classes: *asset* balances and *speculative* balances. The three concepts are related by the identity:

$$M^D_{\text{idle}} \equiv M^D_{\text{asset}} + M^D_{\text{speculative}}.$$

Consider now the demand for asset balances. This is related to money's ability to act as a store of wealth. Money, to put the same point rather differently, *is one form of asset in which an individual may hold his accumulated savings (wealth)*. The demand for asset balances is thus related to an individual's capital account and reflects what is called a *portfolio decision:* that is, a decision regarding the assets over which an individual chooses to distribute his accumulated savings.

In the simple macroeconomic model we are constructing there are by assumption, only three forms of asset: money, bonds, and goods. In our examination of the consumption and investment functions we have already discussed the factors influencing planned expenditure on goods. Hence the demand for idle balances (in general) and asset balances (in particular) is concerned essentially with the decision as to how to distribute a given value of accumulated savings (wealth) over money and bonds: that is the portfolio decision. In what circumstances then will an individual plan to hold some part of his accumulated savings in the form of idle balances: that is, hold money as part of his chosen portfolio?

Suppose the rate of interest on bonds is 4 percent and is expected to remain 4 percent forever. Suppose further, though this is in practice impossible, that the expectation that 4 percent will remain the rate of interest is held with complete certainty. In these circumstances no individual will wish to hold idle balances since, by holding bonds rather than money, he can obtain 4 percent per annum on his accumulated savings *without risk.* Admittedly converting money into bonds or bonds into money costs something in time, trouble, and brokerage fees. It is possible therefore that some persons whose accumulated savings are small or who plan to dis-save in the near future may consider it not worthwhile to purchase bonds. But if we neglect these cases, which are probably rather rare and quantitatively unimportant, our general proposition holds. In the postulated circumstances no individual wealth owner would wish to hold any part of his wealth in money, for money earns no interest and bonds, by assumption, earn 4 percent. Thus the portfolio of John Smith who has accumulated savings of $10,000 would look like this:

Accumulated savings	$10,000	Money (asset balances)	$ nil
Total wealth	10,000	Bonds	10,000
		Total assets	10,000

This example, though, unrealistic, is nevertheless instructive, for in demonstrating that, in our assumed conditions, John Smith will not plan to hold any asset balances, we have provided ourselves with a clue to the explanation of why, in general, people will choose to hold such balances. This is so because the implausibility of our hypothetical example lies in the assumption that John Smith's expectations were held with perfect certainty. In such a situation Smith clearly, because the future rate of interest was expected with complete certainty, ran no risk of a fall in bond prices (rise in interest rates) or rise in bond prices (fall in interest rates). The portfolio of "bonds only" thus emerges in a situation in which there is *no uncertainty* about the future interest rate and thus *no risk* of changes in the value of the bond holding. As we know, complete certainty about the future of the interest rate or anything else is impossible. However confident Smith may feel about his expectation of an unchanged rate, the rate *may* change. Hence, in practice, uncertainty (and thus risk) will always be present in some degree. What happens to the portfolio choice when the existence of uncertainty is admitted? Before examining this problem let us see first the consequence of interest rate changes.

Suppose Smith holds his whole wealth in bonds purchased when the ruling rate of interest is 4 percent; then if the rate rises to 5 percent each $1000 bond he holds will be valued in the market at, say $900. He will have incurred $1000 capital loss—a capital loss sufficient to reduce the market value of his wealth by 10 percent. Conversely, if the rate *falls* to, say, 2 percent, the market value of his bond holding, and thus his accumulated savings, will have risen. We may thus conclude that where there is, as there always will be, uncertainty about the rate of interest ruling in the future, to hold accumulated savings in the form of bonds provides a money income but involves the acceptance of uncertainty and hence the risk of capital gain or loss.

Most individuals seek money income but try to avoid risk. It is therefore likely that Smith will distribute his portfolio between money (asset balances) and bonds in such a way as to give him his preferred combination of interest income and risk. This means that he will tend to hold a *mixed portfolio*—reducing his risk (at the cost of sacrificing some interest income) by holding some of his wealth in the form of money. In short he will heed the ancient adage on the unwisdom of "putting all his eggs in one basket" and distribute them over two: bonds *and* money.

We can perhaps make the argument slightly clearer by a table illustrating three possible portfolio positions.

				PORTFOLIO CHARACTERISTICS
		Portfolio I		
Accumulated		Money	$ nil	Maximum money income
savings	$10,000	Bonds	10,000	Maximum risk
		Portfolio II		
Accumulated		Money	$10,000	Zero income
savings	$10,000	Bonds	nil	Zero risk
		Portfolio III		
Accumulated		Money	$ 2,000	*Less* than maximum income
savings	$10,000	Bonds	8,000	*Less* than maximum risk

Portfolio I provides maximum income *and* maximum risk. It will be selected only by those who are either indifferent to risk or who positively relish it. Portfolio II provides zero income and zero risk. It is unlikely to be selected. Portfolio III represents a mixed portfolio strategy—an attempt to find the optimal income risk combination.

We may thus argue that where individuals seek, as we have assumed John Smith to do, to avoid risk, they will in general hold mixed portfolios of assets and thus will hold some of their wealth in the form of idle (asset) balances. Hence the demand for asset balances arises because (1) the future rate of interest cannot be known with certainty; and (2) individuals are, in general, risk avoiders; although (3) they have no reason to expect the rate of interest to be higher or lower in the future.

Assumption (3) is worth spelling out in slightly greater detail. It is, clearly enough, an alternative way of expressing an assumption that the rate of interest is expected to remain unchanged at 4 percent. Where expectations are of this form—sometimes called neutral—the demand for idle balances is, by definition, purely an asset demand. Money is held as an asset simply to reduce risk.

Suppose, however, that with the rate of interest at 4 percent some individual, say Henry Snodgrass, though uncertain of the future rate of interest (as he must be) expects *not that it will remain unchanged but that it will fall to 3 percent.* Then, by buying bonds now (at 4 percent) and holding them until the rate falls to 3 percent. Snodgrass can obtain not only his interest income but also a capital gain. In short Snodgrass can make a speculative gain from "knowing better than the market what the future will bring forth." As we shall see shortly, it is from considerations of this kind that the *speculative* demand for idle balances arises. In such a case we say that expectations are nonneutral.

The demand for *asset balances* thus gives rise to planned money holdings in excess of planned active balances and arises fundamentally because the future of the rate of interest is uncertain. *It contains no speculative element whatever.* Its basic assumption is that whatever the ruling rate of interest happens to be, so it is expected to remain.

Now for a given degree of risk, a given amount of uncertainty, it is reasonable to argue that the higher is the rate of interest—and thus the stronger the reason for accepting risk—the greater the proportion of accumulated wealth which will be held in the form of bonds and, what is the same thing, the smaller the proportion of accumulated wealth which will be held in the form of money. Hence the planned holdings of asset balances will depend upon (1) the value of wealth (W) or accumulated savings; (2) the rate of interest (r); (3) uncertainty regarding the future value of $r(u_r)$; (4) people's attitudes towards risk and income. In our usual functional notation we may write:

$$M_{p(\text{asset})}^D = L_2'(r, u_r \times W) \tag{12.14}$$

and expect the marginal response coefficients to have the following signs:

$$\frac{\partial M_{p(\text{asset})}^D}{\partial r} < 0 \qquad \frac{\partial M_{p(\text{asset})}^D}{\partial u_r} > 0 \qquad \frac{\partial M_{p(\text{asset})}^D}{\partial W} > 0$$

This, of course, is a very general statement. Since our theory is short-run, we may regard wealth as a constant. Then, given the (constant) value of wealth, we might postulate a familiar linear function thus:

$$M^D_{p(\text{asset})} = T + n \times r + o \times u_r \qquad (12.15)$$

$$M^D_{p(\text{asset})} = \$100 \text{ bil.} - \$6 \text{ bil.} \ r + \$1 \text{ bil.} \ u_r \qquad (12.15n)$$

This formulation presupposes that we can define, and measure, an appropriate index of uncertainty (u_r). Taking a given value for this index (say $u_r = 20$) we can plot the resultant demand curve in Figure 12.4.

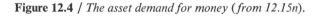

Figure 12.4 / *The asset demand for money (from 12.15n).*

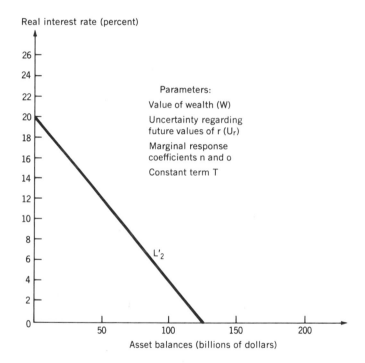

Notice that, at rates of interest above 20 percent, this function makes no economic sense. This is a limitation not of theory but of the functional form which is only an approximation and a very simple one at that.

What are the parameters of the function? Apart from wealth which we have suppressed, they are as usual the value of the constant (T), the value of the marginal response coefficients n and o, and the value of u_r (the uncertainty index). T, n, and 0 reflect the public's preference for holding wealth in money rather than bonds: they thus reflect its preference for liquidity or its liquidity preference. Hence *demand schedules* of this type are frequently referred to as *liquidity preference schedules.*

Suppose the public becomes more anxious to avoid risk. The curve will move to the right. Alternatively suppose, with unchanged preference on the part of the public, the index of risk u_r increases: the curve will move to the right. Similarly if wealth were greater the curve would lie further to the right.

In interpreting this curve it is important to remember that it reflects the assumption that, whatever the rate of interest is, it is expected to remain unchanged. Put another way the curve shows the demand for idle balances when the expected capital gain or loss from holding bonds is zero: that is, gains and losses are equally probable. It supposes a zero speculative demand for idle balances. Hence the L_2' schedule as we have called it is *not* the demand for idle balances but simply a component of it. It is identical with the total demand for idle balances only in the special case in which the public expects no gains from speculation. If it was empirically the case, as the L_2' curve assumes, that whatever the rate of interest ruling the expected capital gain or loss was zero, then the L_2' curve would be identical with the total demand for idle balances. However, as we shall now demonstrate, this is not likely to be the case and the demand for idle balances when account is taken of the speculative element, differs very significantly from the asset demand which assumes neutral expectations.

The Demand for Idle Balances: Speculative Demand / As we have seen, the asset demand for idle balances arises because

　　1) future interest rates (bond prices) are not known with certainty; and

　　2) wealth owners in seeking to reduce the risk of capital losses which then arise will, in general, adopt a mixed portfolio, selecting it so that

　　3) the quantity of idle balances demanded for asset reasons will be greater the smaller is the interest rate.

The fundamental assumption of the asset demand as we have defined it is that whatever the rate of interest ruling in the market is, it is expected to remain unchanged in the future. Expectations in this case are neutral.

The *speculative demand* arises where future interest rates are uncertain, as is always the case, and some people think they know better than the market what the future will bring forth. Thus, for some people at least, *expectations are not neutral.* Accordingly they will buy bonds if they expect rates to fall (and thus anticipate a capital gain) and sell bonds if they expect interest rates to rise (thus avoiding an anticipated capital loss).

In short, where the ruling market rate is above (below) the rate of interest expected to rule in the future, people will *for speculative reasons,* wish to hold more bonds (money) than the analysis of the asset demand would suggest. Or, to put the same point another way, when the rate of interest is expected to rise (bond prices to fall) wealth owners have a *positive* demand for idle money balances on speculative account; when the rate of interest is expected to fall (bond prices to rise) wealth owners have a *negative* demand for idle money balances on speculative account.

We may thus argue that the speculative demand for money depends upon (1) the market rate of interest (r); (2) uncertainty about the rate of interest (u_r); and (3) the rate of interest which is expected to rule in the future ($\hat{r}$); as well as (4) the general attitude of wealth owners towards speculation.

You can now see that, in formulating the asset demand, we made the special assumption that, whatever the value of r, the general expectation was that $r = \hat{r}$: that is, expectations were neutral. The speculative demand arises once this assumption is relaxed so that $r \lessgtr \hat{r}$: that is, expectations can be nonneutral.

Suppose now wealth owners possess a unanimous and firmly held expectation that the "safe" or "normal" rate of interest at long term is 5 percent. The expectation can be regarded as being based on historical experience of interest rates and the current state of the news. Two conclusions emerge immediately:

1) If the ruling rate in the market is 5 percent, the speculative demand for money will be zero. Hence:

$$M^D_{\text{idle}} = M^D_{\text{asset}}.$$

2) If the ruling rate is 6 percent, capital gains will be expected from bond holding and the speculative demand for money will be *negative*. Hence:

$$M^D_{\text{idle}} < M^D_{\text{asset}}.$$

Figure 12.5 v. depicts the demand curve for speculative balances in such a case.

How is this figure to be interpreted? At $r = 5$ percent we have $r = \hat{r}$ and $M^D_{\text{speculative}}$ is consequently zero. As soon as the rate of interest rises *above* 5 percent, we have $r > \hat{r}$. Since we have assumed that expectations are unanimous and firmly held, speculators will move out of asset balances into bonds in order to make a capital gain when r returns to $\hat{r}$. Conversely if r is *below* 5 percent, we have $r < \hat{r}$ and the prospect of a capital loss, and speculators would move out of bonds and into idle (speculative) balances.

Clearly if expectations were unanimous (as we have assumed) and held with perfect certainty (as in practice they cannot be) we should have the curve shown in Figure 12.5—simply a straight line with $r = \hat{r}$. The demand for speculative balances would be infinitely elastic at the rate $r = 5$ percent and the rate of interest could never depart from this value, for if r rose *above* $\hat{r}$ (i.e., above 5 percent) speculators would rush to buy bonds and

Figure 12.5 / *The speculative demand for money.*

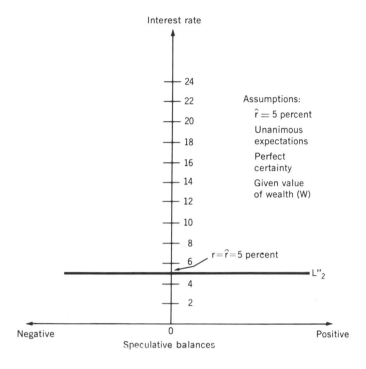

drive up their price until *r* fell to 5 percent. Conversely if *r* was below $\hat{r}$ speculators would rush to sell bonds and their price would fall until *r* rose to 5 percent.

The case depicted in Figure 12.6, though useful expositionally, is extremely artificial because expectations are not likely to be unanimous and because expectations cannot be held with complete certainty.

These two considerations lead us to construct a new curve as in Figure 12.6. This assumes (1) diversity in expectations and (2) incomplete certainty. As a result it shows the speculative demand increasing (negatively) as *r* rises above $\hat{r}$ (which must now be interpreted as an average of the diverse expectations of wealth owners) and increasing (positively) as *r* falls below $\hat{r}$.

This curve also incorporates a further hypothesis to the effect that at some interest rate, which we have called r_{min}, the L_2'' curve becomes completely horizontal. This is the lowest rate of interest acceptable to the community. At this rate, provided speculative balance holdings are greater than or equal to *OZ,* the community is indifferent between money and bonds. In short, because expectations are diverse, the horizontal part of the

Figure 12.6 / *The speculative demand for money.*

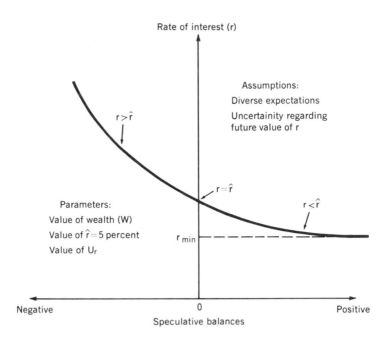

L_2'' function indicates a range along which even the most sanguine speculators expect the capital losses from bond holding to offset so much of the income derived from interest that, allowing for the uncertainty which always attaches to holding bonds, the marginal advantages of holding bonds and money are equal. This idea of a completely elastic range of the liquidity preference curve was introduced into economics by Keynes, who, however, did not think that such elasticity was likely to occur at interest rates actually experienced. It was given more emphasis by some of Keynes' followers, but there is no empirical evidence that we ever actually experienced such a "liquidity trap." And even on theoretical grounds alone, the whole notion has been challenged.[4]

Reverting to our usual functional presentation, we may write the demand for speculative balances (given wealth) as:

$$M_{speculative}^{D} = L_2''(r, \hat{r}, u_r),$$ (12.16)

with $\quad \dfrac{\partial M_{speculative}^{D}}{\partial r} < 0 \qquad \dfrac{\partial M_{speculative}^{D}}{\partial \hat{r}} > 0 \qquad \dfrac{\partial M_{speculative}^{D}}{\partial u_r} > 0.$

4. See Don Patinkin, *Money, Interest, and Prices*, 2nd ed. (New York: Harper and Row, 1965), Chapter 14.

We can now add the asset and speculative demands for money to obtain the total demand for idle balances. To do this we make use of the L_2 and L_2'' curves and the identity:

$$M_{idle}^D \equiv M_{(asset)}^D + M_{speculative}^D$$
$$= L_2'(r, u_r) + L_2''(r, \hat{r}, W, u_r)$$
$$= L_2(r, \hat{r}, W, u_r).$$

Thus our hypotheses are that the demand for idle balances is dependent upon liquidity preference (reflected in the L_2 function itself) and the values of the rate of interest (r), the expected "safe" rate of interest $(\hat{r})$ and the uncertainty of the expectation (u_r). This formulation is, of course, essentially short-run in that it takes as given and constant the value of wealth.

The addition of the asset and speculative demands to obtain the total demand for idle balances is carried out geometrically in Figure 12.7. Interpretation of the figure is simple enough for it is constructed to reflect the hypothesis that

1) with $r > \hat{r}$ $M_{speculative}^D$ is negative;

2) with $r = \hat{r}$ $M_{speculative}^D$ is zero;

3) with $r < \hat{r}$ $M_{speculative}^D$ is positive;

and the constraint that $M_{p(idle)}^D$ cannot be less than zero.

Obviously, from the shape of the L_2 curve, no simple linear function can be used to represent it though if the speculative motive were absent a

Figure 12.7 / *The demand for idle balances.*

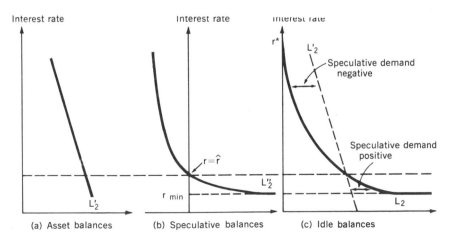

linear relationship might be a plausible approximation (as we have assumed).

Consider now the L_2 curve shown in Figure 12.7. At some interest rate r^*, the sum of the asset and speculative demands is zero: that is, the public would plan to hold no idle balances whatever. As the rate (r) falls below r^*, the demand for idle balances increases until at $r = \hat{r}$ it is equal to the demand shown by the L_2' function. As r falls below $\hat{r}$ the planned holdings of idle balances increase and with $r = r_{min}$ the L_2 curve (like the L_2'' curve and for the same reason) becomes horizontal—that is, infinitely interest elastic.

What are the parameters of the L_2 function? Since the L_2 function depends upon both the L_2' and L_2'' functions, the reader may work the answer to this problem himself and use his answer to explain the circumstances in which an increase or decrease in liquidity preference might be expected. Both changes are illustrated in Figure 12.8.

Figure 12.8 / *The demand for idle balances.*

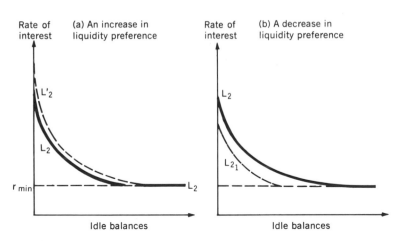

THE DEMAND FOR MONEY AND THE INTEREST RATE

We can now write the total demand for money, given the price level, as:

$$M_p^D \equiv M_{p(\text{active})}^D + M_{p(\text{idle})}^D$$
$$\equiv L_1(Y, r, u_y) + L_2(r, \hat{r}, W, u_r)$$

which, taking u_y, r, and u_r as given, is more commonly written as:

$$M_p^D = L_1(Y) + L_2(r) \qquad (12.17)$$

We know that, in equilibrium,

$$M_p^D = M_p^S \quad \text{and assume that} \quad M_a^S = M_p^S = M_0.$$

Hence if we are given (1) the level of Y; (2) the L_1 and L_2 functions; (3) the money supply; and (4) the price level, we can find the equilibrium value of r—the rate of interest.

To see this look at Figures 12.9(a) and 12.9(b).
From Figure 12.9(a) if $Y = Y_0$ the $M_{p(\text{active})}^D = OQ = \$50$ billion. It

Figure 12.9 / *The determination of the equilibrium rate of interest.*

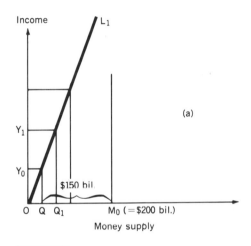

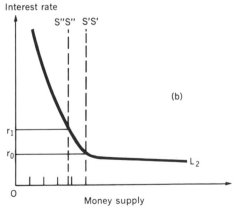

follows that the supply of idle balances is:

$$M_0 - M_{p(\text{active})}^D = \$200 \text{ bil.} - \$50 \text{ bil.} = \$150 \text{ bil.}$$

This supply of idle balances can now be inserted into Figure 12.9(b) as the dotted line $S'S'$. Where this line cuts the L_2 curve determines the rate of interest at r_0. This is easy to see since when income is Y_0 and the rate of interest r_0 we have:

$$M_p^D \equiv M_{p(\text{active})}^D + M_{p(\text{idle})}^D = M_0 = \$200 \text{ bil.}$$

Notice that levels of income higher than Y_0 involve (1) *greater* demands for active balances and so with a fixed money supply (2) a *smaller* supply of idle balances and (2) a *higher* equilibrium rate of interest. How does this come about? Suppose income rises to Y_1. As a result the demand for active balance rises from OQ to OQ'. As a consequence firms and households find their active money holdings too small. Accordingly they try to increase their money holdings by selling bonds. This drives bond prices down and interest rates up until the interest rate reaches r_1. At this rate the demand for money is again equal to the supply.

What happens if the community revises its estimate of $\hat{r}$ upwards? The L_2 curve shifts upwards: that is to the right. At the ruling interest rate people are now holding less as idle balances than they wish. They offer bonds for sale and hence bond prices fall and the interest rate rises.

We can now give a short summary of our interest theory as follows:

1) the rate of interest is determined by the supply and demand for money;

2) the demand for money can be written: $M_p^D = L_1(Y) + L_2(r)$ taking u_y, $\hat{r}$, p, u_r as given and the value of wealth as given;

3) an increase in liquidity preference (upward shift in L_2 function), given the money supply, raises r: a decrease lowers r;

4) an increase in Y raises r:

5) an increase in the money supply (given L_1, L_2) lowers r;

6) the L_2 function is likely to be volatile and respond quickly to changes in the "state of the news."

You should now verify that all these propositions are compatible with our introduction to the theory of interest in the second section of this chapter.

QUESTIONS AND EXERCISES

1. "The essence of the liquidity preference theory of interest is that the rate of interest is the price which brings about equality between the demand for and supply of money." Explain.

2. If the quotation in Question 1 is correct, what relationship would you expect to observe between the ratio of gross national product/money supply and the rate of interest? Give your reasons and construct a rough graph of the relationship you predict.

3. Obtain from the *Economic Report of the President* a series for the average money supply for each year from 1950 to 1970. Selecting other series for the annual interest rate and gross national product, construct a scatter diagram with (a) the interest rate on the vertical axis; (b) the ratio GNP/money supply on the horizontal axis, by plotting a point to represent each year's observation.

   Draw freehand a curve to represent the observations. Does its shape conform with your answer to Question 2? If not is the theory refuted? If so is the story proved?

4. Assume that the demand for active (M_1) balances is given by:

$$M_1^D = KYp \quad \text{where } K = 0.25 \text{ and } p = 1$$

Approximate the demand for idle balances by assuming that $r_{min} = 2$ percent, and that with $r > 2$ percent the following linear relationship is acceptable:

$$M_2^D = T - n \times r \text{ with } T = 1375 \text{ and } \frac{\partial M_2^D}{\partial r} = n = -50.0.$$

Take the money supply as exogenously given, i.e.

$$M^S = M_0 \text{ with } M_0 = 2500,$$

remember that equilibrium in the money market requires:

$$\left\{ \begin{matrix} M^D \\ \text{demand for money} \end{matrix} \right\} = \left\{ \begin{matrix} M^S \\ \text{supply of money} \end{matrix} \right\}.$$

Applying this condition,
   a) find all the pairs of values of Y and r compatible with money market equilibrium;
   b) plot these on a graph with r on the vertical axis and Y on the horizontal;
   c) interpret the curve defined by these points;
   d) explain the relationship between this curve and the curve you constructed from observed data in Question 3;
   e) find the rate of interest when $Y < 4900$;
   f) find the rate of interest when $Y = 6500$;
   g) find the maximum level of Y that the money supply can finance.

5. Using the model of Question 4, show the consequences of an increase of 100 in the money supply; an increase of 100 in the demand for idle balances; a rise in p from 1 to 2. Treat each problem separately and specify clearly the conditions under which your prediction holds.

6. "It is possible to control *either* the money supply *or* the rate of interest but not both." Use the analysis of Chapter 11 to discuss this contention.

7. Using the data of Question 4, what is the interest elasticity of the demand for money when

$$r = 2.0 \text{ percent?}$$
$$r = 5.0 \text{ percent?}$$
$$r = 27.5 \text{ percent?}$$

8. If the rate of interest is 5 percent and expected to fall to 4 percent, a man stands to make a capital gain by holding bonds rather than money. Would he hold *all* his wealth in the form of bonds rather than money? Or would he hold some bonds and some money—a mixed portfolio? Give your reasons.

9. "As long as a wealth owner holds some bonds, the value of his wealth must be inversely related to the rate of interest." Explain. Does this complication modify significantly or even invalidate the analysis of the third and fourth sections of this chapter? Give your reasons.

10. The accounts of John Hawgood on two dates gave the following information:

DEC. 31, 1970 ASSETS		DEC. 31, 1971 ASSETS	
Money	1,500	Money	4,000
Bonds	4,000	Bonds	1,500
House	5,000	House	5,000

Did Hawgood save or dis-save in 1971? If so how much?
Did he invest in 1971? If so how much?
Did his liquidity preference increase/decrease in 1971?
What was his demand for money on December 31, 1970 and December 31, 1971?
On what assumptions and definitions are your answers based?

11. "If there were no speculation, there would be no demand for idle balances." Do you agree? If not why not?

12. A week in advance of its publication your friendly neighborhood spy slips you a government report estimating next year's imports and exports. It shows a 10 percent *increase* in exports and a 2 percent decrease in imports. Your existing portfolio of assets is:

$$\$$$
	$
Money	14,000
Bonds	16,000

You have no inhibitions about using the information you have. Do you rearrange your portfolio? If so in what direction? Give your new portfolio and your reasons for selecting it.

13. How far are the reasons for selecting your new portfolio (in Question 12) compatible with the analysis of Chapter 10 and what light do they throw upon it?

14. "In the short run, wealth is constant." Elucidate. Does this simply reflect the definition of the short run? If it does not, is it correct?

15. "Ultimately it is a question of fact whether it is the speculative or asset motives which dominate the demand curve for idle balances." Elucidate. In what institutional environments would you expect the asset motive to be dominant? Can you suggest a way of testing whether the speculative motive is present?

16. The discussion of the speculative motive runs in terms of *both* diverse expectations and uncertainty. What would the speculative demand curve look like if expectations were diverse and uncertainty *absent?* Give your reasoning fully.

17. What do you think would be the consequences for the L_2 function and the rate of interest, of a statement by the Council of Economic Advisers that the Administration is actively considering ways and means of reducing the rate of interest? Why?

18. "Even with the liquidity preference theory an increase in the propensity to save will reduce the interest rate—through its effect upon income." Elucidate. Are there any limitations to this proposition?

19. "The liquidity preference theory relates to the demand for and supply of a *stock* of money. It is thus formally analogous to the demand for and supply of Rembrandts rather than cabbages." Explain.

20. Can you suggest a method of defining and constructing a measurable index of "uncertainty regarding interest rates (u_r)"?

21. The following hypothetical data relates to John Smith's expectations regarding the future interest rate on two different dates.

DEC. 31, 1970		DEC. 31, 1971	
INTEREST RATE %	EXPECTED WITH PROBABILITY OF	INTEREST RATE %	EXPECTED WITH PROBABILITY OF
3.0	0.1	3.0	0.00
4.0	0.2	4.0	0.10
5.0	0.4	5.0	0.80
6.0	0.2	6.0	0.10
7.0	0.1	7.0	0.00

At each date the ruling rate in the market is 5 percent.
At each date what is the value of $\hat{r}$?
At either date will Smith have a speculative demand for money?
Which set of expectations implies the greater value of u_r?
Assuming no change in Smith's wealth between the two dates, in which situation will Smith have the greater demand for idle balances? Why?
Can you *now* define a measurable index of u_r?

22. Use the current *Wall Street Journal* to obtain the ruling rate of interest on U. S. Treasury $3\frac{1}{2}$% bonds of 1998. Then write

a) the highest rate which you think might rule in a year's time;
b) the lowest rate you think might rule in a year's time;
c) the rate you think most likely to rule in a year's time.

Identify $\hat{r}$. Have you a speculative demand for money? How would you estimate the value of u_r attaching to your expectations?

SUGGESTED READING

A. H. Hansen, *Monetary Theory and Fiscal Policy* (New York: McGraw-Hill, 1949) Chaps. 4–5.

L. Harris, "Regularities and Irregularities in Monetary Economics," in C. Whittlesey and J. Wilson, eds., *Essays in Money and Banking in Honor of R. H. Sayers* (New York: Oxford, 1968), pp. 85–116.

D. Laidler, *The Demand for Money* (Scranton: International Textbook Co., 1969) Chaps. 7–9.

W. T. Newlyn, *The Theory of Money* (New York: Oxford, 1962) Chaps. 4–5.

J. M. Keynes, *The General Theory of Employment, Interest and Money* (New York: Harcourt, Brace, 1936) Chap. 15.

13

The Theory of Income Determination

As a result of our work in Chapter 12, we now have a theory of the determination of the equilibrium rate of interest. Our elementary model is thus complete. It is, therefore, convenient at this point to summarize our argument: that is, to display in full the characteristics of the model at this stage. Once this is done we can see where the model needs further extensions and what prediction it yields.

How then can we conveniently summarize the model we have developed?

CHARACTERISTICS OF THE MODEL: GOODS MARKET

As we have developed it our model consists of two markets: one for goods and services (the *goods market*) and one for money (the *money market*). For the whole system to be in equilibrium, both these markets must simultaneously be in equilibrium. What does this imply?

Consider the market for goods and services. Equilibrium here requires that aggregate demand be equal to aggregate supply: in short, that $C_p + I_p = Y$. To explain C_p and I_p we have a theory of aggregate consumption (developed in Chapters 8 and 9) and a theory of investment (developed in Chapters 10 and 11). These two theories may be written:

$$C_p = f(Y, r, A, \alpha)$$
$$I_p = f(x, r).$$

We take the values of $A \equiv$ real value of households' assets, $\alpha \equiv$ the distribution of income, and $X \equiv$ schedule of marginal efficiency of capital as *given*. This enables us to write:

$$C_p = f(Y, r)$$
$$I_p = f(r)$$

From this it follows that for any given value of r we can determine the rate of real planned investment I_p. Once we know this, since we know the schedule of the propensity to consume, we can determine the equilibrium level of real income (Y). In other words, for any given rate of interest there will be a determinate rate of real planned investment which, *given* the schedule of the propensity to consume, *determines* an equilibrium level of real output.

To see this consider Figure 13.1. On the left we have the familiar 45° diagram of Chapter 8. In the center the theory of investment of Chapter 10. On the right we have a new graph with the rate of interest plotted on the vertical axis and the level of real income on the horizontal.

Figure 13.1 / *The determination of the equilibrium level of income, given the rate of interest, the marginal efficiency of capital schedule and the consumption function.*

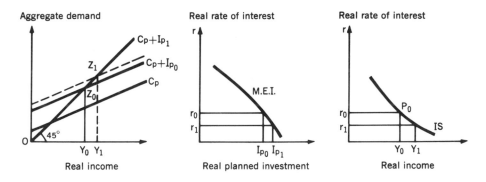

Take any rate of interest r_0. This determines, from the *MEI Schedule,* a rate of real planned investment I_{p0}. This rate can now be transferred to the 45° diagram yielding an aggregate demand schedule $C_p + I_{p0}$. This cuts the 45° line at Z_0 and determines the equilibrium level of income Y_0. The pair of values r_0, Y_0 now define a point (P_0) on the third diagram.

Repeat the process with rate of interest r_1 and rate of planned investment I_{p1} to obtain the equilibrium income Y_1. This yields a second point (r_1, Y_1) in the third figure. Obviously for *any* value of r we can find that level of Y at which the *goods market is in equilibrium* and these pairs of values, plotted on the third diagram will trace out a curve—called the *IS* curve—*which shows all the pairs of values of r and Y at which the goods market is in equilibrium.*

The slope of this *IS* curve is downwards because the higher is r the lower is I_p and the lower is I_p the lower is the value of Y at which the goods market is in equilibrium.

The position of the *IS* curve depends upon (i) the marginal efficiency of investment schedule; and (ii) the schedule of the propensity to consume.

You are invited to work out for yourself the direction in which the *IS* curve will shift in response to shifts in either the propensity to consume schedule or the MEI schedule and to refresh your memory as to why either of these schedules may shift.

CHARACTERISTICS OF THE MODEL: MONEY MARKET

The *IS* curve is not, by itself, sufficient to tell us the equilibrium level of income. All it can say is that *if* the rate of interest is (say) r_0 *then* the level of income at which aggregate demand equals aggregate supply will be Y_0. To find *the* equilibrium level of income we must find the value of r. To do this we turn to the money market.

The equilibrium condition in the money market is

$$M_p^D = M_p^S$$

demand for money = supply of money.

As in Chapter 10 we assume a fixed and invariant supply of money M_0. Hence we require $M_p^D = M_0$. The demand for money, M_p^D, we already know can be written: $M_p^D = L_1(Yp) + L_2(r)$.

Our model takes the value of p ($\equiv$ the price level) as given and constant. Hence real income (Y) and money income (Yp) move together in the sense that any given value of Y implies a single value of Yp. This being so we can think of the demand for money as

$$M_p^D = L_1(Y) + L_2(r) \text{ given } p, W \text{ and } r.[\dagger]$$

Now look at Figure 13.2. As before this is divided into three sections. On the left we have the demand curve for *active balances* (the L_1 function). In the center we have the demand curve for *idle balances* (the L_2 function). On the right we have a diagram with the same axes as we had on the right of Figure 13.1. On the left-hand figure the vertical line *SS* is drawn at a distance along the horizontal axis equal to the given money supply M_0.

[†]In the previous chapter we included the interest rate in the L_1 equation. To simplify the exposition we will ignore it now.

Figure 13.2 / *The LM schedule establishing a relation between real income and the rate of interest, given the liquidity preference, the money supply and the price level.*

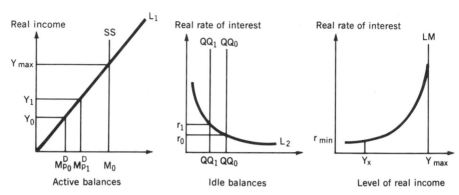

Suppose income is Y_0. Then the demand for *active* balances is $M^D_{p(active)_0}$. Hence the supply of the idle balances is $M_0 - M^D_{p(active)_0}$. This is shown by the curve QQ_0. The equilibrium rate of interest is r_0. Thus (Y_0, r_0) are a pair of values which equate the community's planned holdings of money balances with the money supply.

Now assume income to be Y_1. The new supply curve of *idle* balances is QQ_1. The new equilibrium rate of interest is r_1. Hence (Y_1, r_1) is a second pair of values at which the demand for money equals the supply. Clearly by running through all possible levels of Y—and finding the associated equilibrium values of r, we can trace out a curve—which we call the *LM* curve—showing *all the pairs of values of r and Y at which the money market is in equilibrium.*

The *position* of the *LM* curve depends upon:

1) the L_1 and L_2 functions: the two liquidity functions as they are often called;

2) the quantity of money (M_0);

3) the assumed level of prices (p).

The *shape* of the curve is dominated, as the diagram shows, by the L_2 function. Over a range this curve is horizontal at the rate of interest r_{min}. This tells us that so long as income is equal to or less than Y_x the *demand* for active balances is such that the *supply* of idle balances (the money supply *less* the quantity for active balances) is sufficient to keep interest at the minimum level acceptable to the community.

As income rises above Y_x, and thus the quantity of money demanded for active balances also rises, so does the equilibrium interest rate. This reflects the fact that, to obtain additional active balances, bonds must be sold and to do this their price must now fall since, with the prevailing hold-ing of idle balances, wealth owners are no longer indifferent—as they were to the left of Y_x—between holding money and bonds. At income Y_{max} the *LM* curve becomes vertical. At this income level the whole of the existing money supply is required as active balances. Hence, so long as the L_1 function is unaltered, Y_{max} (given the value of p) is the highest level of *real income* which the community can finance with the given money supply. Attempts to obtain additional active balances, by offering bonds for sale, cannot succeed. They can only drive up interest rates by lowering bond prices.

THE COMPLETE MODEL

Now that we have constructed both the *IS* and *LM* curves we can put them on a single diagram. This is done in Figure 13.3.

Figure 13.3 / *The determination of the equilibrium income and the equilibrium rate of interest, given the LM and the IS schedules.*

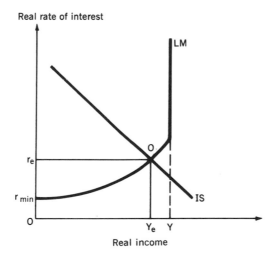

The curves cut at the point O which has coordinates Y_e and r_e. The sig-nificance of this point is clear from the definition of *IS* and *LM*. Because O lies on *IS* then Y_e and r_e are a pair of values at which

$$C_p + I_p = Y$$

and the *goods market is in equilibrium*. Because O lies on *LM* then Y_e and r_e are a pair of values at which

$$M_p^D = M_p^S$$

and the *money market is in equilibrium*.

It follows that Figure 13.3 describes the full equilibrium of the system; in short, it shows how the equilibrium values of the *two* dependent variables, income and the rate of interest, are simultaneously determined by the independent variables which are, *as a first approximation,*

1) the propensity to consume schedule;
2) the marginal efficiency of investment schedule;
3) the liquidity preference (L_1 and L_2) functions;
4) the money supply; and, in the simple version of the model,
5) the given level of prices.

Why do we say "as a first approximation"? Simply because in depicting our system in these terms we need to remember that the first three independent variables—as we are here defining them—are themselves simplifications. For example, our propensity to consume schedule is a relationship between

$$C_p \qquad\qquad Y \qquad\qquad r$$
real planned consumption *and* real income *and* interest rate .

We derived it from a consumption function hypothesis of the form[1]:

$$C_p = Q + cY + dA + e\alpha$$

by taking as given the value of Q, d, A, c, and thus obtaining

$$C_p = [\bar{Q} + \bar{d}\bar{A} + \bar{e}\bar{\alpha}] + cY.$$

Analogously to write the demand for active balances as a function of Y we not only have to take p (the price level) as given, but also u_y, the degree of uncertainty with regard to future income receipts and payments, while to draw the L_2 function we need to take as given the expected ("safe") rate of interest ($\hat{r}$) and the degree of uncertainty with respect to r which we have called u_r.

In short, in interpreting Figure 13.3, the reader needs to keep constantly in mind not only that the IS and LM curves depend on the four independent variables listed above but that these themselves are but convenient simplifications of relatively complicated theories. Provided this is done, Figure 13.3 is a convenient and useful device for thinking about problems in the theory of income determination.

In Figure 13.3 we do not show *directly* the determination of employment. However since we can from the figure determine Y_e—the equilibrium

1. In this form we have omitted the rate of interest for reasons given earlier.

level of real output (income)—we need only to refer back to our short-run production function (Chapter 6) to find the equilibrium level of employment.

WHAT THE MODEL PREDICTS

Now that we have got our model, what predictions does it yield? A prediction, we must recall, is a statement of the form:

if X occurs in context *Y, then Z* will occur.

Our model is not specified quantitatively. Hence our predictions can only be qualitative. Let us generate a few to show how the model operates.

An Increase in the Marginal Efficiency of Investment / This means a *right-ward* shift of the MEI schedule. From Figure 13.1 we see that this shifts the *IS* curve to the *right*. In *general* the new equilibrium will give a higher level of income and a higher rate of interest than the initial level. The precise result, however, will depend upon the nature of the initial equilibrium. The geometry of this is shown in Figure 13.4 where *IS'* is the position of the *IS* curve after the MEI has increased.

What lies behind the geometry?

The rightward shift in the MEI raises the level of planned investment at each interest rate. Hence the multiplier comes into operation to raise income. However, as income rises the quantity of active balances de-

Figure 13.4 / *A shift in the IS curve and the changes in the level of income and the rate of interest.*

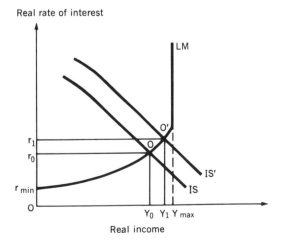

manded increases. To satisfy this demand, bonds are offered for sale and bond prices fall (the interest rate rises). This rise in the interest rate brings about an *induced* decline in investment which thus increases by less than the *autonomous* increase brought about by the shift in the MEI schedule. Our prediction is, therefore, that an increase in the MEI schedule will in general raise *income* and *the rate of interest*.

The conditions we assume for this result are:

1) *given* and *invariant* money supply and price level;
2) *given* and *invariant* propensity to consume schedule;
3) *given* and *invariant* liquidity functions.

An Increase in Liquidity Preference / This is usually interpreted, as a matter of geometry, as an upward shift in the L_2 function which leaves unchanged the level of the minimum acceptable interest rate and, of course, the maximum money income which, given the price level, the given money supply can finance.

How can such a shift come about? The reader can refer to Chapter 12 for the full range of possibilities but two obvious reasons for such a shift are an upward revision in $\hat{r}$ (the expected rate of interest) and an increase in u_r (uncertainty about the future of r). Either can occur separately: alternatively they may occur together. What are the consequences of such an increase in liquidity preference?

As a result of this increased demand for idle balances the *LM* curve shifts to the *left*. The result, as is shown in Figure 13.5, is, in general, a new equilibrium with a higher rate of interest and a lower level of income.

What is the economic mechanism underlying this result?

Figure 13.5 / *An increase in liquidity preference.*

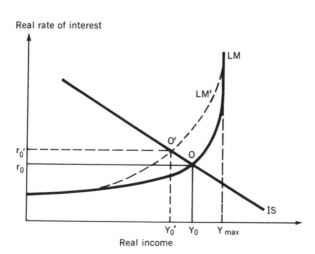

The increase in the demand for *idle* balances means that, at the initial rate of interest and income the community's actual holding of idle balances is now less than their planned holding. Acocrdingly bonds are offered on the market as some people seek to move out of bonds and into money. As a result bond prices fall (interest rates rise). This rise in the rate of interest reduces real planned investment. Hence the multiplier comes into operation and incomes fall. This reduces the quantity of active balances demanded and so increases the supply of idle balances. This rise in the supply of idle balances somewhat reduces the extent to which the rate of interest increases. This is now less than it would have been had income remained constant.

What conditions are we assuming to reach this result? They are:

1) given and invariant propensity to consume schedule;
2) given and invariant MEI schedule;
3) given and invariant money supply and price level.

An Increase in the Money Supply / Suppose the money supply increases because of, let us say, the purchase of bonds from the general public by the Federal Reserve. In this case the additional money enters the system as a result of a capital account transaction. The new money does not enter the system as anyone's income but simply as an asset received for the transfer of another asset (bonds). What happens?

In terms of our diagram the *LM* curve moves to the *right*. Hence the new equilibrium is characterized by a higher level of income and a lower rate of interest than the old. This is shown in Figure 13.6.

Figure 13.6 / *An increase in the money supply.*

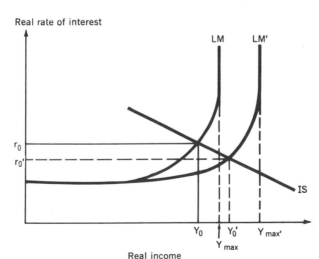

What is the mechanism?

By hypothesis the government is purchasing bonds from the public and giving money in exchange. At the initial equilibrium the public was holding its preferred ratio of money/bonds. To persuade it to *raise* this ratio, the interest rate must fall. Hence as the government seeks to purchase bonds, bond prices rise to persuade those who, at the initial prices preferred bonds to money, to move *out of* bonds and *into* money. A rise in bond prices is a fall in interest rates. The mechanism is thus straightforward.

The fall in the rate of interest induces an increase in investment. This brings the multiplier into operation and raises income. The rise in income increases the quantity of active balances demanded. Hence the final increase in the supply of idle balances is *less* than the increase in the money supply and the fall in the rate of interest *less* than it would have been if income had not changed.

You should work out the conditions we assume to reach this result.

The qualitative predictions set out above have been reached by a highly formal process of reasoning in which the assumed conditions under which they will be valid are stated in some detail. This is a necessary step in economic analysis. But it is very far from being the whole of economics. We must always remember that a shift in one schedule may itself induce changes in others. According to our model such induced changes need not occur. Whether they do so or not is a question of fact. It follows that, after making a prediction from the model and specifying the conditions under which it is valid, it is essential to consider whether, in practice, these conditions are likely to hold or not and, if they are not, in what way we should modify our initial prediction.

To give an example: we predicted that *if* the MEI schedule shifted upward, then *both* income *and* the rate of interest would tend to rise. We reached this result by assuming, among other things, unchanged L_1 and L_2 functions.

Suppose the MEI schedule shifted upward because of a decline in business uncertainty. Might the factors which brought this about not also lead to a decline in the uncertainty regarding future income payments and receipts (thus shifting the L_1 function) or the uncertainty regarding the future expected interest rate (thus shifting the L_2 function)? If so can we be very confident in our prediction that the rate of interest would rise?

This sort of consideration is important. Formal theoretical analysis is the first step in economic analysis. And it is essential. Failure to specify our model and its properties carefully and precisely is simply to invite confusion. The second step, however, must always be to review the assumptions underlying any given prediction. Failure to do this is to risk irrelevance.

WEAKNESSES OF THE MODEL

In its present form the model has four principal weaknesses which we must try to remove in later chapters.

In the first place it is entirely static. This means that we can use it only to compare positions of (short period) equilibrium and not to discuss how the system moves from one equilibrium position to another. For many problems, for example, the stability of the model and for the theory of investment, dynamics are of crucial importance. In short we need at least some elementary dynamic developments.

In the second place the model admits no government activity and assumes that there is no international trade. This reduces its usefulness for the study of policy problems. We need extensions here.

In the third place the model treats the price level as given and invariant: that is, as an *exogenous* variable. This is convenient but no more than that. We need a theory of prices.

All these weaknesses are removed in later chapters.

QUESTIONS AND EXERCISES

1. "If the rate of investment is greater the *lower* is the rate of interest, why is it that, as a matter of observation, the rate of interest is high when investment is high?" Explain.

2. Predict the consequences for income, employment, and the rate of interest of a decrease in liquidity preference. Explain your prediction. State clearly the assumptions on which your prediction is based. Are there any special cases?

3. From the following information construct the *IS* and *LM* curves and graph them. Then find the equilibrium value of income (Y) and the rate of interest (r).

$$C_p = A + bY \qquad \text{when} \quad A = 100 \quad b = 0.8$$

$$I_p = Z - gr \qquad \text{when} \quad Z = 1000 \quad g = 10$$

$$M_1^D = kYp \qquad \text{when} \quad k = 0.25 \quad p = 1$$

$$M_2^D = R - hr \qquad \text{when} \quad R = 1375 \quad h = 50$$

$$M^S = M_0 \qquad \text{when} \quad M_0 = 2500$$

$$r_{min} = 2.0 \text{ per cent.}$$

One way of increasing the equilibrium level of Y is to reduce r to its minimum level. Suppose this is done.

1) What is the new equilibrium level of Y?

2) What is the minimum value of the money supply necessary to equate r to r_{min} at the new equilibrium level of Y?

3) What are the consequences of a shift in the consumption schedule raising A to 200?

4. Using the model of Question 3, assume the investment function to shift upwards so that, in the new situation,

$$I_p = Z + \Delta Z - gr \quad \text{where } Z \text{ and } g \text{ are as before but}$$
$$\Delta Z = 100$$

Calculate the new equilibrium level of: income (Y); interest (r); planned investment (I_p).

What is the value of the multiplier? the *induced* change in I_p?

5. Write down as fully as possible the assumptions underlying the consumption and investment functions of Question 3: What are

the interest elasticity of M_2^D when $r = 4$ percent;

the income elasticity of C_p when income is 5300;

the interest elasticity of investment when $r = 4$ percent?

7. Using the data of Question 3, suppose the price level to double so that $p = 2$. Which curve (IS or LM) is affected? Why? Calculate the new equilibrium values of income and interest.

8. "An increase in the propensity to save does not lower the rate of interest. On the contrary it lowers income."

"An increase in the propensity to save always lowers the rate of interest. In some cases it may also lower income."

Discuss these two statements in the light of the analysis of this chapter.

9. In Question 4 the autonomous change in $I_p \equiv \Delta Z = 100$. According to the simple multiplier theory the change in equilibrium income should be given by:

$$\Delta Y = \Delta Z \frac{1}{1 - c} \quad \text{where } c \equiv \frac{\partial C_p}{\partial H}$$

From Question 3 the value of C is 0.5. Hence we should find

$$\Delta Y = \Delta Z \frac{1}{1 - 0.5} = 2 \Delta Z$$

Reconcile this result with your answers to Question 4. What are the *ceteris paribus* assumptions of the simple multiplier which are not satisfied in the more general model? Illustrate the simple multiplier on the IS/LM diagram. Is there any part of the diagram to which simple multiplier theory is applicable?

10. Suppose the money supply were increased not by purchases of bonds from the general public but by a single payment to all persons reaching their

twenty-first birthday in a given year. How would your analysis differ from the analysis in the text? Why would it differ? Can you predict the change in the interest rate?

11. Reconstruct the model of Question 3 by assuming the speculative demand for money to be absent. Does any part of Question 3 still have meaning? If so, how are the answers to it modified by the new hypothesis?

12. If the MEI schedule is volatile, how will income and the rate of interest behave? Do your conclusions throw any light on Question 1?

13. On what behavior hypotheses would the *IS* curve be a horizontal straight line? Do they seem plausible to you? On what hypotheses would it be vertical?

14. Analyze the consequences for income, employment, and the interest rate of an increase in the equality of income distribution. Illustrate your analysis on the *IS/LM* diagram.

15. "A movement *along* one function may in practice cause a *shift* in another function." Do you agree? Suggest plausible examples.

SUGGESTED READING

G. Ackley, *Macroeconomics Theory* (New York: Macmillan, 1961) Chap. 14.

A. H. Hansen, *Monetary Theory and Fiscal Policy* (New York: McGraw-Hill, 1949) Chaps. 4–5.

W. T. Newlyn, *The Theory of Money* (New York: Oxford, 1962) Chap. 8.

J. M. Keynes, *The General Theory of Employment, Interest and Money* (New York: Harcourt, Brace, 1936) Chap. 18.

J. R. Hicks "Mr. Keynes and the Classics," in *Readings in the Theory of Income Distribution,* W. Fellner and B. Haley (London: Allen & Unwin, 1950). *Advanced reference.*

14

The Public Sector and the International Sector

Now THAT we have developed our static theory of the determination of income and interest in an economy *without* either government economic activity or international trade, we need to extend our model to take account of these elements of the problem.

We begin by introducing government economic activity.

THE PUBLIC SECTOR

Where the system contains a government sector, aggregate demand must be redefined to include the real planned spending of government on goods and services. This we divide into two components, government investment and government consumption, writing:

$$G_p \equiv I_g + C_g. \tag{14.1}$$

Using this notation our equilibrium condition is:

$$Y = C_p + I_p + G_p. \tag{14.2}$$

This modification takes account of government spending. We now take account of the *direct taxes* imposed by government by reframing our consumption hypothesis in terms of personal disposable income rather than national income.

Reference to Chapter 3 tells us that if we disregard the complication of undistributed profits,

$$\text{personal disposable income} \equiv Y - T + R \qquad (14.3)$$

where $\qquad T \equiv$ direct taxes on persons

$\qquad\qquad\qquad R \equiv$ income transfers to households.

We now introduce the consumption function hypothesis by writing:

$$C_p = Q + c(Y - T + R), \qquad (14.4)$$

which relates planned expenditure on consumption to real personal disposable income.

For convenience let us write real planned investment as a function of the rate of interest.

$$I_p = H - br \qquad (14.5)$$

We now assume that the real planned expenditure of government ($\equiv G_p$) is *exogenous*: that is, is unaffected by the value of any other variable in the system. Formally:

$$G_p = \bar{G}$$

Substituting yields:

$$\left.\begin{aligned}
Y &= C_p + I_p + G_p \\
&= Q + c(Y - T + R) + H - br + \bar{G} \\
&= [Q + H + \bar{G} - br + c(R - T)]\frac{1}{1-c}
\end{aligned}\right\} \qquad (14.6)$$

which is an expression for the equilibrium value of output (income) in terms of

the *autonomous* expenditures, $Q, H, \bar{G}, -br, c(R - T)$;
the *rate of interest* (r); and
the *multiplier* $\dfrac{1}{1-c}$.

By examining this expression it is easy to see the effect on the equilibrium value of income of governmental economic decisions.

Suppose, for example, that the government sector increases its expenditure on goods and services (G_p) by an amount ΔG per period. Clearly the resultant increase in income will be:

$$\Delta Y = \Delta \bar{G} \frac{\partial Y}{\partial \bar{G}} = \Delta \bar{G} \frac{1}{1-c}$$

so that the multiplier for government expenditure on goods and services *financed by borrowing*—or the "marginal response coefficient"—is:

$$\frac{\partial Y}{\partial \overline{G}} = \frac{1}{1 - c},$$

(14.7)

the familiar multiplier of Chapter 8.

Why do we say *financed by borrowing?* Expenditure must always be financed in the sense that the money required to undertake it must be made available. The government derives its receipts from two sources: *taxation* and *borrowing*. In our example we have postulated an increase in $\overline{G}$ *without* any increase in T ($=$ tax receipts). Hence the increased expenditure *must be financed by borrowing*.

Notice that $\partial Y/\partial \overline{G}$ is the "marginal response coefficient" relating the increase in income to an increase in G_p with *everything else held constant.* In practice, as we have already shown, an increase in Y raises the quantity of active (M_1) balances demanded and this, with a given money supply, will raise the rate of interest (r). Since a higher level of the rate of interest is associated with a reduced rate of real planned investment by the private sector, the *total change* in income will be *less* than indicated by the simple multiplier of (14.7). We shall illustrate this proposition in a moment by reference to our *IS/LM* diagram.

What is the "simple" (interest rate constant) multiplier for an increase in direct taxation?

Suppose T is increased. A glance at (14.6) shows that the simple multiplier is

$$\frac{\partial Y}{\partial T} = -\frac{c}{1 - c}.$$

(14.8)

This tells us that an increase in taxation *reduces* income (i.e., the multiplier operates in reverse). It also tells us that an increase in taxation does not have the full "simple" multiplier but a smaller one: $c/1 - c$.

We can now show a result known as "the balanced budget" theorem. Suppose the authorities increase government expenditure on goods and services by an amount $\Delta\overline{G}$. From (14.7) the resulting *increase* in income (assuming the rate of interest is held constant) is:

$$\Delta Y_1 = \Delta\overline{G} \frac{\partial Y}{\partial \overline{G}} = \Delta\overline{G} \frac{1}{1 - c}.$$

Assume further that the additional expenditure is financed entirely by taxation. The increase in taxation ΔT *reduces* income. We have:

$$\Delta Y_2 = \Delta T \frac{-c}{1 - c}.$$

The net effect of the *two* transactions is:

$$\Delta Y_1 + \Delta Y_2 = \Delta \bar{G} \frac{1}{1-c} - \Delta T \frac{c}{1-c}.$$

Assume that $\Delta \bar{G} = \Delta T$, i.e., that the whole of the additional expenditure on goods and services is financed by additional taxation. Hence the effect of an increase in government expenditure financed by taxation is:

$$\Delta Y = \Delta \bar{G} \left[\frac{1}{1-c} - \frac{c}{1-c} \right]$$

$$= \Delta \bar{G} \left[\frac{1-c}{1-c} \right]$$

$$= \Delta \bar{G}. \tag{14.9}$$

This tells us that the multiplier effect of an increase in government expenditure financed by taxation is unity.

At first sight this is a somewhat surprising result. A little reflection, however, shows that there is really nothing surprising about it at all. Let us write out the multiplier series of an increase in government expenditure using the method of Chapter 8. We have

$$\Delta Y_1 = \Delta \bar{G} + c\Delta \bar{G} + c^2 \Delta \bar{G} + \cdots + c^n \Delta \bar{G}$$

$$= \Delta \bar{G}(1 + c + c^2 + c^3 + \cdots + c^n) \tag{14.10}$$

The corresponding series for the increase in taxation is:

$$\Delta Y_2 = -\Delta T(c + c^2 + c^3 + \cdots + c^n) \tag{14.10a}$$

The latter series, it should be noted, *lacks the first term found in the government expenditure series. This reflects the fact that an increase in taxation does not reduce household consumption by its full amount but only by that part of the additional tax which would have been spent on consumption.* This is the increase in tax multiplied by the marginal propensity to consume, i.e.,—$c\Delta T$. Subsequent reductions in consumption occur because the initial fall in consumption $-c\Delta T$ reduces incomes by this amount and thus consumption by $-c^2 \Delta T$ and so on.

Obviously if we now add ΔY_1 and ΔY_2 and equate $\Delta \bar{G}$ and ΔT, all the terms in the two series drop out apart from the first term in the government expenditure series. To show this, perform the operation thus:

$$\Delta Y_1 + \Delta Y_2 \equiv \Delta Y$$
$$= \Delta \bar{G}[1 + (c - c) + (c^2 - c^2) + (c^3 - c^3) + \cdots + (c^n - c^n)]$$
$$= \Delta \bar{G}$$

so that we have

$$\Delta Y = \Delta \bar{G}, \tag{14.10b}$$

the result we obtained above.

Still another of the many ways of demonstrating the balanced budget theorem is the following: When the government imposes taxes to finance the new expenditures, some of these taxes come from taxpayers, reducing their saving rather than their consumption. Since an increase in taxes works like any other reduction in disposable income, households cut their consumption by $\Delta \overline{G} c$ and reduce their planned saving by $\Delta \overline{G}(1 - c)$. But since planned investment is constant, actual saving must be constant too. That is, income must rise until the public is willing to increase its saving by $\Delta \overline{G}(1 - c)$, thus offsetting the initial decrease in planned saving; in other words, until $\Delta Y(1 - c) = \Delta \overline{G}(1 - c)$. Hence $\Delta Y = \Delta \overline{G}$.

Before leaving the balanced budget multiplier we should note that when one abandons the assumptions of the model being used here and looks at the actual effect of government expenditures and taxes in a specific situation the balanced budget multiplier need not be unity. Thus the marginal propensities to consume of taxpayers and the recipients of government expenditures may differ, and if so, the balanced budget multiplier will not be unity. Similarly, an increase in government expenditures and taxes may affect private investment and change the income level in this way. Moreover, if the government uses the tax receipts to buy, not newly created goods and services, but existing assets, such as land, the balanced budget multiplier will be less than unity. And if it spends the tax receipts only on transfer payments, then the balanced budget multiplier will be zero. But, nonetheless, the balanced budget theorem teaches us an important lesson. It tells us that, except in the case of transfer payments, an equal increase in taxes and in government expenditures will not be neutral, but will change the level of income.

For simplicity we can tabulate these results as follows:

Table 14.1 / *Various multipliers (interest rate constant).*

ACTION	METHOD OF FINANCE	ΔY	SIMPLE MULTIPLIER	FULL OR TOTAL MULTIPLIER
Increase in government expenditures on goods and services	Borrowing	$\Delta \overline{G} \dfrac{1}{1 - c}$	$\dfrac{1}{1 - c}$	$\leq \dfrac{1}{1 - c}$
	Taxation	ΔG	unity	≤ 1
	Reduction in transfer payments	ΔG	unity	≤ 1
Increase in taxation	—	$\Delta T \dfrac{-c}{1 - c}$	$\dfrac{-c}{1 - c}$	$\geq \dfrac{-c}{1 - c}$
Increase in transfer payments	Borrowing	$\Delta R \dfrac{c}{1 - c}$	$\dfrac{c}{1 - c}$	$\leq \dfrac{c}{1 - c}$

In this table the "full multiplier" is the value of the multiplier allowing for (1) the effect of the increase in income on the rate of interest; (2) the effect of the increase in the rate of interest on the rate of real planned investment by the private sector; (3) the effect of the change in real planned investment on income.

To illustrate the action of the "simple" and "full" multipliers let us go back to our *IS/LM* diagram.

We have, from equation (14.6), the following equilibrium condition in the goods market:

$$Y = [Q + \bar{G} + H - br + c(R - T)]\frac{1}{1 - c}. \qquad (14.11)$$

From this, just as we did previously, we can find all *pairs* of values of r and Y which equate aggregate demand and supply. This gives us a new *IS* curve the position of which now depends on $\bar{G} \times R$ and T: that is, upon the fiscal decisions of government.

The *LM* curve we find in the same way as in Chapter 6. The resulting diagram is set out below. The initial equilibrium is at Y_0, r_0.

Figure 14.1 / *The effect of increased government expenditure on goods and services $(\bar{G})$.*

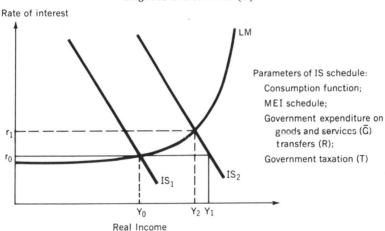

Suppose now the G is increased. The *IS* curve shifts to the right. *If the rate of interest remains unaltered, the new equilibrium of income is Y_1.* The change in income $(\Delta Y \equiv Y_1 - Y_0)$ is the result of the "simple" multiplier operating on $\Delta \bar{G}$. That is,

$$\Delta Y = \Delta \bar{G} \frac{1}{1 - c}.$$

In practice, assuming a constant money supply, the rate of interest will *not* in general remain unaltered. Hence we shall move not to Y_1 but to Y_2. Thus

$$\Delta Y' \equiv Y_2 - Y_0$$

is a diagrammatic representation of the change in income resulting from the operation of the "full multiplier." Except in the special case in which the *IS* curve (before *and* after its shift) cuts the *LM* curve at the minimum rate of interest,—or the *IS* curve is vertical—we shall always have $\Delta Y' < \Delta Y$.

In short, the change ($\Delta Y'$) allows for the effects of the higher level of income on the demand for money; the increased demand for money on the rate of interest; the higher rate of interest on the rate of real planned investment by the private sector and the lower rate of real planned investment on income.

ELEMENTS OF FISCAL POLICY

Now that we know how the government's decisions regarding expenditure on goods and services, taxation, and transfer payments influence income and employment, we can see something of their importance. Suppose, for example, it is the objective of the authorities to maintain the percentage of the labor force unemployed within the range of 4–4½. This objective given the production function defines a range of output (income) $Y_f - Y_f'$ which is shaded in Figure 14.2. Suppose further that income is at Y_0 with unemployment at, say, 5 percent.

Figure 14.2 / *Fiscal policy and full employment.*

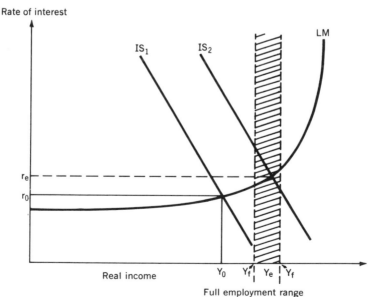

Full employment range

Clearly, by changing $\overline{G}$, R, or T, the authorities can raise the equilibrium level of income to a value Y_e which falls within the range $Y_f - Y_f'$ and thus restore "full employment."

Fiscal policy—defined as the manipulation of government expenditure, transfers, and taxation—is thus a powerful device for controlling the level of output and employment. This is the first lesson to be derived from the formal discussion of the preceding section.

There is, however, a second lesson. This is that there are no simple rules by which, merely by reference to the employment target, we can calculate the "proper" fiscal policy. For example to raise income from Y_0 to a level within the range $Y_f - Y_f'$ the government could

1) increase $\overline{G}$ and finance the increase by borrowing;

2) increase $\overline{G}$ and finance the increase by raising taxation or reducing transfers;

3) reduce taxation;

4) increase transfers, financing the increase by borrowing; or

5) make use of some combination of 1–4.

The point is that *each* of these courses of action will raise Y. Each therefore *can* be used to reach "full employment." The employment objective cannot therefore tell us *which* is the one to choose. It follows that the choice must be made on other grounds. In short, there is an infinite number of "possible" fiscal policies which will raise Y to "full employment" levels. Thus the sort of statement which runs: "To increase income and employment the government should run a deficit (i.e., increase $\overline{G}$ or R and finance the increase by borrowing)" is, at best, a half truth. Such a policy *will* raise employment. But so will an infinity of others. There is, therefore, no rule telling us we must adopt it.

The third lesson is that some policies are obviously inconsistent with the objectives which the authorities seek to attain. To illustrate in terms of an example: if the economy is at Y_0 and the government wishes to restore "full employment" it would be inconsistent to *reduce* $\overline{G}$, raise T, *or reduce R,* for these policies must, if our model is correct, reduce aggregate demand and thus output and employment.

This, no doubt, seems a very obvious conclusion but, it was not always so. Indeed it was not so as recently as the Great Depression of the thirties; as employment and output fell during the Great Depression, governments in many countries sought to *avoid* deficits, to *cut* expenditure, and even, on occasion, to *raise* taxes. As a result they reduced aggregate demand and made the depression, quite unnecessarily, a great deal worse than it need have been. This was usually done on the argument that since an individual family faced by a fall in its income must, to avoid bankruptcy, reduce its expenditure, so too must a nation faced with a fall in national income. The fallacy in this, often called the fallacy of composition, consists in assuming that what is true for an individual is necessarily true for the sum of individuals.

The fourth lesson, which is in reality a special case of the third, is simply that there is no particular virtue in a "balanced budget"; that is, a situation in which $\overline{G} + R = T$. Here again the argument is often derived from the consideration of an individual household and then, via the fallacy of composition, applied to the community as a whole. "No family can, for long, spend more than its income: that is, run a deficit. A nation is a family. Hence what is true for the family must be true for the nation." It is easy to see that this "rule" too is nonsense. This does not mean that there are no arguments in favor of a balanced budget: there are many. But the question of whether to maintain a balanced budget, run a deficit or a surplus, is an open one which has to be considered in relation to the economic objectives of the authorities and the properties of the economic system. It cannot be settled by appeal to some "rule"—and certainly not by appeal to a "rule" which involves a particularly glaring example of the fallacy of composition.

The fifth lesson which we can obtain from our discussion is this. In considering a budget introduced by a particular Administration we must always ask: Will this budget influence aggregate demand in a way consistent with the Administration's employment objectives?

THE INTERNATIONAL SECTOR

We now consider the effect on our theory of introducing international transactions.

Clearly, as we have already learned from national income accounting, some part of the demand for domestic output arises out of the expenditure by foreigners. To a manufacturer it is a matter of indifference whether his output is purchased by a Scotsman, a Scandinavian, a Chinese, or the man next door, as long as the price after deduction of selling costs is the same. A purchase by a foreigner is a purchase which generates income just like any other.

We call the demand for domestic goods by foreigners "planned purchases of exports" (E_p), and assume that foreigners' plans are always carried out. Hence planned exports (E_p) equal actual exports (E) and these constitute an *addition* to domestic demands for domestic output.

Planned expenditure by a nation on goods and services is, as we have already seen, the sum of planned consumption, planned private investment, and planned government expenditure on goods and services. Some part of this expenditure will, however, not be devoted to the purchase of domestic output but to the purchase of output produced by foreigners. This we call imports (Z). Again we shall assume that planned purchases of imports (Z_p) equal actual purchases of imports (Z).

Clearly the purchase of imports does not generate domestic incomes but incomes abroad. Hence, from the point of view of the aggregate demand for domestic output, imports constitute a "leakage" from expenditure of the same type as planned saving. Hence Z, the total of imports, must be *subtracted* from domestic expenditure to arrive at the domestic expenditure on domestic output.

Accordingly our equilibrium condition in the goods market becomes:

$$Y = C_p + I_p + G_p + E - Z. \qquad (14.12)$$

This shows that our expression for aggregate demand now includes a term for exports (E) and imports (Z). This is helpful but we need now a theory to explain the value of exports (E) and the value of imports (Z).

Consider exports first. The exports of the U. S. are part of the imports of the rest of the world. As a first approximation we may think of the rest of the world's expenditures on our products as depending on two variables:

1) the level of real incomes in the rest of the world (Y_w)

2) the price of U. S. goods (and services) in relation to the prices of similar goods and services.

Formally we can write this simple hypothesis thus:

$$E = f\left(Y_w, \frac{P_w}{P_{US}}\right) \qquad (14.13)$$

where

$E \equiv$ actual $=$ planned, purchases of exports

$P_w \equiv$ prices of rest of the world's goods and services in their own currencies

$P_{US} \equiv$ prices of American goods and services in dollars.

The prices of U. S. goods are expressed in dollars. Other countries use other units of account such as the pound, franc, mark, pengo, rupee, and rouble. These prices can only be compared if we know the rate of exchange between the dollar and other currencies. Hence the rate P_w/P_{US} depends upon the rate of exchange. As we have written it, it is meaningless.

Let us call q the rate of exchange and interpret it to mean the price (in terms of foreign currency) of one dollar. A rise in q thus means that the dollar is worth *more* in terms of foreign currency and therefore that, for any given level of P_{US}, U. S. goods and services are relatively *dearer* than they were (to foreigners) and foreign goods and services relatively *cheaper* than they were (to U. S. residents).

Our exports hypothesis is now:

$$E = f\left(Y_w, \frac{P_w}{P_{US}}, q\right). \tag{14.14}$$

What general form do we expect this function to take? If real incomes rise in the rest of the world then, with no change in P_w, P_{US} or q, our expectation is that E will rise. In other words we expect the "marginal response coefficient" $\partial E/\partial Y_w$ to be positive but less than unity.

An increase in q makes American goods and services *dearer* to foreigners. With Y_w and P_w/P_{US} unchanged we would expect this to *reduce* E. Thus we expect the "marginal response coefficient" $\partial E/\partial q$ to be negative.

An increase in the ratio P_w/P_{US} makes U. S. goods *relatively cheaper* to foreigners. We would thus expect $\partial E/\partial(P_w/P_{US})$ to be positive.

The function (14.14) provides a very simple hypothesis with which to try to explain the rate of exports. Obviously many variables (foreign tariffs, trade regulations, and so on) are omitted. For our present purposes it is nevertheless helpful, because of the four variables on which we expect E to depend, *two,* namely Y_w and P_w, are determined in the rest of the world and are thus reasonably regarded as exogenous.

So far we are taking domestic prices to be constant. Hence P_{US} is invariant by assumption. It follows that, as far as the domestic economy is concerned, E can only be varied by alteration in the exchange rate (q). If we assume the exchange rate (q) to be invariant we may then reasonably regard E as an exogenous variable. This we shall do and write:

$$E = \bar{E}. \tag{14.14*}$$

What of imports? We have already argued that our exports (part of foreigners' imports) are likely to be dependent upon the real income of foreigners. By the same reasoning our imports (part of foreigners' exports) are likely to depend upon *our* real income.

Which is the appropriate income concept? If imports consisted entirely of consumption goods, it might be plausible to regard imports, like consumption expenditure itself, as dependent on personal disposable income. But imports consist not only of consumption goods, but include raw materials and other capital goods. The demand for these is much more plausibly related to national income or even gross national product. Accordingly we shall write our import hypothesis:

$$Z = f\left(Y, \frac{P_{US}}{P_w}, q\right) \tag{14.15}$$

and expect

$$0 < \partial Z/\partial Y < 1; \quad \partial Z/\partial(P_{UK}/P_w) > 0 \quad \text{and} \quad \partial Z/\partial q > 0.$$

We are taking P_{US} and q as given and invariant. Let us make the same assumption about P_w. We can then write a linear import function analogous to the linear consumption function

$$Z = F + zY,$$

where

$Z \equiv$ real imports

$F \equiv$ autonomous real imports

$z \equiv$ marginal propensity to import out of real national income $\equiv \partial Z / \partial Y$

$Y \equiv$ real national income.

This is illustrated in Figure 14.3.

Figure 14.3 / *The propensity to import.*

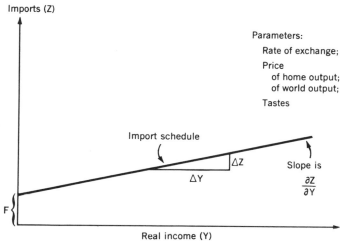

Substituting these relations into the equilibrium condition for aggregate demand, we have:

$$Y = C_p + I_p + G_p + E - Z$$
$$= Q + c(Y - T + R) + H - br + \overline{G} + \overline{E} - F - zY,$$

so that

$$Y = [Q + c(R - T) + H - br + \overline{G} + \overline{E} - F]\frac{1}{1 - c + z} \quad (14.16)$$

Now this expression (14.16) is analogous to our earlier expression (14.11) in that it gives the equilibrium level of income in terms of the *autonomous* items in expenditure; the rate of interest; and the multiplier. The difference between (14.16) and (14.11) occurs because the *autonomous* items now include exports (E) and that part of expenditure on imports which is independent of income (F), while the multiplier now depends upon the marginal propensity to import (z) as well as the marginal propensity to save $(1 - c)$.

Now, as we have remarked, $1 - c \equiv s \equiv$ the marginal propensity to save. Thus where our earlier multiplier was

$$\frac{1}{1 - c} \equiv \frac{1}{s}$$

our new multiplier is

$$\frac{1}{1 - c + z} \equiv \frac{1}{s + z}.$$

In short the appearance of the marginal propensity to import (z) in the multiplier reflects (and justifies) our earlier assertion that, *from the point of view of income determination,* expenditure on imports constitutes a "leakage" from expenditure on domestic output just as does saving. To put the same point slightly differently, the new form of the multiplier arises because the equilibrium condition which, in the simplest model is

planned saving = planned investment

is now

planned saving = planned investment *plus* (exports − imports)

or, explicitly recognizing the existence of the government sector,[1]

$$\left\{ \begin{array}{c} \text{planned saving of households} \\ \text{plus} \\ \text{planned saving of government} \end{array} \right\} = \left\{ \begin{array}{l} \text{planned investment of} \\ \text{private sector } \textit{plus} \\ \text{planned investment of} \\ \text{government sector } \textit{plus} \\ \text{(exports − imports).} \end{array} \right\}$$

The multiplier $\dfrac{1}{1 - c + z} \equiv \dfrac{1}{s + z}$ is often called the "international trade" multiplier. It is the multiplier appropriate to an economy engaging in international trade and maintaining constant interest rates. Thus, for example, the multipliers we have hitherto found become, when the international sector is introduced,

$$\frac{\partial Y}{\partial I_p} = \frac{1}{1 - c + z} \quad \text{investment multiplier}$$

1. The reader should refer to the national accounting identity of Chapter 3, which was
$$S \equiv I$$
$$\equiv I_c + I_g + I_f.$$

$$\frac{\partial Y}{\partial Q} = \frac{1}{1 - c + z} \quad \text{(autonomous) consumption multiplier}$$

$$\frac{\partial Y}{\partial G} = \frac{1}{1 - c + z} \quad \text{government expenditure multiplier}$$

$$\frac{\partial Y}{\partial T} = \frac{-c}{1 - c + z} \quad \text{taxation multiplier.}$$

These propositions the reader may readily verify for himself by carrying out the appropriate operations on (14.16).

We can now ask two questions. First, what effects do changes in international transactions have on the level of income and the balance of payments? Second, what effects do changes in the propensity to consume, private investment, or fiscal decisions have on the balance of payments?

Suppose there is an increase in exports by $\Delta \bar{E}$. Then, from (14.16), the increase in income is given by:

$$\Delta Y = \Delta \bar{E} \frac{1}{1 - c + z}.$$

In other words, given constant interest rates, incomes rise by the multiplier times the increase in exports.

What happens to the balance of payments? Exports increase, by assumption, by $\Delta \bar{E}$. This however raises income which, since imports are a function of income, brings about an *induced* increase in imports. The amount that imports increase depends upon

the rise in income $\Delta \bar{E} \dfrac{1}{1 - c + z}$; and

the marginal propensity to import (z).

Hence, the *change* in the balance of payments is given by:

increase in exports $-$ increase in imports

$$\Delta \bar{E} \quad - \quad z[\Delta \bar{E}] \frac{1}{1 - c + z}$$

$$= \Delta \bar{E} \frac{1 - c}{1 - c + z} = \Delta \bar{E} \frac{s}{s + z}.$$

Since s is greater than zero, this tells us that the balance of payments must improve but will never improve by as much as the increases in exports unless $z = 0$: that is, imports are *independent* of income.

We cannot speak unambiguously of an increase in imports but only of a *shift* (upward or downward) in the *import function*. Suppose the import function shifts upward (the propensity to import increases): what happens? First let us see what this means from the Figure 14.4.

In this figure we have assumed, as we did when discussing an increase

Figure 14.4 / *An upward shift in the propensity to import.*

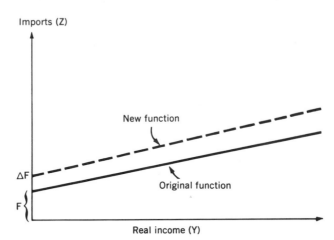

in the propensity to consume, that the shift in the function leaves its slope (z) unaltered. Formally then an increase in the propensity to import is an increase in F—the "constant" term in the import function. A glance at (14.16) tells us immediately that the change in income is

$$\Delta Y = -\Delta F \frac{1}{1 - c + z}.$$

In short, as we would expect, an increase in the propensity to import, like an increase in the propensity to save, *lowers* income.

What happens to the balance of payments? Exports, which are exogenous, do not change. We have, however, two types of change in imports. First the *autonomous increase* (ΔF). Second the *induced decrease* due to the decline in income operating via the marginal propensity to import ($z\Delta Y$). The change in the balance of payments is therefore:

increase in exports *minus* increase in imports

$$0 \quad - \quad [\Delta F + z\Delta Y]$$

$$- \left[\Delta F - z\Delta F \frac{1}{1 - c + z} \right]$$

$$- \left[\Delta F \frac{1 - c}{1 - c + z} \right].$$

Thus the balance of payments *deteriorates* by an amount which is greater than zero (since $1 - c \equiv s > 0$) but less than ΔF (the autonomous increase in imports) since $z > 0$.

What are the consequences of an increase in domestic investment? This means an upward shift in the investment function which, in our notation, is an increase in H. The increase in income is:

$$\Delta Y = \Delta H \frac{1}{1 - c + z}.$$

There is no change in exports so, once again, the change in the balance of payments comes about entirely through the change in imports. This change, *since the import function does not shift,* consists of the *increase* in imports *induced* by the increase in income. This is:

$$z\Delta Y = \frac{z}{1 - c + z} \Delta H,$$

which is the amount by which the balance of payments deteriorates.

It would be tedious, and pointless, to work out the consequences of increases in the propensity to consume, government expenditure on goods and services, taxation, or transfer payments. These you should establish for yourself. Our results can easily be summarized in a few simple propositions of great practical importance.

1) Any change in one (or more) of the *domestic* determinants of income will change income through the multiplier and thus bring about an *induced* change in imports and the state of the balance of payments.

2) Any change in exports will change income and bring about an induced change in imports.

3) Any change in the import function will change income and bring about both an *autonomous* and an *induced* change in imports.

Two points need now to be noticed. The first is that the multiplier $\frac{1}{1 - c + z}$ is the "simple" multiplier which is strictly applicable only when the rate of interest is constant. The "full" or "total" multiplier, assuming an invariant quantity of money, will be less than this because of the effect of the change in the rate of interest on real planned private investment.[2]

The second, and more important, point is that the *equilibrium of income* does not imply the equality of exports and imports: that is, *external equilibrium.* To illustrate this, suppose the economy is operating at 5 percent unemployment and exports = imports so that external equilibrium exists. If the government, in an attempt to reach "full employment," increases expenditure on goods and services, incomes will rise by an amount, assuming the interest rate to be constant, given by:

$$\Delta Y = \Delta \bar{G} \frac{1}{1 - c + z}.$$

The increase in income, however, will increase imports by an amount:

$$\Delta Z = \Delta Y = z\Delta G \frac{1}{1 - c + z}.$$

2. And, if planned consumption is a function of the interest rate, on consumption.

Hence the balance of payments will move into *deficit*. Since no country can, for long, import more than it can pay for by means of its exports, the authorities, in solving the "employment problem," find that they have created a "balance of payments problem."

We can put the same point in a number of different ways, two of which are particularly useful.

The first is to say that the equilibrium level of income and the state of the balance of payments are interdependent, *not* independent. Any change in one entails a change in the other.

The second is to say that the *full* equilibrium of the system requires, once international trade takes place, the simultaneous satisfaction of three conditions:

1) $Y = C_p + I_p + G_p + (E - Z)$
   i.e., aggregate demand = aggregate supply;

2) $M^D = M^S$
   i.e., demand for money = supply of money;

3) $E = Z$
   i.e., external receipts = external payments.

The importance of the interdependence between income and the state of the balance of payments differs in different countries. In the U. S. international trade is relatively unimportant as a component in GNP. Both the average and marginal propensities to import are small—probably of the order of 0.05. In Britain, on the other hand, international trade is of far greater significance and both the average and marginal propensities to import are far greater, the latter probably being of the order of 0.2. This means that while quite a large (absolute) increase in American GNP produces only a small (absolute) increase in imports, this is not so for Britain. As a result the British authorities, in endeavoring to implement a "full employment" policy, have constantly to divert their attention to the state of the balance of payments. Indeed the interdependence of income and the state of the balance of payments, as analyzed above, lies at the heart of many of the difficulties which have beset the British economy since the end of the Second World War.

QUESTIONS AND EXERCISES

1. How important are public sector expenditures in total demand? Prepare a table, using data from the latest *Economic Report of the President,* showing (1) the ratio of $\overline{G}/Y$ in each year; (2) the ratio $\Delta\overline{G}/\Delta Y$ in each year.

2. Suppose the government changes its tax system so that, for a given value of gross national product, direct taxes on income are reduced by $5 billion and indirect taxes increased by $5 billion thus leaving the total tax yield unaltered. What will be the consequences for (1) consumption; (2) aggregate demand; (3) the rate of interest; and (4) output?

3. "To control the economy the Federal Government manipulates tax rates and government spending." Explain. Which do you think is the easier to adjust and why?

4. "The maintenance of 'full employment' does not define the 'optimal' fiscal policy. It simply gives us one condition which the 'optimal' fiscal policy must satisfy." Explain. What other criteria would you wish to take into account in specifying the "optimal" fiscal policy? Why?

5. Analyze the consequences of an increase in welfare payments financed by increased taxation on those with incomes of over $25,000 per year. Why does the formal analysis of Chapter 14, second section, appear to suggest an answer at variance with the analysis of Chapter 8?

6. From the *Economic Report of the President* obtain annual data for U.S. imports and GNP for each year from 1960–1970. Plot each year's observations on a scatter diagram with imports on the vertical axis and GNP on the horizontal axis. Does a linear function usefully describe the observations? If not, why not? If so, fit such a function freehand and measure its slope. On what assumptions is this slope a good estimate of the marginal propensity to import?

7. Suppose import restrictions are imposed and reduce imports by 10 percent. Analyze the consequences for aggregate demand and employment.

8. Examine critically the assumption that the demand for American exports is independent of the level of American imports.

9. The model used to analyze fiscal decisions assumes that both the total revenue from direct taxes (T) and the total of transfer payments (R) are independent of the level of income. This is implausible. Replace these assumptions by the hypotheses

$$T = \hat{T} + tY \quad \text{where } t \equiv \frac{\partial T}{\partial Y} > 0 < 1;$$

$$R = \hat{R} + rY \qquad r \equiv \frac{\partial R}{\partial H} < 0 > -1.$$

Rework the analysis of the first section of this chapter. How do the new hypotheses modify the analysis?

10. A system such as that defined by Question 9 is said to have a measure of "built-in fiscal stabilization." Elucidate this statement and propose an appropriate way of measuring the "stabilization" provided. (Hint: compute the simple multipliers of Question 9 and the text.)

11. Does the "balanced budget theorem" hold for the system of Question 9? Assume an increase of ΔG in government expenditure which is to be

financed by reducing taxation and reducing transfer payments. How much of the additional revenue must be provided by a *shift* in the tax (and/or transfer function) and how much must be *induced* by the change in income for the balanced budget theorem to hold?

12. The model used in the first section, even when modified along the lines of Question 9, is oversimplified. What are its main limitations? How would you seek to develop it?

13. In practice the marginal rate of tax rises with income. Since this is so, is the hypothesis $T = \hat{T} + tY$ reasonable? Can you suggest a more plausible function? If so can you incorporate it in your answer to Question 9?

14. From the *Economic Report of the President* obtain estimates for the annual receipts of the government from direct taxation for each year from 1950–1970. Construct a "scatter diagram" with receipts from direct taxation on the vertical axis and national income on the horizontal axis. Use this scatter to reconsider your answer to Question 13. Is a linear function a reasonable approximation? If so, fit it to the observed points by eye and estimate (1) the marginal response coefficient $\partial T/\partial Y$; and (2) the income elasticity of direct tax receipts for the year 1970.

15. Assume that the U. S. needs to improve its current account balance of payments by $10 billion a year. If exports are exogenously determined and the marginal propensity to import is 0.25, what is the annual cost of doing this by reducing incomes?

16. Suppose a 1 percent devaluation would improve the current balance by $500 million a year. What is your estimate of the relative merits of achieving the $5 billion improvement mentioned in Question 15 by a 10 percent devaluation rather than the method of Question 15?

17. Retaining the quantitative assumptions of Question 16 what fiscal policy would you recommend should accompany a 10 percent devaluation? Give your reasons.

18. Is management of an economy simplified or otherwise by the existence of a numerically small marginal propensity to import? Why?

SUGGESTED READING

F. Brooman and H. Jacoby, *Macroeconomics* (Chicago: Aldine, 1970) Chaps. 8–9.

M. Evans, *Macroeconomic Activity* (New York: Harper and Row, 1959) Chap. 9.

E. Lundberg, *Instability and Economic Growth* (New Haven: Yale University Press, 1968).

15

Prices, Wages, and Output

IN THE PREVIOUS CHAPTERS we took up the determinants of aggregate demand. Now the time has come to look at aggregate supply and to see how the impact of aggregate demand changes is divided between output and prices. We cannot tell from a knowledge of aggregate demand alone the value of real income and of the price level. If we know that aggregate demand will change by a certain amount, we know that money income will change by the same amount, but we do not know how much of the change in money income will be a change in output and how much a change in prices. But, obviously, this is an important question; in fact, it may be the most difficult question in formulating stabilization policy. In a recession the government not only wants to raise money income, it wants this increase in money income to take the form of increased output and employment, not of higher prices. Similarly, in fighting inflation it is necessary to reduce aggregate demand, but the anti-inflation policy will obviously be a failure if its primary effect is to reduce output rather than the rate of price increase. To take a concrete example, in 1970–71, the United States faced a situation of both rising prices and unemployment. This situation would seem to call for both expansionary and contractive policies at the same time. The question facing the Administration was to what extent it could reduce the growth of aggregate demand to curb inflation without increasing unemployment too much.

Unfortunately, the macroeconomic theory of aggregate supply is not as fully developed as aggregate demand theory. In fact, it is quite undeveloped. During the 1930s when Keynes and others developed macroeconomic theory, the problem was one of inadequate demand, and the primary

237

task for economic policy was to raise money income. With large-scale unemployment and excess capacity there was a presumption that the main impact of an increase in aggregate demand would be on output rather than on prices; and even if prices rose, as they in fact did from 1933 on, this would merely offset their previous decline.[1] It was not until well into the postwar period that aggregate supply received much attention from Keynesian economists. And the main rival to Keynesian theory, the quantity theory, which we shall discuss in Chapter 17, has left aggregate supply essentially unanalyzed too. As a result aggregate supply theory is still an unsettled territory, and instead of presenting a single theory we will present two rival views.

THE TRADITIONAL APPROACH

Until a few years ago the standard way of analyzing aggregate supply was to start with the assumption—to be discussed further below—that money wages are fixed and can be taken as given. Each firm decides how much to produce by setting marginal revenue equal to marginal cost. If one works, as Keynes himself did, with a model of perfect competition, marginal revenue is equal to price; so that each firm then produces that output at which marginal cost equals price. As shown in Figure 15.1, we can, in this way, determine how much a firm produces as demand for its product changes. There is, however, a complication here; we cannot obtain *aggregate* supply by adding up the supply curves of various firms. The reason is that when one firm increases its output, it bids up factor and material prices and hence raises the marginal cost curve for other firms. A simple, though not very rigorous, way of getting around this problem is to think of the firm shown in Figure 15.1 as not just any firm, but as a "representative" firm with its marginal cost curve drawn on the assumption that other firms change their output in proportion to this firm's output.

We can now look at this marginal cost curve further. It has two components. One is labor cost and the other is the cost of using the firm's stock of capital. (This *user cost* of capital is less than total depreciation because some depreciation takes place in any case even if the capital equipment is not used.) On the usual assumptions of *micro*economic theory, this marginal cost curve slopes upward mainly because the marginal productivity of labor falls as the firm adds more labor to its existing stock of capital.

Instead of perfect competition one can assume that there are monopoly

1. The GNP deflator (on a 1958 basis) rose from 39.3 in 1933 to 44.5 in 1937, a 13 percent increase. In 1929, it had been 50.6.

Figure 15.1 / *Price output determination.*

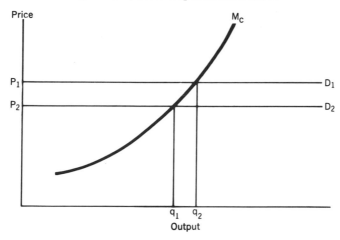

and oligopoly elements in the economy, or that all firms determine their prices, not by equating marginal revenue to marginal cost, but by adding a fixed mark-up to variable costs. This does not change the principle. In either case we can think of the firm as taking its labor and materials cost and adding a certain amount to it regardless of whether this amount is determined by the user cost of capital, by the degree of monopoly, or by the firm's traditional mark-up policy.

We now have to ask what determines marginal labor cost. There are two factors. One is the firm's production function, which we can take as given, and the other is the money wage rate. In traditional Keynesian macroeconomics the money wage rate is usually considered as given too. It depends upon the bargaining power of workers and employers, and is determined by a bargaining process outside the model. One important aspect of this exogenously determined money wage rate is that it is inflexible downward, although it *is* flexible upward. Workers, in the Keynesian model, bargain mainly for a certain money wage, and not a real wage. Hence, even if prices fall, workers resist a corresponding cut in their money wages. And while workers *do* use rising prices as an argument for higher wages, they are much more willing to let their real wage be cut by a price rise than by a cut in their money wages.

Money wages, in the traditional Keynesian model, are rigid, not only if prices fall, but also if employment declines. The labor market is highly imperfect. It acts as a market governed by a traditional minimum "rate for the job" rather than as a freely adjusting competitive market. Workers generally choose unemployment rather than work at less than standard wage rates. This may be due to union wage-fixing, but it need not be. Even prior to the 1930s, when unions accounted for only a small part of the labor force, money wages declined very little, if at all, during recessions.[2]

Thus, traditional Keynesian theory determines the price level in three stages. First, there is an exogenously determined money wage. Second, this money wage when combined with information about the production function determines wage costs per unit of output. Third, businessmen add a mark-up (which may, or may not, be competitively determined) to their labor costs. If one takes the mark-up and the production function as given, one can then say that the price level is determined by the wage rate and by the level of output. The level of output is relevant because with the marginal physical product of labor declining as output rises, labor cost per unit of output rises as output increases.

However, for many purposes it is convenient to simplify the analysis by ignoring the declining marginal product of labor and, further, to assume that until full employment is reached wage rates, as well as mark-ups, are constant. But once full employment is reached, the production function for the economy becomes completely inelastic, since output cannot be increased. As a result any rise in demand results in a proportional increase in prices and no increase at all in output. Such an aggregate supply curve with an "elbow" at full employment is shown by line *A* in Figure 15.2. It

Figure 15.2 / *Output prices and output.*

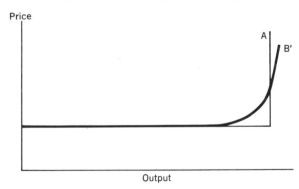

is important to note what this supply curve is and what it is not. It is *not* supposed to be an accurate representation of the way the aggregate supply curve *actually* looks. In actuality wages and prices are likely to start rising well before "full employment" is reached. In any case, due to the possibility of inducing additional workers to enter the labor force by raising wages and making jobs easy to get, and due to the possibility of scheduling over-

2. See Clarence Long, "The Illusion of Wage Rigidity: Long and Short Cycles in Wages and Labor Costs," *Review of Economics and Statistics*, Vol. XLII (May 1960), pp. 140–51.

time work, there is no single point of full employment. Instead of having an elbow, the aggregate supply curve simply becomes steep, as is shown by line *B* in Figure 15.2, though eventually it would become completely inelastic. The simple aggregate supply curve shown by line *A* is what is called an "idealization." Although it is known to be an inaccurate description of the real world, it is for many purposes a convenient simplifying assumption. It allows us to dichotomize the economy into two stages: one, underemployment, in which only output responds to changes in aggregate demand; and the other, pure inflation, in which *only* prices respond. The use of such idealizations is not unique to economics; for example, physicists talk about a pure vacuum.

So far in this chapter we have considered only aggregate supply. Since prices and output are determined by both supply and demand, we should now try to combine aggregate supply and aggregate demand and show their interrelation. But to do this we need a new mechanism.

We can use, with slight modification, a mechanism originally developed by Keynes. Keynes presented his analysis in terms of employment rather than of output, but this does not create a problem, because if we assume a given production function and a given stock of capital (both permissible assumptions for the short run) we have a unique relationship between output and employment.

The amount of employment offered by a single firm depends upon the firm's expectations of demand for its products. Aggregating for the whole economy, we can therefore relate the volume of employment offered by all firms to their expectations of aggregate demand. This relationship, shown in Figure 15.3, is concave upward for two reasons. One is the declining marginal physical product of labor. As the firm expands output, product per worker falls, and hence the greater the existing level of employment, the greater is the number of dollars of additional aggregate demand needed to induce firms to employ an extra worker. The second reason is that as employment increases, money wages rise, and this has an effect similar to decreasing marginal product.

Juxtaposed to this aggregate supply curve is the aggregate demand curve. This curve is constructed as follows. Each level of employment is associated with a certain level of income to the factors of production. Each level of factor income is in turn associated, via the consumption function and the accelerator, with a certain level of aggregate demand.[3] Hence we can relate each level of employment to a given level of aggregate demand. Thus, if firms offer employment of x_1, they get back y_1 as aggregate demand from the factors.

---

3. The aggregate demand curve is drawn concave downward because we assume that the marginal propensity to consume declines as income rises. We could also have discarded this assumption and drawn it as a straight line without changing the substantive results.

Figure 15.3 / *Aggregate supply and demand.*

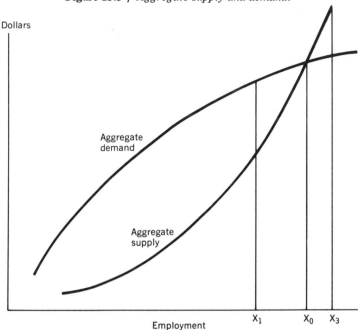

It may be worth emphasizing the distinction between aggregate supply curve and the aggregate demand curve. The aggregate supply curve shows how much aggregate demand firms must expect to make it worth while for them to employ a given number of workers. It tells us how much employment will be offered for each assumed level of aggregate demand. The aggregate demand curve, on the other hand, tells us what aggregate demand will be for each level of employment. In the one case (supply curve) we ask how much aggregate demand is required to validate a given level of employment; in the other case (demand curve) we ask what aggregate demand will actually be at this level of employment.

At the point x_0 where the two curves intercept, firms get back in aggregate demand exactly as much as they need to offer this much employment. It is therefore an equilibrium. By contrast at x_1 firms are receiving back from the public in aggregate demand more than is required to justify this level of employment. In other words, they are making abnormal profits, and, given our competitive assumptions, they expand output until they reach x_0. At x_2, on the other hand, they are receiving back in aggregate demand less than they are paying out to the factors, and so they have losses. Hence, they contract output and employment back to x_0.

We can now go from employment to output and prices. Quadrant I of Figure 15.4 is the same as the preceding figure. Quadrant II tells us how much output will be for each level of employment given the production function and the stock of capital. And Quadrant III tells us the price level corresponding to each level of output. This is the relationship we discussed earlier in this chapter.

Figure 15.4 / *Determination of output and prices.*

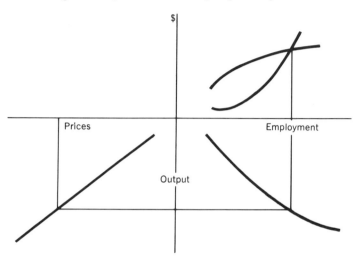

To summarize: in the traditional Keynesian model, in its simplest form, the price level is determined by the level of money wages, and money wages in turn are treated as given. Treating money wages as given is close to treating the price level as given, instead of explaining what determines it. If we had a good theory of wage determination, macroeconomic theory would not have to concern itself with the question of what determines money wages but could simply use this wage theory. But we do not have a good theory of money wages. To say that wages depend on the bargaining power of workers and employers is not an adequate explanation; it is only a caricature of an explanation, and tells us virtually nothing without a theory of what governs bargaining power. It is like predicting the outcome of the World Series by saying that the better team will win. Moreover, it is worth noting that only about one quarter of the U. S. labor force is unionized, so that a bargaining theory of wages would have to deal largely not with the outcome of formal negotiations, but with the factors which cause employers to set wage rates in an unorganized market.

The price level is one of the leading variables which macroeconomics should explain. The fact that the traditional Keynesian theory takes the wage level as exogenous, and that there is no adequate theory of wages to backstop it, is therefore a major weakness of traditional Keynesian theory. In addition, two suppositions of this theory are open to question. One is that wages are *completely* rigid downward, and the second is that workers look at money wages rather than at real wages. To be sure, there is substantial evidence that workers resist cuts in money wages, but all the same, money wages did fall during the Great Depression. Moreover, economic theory should try to explain, as far as it can, the reasons for wage inflexibility and not simply treat it as a fact of life even if some of the resistance to money wage cuts results from the feeling of self-esteem that a worker attaches to his money wage rate, and hence may be outside the purview of economic analysis. The proposition that workers have a money illusion and therefore resist wage cuts is open to question. We generally assume in economic theory that people behave rationally and therefore focus on real rather than money values. Why should workers behave differently? To be sure, one must not indulge in what has been called "the irrational passion for impassionate rationality," and should allow for the fact that people are likely to disregard small price movements in the short run, particularly if there is a good chance that they will be reversed soon. Observation of the behavior of labor markets suggests that there is *some* money illusion.[4] But should one assume an extreme one?

In response to these criticisms, in recent years a number of economists have developed a rich and detailed theory of wage behavior, a theory which does not rely on a money illusion and on unexplained wage rigidity. While it is too early to tell whether this new theory will win out over the traditional Keynesian treatment of wages, it is certainly worth considering in some detail.

AN ALTERNATIVE APPROACH[5]

The new approach to the money-wage problem is to look upon the labor market as essentially competitive but subject to uncertainty. While the traditional view seems to fit most naturally into a world of union-management bargaining, the new view fits best into a world of unionized labor markets

4. See Albert Rees, "The Phillips Curve as a Menu for Policy Choice," *Economica*, Vol. XXXVII (August 1970), p. 235.

5. The theory described in this section is still new. For a detailed description of this theory see Edmund Phelps, *et al.*, *Microeconomic Foundations of Employment and Inflation Theory* (New York: W. W. Norton, 1970), Introduction and Part 1. For criticisms see Albert Rees, *op. cit.*, pp. 227–38, and George Perry, "Inflation and Unemployment," in U.S. Savings and Loan League, *Savings and Residential Financing: 1970 Conference Proceedings* (Chicago: U. S. Savings and Loan League, 1970), pp. 30–45.

where employers set a wage rate and workers either accept or reject job opportunities at these wage rates. Aware that roughly one quarter of the American labor force is unionized, adherents of the new view do not deny that some wages are set by collective bargaining. Rather, they argue that unions, being concerned with maintaining employment for their members as well as with wage rates, act in a way not very different from unorganized workers. Unionized as well as nonunionized workers are looked upon as acting more or less rationally. To be sure, they may be reluctant to take money wage cuts, and they have only vague ideas—which are slow to change—about their equilibrium wage rate. But still, they pay attention to their *real* wages.

In this model the employer sets the wage rate equal to the expected marginal product of labor. If we take product prices, the stock of capital, and the production function as fixed, the money wage which the employer offers depends only (via the curvature of the production function) on his volume of employment; or, conversely, his demand for labor depends on the money wage. And we can readily relate his demand for labor to real wages by assuming that all prices change proportionately. Then, if product prices double, the employer will employ just as much labor as before at a doubled money wage. Hence the real wage depends upon the volume of employment.

Turning to the supply curve of labor, one could very simply treat it as a fixed proportion of the adult population. But such a treatment is unnecessarily crude since it ignores such factors as working overtime, moonlighting, variations in the ages at which workers enter and leave the labor force, and, most importantly, the participation rate of secondary earners such as housewives and students. Despite the rigidity of the standard workday, the household has some choice about the amount of labor it supplies. One obvious factor which enters this choice is the wage rate. However, it is not possible to say *a priori* whether an increase in the wage rate will raise or lower work effort. On the one hand, if the wage rises, the reward for working is greater; but, on the other hand, a higher wage, and hence a higher income, means that workers can afford to enjoy more leisure and work less. We have here an income effect pulling against a substitution effect, and which one dominates is an empirical issue. But now consider a related variable, the ratio of the current wage to the worker's long-run normal wage. If wages go up *temporarily,* the rational worker will work more hours now, and fewer in the future when wages will be lower. In other words, he tends to "buy" his leisure when its price is lowest. Current prices relative to normal or expected prices also play a role in the worker's labor supply function because, since some of the currently earned income will be spent later on, the more prices are expected to rise, the less is the reward for working. Thus we get a supply function of labor which looks as follows:

$$\frac{N_t}{M_t} = a + b\,\frac{W_t}{W^*} + cW^* - d\,\frac{P^*}{P_t} \qquad (15.1)$$

where N_t is the total number of man-hours of labor currently supplied; M_t, the current size of the population; W, current and W^* normal wage rates; P^*, normal prices; and P, current prices.[6] The wage rates are, in accordance with our rationality assumption, real rather than money wage rates. Thus, leaving aside transitional factors, such as lags in the formation of expectations, if prices and wages double, the amount of labor supplied is unaffected, but if only prices rise and money wages do not, the supply of labor would be smaller.

We have thus a demand schedule for labor which, given a fixed stock of capital and a stable production function, relates employment offered to the current real wage. At the same time we have a supply schedule of labor which relates the amount of labor supplied by workers to the current real wage, holding constant the size of the population, normal real wages, current prices, and normal prices. As shown in Figure 15.5, employment and thus the real wage can be determined.

Figure 15.5 shows supply and demand intersecting, thus suggesting that at the equilibrium real wage the market is cleared. At this wage there is no unemployment at all, and there are no unfilled vacancies. This is clearly an unrealistic picture. Despite the great labor shortage during World War II, more than 1 percent of the labor force was unemployed every year. The

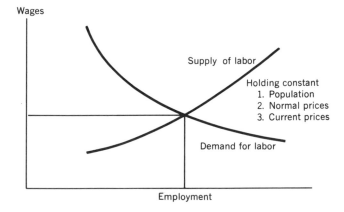

Figure 15.5 / *Equilibrium in the labor market.*

6. This equation comes from R. E. Lucas and L. A. Rapping, "Price Expectations and the Phillips Curve," *American Economic Review*, Vol. LIX (June 1969), p. 343, where it is given in logarithmic form.

labor market is a highly imperfect market. It is not a centralized market analogous to the stock market where supply and demand are matched with almost no friction. As a result there is frictional unemployment. A worker knows his current wage, but he does not know the alternative wage other employers are willing to offer. Often he can find this out only by quitting his present job and looking for another one. And once he does quit his job, it is usually not worth his while to take the first offer he gets; rather he can improve his income over the long-run by spending some time sampling the labor market. Similarly, a new entrant to the labor force is often better off spending considerable time searching for the best job he can get. As a result, even if there are as many, or more, vacancies as unemployed workers, there will be some frictional unemployment. Such unemployment is not necessarily a bad thing. It is necessary to get workers into those jobs where their marginal product is highest.

In this theory—in sharp contrast to the Keynesian theory—workers bargain for real wages rather than money wages. Hence, money wages cannot be treated as fixed. And even real wages are flexible because, according to this theory, unemployed workers are willing to take cuts in their real wages.

Assume that aggregate demand declines. The only way a firm could continue to employ the same quantity of labor would be to cut its product prices or to substitute labor for capital. Both of these imply a decline in the marginal product of labor and hence require a cut in wages. Workers may not be willing to accept wage cuts. They may think that they would be better off leaving their jobs and looking around for other jobs paying a wage greater than the reduced wage their current employer is offering. But many of these workers will be unsuccessful in their search. Since aggregate demand has fallen, other firms will normally be in the same position and will also be offering lower wages or more unpleasant working conditions. Eventually—and it may take a long time—workers will realize the extent to which market conditions have changed and will be ready to accept lower wages. At this point unemployment will decline to its previous level.

But it is important to keep in mind the qualifying word "eventually." There is nothing in the theory just outlined which requires this process to be swift. Workers may reduce their wage demand very, very slowly.[7]

Now assume that demand increases. The equilibrium money wage rises too, but workers do not adjust their wage expectations to the full extent. Frictionally unemployed workers hunting for new jobs now find jobs paying the wages they demand. Frictional unemployment therefore falls below its

7. There is evidence that unemployed workers reduce their wage demands very slowly, perhaps at a rate of about 1 percent every three months or so. See Charles Holt, "Job Search, Phillips Wage Relation and Union Influence: Theory and Evidence," in Edmund Phelps, *et al*, *Microeconomic Foundations of Employment and Inflation Theory* (New York: Norton, 1970), pp. 96–101.

normal level. But after some time workers realize that money wages generally have risen, and hence—particularly if prices have risen too— they adjust their wage expectations. Some workers now quit their jobs to look for better opportunities. These and other unemployed workers look for jobs paying a higher wage and therefore spend more time in this "search unemployment." Once workers have adjusted their wage expectations fully, frictional unemployment is back at its normal level.

Thus, in this model, changes in aggregate demand result initially in changes in frictional unemployment and subsequently in changes in money wages as well as in prices. By contrast, in the traditional Keynesian model, changes in demand at less than full employment result in changes in output, employment, and real wages, while money wages and prices are relatively stable.

This new approach, unlike the traditional Keynesian approach, therefore denies the existence of "involuntary" unemployment. The workers who have lost their jobs are not *involuntarily* unemployed because—leaving aside minimum wage laws—there is some wage low enough at which they could be employed. Hence, it must be conceded that in some sense their unemployment is voluntary. But calling their unemployment voluntary does not eliminate the actual fact of human suffering and of lost production. Moreover, one should not read a moral judgment into the terms "voluntary" and "involuntary" unemployment. A voluntarily unemployed worker is not necessarily lazy or abnormally stubborn about his wage. If demand declines, most workers, according to this new theory, have invalid ideas about their equilibrium wage, and these ideas change slowly. It is not the case that only those who are unusually slow to change will be unemployed.

Besides, an unemployed worker who does not accept the first job offered to him is not necessarily doing the wrong thing. By rejecting this job he may well be raising his discounted lifetime earnings. From the social point of view, as well as from his own, an unemployed worker may be doing the correct thing in waiting for a job at his old wage to come along. To take a strong example, a skilled automobile worker who is unemployed but expects with good reason that he will be rehired in a month would probably be lowering his own yearly income, as well as the nation's productivity, if he were to accept a job as a janitor in another city which he would not be able to leave for some time. Moreover, one could well argue that during a recession the increase in voluntary unemployment is the fault not of the unemployed, but of the government which allowed aggregate demand to decrease, so that workers have to spend time they would otherwise be working, in sampling the job market and learning what their new equilibrium wage is.

Finally, it is worth emphasizing that the theory sketched in this section is still very new. Only time will tell whether it finds widespread acceptance among economists. What may well emerge is a synthesis of the two views.

THE PHILLIPS CURVE

Let us now look at the actual behavior of wages and unemployment. When one charts unemployment and the proportionate rate of increase in wages, one gets a curve, such as *AA* in Figure 15.6, known as the Phillips curve after its discoverer, Professor A. W. Phillips. Such Phillips curves have been fitted to the data for a number of countries, and some economists have tried to improve upon the relationship by introducing other variables, apart from unemployment, which may affect the rate of wage increases. Among such variables are the previous years' price change, profitability, and the rate of change of unemployment.

Figure 15.6 / *Unemployment Phillips curves.*

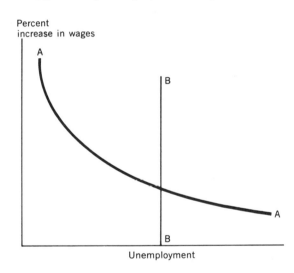

The basic idea that wages rise at a faster rate when unemployment is low is intuitively appealing. In the absence of adequate statistics on job vacancies, we measure the relative magnitudes of supply and demand of jobs by looking only at the unemployment rate. The wage rate is a price, and like any other price it tends to rise when supply is low relative to demand. More specifically, one can look at the Phillips curve in two ways. One is via the bargaining process. According to this interpretation, unions have more bargaining power when unemployment is low, and with low unemployment and generally prosperous conditions, employers are less willing to resist labor's demands. Hence, at a time of low unemployment large wage increases occur in the unionized industries, and these wages increases then spread to unorganized industries. Conversely, in years of high unemployment, unions do not press strongly for large wage increases because they are afraid of even more unemployment if wages rise too much. Moreover, employers feel unable to pass large wage increases forward through higher prices, and with business being rather unprofitable they are less worried about a long strike.

But one can also explain the Phillips curve without recourse to unions. If unemployment is low, businessmen find it more difficult to fill job vacancies. They can react to falling unemployment in three ways. One is to reduce their demand for labor by scheduling overtime work or by reducing output. Another way is to spend more on labor market searches, and the third is to raise wages. As unemployment decreases, more and more firms raise their wage offers, thus, when unemployment declines, wages rise. In addition, a wage increase itself serves to reduce unemployment. This is the case because as wages rise, more frictionally unemployed workers find jobs which pay what they think of as their equilibrium wage. For these reasons it is not surprising that there is a Phillips curve showing that unemployment is low when wages are rising at a fast rate. There is a statistical association between rising wages and unemployment, and this is just what the Phillips curve shows.

In Chapter 5, when discussing the past behavior of the American economy, we presented a chart (Figure 5.3) which shows wages rising faster when unemployment is low, as the Phillips relation predicts. But this figure also shows something apart from the Phillips curve: a tendency for wages to rise faster at those times when prices are rising than when prices are stable. This raises a very basic issue about the Phillips curve: is it fixed in real or money terms? In other words, do price increases have such a strong effect on wage increases that it is best to think of the Phillips curve as relating *real* wages, rather than money wages, to unemployment? In his *General Theory* (published in 1936), Keynes asserted that workers bargain for money wages rather than for real wages. This is more likely to have been the case during the depressed 1930s when workers were reluctant to let money wages decline along with prices, then it is during the postwar inflation, when unions generally argue for cost-of-living increases, and some contracts actually contain formal cost-of-living clauses. Accordingly, many Keynesian economists, while using a Phillips relationship fixed in money terms, have taken account of this tendency of workers to look at real wages as well as money wages. They have done this by including the previous year's price increase as one of the terms in the equation describing the Phillips relationship. The results they have generally obtained this way are that rising prices do lead to higher wages, which is not very surprising. However, they also found that price increases are not completely reflected in subsequent wage increases, that a 1 percent price increase results in wages rising, not by 1 percent, but, say, only by 0.4 percent.

But other economists, particularly those connected with the theory described in the previous section or with the quantity theory described in Chapter 17, have argued that, in the *longer* run, both employers and workers look almost wholly at real wages rather than at money wages. Instead of merely adding a price term to a Phillips equation formulated in money terms, they have reformulated the whole equation in real terms. They do not deny that there is *some* lag in the adaptation of employers and employees to changes in the price level, but they look upon this as merely a transitional phenomenon of imperfect adaptation in the short run. They therefore believe that there exist both short-run and long-run Phillips relations.

The difference between the two approaches can be illustrated by an example. Suppose that during a period in which prices are generally stable, we observe that wages rise at a rate of 3 percent per year if there is, say, 5 percent unemployment, and at a rate of 6 percent if there is 3 percent unemployment. Suppose further that prices now start to rise at a 4 percent annual rate. If workers look only at their money wage and the Phillips curve is fixed in money terms, then the previous relationship would hold; at 5 percent unemployment money wages would rise at a 3 percent rate. But if the Phillips curve is in real terms rather than in money terms, this would not be the case. Workers would demand, and employers would be willing to grant, a 3 percent rise in *real* wages which, given a 4 percent inflation, would require a 7 percent rise in money wages. In other words, the Phillips curve, after a transitional period, becomes vertical. This long-run Phillips curve is shown by *BB* in Figure 15.6.

To be sure, this example makes the conflict appear sharper than it really is. As pointed out above, many economists who use a Phillips relation fixed in money terms include a price change term in their equation. However, they would argue that this price change term shows only a partial, not a full, adjustment to inflation, so that given, as in the above example, 5 percent unemployment and 4 percent inflation, wages would rise neither by 3 percent, as in the complete-money-illusion case, nor by the 7 percent of the no-money-illusion-at-all case, but say, by 5 or 6 percent. On the other hand, those economists who believe that the Phillips curve is fixed in real terms realize that people's expectations of price increases tend to lag behind actual price increases. Hence, *in the short run,* with 4 percent inflation, the equilibrium money wage at 5 percent unemployment would be less than 7 percent. But ultimately, it would approach this equilibrium value.

The question whether the Phillips curve is fixed in money or real terms is not only a matter of theoretical interest, but has an extremely important policy implication. Suppose the Phillips curve is fixed in nominal terms. In this case we have an important choice to make, since we can trade off price stability against full employment. Suppose we raise aggregate demand enough to bring unemployment down, say, from 5 percent to 3 percent. In our example, wages now rise at a 6 percent rate, and assuming that productivity is rising at a 3 percent rate too, and that other real factor shares are constant, prices rise at a 3 percent rate. We are therefore trading off a 2 percent reduction in employment against a 3 percent inflation. Whether or not such a trade-off is desirable involves difficult value judgments as well as technical issues, but in any case, *if* we want to use it, we have such a trade-off available to us. But suppose that the Phillips curve is fixed in real terms. Then, except as a transitional phenomenon, this type of trade-off does not exist. If we raise aggregate demand and try to get the unemployment rate down to 3 percent, we will not succeed; there exists an equilibrium, or natural unemployment rate of 5 percent. The reason for this is that as prices rise by 3 percent, such a 3 percent increase will become built into the expectations of workers and employers. Thus, if unemployment declines to 3 percent, they will seek a 6 percent rise in *real* wages, which, with a 3 percent inflation means a money wage increase of 9 percent. And if the government were then to increase aggregate demand enough to make employers willing to raise wages by 9 percent, given a 3 percent increase in productivity, prices would rise by 6 percent. So, now with prices rising by 6 percent, it would take a 12 percent increase in money wages to raise real wages by 6 percent and keep unemployment down to 3 percent. And, in the next period with prices rising by 9 percent, it would take a 15 percent wage increase. Clearly, what we have here is an explosive inflation. Hence, except in the short run, until expectations adapt, we cannot reduce unemployment by letting prices rise. In the long run there is no feasible trade-off. We simply get more and more inflation, and once we stop the inflation, unemployment will be the same as it was before the inflation. One very unpleasant fact which should be faced in this connection is that the natural rate of unemployment *may* be very high, and may exceed the socially acceptable rate of unemployment. In this case—particularly if continually accelerating inflation is also not acceptable to society—a change in the organization of the labor market is necessary. But this too may be unacceptable to society.

QUESTIONS AND EXERCISES

1. If you have ever been, even temporarily, in the labor market, think back on how you obtained your job. Describe your experience with "search unemployment."

2. Discuss: "An unemployed individual could always obtain a job if he would only be willing to work for less. Hence, if he is unemployed it is his own fault, and he deserves no public sympathy."

3. Discuss: "Unemployment compensation is a bad thing, because by making frictional unemployment less painful for the worker, it makes him less willing to take a job and hence it increases unemployment."

4. Discuss: "Whether we call it 'frictional unemployment' or 'involuntary unemployment' is just a matter of terminology and should not change the way we actually view large-scale unemployment."

5. What does it mean to say that a person suffers from a money illusion? Give a precise definition.

6. Which, if any, of the following consumption functions implies a money illusion? Explain carefully.

$$Cp = A + cY + b(M/p)$$
$$Cp = A + c(Yp) + b(M/p)$$
$$p(Cp) = pA + c(Yp) + bM$$

Cp is real consumption, A is a constant, Y is money income, Yp real income, M is the money stock (measured in nominal terms).

7. Can you think of any reason why workers are more likely to have a money illusion than other people?

8. How realistic do you think it is to say that workers bargain for real wages? How about employers?

9. Considering the overall U.S. economy, would you expect that wage rates are determined more by union wage bargains or by wage setting in unorganized industries? What do you think is the impact of union wage bargains on wages in unorganized industries?

10. Discuss: "If the number of vacancies just equals the number of unemployed workers, then obviously there is no upward pressure on wage rates, and wages are stable."

11. From the *Economic Report of the President* chart yearly wage rates and unemployment rates for the last ten years. Do you find a Phillips curve?

12. Can you think of some reasons why labor is unwilling to take cuts in money wages at the cost of unemployment? Would you modify your answer if prices were falling?

13. Are there any reasons why employers might be reluctant to cut money wages?

14. Even at what we normally think of as full employment, the aggregate supply curve does not become completely vertical. Can you think of some reasons for this?

15. Can you think of some ways in which we could improve the functioning of the labor market to reduce frictional unemployment?

16. Discuss: "Reducing frictional unemployment would be a very unwise policy. We rightly complain if the vacancy rate of apartments is less than one percent in a city, and, for the same reason, we should be unhappy if unemployment is too low."

17. "He also serves who only stands and waits." Does this provide a reason why an unemployed worker should maintain his self-respect? Does it furnish a justification for paying unemployment compensation almost equal to a worker's previous wage?

18. Assume that people enjoy working, and that, therefore, there is no problem of work incentives. Would there be any disadvantage in paying unemployment compensation practically equal to a worker's wage? Would it interfere with efficient resource allocation?

19. What factors determine how long an unemployed worker should spend in search unemployment from (a) his point of view, (b) the point of view of society?

20. Which do you prefer, the traditional Keynesian treatment of the labor market and unemployment, or the new theory? Explain carefully.

SUGGESTED READING

C. Schultze and J. Tryon, "Prices and Wages," in J. Duesenberry, G. Fromm, L. Klein, and E. Kuh, eds., *The Brooklings Quarterly Model of the United States* (Chicago: Rand McNally, 1965), pp. 281–333. *Advanced reference.*

E. Phelps, *et al., Microeconomic Foundations of Employment and Inflation Theory* (New York: W. W. Norton, 1970), Introduction and Part 1.

G. Perry, "Inflation and Unemployment," in U.S. Savings and Loan League, *Savings and Residential Financing: 1970 Conference Proceedings* (Chicago U.S. Savings and Loan League, 1970), pp. 30–45.

G. Perry, "The Determinants of Wage Rate Changes," *Review of Economic Studies,* Vol. XXXI (October 1964), pp. 287–308. *Advanced reference.*

A. Rees, "The Phillips Curve as a Menu for Policy Choice," *Economica,* Vol. XXXVIII (August 1970), pp. 227–38.

R. Gordon, "The Recent Acceleration of Inflation and Its Lessons for the Future," in Brookings Institution, *Brookings Papers on Economic Activity,* #1, 1970, pp. 8–47. *Advanced reference.*

16

Keynesian Theory and
Its Predecessors

IN CHAPTERS 6 through 15 we have gradually developed a macroeconomic model which is, in all essentials, derived from the work of John Maynard Keynes. In developing this model there is a risk that, in our detailed examination of its component parts, we have lost sight of its overall characteristics. To guard against this, in this chapter we take, as it were, a step back and attempt to set out the principal characteristics of the model as a whole. We begin by looking at its structure.

THE STRUCTURE OF THE MODEL

In considering the structure of any theory the first step is to ask two questions:

Which variables does the model explain or determine? These we call the *endogenous* variables.

Which variables does the model take as given—that is determined outside the system? These we call the *exogenous* variables.

Let us now look at the first of these questions, remembering that any model of this type is constructed not only of a set of *hypotheses* about behavior but also of a set of assumptions about the institutional environment.

As we already know from our manipulation of the model, it contains nine endogenous variables. These are:

$Y \equiv$ real output

$C_p \equiv$ real planned consumption

$I_p \equiv$ real planned investment

$r \equiv$ rate of interest

$p \equiv$ price of a unit of output

$N \equiv$ quantity of employment demanded (employed)

$\dfrac{W}{p} \equiv$ real wage rate

$U \equiv$ the quantity of involuntary unemployment

$M^D \equiv$ quantity of money demanded.

To determine the equilibrium values of these variables we need to know (1) the values of the *exogenous* variables; (2) the functional relationships which constitute the behavioristic hypotheses of the theory; and (3) any relationships between the variables which exist by definition.

In the short-run model, the variables which we take to be given—that is, determined outside the system and hence by definition *exogenous*—are:

$M^S \equiv$ the nominal quantity of money—determined by central banking policy and the commercial banking system

$W_h \equiv$ the value of the money wage rate—determined by an institutionalized process of bargaining between employers and employees

$K \equiv$ the real capital stock

$T \equiv$ the state of technology

$N_{FE} \equiv$ the "full employment" labor force

$A \equiv$ the real value of households' assets

$\alpha \equiv$ the distribution of income.

Notice here that, in purely formal terms, the variables we take to be *exogenous* are a matter of choice. It would, for example, be a simple matter to regard the money supply (M^S) as *endogenous*. To do this we would need to formulate behavior hypotheses for the central bank and for commercial banks, which would permit us to write the money supply as a function of some endogenous variables on which the central bank bases its policy. A simple, but not necessarily plausible hypothesis, might regard the central bank as providing a greater nominal quantity of money the higher is the market rate of interest. This would give us a behavior function of the form: $M^S = f(r)$, with $\partial M^S / \partial r > 0$, to replace our more familiar formulation $M^S = M_0$. Equally we could develop a hypothesis about the labor market which would make W_h an endogenous variable. This, at this stage of our analysis, we do not choose to do

Though we shall proceed retaining our classification of M^S and W_h as *exogenous,* it should be clear to the reader that since we need not do so, part of the skill in building models is concerned precisely with deciding *which* variables are to be taken as exogenous. A sensible decision depends partly on knowledge of the institutional and social environment in which our model is to operate and partly upon the type of problem on which we wish our model to throw light. What is involved is "judgment"; there are therefore no rules—simple or complex—which can be set out to insure that any model constructed will be relevant.

Once we have taken our decision on this matter, in addition to the values of the *exogenous variables* we require certain behavior assumptions. These are:

1) a consumption hypothesis which explains consumption behavior;

2) an investment hypothesis which explains investment behavior;

3) a liquidity preference hypothesis which explains behavior with respect to the demand for money;

4) a profit maximization hypothesis which explains the demand for labor in terms of the real wage rate and also underlies some versions of item (2);

5) a labor supply hypothesis which explains the supply of labor; and

6) the "technical" relation, specified by the production function, which relates the inputs of labor (N) to quantities of real output (Y).

Our model, despite its heroic level of simplification, thus contains *fifteen* variables of which nine are endogenous and six exogenous. An elementary knowledge of mathematics tells us that, to determine the value of any variable, a single equation is required; for two variables we need two independent equations; for fifteen variables fifteen independent equations. Hence, if we wish, and it is often convenient to do so, we can write down our model in terms of 15 equations. These equations, which the reader will readily recognize from the previous chapters, are set out in Table 16.1.

Though this mathematical method of expressing a model is undoubtedly convenient and useful, it may also help to set out the model in terms of a diagram. This is done in Figure 16.1. (Notice that though the figure does not explicitly show the interdependence of the three markets, certain variables are shown as affecting more than one market. This reflects the interdependence which is a feature of the model.)

Taken together, the table and the figure make it clear what the structure of our system is. They also make it plain that by (1) taking as given the values of *six* exogenous variables; (2) assuming *six* functional relations

Table 16.1 / *The Keynesian model.*

EQUATION	MEANING	CHAPTER REFERENCES
1. $Y = C_p + I_p$	Equilibrium in goods market	7
2. $C_p = f_1(Y, A, \alpha, r)$	Consumption hypothesis	8 and 9
3. $I_p = f_2(K, r)$	Investment hypothesis	10 and 11
4. $M_p^D = L_1(Yp) + L_2(r)$	Demand for money hypothesis	12
5. $M^S = M_0$	Supply of money assumption	12
6. $M^D = M^S$	Equilibrium in money market	12
7. $N^D = f_3(W/p)$	Demand for labor depends upon the real wage	15
8. $N^S = f_4(W)$	Supply of labor depends upon money wage	15
9. $Y = f_5(T, K, N)$	Production function hypothesis	6 and 15
10. $W = W_h$	Money wage rate determined by "historical" bargaining process	15
11. $T = T_0$	State of technology given	10 and 15
12. $K = K_0$	Stock of capital given	10 and 15
13. $A = A_0$	Real value of household assets given	8
14. $\alpha = \alpha_0$	Income distribution given	8
15. $U \equiv N^S - N^D$	Definition of involuntary unemployment	15

The subscripts after the function signs inserted in equations 2, 3, 7, 8 and 9 are used merely to remind the reader that the functions are not the same in each equation.

which reflect behavior; (3) adding the *two* equilibrium conditions for the goods and money markets; and (4) *one* definitional identity, we can determine the equilibrium values of each of the fifteen variables and hence of the nine *endogenous* variables. Suppose we operate the model in this way and the resulting equilibrium levels of output and employment are Y_0 and N_0. Suppose further that $N_0 < N_f$ so that involuntary unemployment (U) exists. Is it natural to ask: what "causes" this involuntary unemployment?

If we look at our system we immediately notice two important characteristics. First, *the equilibrium values of all the endogenous variables are simultaneously determined.* Hence, *in a system of this type, crude notions of causation are obviously inappropriate simply because the value of any endogenous variable depends upon the value of all the exogenous variables and all the assumed functional relations.*

For example to "explain" the existence of involuntary unemployment (U) we can point to (1) too small a money supply; (2) too high a money wage rate; (3) too low a propensity to consume schedule; (4) too low a marginal efficiency of capital schedule; (5) too high a liquidity preference schedule; or (6) some combination of all these. The conclusion is that, if it makes sense to speak of "causation" at all in a system of this kind, no single "cause" can in general be isolated to explain the equilibrium value of any single endogenous variable. The reader is thus well advised to drop the concept of causation and think instead merely of the properties of the system. This means that instead of asking what "causes" involuntary un-

Figure 16.1 / *The model in outline.*

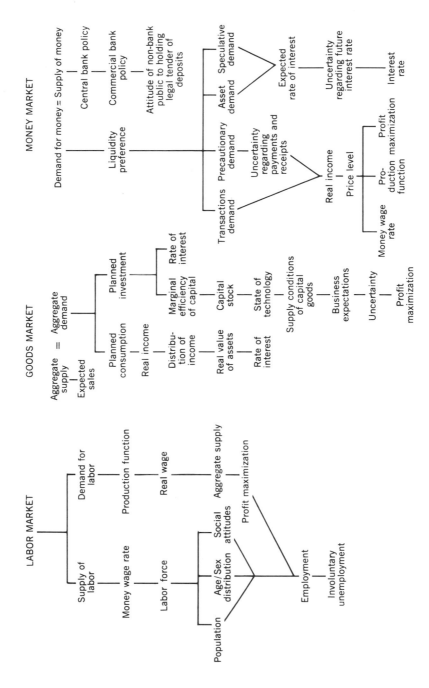

employment, we ask what would be the result, for the equilibrium value of U, if say some exogenous variable changed or some functional relationship shifted. This, as the reader will recall, is precisely the form of question we have in fact been asking.

The second point to notice is that this is the only form of question it is meaningful to put to the model.

It is obviously not meaningful to ask, for example, what would happen if the rate of interest (r) changed, for r is an endogenous variable determined within the system. It therefore cannot change its equilibrium value unless some change occurs in the exogenous variables and/or the functional relations. This does not mean, and must not be interpreted to mean, that it is not meaningful to ask how a businessman (or a group of businessmen) would behave, in given and specified circumstances, when confronted by different interest rates. We asked precisely this form of question in building up our investment function. But in this case we were considering only investment behavior. We thus treated planned investment (I_p) as a dependent variable and the rate of interest, r, as an independent variable. In the system as a whole, however, the equilibrium values of *both* I_p and r are dependent variables. Endogenous variables are, in short, dependent variables *within the system as a whole*. This point, which is sometimes hard to grasp, is important. The reader will find the figure helpful in this context and he will also find it instructive to work the exercise at the end of this chapter.

PRE-KEYNESIAN MACROECONOMICS

In contrast with our "Keynesian" type model, pre-Keynesian macroeconomic theory predicted that the equilibrium level of output would always be such as to provide "full employment" in the sense that everyone willing to work at the real wage rate ruling in the economy was able to do so. Thus the principal prediction of pre-Keynesian macroeconomics was that, in equilibrium, involuntary unemployment (U) would be zero. How was this result reached? In what main way, or ways, did pre-Keynesian macroeconomics differ from Keynesian?

According to pre-Keynesian theory in its simplest form, the economy consisted of three markets: those for labor, goods, and money. To show the nature of pre-Keynesian theory we consider each in turn.

In the labor market the quantity of labor *demanded* by businessmen is taken to be a *decreasing* function of the real wage. This proposition, which we have already discussed in Chapter 15, assumes that businessmen maximize profits and that there is a given short-run production function exhibiting diminishing marginal physical productivity of labor. Hence,

$$N^D = f^D \left(\frac{W}{p} \right). \tag{16.pK 1}$$

On the supply side of the market individuals are assumed to offer their labor until the real wage exactly offsets the marginal disutility of working. If, as seems plausible, the marginal disutility of work rises as the amount of work done increases, then the quantity of labor offered by a given labor force will be an *increasing* function of the real wage. Hence

$$N^S = f^S \left(\frac{W}{p} \right) \tag{16.pK 2}$$

For equilibrium in the labor market we require

$$N^S = N^D \tag{16.pK 3}$$

Hence when the labor market is in equilibrium we have a determinate (and equal) quantity of labor supplied and demanded and a determinate real wage. This is illustrated in the figure below where

N_0 is the equilibrium quantity of employment

$\left(\dfrac{W}{p_0} \right)$ is the equilibrium quantity of real wage.

Note that since, at N_0, *all those who wish to work at the real wage* $(W)/p_0$ *are doing so, there is no involuntary unemployment. N_0 thus*

Figure 16.2 / *The equilibrium in the labor market.*

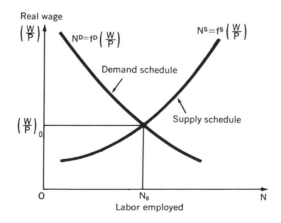

corresponds to *full employment*. Given our production function and taking, as we must in short-run analysis, K and T as given, it is easy to see that the equilibrium level of real output (Y_0) is determined once N_0 is known. This is demonstrated in Figure 16.3.

We now know the value of output ($=$ income). Will planned expenditure equal this value in real terms? If this is so then

$$I_p = S_p. \qquad \text{(16.pK 4)}$$

We now need two functional relations, expressing behavior, to explain I_p and S_p. Let us write, as we did before,

$$I_p = f(r) \qquad \text{(16.pK 5)}$$

$$S_p = f(Y, r, A) \qquad \text{(16.pK 6)}$$

As before we treat A, the real value of households' assets, as *exogenous*. From 16.3 we already know $Y = Y_0$. Hence, given A and Y_0, we can draw, on Figure 16.4, both planned investment and planned saving as functions of r (the rate of interest). We thus find r_0, the equilibrium value of r, and S_{p0}, I_{p0} the equilibrium values of S_p and I_p.

In the money market, as before, we take the nominal money supply to be exogenous.

$$M^S = M_0. \qquad \text{(16.pK 7)}$$

To explain the demand for money, pre-Keynesian theory assumed that the public wants to hold as money balances a fixed proportion of its money

Figure 16.3 / *The determination of output.*

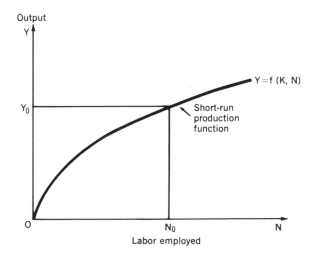

Figure 16.4 / *Equilibrium in the goods market.*

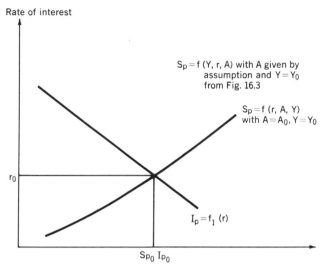

Rate of interest

$S_p = f(Y, r, A)$ with A given by
assumption and $Y = Y_0$
from Fig. 16.3

$S_p = f(r, A, Y)$
with $A = A_0, Y = Y_0$

r_0

$I_p = f_1(r)$

$S_{p_0} I_{p_0}$

Planned saving (S_p); planned investment (I_p)

income. While many of the better pre-Keynesian economists realized that
the quantity of money the public wants to hold depends upon the rate of
interest, this was often forgotten in practice. Hence, we can write a crude
pre-Keynesian substitute for the liquidity preference relationship as follows:

$$M^D = LpY, \qquad (16.pK\ 8)$$

where L is the proportion, assumed to be constant, of their money incomes
(pY) that people wish to hold command over in the form of money. Notice
that (16.pK 8) entails a *behavior* assumption—namely that people *do* hold
L constant.

Finally we impose the equilibrium condition

$$M^S = M^D \qquad (16.pK\ 9)$$

These three equations enable us to determine M^S, M^D and equilibrium
money income $(pY)_0$ which, since we already know Y_0, immediately gives
the equilibrium price level p_0. This is shown in Figure 16.5.

Clearly once we know p_0—the equilibrium price level—we also know
W_0—the equilibrium money wage rate—for, from 16.2, we already have
W_0/p_0 (the ratio of the money wage rate to the price level) whence, knowing the absolute price level (p_0) we can easily find the equilibrium absolute
money wage rate (W_0).

Figure 16.5 / *The determination of money income.*

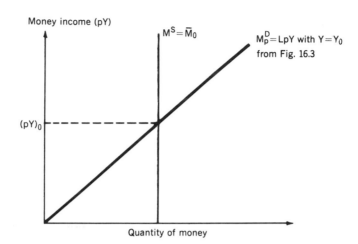

It is not our purpose to give a detailed analysis of this pre-Keynesian system. Certain of its properties are, however, of great interest. For example:

1) If the labor market is permitted to operate freely—on the usual competitive assumptions—equilibrium in this market will *always* be at full employment in the sense that all those who wish to work at the ruling real wage are able to do so. In short there can in equilibrium be no involuntary unemployment. This conclusion was often expressed in the form of "Say's Law" (named after Jean-Baptiste Say, 1767–1832, a major French economist) that "supply creates its own demand." This means that if a man produces and sells goods and services, he will, in turn, use the proceeds of this sale to purchase goods and services from someone else rather than adding them to his money balances. While classical economists are often accused of holding this proposition in the rigid sense that none of the proceeds are ever added to cash balances, there is some evidence that they really espoused a looser version of Say's Law, a version which made it a long-run tendency rather than a proposition which holds fully at all times.[1]

2) This suggests that involuntary unemployment, if it occurs, reflects some intervention in the working of the labor market.

This possibility is illustrated in Figure 16.6, which again depicts the labor market. If the real wage, say because of governmental or union intervention, is fixed at $\overline{W}/p$ then the quantity of labor demanded is N_1^D and that offered is N_1^S. Involuntary unemployment is then $N_1^S - N_1^D \equiv U$.

1. See Joseph Schumpeter, *A History of Economic Analysis* (New York: Oxford University Press, 1954) pp. 615–25, and Don Patinkin, *Money, Interest and Prices* (New York: Harper and Row, 1965), pp. 645–50.

It is easy to see that a policy *implication* of pre-Keynesian theory was that, to eliminate involuntary unemployment, the appropriate action was to *eliminate intervention* in the labor market, allowing the forces of competition to push real wages down to W_0/p_0 and thus restore full employment. Again when the wage rate was not flexible, the implication of pre-Keynesian macroeconomics was that a cut in money wages—by reducing the real wage rate—would restore full employment which, as we have seen, is not necessarily so in our (Keynesian) model. In addition it is worth noting that, in preKeynesian macroeconomics, the quantity theory of money holds. Suppose, for example, the money supply is doubled. Then, from (pK 8) or Figure 16.4, equilibrium money income $(pY)_0$ also doubles. Since equilibrium real income (Y_0) is determined by the level of employment, which depends only on the real wage, then if both p_0 and W_0 also double, the system will once again be in equilibrium with prices and money wages twice their previous level but with employment, output, the real wage and the rate of interest unaffected. It follows that the *equilibrium* values of these variables, and of S_p and I_p, do not depend upon the money supply, which influences only the equilibrium value of p and W—*absolute* prices and money wages. For this reason it is sometimes said that in pre-Keynesian macroeconomics "money was a veil." The pre-Keynesian system also carried the implication that rising prices (inflation) were to be explained by an increasing money supply.

Figure 16.6 / *Involuntary unemployment.*

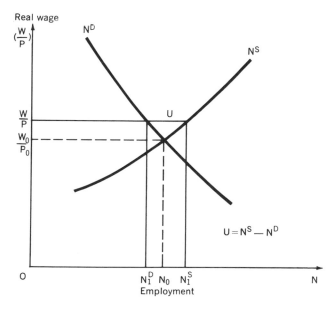

Though our formal analysis shows the quantity theory of money to hold when the nominal money supply is doubled, at least one mystery remains. Plainly, in the new equilibrium we must have

$$M^D = 2p_0 Y_0,$$

but this simple deduction leaves unexplained the *mechanism* which raises prices from p_0 to $2p_0$. To put the same point rather differently: since, in a competitive system, prices rise only if aggregate demand exceeds aggregate supply, just *how* does the doubling of the money supply cause aggregate demand (at p_0) to exceed aggregate supply (at p_0)? Equations (pK 5) and (pK 6) appear to provide no explanation. Nor, since (pK 8) hypothesises that the demand for money is *not* a function of the interest rate, can the interest rate mechanism be the explanation? This is the mystery.

A simple and appropriate solution to the mystery is provided by rewriting (pK 6). This involves recalling that A ($\equiv$ the real value of households' assets) must, in a model containing only three types of assets, be capable of disaggregation as follows:

$$A \equiv \frac{M^S}{p} + \frac{B_0}{p} + K,$$

where

$$\frac{M^S}{p} \equiv \text{real value of households' money balances}$$

$$\frac{B_0}{p} \equiv \text{real value of households' bonds}$$

$$K \equiv \text{households' holdings of real assets.}$$

Then, with B_0/p and K held constant, a doubling of M^S from M_0 to $2M_0$ must raise A by doubling M^S/p. This shifts the savings (consumption) schedule. We expect the marginal response coefficient relating planned consumption (C_p) to real assets (A) to be positive. Hence $\partial S_p/\partial A$ will be negative. Hence because of the "cash balance" effect subsumed in (pK 6) there *is* a mechanism which will cause excess demand at the initial price level p_0—though the existence of such a mechanism is not obvious at first glance.

In short, the "classical pre-Keynesian" model's central hypothesis was that an increase in real money (real cash) balances caused households to substitute money for goods. By contrast the Keynesian model implies that an increase in real cash balances M/p leads households to substitute money for bonds.

The remaining properties of pre-Keynesian macroeconomics the reader can readily establish himself by manipulating the model set out in the Questions and Exercises at the end of this chapter.

What is the structure of pre-Keynesian macroeconomics? The *exogenous* variables are:

$M^S \equiv$ the nominal quantity of money
$K \equiv$ real capital stock
$T \equiv$ state of technique
$A \equiv$ real value of households' assets.

The *endogenous* variables are:

$Y \equiv$ real output
$C_p \equiv$ real planned consumption
$I_p \equiv$ real planned investment
$r \equiv$ rate of interest
$p \equiv$ price of a unit of output
$N^D \equiv$ quantity of labor demanded
$N^S \equiv$ quantity of labor supplied
$W/p \equiv$ real wage rate
$M^D \equiv$ nominal quantity of money demanded;
$U \equiv$ the quantity of involuntary unemployment.

There are thus *fourteen* variables, *ten* endogenous and *four* exogenous. To determine them we have the nine equations (16pK 1–16pK 9) *plus*

$$K = \bar{K} \qquad \text{(16.pK 10)}$$
$$T = \bar{T} \qquad \text{(16.pK 11)}$$
$$A = \bar{A} \qquad \text{(16.pK 12)}$$

the production function and the definitional identity $N^S - N^D \equiv U$. This gives us the fourteen equations we need.

KEYNESIAN AND PRE-KEYNESIAN MACROECONOMICS: THE "KEYNESIAN REVOLUTION"

In the broadest of comparisons both our "Keynesian" model and the model we have called "pre-Keynesian" are alike in that given (1) the values of certain *exogenous* variables, (2) a number of behavior assumptions, including a production function, and (3) any necessary definitions, each determines the equilibrium values of the *endogenous* variables. However the models differ sharply in their *predictions*. As a result they differ sharply in their *policy implications*. Because of this it is not uncommon to describe the development of modern macroeconomics as originating in or amounting to a "Keynesian revolution." To see why this is so, let us look at the principal results of the two systems.

According to our (Keynesian) model, the equilibrium of the system may occur at any level of employment within the upper limit imposed by the size of the work-force. There is *no* mechanism which makes the system automatically tend towards a full-employment equilibrium. This result, which was obviously easy to reconcile with the severe involuntary unemployment of the interwar years, carried the general policy implication that to attain full employment, conscious intervention in the working of the economic system was necessary.

By implication, therefore, Keynesian macroeconomics justified intervention, for it not only showed that appropriate forms of intervention *could* raise the equilibrium of level of employment but also insisted that full employment—as simply one of a number of equally probable equilibria—would otherwise occur only as a fluke.

In direct contrast pre-Keynesian macroeconomics asserted that (1) the economic system tended *always* towards a full-employment equilibrium; and hence implied that (2) intervention in the working of the system to attain full employment was *unnecessary*—indeed possibly harmful.

In short, Keynesian macroeconomics was by implication in favor of governmental action to control aggregate demand, pre-Keynesian economics by implication in favor of *laissez-faire*.

In the 1930s it was, of course, not easy to reconcile the principal assertion of the pre-Keynesian model with the chronic persistence of involuntary unemployment on a massive scale. But where such unemployment was observed, pre-Keynesian macroeconomics inevitably tended to focus attention on the failure of the labor market to behave competitively. As a result the pre-Keynesian macroeconomics emphasized *wage flexibility* and implied, though this was not so often advocated, that a reduction in the money wage, leading to a reduction in the real wage, would restore full employment. Hence the pre-Keynesian approach was to argue that since involuntary unemployment was (cf. Figure 16.6) incompatible with a *competitive* labor market, the labor market should be *made* competitive. In formal terms it predicted that *flexible* money wages, which fell if $N^S > N^D$, would always restore full employment while the Keynesian model predicted that *flexible* money wages would restore full employment *if,* and only *if,* the rate of interest necessary to attain full employment (r_{FE}) was greater than the minimum rate of interest acceptable to the community (r_{min}). And while this would normally be the case, a wage cut has a number of unfavorable effects on employment. Hence, even if a wage reduction would, *in principle,* be able to restore full employment, it would be an awfully clumsy way to do it.

It followed that, as a means of eliminating involuntary unemployment the Keynesian approach tended to emphasize the manipulation of government expenditure and tax rates (fiscal policy) and the manipulation of the money supply and hence interest rates (monetary policy) while the pre-Keynesian approach tended to emphasize wage policy. The "revolution" in theory brought about a "revolution" in policy.

In sum, the development of Keynesian macroeconomics had important consequences not only for social attitudes toward economic policy but also for the forms of policy. Nowadays many of us, irrespective of political allegiance, expect the government to manage aggregate demand either by fiscal or monetary policy so as to maintain "full employment." That we do so is, at least, in part the result of the "Keynesian revolution."

It is not possible to say to what degree our relatively greater success in maintaining "full employment" after World War II (as compared with the period after World War I) is due to the Keynesian revolution. It seems safe, however, to say that some part of it is. If this is so, two conclusions follow. First, the Keynesian revolution has made a significant impact on all of our lives. Second, few men can, by their work, have given greater benefits to the world, particularly the developed Western World, than Lord Keynes.

SUMMARY

In this chapter we have presented a comparison between "Keynesian" and "pre-Keynesian" macroeconomics. In two important senses this comparison has been unfair to pre-Keynesian economists. In the first place, our comparison gives no hint of the very considerable debt Keynes owed to his predecessors upon whose work he necessarily built. In the second place, while we have devoted many chapters to building the Keynesian model, pre-Keynesian theory has been expounded in a few pages. Inevitably, this has done it less than justice. As a result the pre-Keynesian theory has been oversimplified and the contrast between the two theories made not only too stark but too one-sided.

The reader should take careful account of these limitations of our treatment. Simplification is a legitimate device of exposition provided it does not involve distortion. Our comparison is designed to bring out the essential features of—and thus the significant differences between—the two systems. It does *not* seek to show how pre-Keynesian economics developed into Keynesian economics. Nor does it seek to give a comprehensive account of pre-Keynesian macrotheory. Readers who require a more comprehensive account of Keyne's great predecessors must look elsewhere.

As we have presented them, both theories are logically consistent: each contains sufficient independent equations to determine the variables it contains. Nevertheless, as the reader may easily verify, the two theories generate different predictions. These differences can arise only because the two theories contain different behavior hypotheses. And in the next chapter we will discuss the behavior hypotheses of the quantity theory.

QUESTIONS AND EXERCISES

1. "In pre-Keynesian economics the rate of interest was the variable which equated planned saving with planned investment. In Keynesian economics the variable which does this is income." Explain.

2. In the pre-Keynesian model on pages 261–62, what would be the consequences of a government deficit? Does pre-Keynesian theory tend to support the notion of a balanced budget? If so, why?

3. "Variables are properly classified as exogenous or endogenous only in relation to an economic *model* containing a number of equations. The classification dependent and independent by contrast refers to a single equation." Do you agree? Illustrate your answer by reference to Keynesian and pre-Keynesian theories.

4. Use the pre-Keynesian model below to find the equilibrium values of

$$Y; \frac{W}{p}; \quad W; \quad p; \quad S_p; \quad I_p.$$

From it develop predictions of the consequences of
1) an increase in autonomous consumption of 100 per period;
2) an increase in the desired ratio of money to money income to 0.5;
3) a shift in the investment function amounting to 100 per period.

   Compare your predictions with those you would derive from a Keynesian model.

Pre-Keynesian Model

$$\left.\begin{array}{l} S_p = -A + (1 - c)Y \\ I_p = H - br \\ S_p = I_p \end{array}\right\} \text{ goods market}$$

$A = 100, (1 - c) = 0.2$
$H = 1000, b = 10$

$$\left.\begin{array}{l} M^S = M_0 \\ M^D = KY_p \\ M^D = M^S \end{array}\right\} \text{ money market}$$

$M_0 = 2650$
$K = 0.25$

$$\left.\begin{array}{l} N^D = X - l\left(\dfrac{W}{p}\right) \\ \\ N^S = Q + n\left(\dfrac{W}{p}\right) \\ \\ N^S = N^D \end{array}\right\} \text{ labor market}$$

$X = 500, l = 50$
$Q = 20, n = 10$

$$Y = F + eN - fN^2 \quad \text{production function}$$
$F = 4400, e = 10$
$f = 0.01$

5. "In pre-Keynesian economics the function of the rate of interest was to determine how a given output should be distributed between consumption and capital accumulation." Explain.

6. In what sense, if any, is it true to say that pre-Keynesian macroeconomics *assumed* full employment?

7. "Saving is spending just as much as consumption is. Moreover since saving entails capital accumulation—which in the *long run* makes us all better off —we should encourage saving at the expense of consumption." What sort of theory is implied by these statements?

8. Which hypotheses of pre-Keynesian macroeconomics seem to you most open to objection? Can you devise tests for them?

9. If A (the real value of households' assets) is interpreted as $A \equiv M/p + B_0/p + K$, is it still correct to say that, in a Keynesian model, flexible wages will restore full employment if and only if $r_{\text{FE}} > r_{\text{min}}$? If not, why not?

10. Rewrite the pre-Keynesian model on pages 261–62 by replacing equation (pK 8) with:

$$MD = L_1(pY, r), \qquad \text{(pK 8*)}$$

where L^1 is now a liquidity function such that $\partial MD/\partial r < 0$. Show that the quantity theory of money still holds and reinterpret the mechanism whereby a doubling of the money supply produces excess demand in the goods market.

11. "In a Keynesian system with no cash balance effect, an increase in the money supply leads households to substitute money for bonds. In the pre-Keynesian system the substitution was in favor of goods." Explain. Construct a more general model containing both forms of substitution. In such a model will money wage cuts eliminate involuntary unemployment?

12. In Question 9 B_0/p denotes the real value of bond holdings and B_0 the nominal values. Hence B_0 depends upon B, the *quantity* or irredeemable bonds in the system and r, the rate of interest such that:

$$B_0 \equiv \frac{\bar{B}}{r},$$

where $\bar{B}$ is the quantity of irredeemable bonds each paying a coupon income of \$1 per year in perpetuity. Explain the identity above. What assumption is entailed in the statement on page 266 that B_0/p is constant? What difficulties would arise if it were not made?

13. Many pre-Keynesian economists emphasized the role of discretionary monetary policy in controlling the economy. Using the model on pages 261–62 as amended by Question 10, discuss the relevance of discretionary monetary policy.

14. Marginal productivity theory suggests that marginal product falls as employment increases. Yet our data show that output increases more than proportionately to employment during a cyclical upswing. How would you explain this apparent conflict?

SUGGESTED READING

J. Robinson, Economic Philosophy (Baltimore: Pelican, 1964) Chaps. 4–6.

G. Ackley, *Macroeconomic Theory* (New York: Macmillan, 1947) Chaps. 5–8.

L. Klein, *The Keynesian Revolution* (New York: Macmillan, 1947) Chaps. 2, 6–7. *Advanced reference.*

R. Harrod, *The Life of John Maynard Keynes* (New York: Macmillan, 1951) particularly Chap. 2.

R. Harrod, *Economic Essays* (New York: Macmillan, 1952) Chap. 12.

R. Meek, *Economics and Ideology and Other Essays* (London: Chapman & Hall, 1967), pp. 179–95.

P. Samuelson, "The General Theory," in S. Harris, *The New Economics* (New York: Knopf, 1947).

J. Schumpeter, "Keynes the Economist," in S. Harris, *The New Economics* (New York: Knopf, 1947).

J. Schumpeter, *History of Economic Analysis* (New York: Oxford University Press, 1954) Part IV, Chap. 8.

17

The Monetarist Challenge

ALTHOUGH THE Keynesian model discussed in the previous chapters of this book has become the dominant approach in modern macroeconomics, it has been strongly challenged in recent years by a revival of the quantity theory. But this revived quantity theory is also a revised one. While it keeps the old quantity theory's emphasis on the quantity of money as the main engine of change in money income—and is therefore often called "monetarism"— it is a theory which has learned a great deal from the Keynesian revolution. In fact, it has been argued that in many ways it is closer to the Keynesian theory than to the old-fashioned quantity theory.[1] While it is still a theory accepted by only a minority of economists, it has gained many adherents in recent years and has had widespread influence beyond the narrow circle of monetarists. It therefore deserves serious study. For reasons of space we will focus mainly on only one version of the new quantity theory: the version presented by Professor Milton Friedman of the University of Chicago and by members of the so-called "Chicago school."[2]

The quantity theory, like the Keynesian theory, looks at the determinants of total expenditures. Where it differs from the Keynesian theory is in asserting that, as an empirical matter, changes in expenditures are primarily due to changes in the quantity of money. In the Keynesian system, changes in expenditures and in money income can be due to

1. See Don Patinkin, "The Chicago Tradition, the Quantity Theory, and Friedman," *Journal of Money, Credit and Banking*, Vol. 1 (February 1969), pp. 46–70. For Professor Friedman's acknowledgment of the Keynesian influence, see his *The Optimum Quantity of Money and Other Essays* (Chicago: Aldine Publishing Co., 1969), p. 73.
2. For an alternative version closer to the Keynesian theory in its conclusion, see the work of Karl Brunner and Allan Meltzer cited in the "Suggested Reading."

changes in any of the following six factors: the quantity of money, liquidity preference, the marginal efficiency of investment, the marginal propensity to consume, government expenditures, and foreign investment. While it would be an overstatement to say that in the monetarist theory only one of these factors, the quantity of money, does affect income, it *is* correct to say that the quantity theory attributes a predominant influence to changes in the quantity of money. The modern quantity theorist accepts the Keynesian proposition that liquidity preference, the MEI, and the MPC are subject to change and that changes in these parameters will affect money income. However, he does not treat such changes as being exogenous. Instead, he argues that such changes are frequently the result of prior, or anticipated, changes in the quantity of money, so that changes in the quantity of money are much more basic than changes in other variables used in Keynesian theory.

To challenge the Keynesian theory effectively a quantity theory must do two things. First, it must show that it can explain changes in money income better than does the Keynesian theory. Second, it must be able to show that a price-flexible *laissez-faire* system would find its equilibrium only at full employment; that except for a transition period, until prices and wages have adjusted, mass unemployment is impossible. The old quantity theory was largely abandoned in the 1930s when the Keynesian theory of underemployment equilibrium seemed much more capable of explaining mass unemployment. To reverse the Keynesian revolution the quantity theory should therefore show that mass unemployment is due either to price inflexibility or unwise government policies (such as allowing a great reduction in the money stock) rather than to an inherent failure of a price-flexible *laissez-faire* system. We will first deal with the problem of determining the level of money income, and then treat the problem of underemployment equilibrium. But, before turning to these issues, it may be useful to discuss a very basic point which permeates the quantity theory, old as well as new.

NOMINAL MONEY AND REAL MONEY

This point is the distinction between the nominal quantity of money and the real quantity of money. The monetarist continually emphasizes the distinction between the two; to him this distinction provides the central point of macroeconomics and monetary theory. The *nominal* quantity of money (that is, the quantity of money in money terms) is the result of actions taken by the Treasury, the Federal Reserve, and the banking system. The Federal Reserve makes available to the banks a certain volume of reserves, and the banks, in turn, use these reserves to create a certain quantity of deposits, and these deposits plus the currency stock are our *supply* of nominal money. Now the *demand* for nominal money consists simply of the amount which all economic units (households, firms, and governments) want to hold. In equilibrium, supply must equal demand, but what brings this about? What makes the nominal quantity of money that economic units want to hold just equal to the quantity which the Treasury, the Federal Reserve, and the commercial banks have created? Suppose, for example, that the money-creating agencies have created more nominal money than the economic units want to hold. In this case some economic units find themselves holding more money than they want to hold relative to their other assets. Hence, they spend this money either on consumption or on assets. This brings their money holdings into equilibrium, but now the sellers of goods or assets have more cash. Since their money holdings were presumably in equilibrium before, they now find that they are holding excess money, so *they* increase their money outlays. The process continues; the excess money is a hot potato which gets passed from one holder to another. But in the process of passing on these nominal money balances, something important happens. If the economy is not already at full employment, then the increased expenditure induces firms to raise output and employment; in other words, real income goes up. As real income rises, the public is wealthier, so that it feels able to afford holding larger money balances. This is one way in which an increase in the supply of nominal money can lead to an equivalent increase in demand.

A second possibility is that economy is already operating at full employment. In this case, instead of output increasing, prices rise.[3] The public wants to hold, not a certain *nominal* quantity of money, but a certain *real* quantity of money. Hence, if prices rise by, say, 10 percent, the public will want, as a first approximation, to hold 10 percent more nominal money. In this way equilibrium is restored. If the money-creating institutions increase the nominal quantity of money by *x* percent at full employment, prices rise by *x* percent at which point economic units find themselves holding the same *real* quantity of money as before, and are therefore back in equilibrium.

So far, we have considered two cases, one in which only output rises, and another in which only prices increase. Obviously, there is an intermediate case in which part of the increase is in output and part in prices. In this case it is increases in both prices and output which induce economic

3. Actually what is relevant is not whether or not the economy is at full employment, but whether prices rise or are stable. Prices may start to rise when there is still considerable unemployment. In terms of economic analysis the important distinction is between situations in which prices are stable (so that changes in real and nominal magnitudes are the same) and those in which prices change. However, we will follow the widespread practice of calling conditions of rising prices full employment.

units to hold the additional money. In the opposite case, where the supply of nominal money is reduced, prices and/or output fall. (The detailed analysis of this case is left to the reader.)

The above analysis can be expressed symbolically, by the so-called Cambridge, or cash balance, equation: $M = kPT$ or $M = kY$, where M is money, P is the price level, T real income, Y money income, and k, often called "the Cambridge k," is the proportion of their income which economic units want to hold in the form of money. For example, if they want to hold one month's income in the form of money, then (on an annual basis) k is one-twelfth. Suppose now that the supply of money is increased. Unless the Cambridge k somehow rises enough, either P or T must rise. In the old-fashioned pre-Keynesian quantity theory k was usually treated as constant, and due to the presumption of full employment, T was treated as unaffected by M too. Hence, it seemed to follow that P has to rise in proportion to M. Nowadays we have abandoned the full-employment presumption and know that T is also variable. Hence, we tend to use the form $M = kY$ since Y includes changes in both T and P.

The moral of this story is that the money-creating institutions determine the supply of nominal money, and that, to bring the demand for money into equality with the supply of money, money income (that is to say, output and/or prices) must change. This means that, if the demand for real money is stable, changes in money income will depend upon, and be explainable by, changes in the supply of nominal money. In the case of full employment, where all the change is in prices, one can formulate this principle more dramatically as follows: the monetary institutions determine the nominal quantity of money in existence, but the public determines the real quantity of money, and the price level is the result of this tug-of-war.

The above analysis is very much in the spirit of the quantity theory. To what extent does it differ from the Keynesian theory? In principle a Keynesian accepts most of the above, but he attaches much less importance to it than does the quantity theorist. The Keynesian accepts the proposition that changes in the supply of nominal money change income, but he believes that the greater part of income fluctuation is due to other factors. The Keynesian does not seek to deny $M = kY$. Instead he argues that factors such as increases in the marginal efficiency of investment, for example, tend to raise Y. This increase in Y, via the L_1 relationship, increases the rate of interest, and the rise in the rate of interest induces the public to hold less money per dollar of income—i.e., it lowers k. (In addition, with rising interest rates banks may reduce their excess reserves, thus raising M.) Moreover, the central bank is likely to try to moderate the increase in interest rates by increasing the quantity of bank reserves and hence money. Thus M tends to be endogenous rather than exogenous. Hence, the Keynesian argues, while the $M = kY$ proposition is valid, it is a formulation which hides rather than elucidates the main causes of income change. Thus the Keynesian would describe differently the process of an increase in the supply of money discussed above. Instead of talking about the public spending excess balances, he prefers to talk about the public lending excess balances and thereby reducing the rate of interest, so that investment increases. And since the liquidity preference curve is not completely interest-inelastic, and the marginal efficiency of investment curve is not very interest-elastic, an increase in the quantity of money does not raise income proportionately. Instead, the liquidity preference relation insures that with the lower rate of interest the increase in the quantity of money is *partly* offset by more money being held idle. (We shall return to this point in greater detail below.)

DETERMINANTS OF INCOME

The modern quantity theory is a theory of the demand for money. To understand this statement, consider the Cambridge equation $M = kY$. In this equation, Y is the unknown that has to be determined. M, on the other hand, is treated as a "given"; that is, it is taken as essentially determined by the central bank's policy. To relate Y to this exogenously fixed M we have to know the value of k, the gearing ratio of money to income. For example, if k is very stable, then we can predict income very well from a knowledge of the money supply. And this assumption of a stable k was, in fact, generally made by the old quantity theory. It was taken to be stable (or rather changing at a steady and predictable rate over time) because it depended upon the marginal utility of holding means of payments, and hence on presumably stable habits and institutions.

But this old quantity theory belief in the stability of k was largely destroyed in the 1930s. This was due to two factors. On the one hand, conditions prevailing during the Great Depression seemed to disconfirm it, and on the other hand the development of Keynesian theory, with its notion of liquidity preference, suggested that a belief in a stable k is not very good economic theory. By relating the quantity of money demanded to the rate of interest, Keynes gave a cogent reason why k should vary from time to time, since clearly the rate of interest does so.[4] Second, by stressing the importance of the speculative motive, and of rapidly changing expectations, Keynesian theory suggested that the whole demand schedule for money is unstable. Hence, one cannot predict Y from a knowledge of M because

4. That the rate of interest affects the quantity of money the public wants to hold was known to some of the older quantity theorists, but they did not stress it, and did not work out its implications.

k is not a constant. Changes in marginal efficiency of investment and the propensity to consume cause the interest rate to change, and changes in the interest rate, in turn, change k, as do changes in the public's expectations about the future course of interest rates.

The modern quantity theory has accepted some of this Keynesian criticism. It concedes that k is not *numerically* stable in the sense of being a stable number, such as 3. Instead it asserts a quite different type of stability for k. It claims that k is a stable *function* of a limited number of variables. That is, k will vary from time to time, but this variation is not arbitrary; it can readily be explained by looking at changes in a limited set of variables such as income or interest rates. The modern quantity theorist therefore does not say: "If I know M, I can predict Y"; instead he says: "If I know M, and if I know the values of a limited number of ascertainable variables, then I can predict k, and therefore also income." It is a much more complex and sophisticated theory than the old quantity theory.

The modern quantity theory differs from the old quantity theory in one additional way. The old quantity theory assumed that prices are very flexible. Hence if aggregate demand falls, output and employment will decline only very temporarily; after a short time the economy will return to full employment with only prices having fallen. In the traditional Keynesian theory, on the other hand, as we saw in Chapter 15, it is output which changes while prices are stable. In the modern quantity theory *both* output and prices adjust when aggregate demand changes. To what *extent* the change takes place in output, and to what extent in prices, is an issue on which the modern quantity theory is agnostic; the change could be in either variable. It therefore takes an additional theory, quite apart from the quantity theory, to determine the separate change in prices and in output when the quantity of money changes. In other words, whereas the old quantity theory was a theory which tried to explain prices—perhaps because it tended to stress the long run—the modern quantity theory is a theory of money income. It tries to explain money income rather than the price level. In this respect, its difference from the Keynesian theory is a subtle one. Keynesians, too, try to explain the level of money income, but they stress, though not exclusively, changes in real output much more than changes in prices. In much Keynesian analysis the price level is not given much emphasis, and is sometimes, though certainly not always, treated as constant.[5] The quantity theorist, on the other hand, is very much aware of the fact that the change in money income may be a change in prices rather than in output.

The demand function for money is basic to the quantity theory. Let us therefore look at it in some detail. The quantity theorist treats money as one of several forms in which the public can hold its wealth. The other forms of

5. Keynesian theory can be used to analyze price changes, and we will take up in Chapter 20 the Keynesian theory of inflation.

holding wealth are (1) bonds and other claims fixed in nominal units such as Savings and Loan shares, Treasury bills, etc., (2) equities, (3) physical goods and human capital (such as education). The way the public allocates its wealth among these types of assets depends, among other things, on the yields it expects to receive from them. Hence, other things being equal, the demand for money depends upon the total stock of wealth held by the public, and on the relative yields of the various types of assets. The yields on directly held physical goods and on human capital are hard to measure, and the same is true for equities, since one of the components of the return on equities, expected capital gains, is very difficult to estimate. Hence, let us simplify by assuming that the rates of return on bonds, on other claims fixed in nominal units, on equities, on physical goods, and on human capital all move together. To the extent that this is so, we can use the interest rates paid on bonds to represent all the other interest rates. We can then measure the cost of holding money; that is, the interest foregone by holding money instead of another asset, by this rate of interest on bonds.

In addition to the cost of holding money we need a scale variable in our demand function. One possibility is to use total (human plus nonhuman) wealth. Since we are looking at money as one form in which the public is holding its total wealth, there is much to be said for using total wealth as a major determinant of money holdings. Unfortunately, since there is no reliable way of measuring human wealth, we cannot measure total wealth and hence cannot use it in empirical work. Fortunately, there is a way out. Wealth is something which yields income, and we can therefore use income as a substitute measure of wealth. But the rate of return which the public earns on its human and nonhuman wealth varies from year to year, so that income is much more variable than is the stock of wealth. This difficulty can be avoided by using as a measure of wealth, not the income of any one year, but the income of many years—so-called "permanent income." (This is the same income concept as is used in the permanent income theory of the consumption function discussed in Chapter 9.) Another alternative, used by some quantity theorists, is to use, instead of a measure of human and nonhuman wealth, just nonhuman wealth, a variable on which data are available. Moreover, it is also possible to use neither permanent income nor nonhuman wealth, but to use just annual income. Using annual income can be rationalized as tying the demand for money more closely to transactions needs than is true for permanent income and nonhuman wealth. Which one of these three variables one uses is not really basic to the quantity theory. Hence, to avoid getting lost in complex details, let us just use an income measure without specifying whether it is annual or permanent income or nonhuman wealth we mean.[6]

6. An additional measurement problem arises from the definition of money. The most common way of defining money is to say that it is the sum of two items, currency and demand

We now have a demand function for money which looks as follows: $M = f(Y, i)$, or more specifically, $M = a + bY - ci$. You will note that this is essentially the same as the Keynesian liquidity preference function, though in the quantity theory we do not separate the demand for money into components such as transaction demand, etc.

If the quantity theory's demand function for money is essentially the same as the Keynesian one, how do the two theories differ? Why don't they reach the same conclusion? This is a rather complex question. One aspect relates to what each theory assumes about the interest elasticities of the demand for money on the one hand, and of investment and consumption on the other. Another aspect relates to the assumed degree of price flexibility and the extent to which one must distinguish between real and nominal money balances. These points are not simple and need considerable explaining.

Let us look first at the interest elasticity of the demand for money; i.e., at c in the above equation. To see its significance, consider first two extreme cases. One is the situation of absolute liquidity preference discussed in Chapter 12. In this case changes in the quantity of money have no effect at all on income. As Figure 17.1(a) shows, an increase in the quantity of money does not lower the rate of interest, and hence it does not raise income.[7] In this case the quantity theory is completely invalid. To relate this case to the above discussion of the demand function for money, it is convenient to rewrite the above equation making the rate of interest the dependent variable (and substituting the supply of money in place of the demand for money) so that it reads $i = d - eM + fY$. Absolute liquidity preference then means that the coefficient e has a value of zero; regardless of what happens to M, i is constant. This is the extreme anti-quantity theory case.[8]

At the other extreme, illustrated in Figure 17.1(b), assume that the interest elasticity of demand for money is zero so that in the equation

---

deposits. However, this is not the only way to define it. Some economists—for example Professor Friedman, the preeminent exponent of the quantity theory—use a broader definition of money. They include not only currency and demand deposits but also commercial bank time deposits. They do this, in part, because they believe that time deposits in commercial banks are a very close substitute for demand deposits, and in part for statistical reasons. Until the Banking Act of 1933 prohibited the payment of interest on demand deposits, there did not exist a reliable breakdown of total bank deposits into demand deposits and time deposits. Hence, in undertaking statistical analysis covering many years there is an advantage to including commercial bank time deposits in the definition of money. But, in any case, the definition of money is a peripheral rather than a central issue for the quantity theory. In fact some quantity theorists, such as Professors Karl Brunner and Allan Meltzer, use the more traditional, narrow definition of money, while, on the other hand, Keynes himself essentially used the broad definition of money.

7. Later on in this chapter we will discuss the point that changes in the supply of money can affect income in ways other than through the rate of interest. For the time being we are ignoring this point.

8. For reasons discussed below the extreme anti-quantity theory case can also be obtained by assuming that, while the demand for money is not completely interest elastic, the marginal efficiency of investment and consumption are completely interest inelastic.

Figure 17.1 / *Liquidity preference functions: (a), absolute liquidity preference; (b), completely interest-inelastic liquidity preference.*

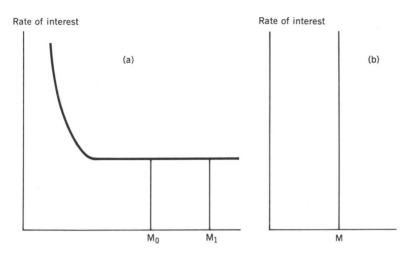

$M = a + bY - ci$, c is zero. In this case the quantity theory is perfectly correct and the Keynesian theory is completely invalid. With c being zero in the preceding equation, the only thing which can induce the public to hold any additional money that has been created is a change in Y. Money income *must* therefore rise proportionately to changes in the money stock. Similarly, if the quantity of money declines, rising interest rates do not induce the public to give up any part of its money holdings. Only a fall in income can do so.

The available empirical evidence strongly suggests that the interest elasticity of the demand for money is neither zero nor infinity; so let us now look at this in-between case. It is more complex than the two previous cases, because with the interest elasticity of the demand for money being neither infinity nor zero, we have to look at its magnitude, not in an absolute sense, but relative to other magnitudes. These magnitudes are the interest elasticities of the investment function and the consumption function. To see this, consider what happens to income if the interest rate drops by a given amount as the quantity of money is increased. If investment and consumption are completely interest-inelastic, even a very large increase in the money stock and a great reduction in the interest rate will not have any effect on income. On the other hand, if investment and consumption are highly interest-elastic, then even a very minor reduction in the interest rate has a substantial effect on income. Figure 17.2 illustrates these possibilities. (For the sake of simplicity both investment and consumption have been combined into a single expenditure curve in this figure.) Thus, the interest

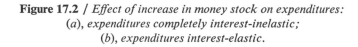

Figure 17.2 / *Effect of increase in money stock on expenditures:*
(a), expenditures completely interest-inelastic;
(b), expenditures interest-elastic.

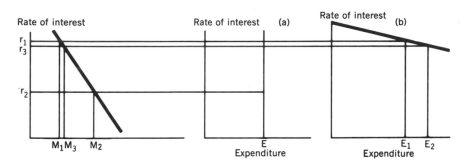

elasticities of both the demand for money and expenditures are relevant for determining by how much a given change in the quantity of money affects money income.[9]

The quantity theory asserts that changes in the money stock have a very important effect on income. This result can be obtained if the demand for money is much less interest-elastic than expenditures. On the other hand, if the demand for money is much more interest-elastic than expenditures, then changes in the money stock have only a relatively small effect on income. In this case changes in other factors, such as government expenditures and the marginal efficiency of investment, may well overshadow changes in the money stock.

It is worth noting that the *stability* of the demand for money, as well as its interest-elasticity, is important for the quantity theory. If the demand function for money fluctuates unpredictably a great deal, it may still be true that changes in the money supply have major effects on money income, but it would no longer be correct to say that one can predict income well from a knowledge of the money supply. But if the demand for money is a stable function with very low interest elasticity, and if expenditures have a high interest elasticity, then one can predict changes in money income very well by looking at changes in the money stocks.

But, though a combination of a highly interest-inelastic and stable demand function for money and a highly elastic expenditure function will yield quantity theory results, these are not *necessary* conditions for the quantity theory. One can get quantity theory results even if the demand

9. These are not the only relevant factors. The magnitude of the multiplier also helps to determine by how much income responds to a given change in the money stock, as do the relative magnitudes of the money stock, investment, and consumption.

curve for money has substantial interest elasticity and the expenditure curve is relatively interest-inelastic.

To see this consider the effect of an increase in the money stock in an economy which is already at full employment.[10] The initial effect of the increase in the money supply is that the interest rate falls. This decline in the rate of interest causes money expenditures to increase. Given that we are already at full employment, the increase in expenditures means that prices are rising. This rise in prices, in turn, results in a reduction of the real money stock. And this reduction in the real money stock then raises the rate of interest, since, as discussed in Chapter 12, the rate of interest is a function of liquidity preference and the real stock of money. The initial interest rate we started out with was one required to obtain full employment at stable prices. As long as the rate of interest is below this initial rate, investment and aggregate demand in general will be greater than is consistent with price stability, and hence prices will rise. With prices rising, the quantity of money in real terms continues to fall and the nominal interest rate rises. Only when the interest rate is back to its initial full-employment-price stability level will prices stop rising. In other words, starting with a position of full employment, an increase in the money supply reduces the rate of interest only temporarily. This initial "liquidity effect," as it is called, is then offset by a second effect, the "price and income effect" just sketched.[11]

Figure 17.3 illustrates these effects. As we increase the money stock from M_0 to M_1 the interest rate initially falls from its full employment price stability level r_0 to r_1. But it does not stay there. With investment and aggregate demand exceeding their full employment equilibrium level, prices rise, and this price rise reduces the real quantity of money to, say, M_2. The rate of interest now rises to r_2. But since r_2 is still less than r_0, it is not an equilibrium rate: aggregate demand is still greater than is consistent with price stability so that prices continue to rise. As a result the real money stock falls to M_3, and the interest rate rises to r_3. This process continues as long as the interest rate is below r_0. Once it reaches r_0 the economy is back in equilibrium. Since we chose r_0 so that at this point prices are stable, the real quantity of money ceases to fall, and hence the interest rate ceases to rise. This is the end of the equilibrating process. The fact that the real quantity of money has returned to its previous level implies that prices have risen in proportion to the rise in the nominal money stock. (If the nominal

10. Actually, the money stock is generally rising to balance the increase in potential output. We will ignore this complication, and when we talk about an increase in the money stock from now on we will mean an increase relative to the trend.

11. In addition, there is a third effect, which operates very slowly. This is that with prices rising the public expects inflation to continue and takes this into account when setting nominal interest rates. As we explained in Chapter 12, the nominal rate of interest is equal to the real rate plus the percentage increase in prices. With the public expecting price increases to occur, the nominal rate is higher than it otherwise would be.

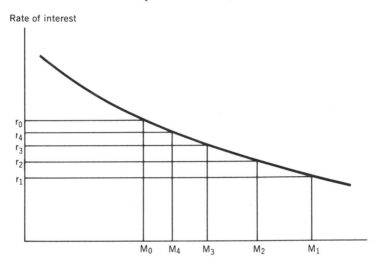

Figure 17.3 / *Effect of increase in the quantity of money on the interest rate.*

money stock has risen by, say, 10 percent, and the real money stock is constant, this implies that prices have risen by 10 percent too.) Since output is constant (we are dealing with a full employment situation), this means that money income (equal, of course, to prices times output) has also risen in proportion to the rise in the nominal money supply. Thus we reach the strict quantity theory conclusion that an increase in the nominal money stock raises money income proportionately. Note that this is so despite the fact that, as Figure 17.3 shows, the demand for money has some interest elasticity.

Put another way, the strict quantity theory asserts that an increase in the nominal money supply is not partially offset by a rise in the Cambridge *k* (or what is the same thing, a fall in velocity). Since an increase in the quantity of money *initially* lowers the rate of interest, this assertion must be supported in either of two ways. One is to say that the public's demand for money is (almost) completely interest-inelastic, so that the decline in the interest rate does not raise the Cambridge *k* significantly. The other way is to say that the decline in the rate of interest is only temporary. If the rate of interest quickly returns to its previous level, then so does the quantity of real money the public wants to hold, regardless of what the interest elasticity of the demand for money is.

The monetarist's argument that *at full employment* an increase in the nominal quantity of money leads to a proportional increase in the price level is something the Keynesian accepts too. The Keynesian theory of inflation does not differ very much from the quantity theory's. The big dispute between the quantity theory and the Keynesian theory is about what takes place under conditions of less than full employment. In the Keynesian system prices are stable until full employment is reached. Hence if the quantity of money is increased under conditions of less than full employment, which is the normal situation in our economy, the price level does not rise. Instead of prices rising, output increases. Now the increase in output raises the demand for money because, via the L_1 relationship, the quantity of money demanded by the public is a function of the income level. But the rise in output does not increase the demand for money enough to raise the interest rate back to its previous level. Instead, it reaches a new equilibrium at an intermediate level, such as point r_3 in Figure 17.3. To see why the interest rate does not return all the way to its previous equilibrium level when prices are stable and output rises, assume that it were to do so. If the rate of interest were to return to r_0 then expenditures would fall back to their previous level. But if expenditures return to their previous level, output would fall back to its previous level too. It follows that the interest rate returning to its previous level is not an equilibrium situation when it is real income rather than prices which adjust. Instead, the new equilibrium requires an interest rate between the old rate which existed before the money stock was increased and the lower interest rate which prevails right after the money stock increased. In the Keynesian theory, therefore, money income under conditions of less than full employment does not rise in proportion to the nominal money stock. Since some of the increase in the money stock is held because the rate of interest is lower, money income does not have to rise that much to insure that the public is willing to hold all the additional money. Part of the increase in the money stock is dissipated in an increase in idle balances.

The Keynesian therefore does not accept the proposition that under conditions of less than full employment an increase in the money stock leads to a proportional increase in money income *in the short run*. As far as the very long run is concerned, however, Keynesian theory is much more hospitable to the idea that money income rises in proportion to the nominal money stock. This is so because sooner or later, during a cyclical upswing, due to factors other than the increase in the money stock, the economy does reach full employment, and then the previous increase in the money stock raises prices. And, as discussed above, when prices rather than output rise, then income rises proportionately to the money stock. But the Keynesian believes that it takes so long for changes in the quantity of money to bring about proportional changes in income that for most practical purposes (such as forecasting income a few years ahead, or formulating monetary policy) one can assume that money income does *not* rise in proportion to the money stock. Hence an increase in the money stock does effectively reduce the rate of interest. Moreover, the Keynesian argues since prices are sticky, a *decline* in the nominal money stock does not lead to a price decline in the foreseeable future. Instead, it simply results in higher interest rates and lower output. The monetarist, on the other hand, believes that money income rises proportionately to increases in the money stock in a much shorter period than this. He envisages that it takes two years or less until money income has risen proportionately to an increase in the money stock.

An additional difference between the monetarist and the Keynesians relates to the mechanism by which changes in the quantity of money affect income. The Keynesian description of this process has been presented in previous chapters: an increase in the money stock lowers the rate of interest, and the lower rate of interest, in turn, raises investment. Both directly, and indirectly via the multiplier, this results in an increase in money income. The quantity theorist, on the other hand, describes the process differently, as follows: an increase in the money stock, resulting, say, from an open market purchase of securities by the Federal Reserve, results in the sellers of these securities holding more money than they want to hold. Consequently, they get rid of this money by buying securities. But in this process they increase someone else's money stock, who then, in turn, runs it down again. This process raises asset prices and makes it profitable to create new assets, i.e., to invest. At the same time it also raises consumption, as a result of consumer credit being more readily available and of households holding a larger stock of money. There is no presumption in the quantity theory that all, or even most, of the direct effect on expenditures comes through investment rather than consumption.[12]

The monetarist describes this whole process in terms of an excess supply of money rather than in terms of a decline in the rate of interest. *In principle,* this is not a material difference; since the price and quantity of any good are linked via the demand curve, it does not really matter, in principle, whether one describes a given change in terms of price or quantity. But, the monetarist argues, the rate of interest we actually observe in our data, e.g., the rate on government bonds, is a very bad measure of what we mean by the term "rate of interest" in economic theory. One reason for this is that our data cover only a few of the many interest rates which are relevant, primarily interest rates observed in the organized markets. For example, they do not include such interest rates as the discount rate which households apply to a future stream of income. Moreover, the interest rates given by our data are nominal interest rates, while the relevant rate is the *real* rate of interest.

---

12. Since consumption is much larger in dollar terms than is investment, an increase in the quantity of money (or a reduction in interest rates) may have a bigger dollar effect on consumption than on investment even if the interest elasticity (a pure number, not a dollar measure) is substantially smaller for consumption than for investment.

Another difference between the Keynesian and the quantity theorist relates to the effect of fiscal policy. In the Keynesian model considered in the previous chapters, an increase in government expenditures is expansionary, as is a cut in taxes. In the monetarist model this is not the case. Suppose the government increases expenditures and finances these expenditures by selling bonds rather than by creating new money (if new money is created, the monetarist would agree that money income will go up, but would attribute this to the money supply increase rather than to the fact that the government is spending). As the government borrows, it reduces the public's money stock and hence raises the rate of interest. If the liquidity preference schedule is *highly* interest-inelastic, and the expenditure schedule is *highly* elastic, then the bulk of the funds borrowed by the government will come from a reduction in private expenditures rather than from a reduction in the amount of money held per dollar of income. In other words, government expenditures simply crowd out an approximately equivalent amount of private expenditures, and hence aggregate demand is but little changed by government expenditures. Similarly, changes in tax rates do not have much effect on money income. If the government cuts taxes and keeps expenditures constant, it has to borrow (unless it creates new money), and this borrowing again crowds out an approximately equal amount of private expenditures.

A similar result can be reached if the liquidity preference schedule is not highly inelastic, but if prices are flexible. Then an increase in government expenditures initially raises prices, and hence the *real* money stock declines. As a result, private expenditures, once again, are crowded out. Monetarists argue that empirical observation supports their belief that fiscal policy has little, if any, effect on the level of money income. Rather, they claim, it is changes in the quantity of money which account for much of the change in income.[13]

As you should have noted by now, the dispute between monetarists and Keynesians is not so much a dispute about economic theory as it is a dispute about empirical magnitudes. By making monetarist assumptions about the interest elasticity of the liquidity preference and expenditure schedules, or about price flexibility, one obtains quantity theory results even if one formulates the theory in Keynesian terms. Conversely, if one makes Keynesian assumptions about the relevant interest elasticities and about price flexibility, one gets Keynesian results regardless of whether one formulates the theory in Keynesian terms or in terms of the Cambridge equation, $M = kY$.

13. This does not mean that monetarists necessarily support the use of monetary policy as a countercyclical device. Many monetarists oppose such a policy because they argue that monetary policy is so clumsy that it does more harm than good. The reasons they give for saying that monetary policy is clumsy are, first, that monetary policy often tries to serve several incompatible goals at the same time; and, second, that it affects income only with long, unpredictable lags.

The issue can therefore be settled only by empirical testing. Such testing consists of drawing certain implications from each theory and confronting these implications with observed events. Much work along these lines has been done and is still taking place, and we hope that substantial agreement will be reached in the not too distant future. Since this book deals with economic analysis rather than with empirical tests, this is not the place to review the empirical evidence. We can just indicate that monetarists have succeeded in showing that there is a close relationship between changes in the quantity of money and changes in money income. Two things, however, are still open to dispute: whether this relation between money and income is closer than the relation between the Keynesian variables and income; and, second, whether money is the cause or the effect. In other words, does the correlation between money and income demonstrate the effect of changes in the money supply on income, or does it instead reflect the effect which changes in income have on the money supply? Strange as it may seem, the available data and statistical tools do not make it easy to get agreement on these questions.

UNDEREMPLOYMENT EQUILIBRIUM

Pre-Keynesian classical theory was a theory of full-employment equilibrium. In the absence of wage-fixing either by the government or by unions, wages, like any other price, adjust until supply equals demand, so that only frictional unemployment is possible. Large scale unemployment is impossible because if workers are willing to reduce their wage demands, firms will find it profitable to hire more labor. They find it profitable because a wage reduction cuts costs but not demand. Demand depends not on wages, but on the quantity of money and the Cambridge k. And a wage cut reduces neither of these. Any persistent large-scale unemployment should therefore be blamed on wage rigidity rather than on inadequate demand. This position was, of course, challenged by Keynesian economics, which argued that, even with wage flexibility, there may be no mechanism by which a capitalistic economy can restore full employment, so that underemployment can be an equilibrium. In the postwar period the Keynesian criticism of the classical position has, in turn, been powerfully challenged by modern quantity theorists who have revived the classical conclusions in a much more sophisticated and subtle form.

We have discussed the pre-Keynesian classical position in the previous chapter. In brief it was that the rate of interest brings desired saving and investment into equality. If unemployment develops, workers should accept wage cuts, and these wage cuts will result in lower prices, a greater stock of real money, and hence a lower interest rate. If wages are cut enough, the rate of interest will fall enough to restore full employment.

The Keynesian answer to this argument was that the rate of interest does not function so as to bring desired saving and investment into equilibrium at full employment income. Instead, the rate of interest equates liquidity preference with the quantity of money. But the liquidity preference theory agrees with pre-Keynesian theory that a decrease in wages and prices generally reduces the interest rate. To this extent Keynes agreed with classical theory. But he did not stop there. He pointed out that the reduction in the rate of interest is only one of many effects of a wage cut. For example, a wage cut redistributes income from wage earners to firms, and therefore lowers the overall propensity to consume. In addition, if businessmen expect wages to be cut again in the near future, they will tend to refrain from investment until wages are, in fact, cut further. A wage cut has many effects on employment; some are favorable and some are unfavorable. One should not select the one particular effect which is favorable and ignore all the unfavorable effects of a wage cut. Moreover, there is the possibility of absolute liquidity preference. In this case, a wage cut cannot reduce the rate of interest. Hence Keynes rejected the "conventional wisdom" of his day which advocated wage cuts as a cure for unemployment. Instead, he urged a policy of achieving full employment by holding money wages constant and raising aggregate demand.[14]

Classical economists eventually responded to this challenge in two ways. First, they agreed with Keynes that one cannot rely for full employment on the effect of a wage cut on the rate of interest. But they developed another way of showing that, in principle, a wage cut, *if it were large enough,* could restore full employment. This way is known as the "Pigou effect" after one of its originators, Professor A. C. Pigou.

The Pigou effect works through the consumption function, more specifically through the asset term of the consumption function. The larger the household's stock of assets, the less incentive it has to accumulate additional assets by saving. Hence, if there is some mechanism by which wage and price cuts raise the public's stock of assets, then it follows that wage cut raises consumption and could, if large enough, restore full employment. And such a mechanism does exist. The public's assets can be divided into three components. One consists of capital goods held directly or in the form of equities (i.e., claims to capital goods), the second consists of claims on other members of the public (e.g., corporate bonds, Savings and Loan shares, etc.), and the third consists of claims on the government, mainly currency and government securities. Suppose now that all wages and prices

14. In addition, Keynes argued that even if it were possible to restore full employment through wage cuts, it would be an extremely awkward way of obtaining full employment. Most contemporary economists would agree with this judgment.

fall proportionately. The real value of capital goods is not affected since their prices change along with those of other goods. The real value of claims on other members of the public rises, of course, when prices fall, and in this way the real value of household assets increases. However, this is completely offset by a rise in the value of debts; what one person gains another loses. But the third category, claims on the government, is quite different. These claims, like claims on other members of the public, are fixed in nominal terms. Hence, as wages and prices fall, their real value rises. The public, as a whole, has an increase in the real value of its assets, and it therefore raises its consumption. To be sure, the government is poorer as the real value of outstanding bonds rises, but we can assume that the government (and taxpayers) do not, for this reason, cut their expenditures. (And, at least to some extent, a similar thing *may* be true with respect to the claim in the form of demand deposits which the public has on commercial banks.)[15] Thus wage and price cuts raise the public's overall wealth, and hence shift the consumption function upward. Since, *in principle,* there is no limit to the percentage by which wages can be cut, it is, *in principle,* possible to restore full employment in this way almost regardless of the other effects which a wage cut has on employment. This certainly does *not* mean that contemporary quantity theorists generally favor wage cuts as a practicable full-employment policy. The dispute about the effects of a wage cut on employment is a dispute not so much about policy as about a theoretical principle. Keynes claimed that, even in principle, a wage cut may not restore full employment. What the Pigou effect has done is to show that this claim is invalid, even though, as a policy measure, a wage cut may be an extremely inefficient way of restoring full employment. One can even go further than this and argue that the type of wage and price flexibility required to restore full employment *may,* at times, be so large that our economic system could not survive it. Some Keynesians have argued that such extreme fluctuations in the value of money would, in large part, destroy the usefulness of a monetary system. The question of how much wage and price flexibility would actually be needed is, of course, ultimately an empirical issue and, unfortunately, an unsettled one.

One can therefore argue that while Keynes was wrong in principle when he denied that a wage and price cut would restore full employment if it were only large enough, he was right in the practical context of wage cuts which are feasible in our economy. The proposition that a wage and price cut large enough to reduce the price of the Empire State Building to one dollar would restore full employment is not a helpful guide to policy.

15. Whether or not there is a Pigou effect with respect to demand deposits is a complex issue which must be passed by here. See Boris Pesek and Thomas Saving, *Money, Wealth and Income* (New York: Harcourt, Brace, 1967) and Don Patinkin, "Money and Wealth: A Review Article," *Journal of Economic Literature*, Vol. VII (December, 1969), pp. 1140–60.

Hence, although Keynes was "wrong" on a matter of economic principle, most economists do not advocate wage cuts as a cure for a recession.

The development of the Pigou effect has made it possible to reformulate pre-Keynesian macroeconomic theory in a very elegant and rigorous manner. This has been done by Professor Don Patinkin, who combined the Pigou effect with the Keynes effect, discussed above, into what he called the "real balance effect." In his model the direct determinants of expenditures are not the marginal efficiency of investment and the propensity to consume, but rather the difference between actual and desired real balances. Patinkin has been able to formulate macroeconomics around this principle. His model yields quantity theory results, but since it is a very abstract model, Patinkin does not claim that this necessarily invalidates the use of Keynesian remedies for practical problems.

SUMMARY

In this chapter we have looked at an alternative approach to macro-economic problems, the monetarist approach. Like the Keynesian approach discussed in the previous chapters, it focuses on the determinants of expenditures. But unlike the Keynesian approach, it treats as the engine of change in expenditures the discrepancy between the public's actual and desired stocks of real balances. Such a discrepancy also changes expenditures in the Keynesian system, but in the Keynesian system it is not the only, or even the predominant, motivator of expenditure change. Moreover, in the usual Keynesian model the effects of this discrepancy are mediated by a comparatively large interest elasticity of liquidity preference and a comparatively low interest elasticity of investment.

Since the quantity theory attempts to predict money income by looking at changes in the nominal money stock, it is vital for the quantity theory that there be a stable demand function for money. Moreover, to obtain the monetarist result even from a stable demand function for money, it is necessary *either* that the interest elasticity of the demand for money be very low and the interest elasticity of expenditures be very high, *or* that the interest rate be only very temporarily reduced by a rise in the money stock, and very temporarily raised by a reduction in the money stock.

We then looked at the question of whether a capitalistic economy with price and wage flexibility could be in a state of underemployment equilibrium. The answer is *no*—on this point Keynes was definitely wrong. But this does not mean that wage flexibility is necessarily a cure for unemployment, only that unlimited wage flexibility could, *in principle,* cure unemployment.

QUESTIONS AND EXERCISES

1. What are the main points of distinction between the modern quantity theory and (a) the old pre-Keynesian quantity theory, and (b) the Keynesian theory?

2. Suppose you were asked to undertake an empirical test of the monetarist vs. Keynesian view. How would you go about it?

3. From the *Economic Report of the President* prepare a chart showing prices, real income, and the money stock, 1948 to date. How would you interpret this chart?

4. During World War I some people used the quantity theory in the following way: They urged the public to reduce their Cambridge k because if k falls it would not be necessary to increase the money stock so much to finance the increased activity. And if the money stock would not rise so much, there would be less inflation. Discuss this plan.

5. Draw a completely interest-inelastic liquidity preference schedule. What happens in this diagram if the quantity of money is increased?

6. Suppose the federal government undertakes public works financed with newly created money. Sketch what will happen to income for several periods according to (a) the quantity theory and (b) the Keynesian theory.

7. If the stock of money increases when output is constant, prices (and hence money income) rise proportionately. Suppose we start with an underemployment situation and that real income rises rather than prices. Would you still expect the rise to be proportional? If not, under what conditions would it be proportional?

8. What variables do you think should be included in the demand function for money? How important do you think each of these variables is?

9. Describe the factors which have influenced your own money holdings over the last three years. How much money do you think you will hold in the next three years? Why? Discuss the interest elasticity of money in a realistic context by reference to your own money holdings.

10. "Commodities are bought not only with money, but also on credit. Hence we should include available credit in the definition of money." Discuss.

11. Suppose it were shown that there is a stable relationship between wage rates and nominal income of the form $Y = a + bW$, such that b is much stabler than k in the Cambridge equation. Would such a wage theory of income determination be a better theory than the quantity theory?

12. Suppose that in a one-crop economy, a disaster destroys half the crop. What would happen to prices? Describe the process using (a) the monetarist approach and (b) the Keynesian approach.

13. Use the quantity theory to describe the effects of business mergers on the price level.

14. Write a brief essay arguing either that (a) a tax cut raises aggregate demand *or* (b) a tax cut does not raise aggregate demand. Then write a brief essay to refute the view expressed in the first essay.

15. From the *Economic Report of the President,* calculate the Cambridge *k* and the interest rate. What do you think accounts for the behavior of *k?*

16. From the *Economic Report of the President* chart the interest rate, the stock of money, and GNP. What do you think accounts for the behavior of the interest rate?

17. Draw the IS, LM diagram on quantity theory assumptions. State these assumptions.

18. "For an exogenous change in the nominal money supply to have a predictable effect on GNP, we require *more* than a stable demand function for money." Discuss.

SUGGESTED READING

M. Friedman, "Money: Quantity Theory," *International Encyclopedia of the Social Sciences* (New York: Macmillan and Free Press, 1968), Vol. 10, pp. 432–46.

M. Friedman, *The Optimum Quantity of Money and Other Essays* (Chicago: Aldine Publishing Co., 1969) Chaps. 2, 5, 10, 12 (particularly Chaps. 2 and 5).

M. Friedman, "A Theoretical Framework for Monetary Analysis" (National Bureau of Economic Research, *Occasional Paper* #112, Columbia University Press, 1971). *Advanced reference.*

C. Warburton, *Depression, Inflation and Monetary Policy* (Baltimore: Johns Hopkins University Press, n.d.) Chap. 4.

K. Brunner and A. Meltzer, "Predicting Velocity, Implications for Theory and Policy," *Journal of Finance,* Vol. XXVIII (May 1963), pp. 319–54. *Advanced reference.*

W. Gibson, "Interest Rates and Monetary Policy," *Journal of Political Economy,* Vol. 78 (May/June 1970), pp. 431–54. *Advanced reference.*

L. Andersen and J. Jordan, "Monetary and Fiscal Actions: A Test of Their Relative Importance in Economic Stabilization," Federal Reserve Bank of St. Louis, *Review,* November 1968, pp. 11–24. *Advanced reference.*

E. Gramlich, "The Usefulness of Monetary and Fiscal Policy as Discretionary Stabilization Tools," *Journal of Money, Credit and Banking,* Vol. III (May 1971), Pt. 2, pp. 506–32. *Advanced reference.*

D. Fand, "Some Issues in Monetary Economics," *Banca Nazionale del Lavoro Quarterly Review,* September 1969, pp. 215–47.

H. Johnson, "The Keynesian Revolution and the Monetarist Counter-Revolution," American Economic Association, *Papers and Proceedings,* Vol. LXI (May 1971), pp. 1–14.

D. Patinkin, "Price Flexibility and Full Employment," reprinted in American Economic Association, *Readings in Monetary Theory* (Chicago: Richard D. Irwin, 1951), pp. 252–83.

D. Patinkin, "Keynesian Economics and the Quantity Theory," in K. Kurihara, ed., *Post-Keynesian Economics* (Brunswick, N.J.: Rutgers University Press, 1954), pp. 123–52.

D. Patinkin, *Money, Interest and Prices* (New York: Harper and Row, 1965), particularly Chaps. 1–12, 14–15. *Advanced reference.*

18

Economic Growth

IN DEVELOPING THE analysis of earlier parts of this book, we made use of the assumption that the capacity of the economic system to produce output was given. We justified this convenient simplification by explicitly confining our analysis to a "short run"—defined as a period over which capacity was invariant—and arguing that this assumption, over a time span of, say, one or two years, though it obviously introduced an error, did not introduce an error so great as to vitiate the analysis. The empirical justification for this position was, of course, that though capacity does grow continuously, it grows very slowly.

The theory of the third part of this book is thus, in essentials, a theory of aggregate demand. It explains how much of the (given) productive capacity will be utilized. In the short-run theory, output can be increased— up to the limit imposed by "full capacity"—only by increasing the extent to which the given capacity is utilized—that is, by increasing employment. An alternative way of describing the theory is thus to call it a theory of employment, or a theory of capacity utilization.

In the long run, by contrast, capacity itself must be treated as a variable simply because, though it grows slowly, slow growth over a long period is significant. It is, indeed, not much of an oversimplification to say that (1) in the short run, output grows only when the extent to which capacity is utilized increases; and (2) in the long run, it grows because capacity itself increases.

In Figure 18.1 we have plotted the behavior of the gross national product of the United States in real terms between 1948 and 1969. On the same figure we have plotted the percentage of the civilian labor force em-

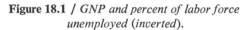

Figure 18.1 / *GNP and percent of labor force unemployed (inverted).*

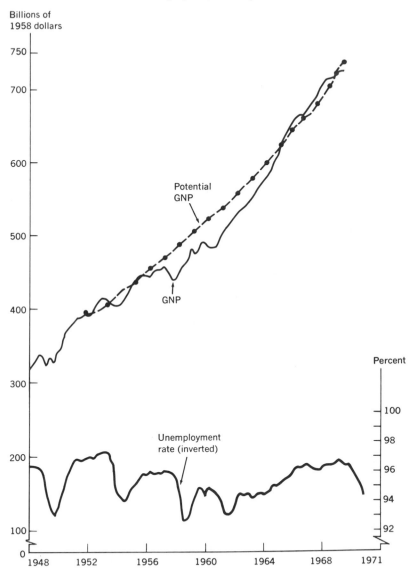

Sources: U. S. Department of Commerce, *Long Term Economic Growth, Business Conditions Digest,* December 1968, December 1970, September 1971; Executive Office of the President, *1971 Economic Report of the President.* Potential GNP is Council of Economic Advisers estimate.

ployed. This figure brings out the distinction between the two types of changes in GNP, the short-run cyclical changes reflecting changes in the proportion of the labor force employed, and the secular changes reflecting the growth of resources and productivity.

We now see rather more clearly what we sketched in outline in Chapter 5: that to explain the behavior of output we need (1) a theory to explain the rate at which *capacity grows;* and (2) a theory to explain why the *proportion of capacity utilized fluctuates.* In this chapter we concentrate on the first of these problems—the problem of *economic growth.*

Now both growth and fluctuations are essentially *dynamic problems*—that is, they involve the time *rates of change* of such variables as income, employment, investment, consumption, and so on. The purely *static* analysis of the third part of the book does not permit the introduction of rates of change. It runs only in terms of equilibrium levels. Hence our earlier analysis, though essential and valuable, necessarily requires extension to deal with these new problems. The nature of these extensions will become clear as we proceed in this and the following chapter.

THE DEFINITION OF ECONOMIC GROWTH

In developing our theory of "economic growth" we need to be as precise as possible. The term "growth" is usually used in relation to real output. There are, however, a variety of "growth concepts" even in relation to output. Are we, for example, interested in gross or net output? Is it simply real output which interests us or is it output per head of the population? Alternatively should we look at output per head of the labor force or, recognizing that hours worked on the average per year per worker have a long-run tendency to decline, should we look at output per man-hour year? Do we mean by growth the absolute or proportional (percentage) increase in the variable which interests us?

There is no single correct answer to these questions for the excellent reason that the concept which is relevant depends, as always, upon the question we are asking. For example, if our concern is with *economic welfare,* net output per head is probably the appropriate variable, while if we are interested in productivity we may prefer gross output per man-hour year.

In the present context our concern is with the broad aspects of "economic growth." We shall therefore discuss the determinants of the proportional (percentage) rate of growth in the capacity of the economy to produce real net output.

THE GROWTH OF PRODUCTIVE CAPACITY

As far back as Chapter 6 we introduced, and in some degree explored the meaning of, the concept of a production function. The notion behind this function, it will be recalled, was that, assuming businessmen to employ labor and capital optimally—that is, to obtain maximum output from any given inputs—there was a stable relationship between real net output (Y), the real capital stock (K), the quantity of labor employed (N) and the state of technique or productive know-how (T). In formal terms this hypothesis was expressed in functional notation by writing:

$$Y = f(K, N, T). \tag{18.1}$$

In Chapter 16 we made use of this hypothesis—though, since our analysis was *short run,* we took both the capital stock (K) and the state of technology (T) to be given and constant. Now, working in the *long-run* context, we treat all three as variables. Hence, thinking now of "full capacity" output and writing this as Y_c we can state that:

$$Y_c = f_1(K, N_f, T), \tag{18.1a}$$

where $N_f \equiv$ quantity of labor input corresponding to "full employment."

It is intuitively obvious that if (18.1) is a meaningful way of expressing a relation between capital, labor, and net output—and we shall assume that it is—then the proportionate rate of growth in full capacity output must depend in some way upon the proportionate rates of growth in capital, the labor-force, and the state of technology. Formally, using lower case letters for proportionate rates of growth in the variables, we may say that

$$y_c = f_2(k, n_f, t). \tag{18.2}$$

This conclusion, which we stated much earlier in Chapter 6, is, as we noted above, intuitively obvious. Nevertheless, it immediately suggests a question: just how much did k (the rate of capital accumulation), n_f (the rate of growth of the labor-force) and t (the rate of improvement in technology) contribute to our growth in capacity? This question clearly has important implications for policy—particularly if we want to accelerate economic growth. It is also important because it is an issue on which economists are by no means unanimous. In explaining the rate of capacity growth, some economists emphasize the role of capital accumulation; others emphasize technical improvement. Plainly both these factors—and the rate of growth of the labor-force—play *some* part in explaining growth. The issues are their relative importance and the degree to which they are independent of each other.

A PRODUCTION FUNCTION HYPOTHESIS

The question of the relative importance of technical change, capital accumulation, and growth in the labor-force in determining the rate of growth in capacity is an empirical one. We must therefore look at our observations of what *has* happened and, from them, try to discover the contributions to past growth of each factor. To do this effectively we must approach the data with a theory formulated precisely enough to permit us to measure the parameters of the production function itself. There is a precise analogy here with our theory of consumption. In developing this theory we began first with a very general notion of a consumption function. Next we postulated a *particular form* of consumption function which permitted us to estimate the value of the "marginal response coefficients" relating real planned consumption to such variables as real income, the real value of households' assets, and the rate of interest. How can we proceed from the general notions of the previous section to a particular production function hypothesis?

In order to develop the notion of the consumption function we placed restrictions upon it which seemed to us, for various reasons, to be plausible. Thus we argued that $\partial C/\partial Y$ ($\equiv$ marginal propensity to consume) would be positive but less than unity. What restrictions can we place on the form of the production function?

Economic theory tells us that, if businessmen maximize profits, they will employ labor until the marginal physical product of labor is equal to the real wage. It follows that—at least over the observed range—the marginal product of labor ($\equiv \partial Y/\partial N$) must always be positive. We also expect that the marginal product of labor will fall if, with the capital stock and technology constant, additional labor is employed.

Symmetrically we are entitled to argue that, if businessmen try to maximize profits, they will employ capital up to the point at which *its* marginal product ($\equiv \partial Y/\partial K$) is equal to *its* cost to the businessman. Since the latter is positive, so too will be the former. Moreover we may expect the marginal product of capital to fall if, with a given labor-force and state of technique, additional capital is employed.

These considerations give us *four* conditions which we can immediately require any new—and less general—production hypothesis to satisfy.

In Chapter 6 we introduced, and to some degree discussed, a *particular* production function of the form:

$$Y = TK^{\alpha}N^{1-\alpha}, \qquad \text{where } 0 < \alpha < 1. \qquad (18.3)$$

This function, as we showed in Chapter 6, satisfied each of the four requirements we have set out above. Are there any other conditions we can impose?

As a matter of empirical observation the share of the national income accruing to wage earners seems to be relatively constant over long periods of time.[1] This means that, since with only two factors of production what does *not* go to labor *must* go to capital, we can plausibly require the additional condition that (1) our function must be such that the shares of labor and capital are constant; if (2) each factor is paid its marginal product.

A businessman who aimed at maximizing profit would employ labor until the marginal product of labor (in real terms) was equal to the real wage. If each worker is paid this real wage, then the total receipts of labor (wage bill) are given by:

$$\text{wage bill} \equiv \text{no. of employed workers} \times \text{real wage}$$

$$= \text{no. of employed workers} \times \text{marginal product of labor}$$

$$= N \times \frac{\partial Y}{\partial N}.$$

Analogously the *share* of wages is given by:

$$\frac{\text{wage bill}}{\text{real income}} = \frac{N \times \partial Y/\partial N}{Y}.$$

Now *if* the function (18.3) entails, on this reasoning, a *constant share of wages* (and profits) in the national income, it will, on assumptions which, at this level of generality, are quite plausible, satisfy *five* restraints which empirical observation and economic theory suggest that we should impose. It would therefore seem a reasonable function in terms of which to seek to explain growth—at least as a first approximation. In practice it is easy to show that, on our assumptions about factor rewards, the function at (18.3) *does* entail constant shares of wages and profits. Indeed, as an arithmetic example easily illustrates, the following conditions always hold:

$$\frac{\text{wages bill}}{\text{income}} = 1 - \alpha \qquad \frac{\text{profit bill}}{Y} = \alpha. \qquad (18.4)$$

For a numerical illustration put $\alpha = 0.5$, $T = 10$, $K = 100$, and $N = 10{,}000$. Then

$$Y = TK^\alpha N^{1-\alpha} = 10 \times (100)^{1/2} \times (10{,}000)^{1/2}$$
$$= 10 \times 10 \times 100$$
$$= 10{,}000.$$

The marginal product of labor is given by the expression

$$\frac{\partial Y}{\partial N} = (1 - \alpha)TK^\alpha N^{-\alpha}{}^\dagger = 0.5 \times 10 \times 100^{(1/2)} \times 10{,}000^{-(1/2)}$$
$$= 5(\tfrac{10}{100})$$
$$= 0.5,$$

1. A warning about the constancy of the capital share is in order. Since the labor share is equal to roughly twice the capital share of income, a 2 percent variation in the labor share means a 4 percent variation in the share of capital.

†This formula is obtained by differentiating the production function partially with respect to N.

whence
$$\text{the wage bill} \equiv N \times \frac{\partial Y}{\partial N}$$
$$\equiv 10{,}000 \times 0.5$$
$$= 5000.$$

The *share* of wages is given by:

$$\frac{\text{wage bill}}{Y} \equiv \frac{N \times (\partial Y/\partial N)}{Y} = \frac{5{,}000}{10{,}000} = 0.5 = 1 - \alpha$$

which is the proposition set out at (18.4).

It follows that the function $Y = TK^{\alpha}N^{1-\alpha}$ satisfies the *five* important conditions which we can reasonably require of it. To what "growth hypothesis" [analogous to (18.2)] does this function lead? By making use of fairly elementary mathematics this is easily found to be:[2]

$$y_c = t + \alpha k + (1 - \alpha)n_f. \tag{18.5}$$

To check (18.5) as before put $\alpha = 0.5$, $T = 10$, $K = 100$, $N = 10{,}000$. Then $Y_0 = 10{,}000$, as we showed in the paragraph above.

Now put $T = 10.001$, $K = 121$, $N = 12{,}100$. We have

$$Y_1 = 10.001 \times (121)^{1/2} \times (12{,}100)^{1/2}$$
$$= 10.001 \times 11 \times 110$$
$$= 12{,}101.210.$$

According to (18.5) we have

$$y_c = t + \alpha k + (1 - \alpha)n_f \tag{18.5}$$
$$= \frac{.001}{10.0} + \alpha \left(\frac{21}{100}\right) + (1 - \alpha)\frac{2{,}100}{10{,}000}$$
$$= 0.01 \text{ percent} + 0.5 \,(21 \text{ percent}) + 0.5 \,(21 \text{ percent})$$
$$= 21.01 \text{ percent}.$$

Now the percentage increase in Y is given by:

$$\frac{Y_1 - Y_0}{Y_0} = \frac{12{,}101.210 - 10{,}000}{10{,}000} = \frac{2{,}101.210}{10{,}000} = 21.0121 \text{ percent},$$

which, taken correct to two decimal places, is the result obtained from (18.5).[3]

It follows that the function (18.3) first introduced in Chapter 6 is not only plausible (since it meets the *five* requirements we put upon it) but also

---

2. This formula holds precisely only for indefinitely small values of the independent variables. It is obtained by logarithmic differentiation of the production function.
3. Which, we recall, does not hold precisely for other than indefinitely small changes.

leads to a simple "growth hypothesis." This simple growth hypothesis tells us that

$$\frac{\partial y}{\partial k} \equiv \begin{array}{c} \text{marginal response coefficient} \\ \text{relating the rate of growth} \\ \text{in output to the rate of} \\ \text{capital accumulation} \end{array} = \begin{array}{c} \text{share of profits in the} \\ \text{national income} \end{array}$$

$$\frac{\partial y}{\partial n} \equiv \begin{array}{c} \text{marginal response coefficient} \\ \text{relating the rate of growth} \\ \text{in output to the rate of} \\ \text{increase in the labor force} \end{array} = \begin{array}{c} \text{share of wages in the} \\ \text{national income.} \end{array}$$

This means that it is not difficult to estimate the marginal response co-efficients—a result which puts us well on the way to calculating the relative importance of k, n, and t in explaining the rate of growth in actual output and thus, adding the full employment assumption, the rate of growth of *full capacity* output.

THE GROWTH IN OUTPUT AND CAPACITY OUTPUT

The previous section of this chapter, though rather difficult, is an essential preliminary to an attempt to assess the relative importance of t, k, and n in explaining growth. If we accept the rather heavy load of assumptions entailed in this section, we can now write our growth hypothesis:

$$y = t + \text{share of profits} \times k + \text{share of wages} \times n. \qquad (18.5)$$

The two shares can readily be obtained from national income estimates.

$y \equiv$ the rate of growth of actual output—is conceptually measurable and, indeed, data exist in most countries which enable us to estimate it.

$k \equiv$ the rate of growth of the real capital stock—is also conceptually measurable and in some countries data exist which enable us to estimate it.

$n \equiv$ the rate of growth of labor input—is similarly capable of estimation.

Hence in (18.5), of the *six* terms, five are susceptible to measurement (in principle) and estimation (in practice). It follows that t—the rate of change of technique—can be estimated as a residual: that is, as the difference between the *observed* rate of increase in output and the contributions explained by the observed rate of increase in capital (multiplied by its marginal response coefficient) and the observed rate of increase in labor (multiplied by its marginal response coefficient).

There are now several studies of the growth in output which are based on production functions of the form of (18.3) and growth hypotheses of the form (18.5). Many of them are rather technical. In what follows we set out some of their results adjusted so as to fit our model. Because of the need for adjustment the results are illustrative only.

According to one set of data, the share of wages (the marginal response coefficient of the growth in employment) is about 0.77. The corresponding marginal response coefficient for the growth of capital is therefore 0.23. Between 1929 and 1957, real national product grew at the compound rate of 2.93 percent per annum. During the same period employment grew at an estimated 1.31 percent. However the average hours worked per employee fell. Hence the input of labor (corrected for the change in hours) grew at only 1.08 percent. Over the same period capital accumulated at the rate of 1.88 percent. Hence, rewriting (18.5) we have:

$$t = y - \text{share of profits} \times k - \text{share of wages} \times n$$
$$= 2.93 - (0.23 \times 1.88) - (0.77 \times 1.08)$$
$$= 2.93 - 0.4324 - 0.8316$$
$$= 1.666.$$

Thus, on this calculation it seems that something like 57 percent (i.e. $1.67/2.93 \times 100/1$) of the growth in national product between 1929 and 1957 is to be explained by the process of technical improvement. Capital accumulation accounts for only a little more than 14 percent while the growth of labor input accounts for about 28 percent.

The calculation set out above, though it has the appearance of precision, is in reality extremely crude. If these figures are meaningful at all—and the reader should by now be aware that the method involves a heavy load of assumptions by which it stands or falls—they do no more than indicate orders of magnitude. Nevertheless *if* these orders of magnitude are even approximately correct, they are interesting, for they suggest that the role of capital accumulation in promoting growth may be less significant than is commonly supposed. Suppose we assume that they are both meaningful and accurate as far as orders of magnitude are concerned. Then, plainly, provided we can calculate the rate of growth of the full employment labor input we can readily calculate the rate at which full capacity grew in the period. It follows that, in explaining the rate at which actual output grew we have developed—in operational terms—a method of explaining the rate of growth in "full capacity" output. But although we have a method, it is by no means clear that we have surmounted the technical measurement problems, and that the numerical values we have used above are really reliable. We have presented them as illustrations of the fact that the theory can be quantified rather than as reliable estimates. Different measuring techniques can yield quite different results. Thus a recent study made some adjustments to these techniques which reduced the growth rate of total factor productivity from 1.6 percent per year to 1.0 percent.[1] This very

1. D. W. Jorgenson and Z. Griliches, "The Explanation of Productivity Changes," *Review of Economic Studies*, Vol. 24 (July 1967), pp. 249–84.

substantial reduction of the residual implies that capital accumulation is much more important than is indicated above.

At this stage we ask you to take note of two points:

1) The estimated contribution of technical progress to observed growth reflects the assumptions involved, and in particular the assumption that the rate of technical progress is independent of the rate of capital accumulation and labor-force expansion.

2) The method we have employed has been subjected to very con- siderable criticism on this and other grounds in the professional literature.

Unfortunately many of the criticisms of the method are technically difficult and thus beyond the scope of this book. The reader, therefore, is asked to consider our results *not* as generally accepted estimates of what are agreed to be the relevant coefficients, but rather as an illustration of *one way among many* in which the production function concept can be made operational and the results which follow from adopting it. It is cer- tainly not claimed that the method used is the best way of approaching the problem. Nor are we arguing that economists as a whole are agreed that it is the best way or that the best way of approaching the problem is pres- ently the subject of a professional consensus.

QUESTIONS AND EXERCISES

1. "The production function $Y = TK^\alpha N^{1-\alpha}$ assumes that the rate of technical progress is independent of the rate of capital accumulation. This is absurd." Discuss these statements.

2. In a group of firms which employed business consultants the average in- crease in net productivity achieved, as a result of their advice, was of the order of 50 percent. Does this surprise you? What light, if any, does it throw upon the production function used in the text?

3. One reason for using the production function $Y = TK^\alpha N^{1-\alpha}$ is that, if each factor is paid its marginal product, the shares of the factors are invariant at α and $1 - \alpha$. Is this marginal productivity assumption reasonable?

4. How "stable" is the share of labor? Use the *Economic Report of the Presi- dent* to calculate the share of labor for each year from 1950–70. Plot your results on a graph. Is there a trend? Is the share "stable?" What is the esti- mated value of $(1 - \alpha)$?

5. In discussing the sources of growth in capacity we have *assumed* a produc- tion function of the form $Y = TK^\alpha N^{1-\alpha}$. Obviously this assumption could be wrong. How could it be tested?

6. The following hypothetical data is observed for the economy of Erewhon. What is the production function? What results would we get if we assumed it was of the form $Y = TK^{\alpha}N^{1-\alpha}$?

Capital employed.

YEAR	Y	CAPITAL STOCK (K)	EMPLOYED PERSONS (N)	WAGE BILL	PROFITS
t	350	500	100	175	175
$t+1$	356	520	96	178	178
$t+2$	355	530	90	177.5	177.5
$t+3$	357	534	90	178.5	178.5
$t+4$	365	540	95	182.5	182.5
$t+5$	375	550	100	187.5	187.5
$t+6$	390	560	110	195	195

In the light of your answer reconsider Question 5.

7. In the exercise of Question 6 which assumption in our earlier analysis must be abandoned? Why? What is your estimate of the average propensity to save? How do you obtain it?

8. "The present preoccupation with economic growth is simply a fashion. If people were aware of the economic and social costs of growing faster, the fashion would be very short-lived indeed." Discuss in the light of (1) our earlier analysis; (2) your own social preferences.

9. "The so-called 'technical progress coefficient' we derive from assuming a production function and applying it to observed data is really nothing more than a measure of our ignorance." Elucidate and appraise.

10. "The Soviet Union is a major industrial power today only because its planners imposed immense privations on its people during the interwar years." Explain.

11. "Faster growth will require greater 'mobility' of labor. Hence if we are serious about trying to grow faster, far from *reducing* immigration, we should be trying to increase it." Discuss with particular reference to the meaning of "mobility."

12. In Figure 18.1 draw in a straight line to represent the constant percentage rate of growth of capacity. This is correct only if national product is measured on a logarithmic scale. Why? How big is the error involved? Show that the error is a function of the time span of the graph.

13. "The rate of growth of *capacity* output, since it depends on net investment, must depend upon the rate of growth of *actual* output. It therefore depends upon demand as well as supply considerations." Elucidate and appraise.

14. Critically examine the assumptions underlying our method of estimating the rate of growth of capacity output.

15. "If businessmen expected the U. S. economy to grow faster, they would act in such a way as to insure that it did." Elucidate. Do you agree?

16. "In most British industries the least efficient firm is only about one-quarter as efficient as the most efficient." If this is correct, what does it suggest about the process and rate of innovation and what policy measures might bring about an increase in it?

SUGGESTED READING

E. F. Denison, *The Sources of Economic Growth in the United States and the Alternatives Before Us* (Washington: Committee for Economic Development, 1962).

D. Jorgenson and Z. Griliches, "The Explanation of Productivity Changes," *Review of Economic Studies,* Vol. 34 (July 1967), pp. 249–84. *Advanced reference.*

S. Kuznets, *Economic Growth of Nations* (Cambridge: Harvard University Press, 1971).

19

Fluctuations in Economic Activity

IN CHAPTER 18 we developed an account of the process whereby, over the long run, the capacity of the economy to produce output grows. In this chapter we consider why, as a matter of observation, the growth path followed by the economy involves *fluctuations* in the extent to which, in any given year, *the available capacity* is utilized. The problem of economic *fluctuations* is often discussed under the heading of the theory of economic *cycles*. What then is a cycle?

A cycle may be defined as a repeated wave-like movement in the value of any economic variable over time. Most economic series when plotted against time exhibit such movements. The cycles, however, are not regular; that is, their *periodicity*—the length of time over which they repeat themselves—and their amplitude are not constant. Nor do the individual series move in step. Nevertheless the wave-like movements exhibit a sufficient degree of regularity to make it reasonable to speak of "cycles."

In this chapter we shall be concerned only with cycles in *macroeconomic variables*. Microeconomic variables such as the output of new houses, pigs, machine tools, and many others also display cyclical fluctuations and these variables sometimes display a pattern of fluctuations dissimilar to that of the macroeconomic concepts.

In Figure 19.1 are plotted quarterly estimates of real GNP and potential GNP which for our purposes we can treat as a trend. Clearly output exhibits considerable fluctuations. In short, there is a cycle in gross national product. This in some periods, for example the year 1964, rises *faster* than the trend while in others, for example 1956, it either rises more slowly or even, as in 1960 actually falls. Obviously whenever output grows faster

Figure 19.1 / *Actual GNP, potential GNP, and unemployment (inverted) 1948–1970.*

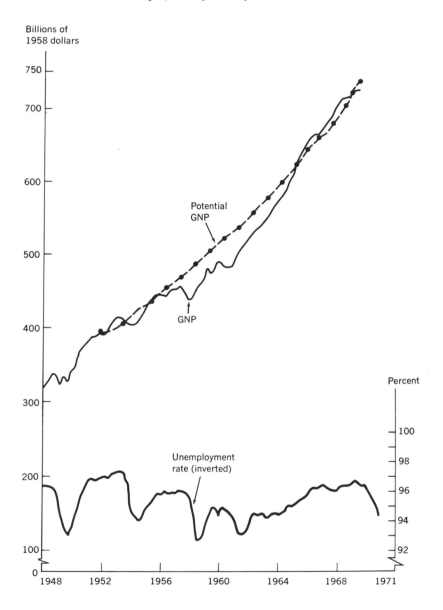

Sources: Same as for Fig. 18.1.

than the trend rate of increase in capacity, the proportion of capacity employed rises. It follows, therefore, as indeed was noted in Chapter 18, that fluctuations in the output of the economy *around its rising trend* can be viewed as fluctuations in the proportion of productive capacity employed. Since the theory which we developed in Chapters 7–13 argued that aggregate output would adjust, up to the limit of "full capacity," to aggregate demand, it is clear that, to explain why cycles of this kind occur, we need to explain why aggregate demand fluctuates over time. In short, we have to try to explain the determinants of *the time rates of change* of such variables as consumption, investment, exports, and government expenditure. Our earlier analysis was *static* and *timeless* and sought to explain only the equilibrium levels of these variables. Hence in this chapter we need to develop our theory in a *dynamic* way—that is, a way which *essentially and explicitly involves time*.

In Figure 19.2 we have plotted the behavior of employment, gross private nonresidential and residential investment and inventory investment. You should notice that though these series too exhibit fluctuations, the timing and form of these does not correspond at all precisely to the fluctuations in gross national product. In some cases the fluctuations are more marked. In others they are less. Fluctuation, however, is general.

THE TERMINOLOGY OF FLUCTUATIONS

In order to discuss cycles in economic activity we need a terminology with which to do so. This terminology is a matter of choice. But if we do not adopt one, we run the risk of confused description from which can come only a confused and confusing analysis.

In the figure below is set out an "ideal" cycle in gross national product around a rising trend. This cycle we divide into two main *phases:*

1) the *upswing:* in which output rises *faster* than the trend and, as a result, the proportion of capacity employed is *rising;*

2) the *downswing:* in which output rises *more slowly* than the trend and, as a result, the proportion of capacity employed is *falling.*
The reader should notice that output may not fall absolutely in the *downswing:* it may not even cease to rise. What falls is the *proportion of capacity employed.* At some point the upswing ceases and becomes a downswing. This we call the *upper turning point:* represented by points A, A' and A'' on the graph. Equally, at some point the downswing ceases and becomes an upswing. This we call the *lower turning point:* represented by points B, B' and B'' on the graph. A single cycle runs from upper turning point to upper turning point (or lower to lower). The time taken for this cycle

Figure 19.2 (a) / *Fluctuations in employment, fixed investment, and inventories, 1948–70 (yearly).*

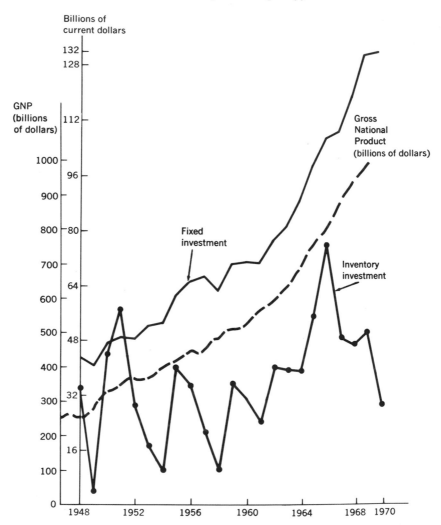

Source: Executive Office of the President, *1971 Economic Report of the President*.

we call the *length or periodicity of the cycle:* this is represented by the distances $A\,A'$, $A'A''$, $B\,B'$, $B'B''$ on the graph.

Notice that, as we have constructed our Figure 19.3, the periodicity of the cycle is constant. In practice, as Figures 19.1 and 19.2 make clear, the

Figure 19.2 (b) / *Components of gross private domestic investment and employment (quarterly).*

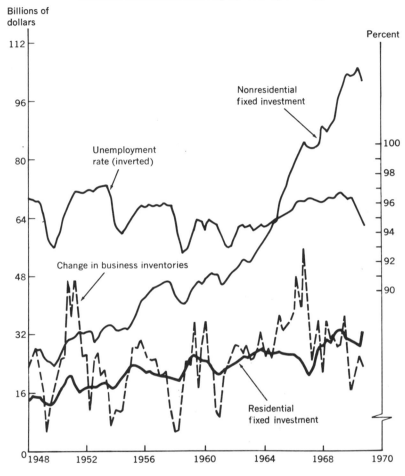

Source: U. S. Department of Commerce, *Business Conditions Digest*, August 1971; *Survey of Current Business*, July 1971; Executive Office of the President, 1971 *Economic Report of the President*.

periodicity of economic fluctuations is *not* regular.

We need a concept to enable us to compare the extent to which different economic variables fluctuate during the cycle. We call the extent of the fluctuation in any time series its *amplitude*. This we shall measure by average deviation (expressed as a percentage) of the variable around its trend.

To illustrate the use of this terminology, let us return to Figure 19.1.

The observations in Figure 19.1 are nothing like as well behaved as those of our "ideal" cycle. Turning points cannot be unambiguously identi-

Figure 19.3 / *"Ideal" cycle in gross domestic product*
around a rising trend.

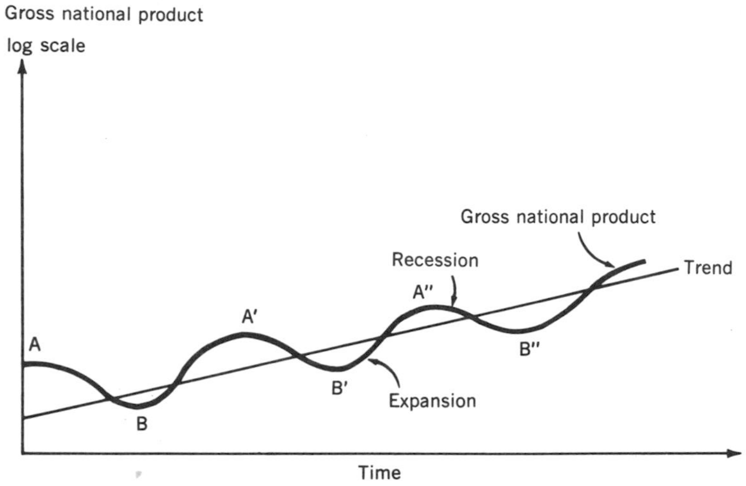

fied. To some degree, therefore, we must take arbitrary decisions about the turning points of the individual cycles in real gross national product. Accordingly we shall classify U. S. postwar experience as follows:

NUMBER OF CYCLE	TROUGH	PEAK	DURATION IN MONTHS CONTRACTION[a]	EXPANSION[b]
1	Oct. 1945	Nov. 1948	8	37
2	Oct. 1949	July 1953	11	45
3	Aug. 1954	July 1957	13	35
4	Apr. 1958	May 1960	9	25
5	Feb. 1961	Nov. 1969	9	105

a. Trough from previous peak
b. Trough to peak
Source: U. S. Department of Commerce, *Business Conditions Digest*, December 1971.

On the basis of this classification it seems that the economy in the postwar period has (i) completed *five* cycles and is now in its sixth, while (ii) the periodicity of the completed cycles varies between 8½ and 26 quarters.

These postwar cycles in U. S. economic activity are, of course, a great deal less severe than those experienced in the interwar years. The cycle, however, has obviously not disappeared. It therefore requires explanation. What does a theory of cyclical fluctuations need to provide?

First, any such theory must explain why, at some point, a cumulative upward movement begins. Second, it must explain why, at some point, the cumulative upward movement ceases and in some cases (e.g. 1957 and 1960) reverses itself.

ELEMENTS OF CYCLE THEORY

According to our static theory of aggregate demand, the principal elements in demand independent of the level of income (output) are (1) investment; (2) exports; (3) government expenditure. It is these elements which, given stable propensities to consume and import, the money supply, the two liquidity functions, the money wage rate, and the production function, determine the equilibrium level of output. This suggests that it is likely to be *fluctuations* in these elements—or some of them—to which we must look to explain fluctuations in output.

In developing our theory of investment we emphasized the subjective nature of the schedule of the marginal efficiency of capital. In particular we pointed out that the position of the schedule depended upon (1) businessmen's *expectations* (which could be optimistic or pessimistic); and (2) businessmen's *uncertainty* regarding their expectations. One possible explanation of fluctuations in planned investment over the cycle thus runs in terms of expectations and uncertainty. Suppose, for example, the economy starts upwards from its lower turning point as a result, let us say, of an expansionary budget. Since, by assumption, there is plenty of spare capacity, output and employment expand. The multiplier operates and a cumulative recovery begins. This tends to raise profits, to make businessmen more optimistic, and to reduce their uncertainty regarding prospects over, say, the next two or three years. In these circumstances it seems entirely plausible that the MEI schedule should shift to the right. If it does, investment increases, thus adding the effect of the investment multiplier to the budget multiplier. And this may further increase investment by producing greater optimism and reducing uncertainty.

In upswings, output expands faster than capacity. In the early stages, when excess capacity is present, the additional output can be produced from the capacity already in existence. As expansion proceeds, and excess capacity is reduced, businessmen need to increase their capacity by undertaking investment. This takes two forms. First, there is investment in fixed capital such as factory buildings, plant, and equipment. Second there is investment in inventories which must be increased, as output rises, if the process of production is to proceed smoothly.

Thus to our *expectational* (or psychological) explanation of fluctuations in investment we can add a second or *capacity* element which is primarily technical in character. These two elements provide a plausible explanation of why, once a recovery has started, it will be fed and sustained by an expansion of investment in fixed capital and in stocks. The result is a cumulative process of expansion—the upswing—which proceeds from recovery to boom.

The pattern of investment behavior explains the cumulative process of expansion. It does not, however, explain why expansion ceases and possibly gives way to contraction. Why should expectations reverse themselves? Why should businessmen suddenly plan to reduce the rate at which they add to capacity? A theory which seeks to answer these questions is set out in later sections. In the meantime, however, we need simply note that if investment behaves as we suggest, the cumulative upswing and the cumulative downswing are not hard to understand. The awkward problems are the turning points.

This brief sketch of the generation of cyclical fluctuations leaves us with three problems to explain: (1) why an upswing halts; (2) why it reverses itself; (3) why recoveries begin.

COMBINING THE ACCELERATOR AND THE MULTIPLIER

In Chapter 11 we developed the accelerator theory of investment. We will now use this theory, in combination with the multiplier to explain fluctuations in income.

The final equation for fixed investment which we discussed in Chapter 11 was

$$I_t = V(Y_t - Y_{t-1}) \tag{11.2f}$$

where I is investment, Y income, and V the accelerator coefficient which combines the optimum capital output ratio (α) with the adjustment coefficient (λ).

We then showed that the same equation holds for inventory investment (I_{st}) so that:

$$I_{st} = V'(Y_t - Y_{t-1}) \tag{11.2h}$$

In the United States the ratio of stocks to gross domestic product (at annual rates) is about 0.2. Since businessmen probably plan to adjust stocks fairly quickly, the speed of response coefficient is probably close to unity. Hence V' may, with some degree of plausibility, be thought of as being about 0.2.

Adding the two components of accelerator net investment, we obtain:

$$I_t + I_{st} = (V + V')[Y_t - Y_{t-1}] \qquad (19.2\text{i})$$

for the sum of accelerator investment. This, simply because it is investment *induced* by the change in output, is often called *induced investment*. Naturally enough *some* net investment is only very loosely related to changes in output. This is the case with very long-range investment. It is also likely to be the case with investment aimed at the production of new products. Net investment which is not induced in this way we call *autonomous*. This we shall write as H.

Our complete investment hypothesis may now be written as:

$$\left.\begin{array}{l} \text{gross investment}_t \equiv \text{net investment}_t + \text{replacement}_t \\ \qquad \equiv H_t + I_t + I_{st} + R_t \\ \qquad = H_t + (V + V')(Y_t - Y_{t-1}) + R_t, \end{array}\right\} \qquad (19.2\text{j})$$

where R_t depends upon the proportion of the capital stock requiring replacement in any year. Since R_t probably changes only slowly, it follows that it is the induced component plus any changes in autonomous investment due to changes in business expectations which, on our hypothesis, explains the cyclical fluctuations in gross investment.

The impact of the *accelerator* may best be seen by combining it with the simple multiplier. To do this we take autonomous investment and replacement as constant and specify the following model:

$$
\begin{array}{ll}
R_t = \bar{R} \text{ for all periods} & \bar{R} = 20 \\
H_t = \bar{H} \text{ for periods } t, t - 1, \text{ and } t - 2 & \bar{H} = 30 \\
H_t = \hat{H} \text{ for periods } t + 1 \text{ and thereafter} & \hat{H} = 40 \\
I_t = V(Y_{t-1} - Y_{t-2}) + H_t + R_t & V = 0.8 \\
C_t = A + cY_{t-1}\dagger & A = 100 \quad c = 0.5.
\end{array}
$$

Two points are worth noticing about this model. First, we have made *induced investment* (I_t) depend upon the *past* change in output rather than the current change. This is probably more realistic. Second, we have assumed that households base their current expenditure on consumption on the *last* period's income.

We can now write the equation for gross output as:

$$Y_t = A + cY_{t-1} + V(Y_{t-1} - Y_{t-2}) + R_t + H_t. \qquad (19.2\text{k})$$

In equilibrium, by definition, output is constant. Hence $Y_t = Y_{t-1} = Y_{t-2}$. Call the *initial* equilibrium level $\bar{Y}_1$. We obtain, on substituting this into (19.2k),

†Notice that this model contains a *consumption lag* and no output lag.

$$\bar{Y}_1 = A + c\bar{Y}_1 + V(\bar{Y}_1 - \bar{Y}_1) + \bar{R} + \bar{H} \qquad (19.2k1)$$

$$\bar{Y}_1 = [A + \bar{R} + \bar{H}]\frac{1}{1-c}$$

$$= [100 + 20 + 30]\frac{1}{1-0.5}$$

$$= 300.$$

In the new equilibrium ($\bar{Y}_2$) we have:

$$\bar{Y}_2 = A + c\bar{Y}_2 + V(\bar{Y}_2 - \bar{Y}_2) + \bar{R} + \hat{H} \qquad (19.2k2)$$

$$= [A + \bar{R} + \hat{H}]\frac{1}{1-c}$$

$$= [100 + 20 + 40]\frac{1}{1-0.5}$$

$$= 320.$$

Two points emerge from this elementary substitution. They are: (1) the *equilibrium* levels of output are unaffected by the accelerator; and (2) the *change* in equilibrium levels is given by the simple static multiplier with which we became fully familiar in Chapter 8.

To illustrate the *dynamic* behavior of the system—how it moves over time—the simplest procedure is to construct a table.

Examination of this table brings out a number of points:

1) On our assumptions the system moves to its new equilibrium by a series of fluctuations.

2) The movement begins with an upswing which lasts until period $t + 4$. But as the rate at which output rises during this upswing falls away, as it does by period $t + 3$, the rate of induced investment begins to fall as it does in period $t + 4$.

3) This fall in induced investment itself slows the rise in output and, by period $t + 5$, causes output actually to fall.

4) By period ? the fall has been checked and output has once again started upward.[1]

You should also notice that though net investment depends upon output via the accelerator relation, its induced component nevertheless begins to fall *before* output. This is, of course, because it depends not on the *level* of output but *its rate of change*.

This table demonstrates, which is certainly interesting, that a model which contains *both* the multiplier and the accelerator may generate quite realistic cycles. Thus the accelerator-multiplier model *can* explain why, if

---

1. You should calculate the period for yourself.

Table 19.1 / *Dynamic multiplier and accelerator.*

| | | GROSS INVESTMENT | | | | | |
PERIOD	INCOME	PLANNED CONSUMPTION	REPLACE- MENT	AUTONO- MOUS	ACCELERATOR INDUCED	PLANNED SAVING	ACTUAL SAVING
	Y	C_p	R	H	$I = V(Y_{t-1} - Y_{t-2})$	S_p	S_A
t	300	250	20	30	nil	50	50
$t+1$	310	250	20	40	nil	50	60
$t+2$	323	255	20	40	8	55	68
$t+3$	331.9	261.5	20	40	10.4	61.5	70.4
$t+4$	333.07	265.95	20	40	7.12	65.95	67.12
$t+5$	327.47	266.585	20	40	0.936	66.435	60.936
$t+6$			20	40			
$t+7$			20	40			
$t+8$			20	40			
$t+9$							
$t+10$							
$\vdots$							
$t+n$	320	260	20	40	nil	60	60

Data: $\dfrac{\partial C_p}{\partial Y} \equiv C_p = 0.5$

$V = 0.8$

Assumptions: constant prices; constant interest rates.
You are invited to work out period $t+6$, $t+7$, $t+8$ for yourself from the equation:

$$Y_{t+6} = A + cY_{t+5} + \bar{R} + \hat{H} + V[Y_{t+5} - Y_{t+4}].$$

Table 19.2 / *Dynamic multiplier and accelerator.*

| | | GROSS INVESTMENT | | | | | | |
PERIOD	INCOME	PLANNED CONSUMPTION	REPLACE- MENT	AUTONO- MOUS	ACCELERATOR INDUCED		PLANNED SAVING	ACTUAL SAVING
	Y	C_p	R	H	$V(Y_{t-1} - Y_{t-2})$	I_p	S_p	S_A
t	300	250	20	30	nil	50	50	50
$t+1$	310	250	20	40	nil	60	50	60
$t+2$	345	255	20	40	30	90	55	90
$t+3$	437.5	272.5	20	40	105	165	72.5	165
$t+4$	652.25	318.75	20	40	277.5	333.5	118.75	333.5
$t+5$								
$t+6$								
$t+7$								
$t+8$								

Data: $\dfrac{\partial C_p}{\partial Y} \equiv C_p = 0.5$ $V = 3.0$

You are invited to work out periods $t+5$, $t+6$, $t+7$ from the equation:

$$Y_{t+5} = A + cY_{t+4} + \bar{R} + \hat{H} + V[Y_{t+4} - Y_{t+3}].$$

output starts on an upswing, it will reach an upper turning point and why, if it starts on a downswing, it will eventually turn up—that is reach a lower turning point.

The results in Table 19.1, however, depend upon the particular values we have selected for the marginal propensity to consume ($c = 0.5$) and the accelerator coefficient ($V = 0.8$). Both these values are probably on the low side. Suppose we take a more realistic value for V. What would happen?

V is, as we have shown, the (marginal) capital/output ratio. If this is equal to the average ratio, a plausible guess would put its numerical value around 3.0. Retaining all our other assumptions unchanged, how does the model behave now? We can easily construct a table to show.

A glance at this table shows that the system now behaves very differently. The system starts upward, as before, in period $t + 1$. But it never turns down. In short, it rises without limit or, as the same point is usually put, it *explodes. Notice also that the two models differ only in their dynamic behavior, for the static equilibria described by both are identical.*

In fact, with our basic equation (19.2) there are a number of possible dynamic paths of output. Which is relevant depends on the values of c (the marginal propensity to consume) and V (the accelerator coefficient). The possibilities can be classified as follows:

Type I. Damped fluctuations ultimately converging to new equilibrium (Table 19.1).

   II. Explosion without fluctuations *never* converging to new equilibrium (Table 19.2).

   III. Constant fluctuations around new equilibrium *never* converging to new equilibrium (Fig. 19.4).

   IV. No fluctuations: smooth convergence ultimately reaching new equilibrium (Fig. 19.4).

   V. Explosive fluctuations *never* reaching new equilibrium (Fig. 19.4).

This is decidedly awkward, for we can hardly suppose that the values of c and V are likely to be precisely those required to produce path Type III—the only path generating cycles of constant amplitude such as, in broad terms, we tend to observe. This makes the accelerator-multiplier model a much less satisfying explanation of the cyclical fluctuations in output though it has its place in any full explanation. For we obviously cannot exclude values of V of the order of 3.0. And such values, when inserted into our model, make it *dynamically unstable*. It does not fluctuate (as we would like it to). Nor does it ever reach its new static equilibrium of 320. Since an *explosive* system seems, empirically, absurd while it equally seems that empirically plausible values of V imply an explosive system, it is

Figure 19.4 / *Classification of dynamic paths of output:*
multiplier accelerator model.

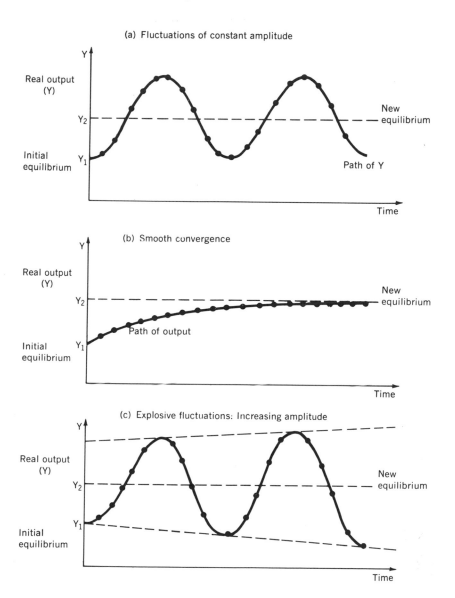

(a) Fluctuations of constant amplitude

Y

Real output
(Y)

New
equilibrium

Y_2

Initial
equilibrium

Y_1

Path of Y

Time

(b) Smooth convergence

Y

Real output
(Y)

New
equilibrium

Y_2

Path of output

Initial
equilibrium

Y_1

Time

(c) Explosive fluctuations: Increasing amplitude

Y

Real output
(Y)

New
equilibrium

Y_2

Y_1

Initial
equilibrium

Time

Note: Individual observations (denoted by dots) have been linked by a smooth curve.

clear that we need to find some way of (1) putting a *ceiling* to the upswings of a *potentially* explosive system and explaining why it should ever turn down, and/or (2) putting a *floor* to the system's downswings and explaining why it should ever turn upward. This we shall attempt in the next section.

Before we discuss the problem of *ceilings* and *floors* we need to make one or two points about the accelerator itself.

Both in our tables and in our exposition we have given a formal and mechanical interpretation of the accelerator. Pedagogically this is permissible. The accelerator hypothesis, however, seeks to describe human behavior. Purely mechanical interpretations should therefore be avoided. In particular the following points, glossed over in our discussion, should be kept in mind.

1) The accelerator theory is a *capacity* theory of investment. The accelerator coefficient may therefore take a lower value in recovery (where there is *ex hypothesi* considerable excess capacity in the economy) than in booms (when excess capacity is far less and still diminishing). Our model in treating V as constant may therefore seriously oversimplify matters.

2) The accelerator theory also contains room for the influence of *expectations* and *uncertainty*. In the early stages of recovery though businessmen may *observe* a given change in output, they may not *expect* the new level of output to persist or, if they do expect it to do so, they may not be very *confident* of their expectation. Hence they may not revise their optimal capital stock (K^*) fully in accordance with the new level of output or, alternatively, may proceed cautiously in adjusting actual K to K^*.[2] Either attitude would reduce the value of V in the early stages of an upswing, a possibility of which we take no account in our table.

3) It is obvious that gross investment in fixed capital can never be negative. This means that induced net investment, which according to the accelerator theory will be negative in the downswing if output falls, cannot exceed, in absolute value, the value of replacement investment (R_t). To put this formally we have $I_t = V(Y_{t-1} - Y_{t-2})$ in the upswing and $I_t = V(Y_{t-1} - Y_{t-2})$, provided $R_t + I_t \geqslant 0$, in the downswing.

This obvious constraint implies that, over the cycle as a whole, the accelerator may behave *asymmetrically*. In short, if the fall in income is very fast in the downswing, since gross investment cannot fall below zero, negative net investment cannot exceed R_t in absolute value, and may therefore not be able to reach the value indicated by our accelerator equation.

Despite these qualifications and the theoretical complications involved in realistic values for V, there is no doubt that the *capacity* element in dynamic investment theory is an important one.

2. Our tables assume $\lambda \equiv$ speed of response parameter to be a constant equal to unity. In fact λ may vary over the cycle.

CEILINGS AND FLOORS

In the last section we came up with the awkward problem that realistic values of the accelerator coefficient imply *explosive* systems. How can we constrain such systems?

In an upswing real output can rise as fast as it likes up to the position of "full capacity." At this point it has reached its *ceiling*. The maximum rate of increase then becomes the rate of increase in capacity—roughly 4 percent per year. This rate of increase must be less than the rate enjoyed during the upswing, for, if it were not, "full capacity" would never be reached. Hence the annual percentage increments in real output along the ceiling must be less than those in the upswing. Thus accelerator-induced investment must fall and a downswing begin.

The existence of a full capacity ceiling thus serves two purposes in our theory. First it explains why a theoretically explosive system cannot proceed upward without limit. Second it explains why, if the economy attempts to "crawl along the ceiling," it will eventually turn downward: that is, it explains why there will be an upper turning point.

Why does the downswing not proceed forever? What checks this? In the first place though gross investment *can* fall to zero, it is unlikely to do so, for this implies that *all* firms in the economy have zero gross investment. This is improbable. If some do not have zero gross investment, then since none can have *negative* gross investment, gross investment as a whole will be positive. Moreover, even if gross investment *does* fall to zero, there will still be a floor to income since, on our usual consumption function hypothesis there will be some level of income so low that, for the community as a whole, all income will be consumed (i.e., $C_p = Y$). In the second place some net investment is, in our terminology, *autonomous:* that is, unaffected by the recent behavior of output. A part at least of this will continue even in depressions. Hence gross investment will not, in general, fall to zero in a depression but to some positive value which we may call I_{min}. It follows that, with a given consumption function, the minimum level of output is:

$$Y_{min} = \left[I_{min} \times \frac{1}{1-c} \right] + \frac{A}{1-c},$$

where $A \equiv$ autonomous consumption, and c, as usual, denotes the marginal propensity to consume.

Once Y reaches Y_{min} it ceases to fall. Hence the induced net investment due to the accelerator, which was *negative* when income was falling, *rises* to zero. As a result output rises above Y_{min} and, probably after some time lag, accelerator-induced investment becomes positive.

Thus even when the value of the accelerator coefficient implies, mathematically, an explosive system, there are good reasons for thinking that the existence of a full capacity ceiling and a minimum level of output will not only constrain fluctuations in a manner more in accordance with experience but also explain both the upper and lower turning points.

GROWTH AND FLUCTUATIONS

In this chapter, by means of a rather brief excursion into dynamics, we have sought to set out the elements of a theory which explains cyclical fluctuations in aggregate demand and thus in output and the proportion of productive capacity employed. In the previous chapter we discussed some aspects of the rate at which, in the long-run, "full capacity" output grew over time. This separation of the related problems of growth and fluctuations is legitimate up to a point. It carries, however, a risk that the reader may unconsciously assume that the two problems are independent. To see the importance of this consider the proposition:

If we could eliminate the cyclical fluctuations in output, then we could grow just as fast as we have done in the past.

This implies that the long-term "trend" rate of growth in capacity is entirely independent of the cyclical process. This may or may not be the case. At present economists cannot give a very confident answer one way or the other. It is possible that, by reducing or eliminating fluctuations, we might grow faster. Equally it is possible that we might, as a result, grow more slowly. The cycle may be the cost of growth: or it may not. Our discussion throws no light on this issue. Nor does it imply one answer rather than another. Two things are, however, sure. The first is that in estimating the long-term rate of growth in capacity we are using observations obtained from the fluctuating path followed by the U. S. economy. Our estimate is, therefore, not independent of the cycle. The second point is that the question is one of considerable practical importance for, during the last few years, the elimination of the cycle and the maintenance of steady, sustainable growth have become avowed objectives of official policy.

MORE ABOUT THE CEILING

In our rather formal discussion of the cycle we have sketched a theory which regards the dynamic structure of the economic system as *explosive* but *constrains* the system within a "ceiling" and a "floor." Hitherto we have interpreted the upper constraint as being the "capacity" of the economy to produce output. However, once we admit the possibility of government intervention, "capacity" becomes only one of a number of possible upper constraints. We must now ask, with the U. S. economy particularly in mind, is "capacity" the relevant upper constraint?

One possible upper constraint may be thought of, rather loosely, as the "inflation" constraint. We shall discuss the problem of rising prices more fully in the next chapter and in this discussion seek to make the notion of "inflation" rather more precise. Nevertheless, without anticipating the work of Chapter 20, we can argue that if, as the economy approaches full "capacity" in the upswing, the rate of increase of prices *either* accelerates *or* is expected by the government to accelerate, the government may again take action to check the upswing before "capacity" is reached. If the government acts in this way, because it regards "rapidly" rising prices as objectionable in themselves or fears their impact on the balance of payments (or for both reasons together), then the effective constraint is *not* "capacity" but "inflation."

There is little doubt that the federal government has at times acted to check expansions before the economy has reached "full capacity." In practice, therefore, it has not always been the "capacity" constraint which has imposed the upper limit of expansions.

It would, of course, be entirely wrong to interpret the cycle as though the role of the government in seeking to conduct macroeconomic policy were limited to checking expansions. Presumably, on the assumption that the inflation constraint is effective, the aim of the government would be to manage the economy, by fiscal and monetary means, so that it moves through time as nearly as possible along the line *pp* in Figure 19.5 which is drawn to represent the notion of the inflation constraint. This, of course, is simply its *short-run stabilization objective* and amounts to attempting to reduce the amplitude of the cycle. Its *long-run* objective is to insure that the "constraint line" *pp* has the maximum attainable slope.

Stabilization involves managing aggregate demand *countercyclically*. Thus in the later stages of upswings, the government if it aims to reduce the amplitude of the cycle, should use fiscal and monetary means to restrain demand: conversely in downswings it should aim to expand demand. This raises difficult problems of *timing*. If the government imposes restraint too late, it may make its *impact* when the economy has already reached (or even passed) its upper turning point. (Note that what is relevant here is the time when the restraint becomes *effective,* not the time when it is imposed.) If this happens, it will serve only to steepen the downswing. Conversely if the government expands demand too late—after the lower turning point is passed—it may cause the expansion to become unmanageably fast. The road to increasing instability is paved with good intentions. We know, in quantitative terms, far too little about the parameters of the economic sys-

Figure 19.5 / *The growth cycle: schematic presentation.*

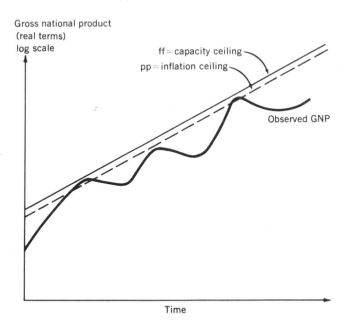

tem including the way in which it responds through time (its dynamic
properties) to make stabilization simple. As a result there have almost certainly been important errors by the government in both the magnitude and
timing of its interventions. Hence the observed behavior of U. S. output, and
hence the U. S. cycle, is probably at least in part the result of government
intervention which has, on occasions, been destabilising rather than stabi-
lising. In fact, some economists have argued that so called stabilization
policy is generally destabilizing rather than stabilizing. Others, have, of
course, denied that this is the case.

The theory we have sketched suggests, you will recall, that the economic
system is potentially explosive (in the sense of Table 19.2 and Figure 19.4).
As we know, this depends on the values of certain parameters. What values
these parameters take is a question of fact. They might be such as to give
rise to a system characterized by damped fluctuations (Table 19.1). In this
case the observed cycle can be explained by the impact on such a system of
a series of exogenous *shocks* occuring in a random manner over time. These
shocks could take any form. A war in the Middle East, a shift in the domestic MEI schedule, or an increase in government expenditures are some of
the numerous possibilities. Whether such a system—or the one we have
outlined—is a more accurate explanation of the U. S. cycle is a question of

fact and we do not know enough, in quantitative and dynamic terms, about the U. S. economy to form a confident judgment as to the answer. In either system, however, there are good grounds for thinking that government action is a significant contributory factor to the observed cycle.

SUMMARY

The aim of this chapter has been to explain why "mixed-capitalist" economies in general, and the United States in particular, experience fluctuations in the level of economic activity which may, rather loosely, be termed "cyclical." To do this we sketched a dynamic theory of investment based, in large measure, upon the accelerator hypothesis. Since the accelerator hypothesis suggested an unstable economic system, we found reasons for thinking that the fluctuations of the system were constrained by (1) the ceiling of "full capacity" growth and (2) the floor provided by a minimum level of output. In discussing the accelerator hypothesis we provided an illustration of the distinction between dynamic and static economic models, for though both our accelerator models (of Tables 19.1 and 19.2) yielded identical static equilibrium results, the first model (with $V = 0.8$) was *stable* while the second (with $V = 3.0$) was *unstable*. From this it is possible to deduce that a wide range of dynamic models, with differing *dynamic* behavior, nevertheless yield *the same equilibrium results*. From this it may be inferred that the *comparative static* method of analysis employed in earlier chapters is valid if, and only if, the model being discussed is *dynamically stable*.

The whole analysis was conducted in real terms and assumed constant prices and interest rates.

QUESTIONS AND EXERCISES

1. Interpret the following two models. Give a verbal explanation of each equation.

Model I	Model II
$Y_t = C_t + I_t$	$Y_t = C_t + I_t$
$C_t = A + cY_{t-1}$	$C_t = A + cY_t$
$I_t = H_t + R_t + v(Y_t - Y_{t-1}).$	$I_t = H_t + R_t + v(Y_{t-1} - Y_{t-2}).$

Using the values of c, v, H_t, R_t given in the text, construct tables showing the behavior of both systems from periods t to $t + 8$. What are the static equilibria of the two systems? Do they differ? Are both systems stable?

2. "The accelerator coefficient is simply the marginal capital/output ratio." Do you agree? If not, why not?

3. "Since the accelerator depends on the ratio K/Y while K is a *stock* independent of the length of the period for which Y (which is a *flow*) is defined, the accelerator coefficient with respect to monthly income is *four times* as large as the accelerator with respect to annual income. It is therefore meaningless to talk of stability in terms of the accelerator coefficient." Examine this view.

4. How would you attempt to test the accelerator hypothesis? Write down a function for investment in fixed capital incorporating the accelerator hypothesis and any other hypotheses which seem to you to be worth investigating.

5. Plot on a graph the quarterly figures for real investment in inventories 1965–1970. Are there any difficulties in interpreting this series? Is it consistent with the hypothesis that businessmen seek to maintain a constant ratio of stock to output? What leads you to take your view? [Use data from the *Survey of Current Business*.]

6. "Booms in investment in fixed capital reflect waves of innovation. Hence if there were no investment booms, there would be no technical progress." Do you agree?

7. In the market for peanuts we have (1) a relation between the quantity demanded and price of the form: $Q_t^D = A + bP_t$ where $b < 0$; and (2) a relation between the quantity supplied and price of the form: $Q_t^S = Z + gP_{t-1}$, where $g > 0$; $P(t) \equiv$ price in period t.

   Find the equilibrium price in terms of A, Z, g, and b. Since the equilibrium price must be positive, what must be the sign of $A-Z$ and what does this mean in economic terms?

   Assign numerical values to A, b, Z, and g and plot the resulting demand and supply curves on a graph. Assume that, in some period $t = 0$ price departs from equilibrium. Trace out the subsequent movements of price and quantity. Is your system stable? What is the economic interpretation of the lag between supply and price?

8. "In the United States investment turns up after output and turns down after output has flattened out." Is this so? If it is, what kind of investment theory does it suggest? What starts U. S. expansions and what stops them?

9. "Observed investment in stocks consists of both planned and unplanned elements. Since we can never identify these two components, we can never hope to test any theory of planned investment in inventories." Do you agree? Can you suggest any way of estimating unplanned inventory accumulation?

10. "The desired ratio of stocks to output must, if businessmen are rational, depend significantly upon the cost of borrowing." Explain. If this is so, what implications has it for our inventory accelerator?

11. Assume that K_t^* (the desired level of inventories at the end of period (t) responds both to output (Y_t) and the rate of interest (r_t). So that

$$K_t^* = f[Y_t, r_t].$$

Assume further that planned investment in inventories in period $t(I_{pt})$ depends upon the difference between the inventories desired at the end of period $t(K_t^*)$ and actual inventories at the end of period $t-1$ (K_{t-1}) so that

$$I_{pt} = \lambda[K_t^* - K_{t-1}].$$

Unplanned inventory accumulation (I_{ut}) is simply the difference between output in period t (Y_t) and demand in period t (D_t) so that

$$I_{ut} = Y_t - D_t.$$

Since businessmen adjust output to expected demand D^* we have

$$I_{pt} + I_{ut} \equiv \text{observed investment in inventories}$$
$$\equiv \lambda[K_t^* - K_{t-1}] + D_t^* - D_t.$$

Which of these variables are observable?
What is the meaning of λ?
Can you offer an explanation of D_t^* in terms of observable variables? (Hint: refer to the beer production model of Chapter 2.)
In the light of your answers reconsider Questions 9 and 10.

12. What is meant by "autonomous" investment? What kinds of investment do you think are likely to fall into this category? If you can think of none, does this mean that you think that all investment is "induced"?

13. It is stated in the text that V ($\equiv$ the accelerator coefficient) is equal to the marginal capital/output ratio. On what assumptions is this correct? In the text what unstated assumption is being made about the value of $\dot{\lambda}$ ($\equiv$ speed of response)? What is the relation between V and $\partial Y/\partial K$?

14. Using the hypothetical cycle of Fig. 19.5 write a memorandum which explains the objectives of short and long-term economic policy. What value judgments underlie your memorandum?

15. Use the theory of the production function to relate the coefficient α of equation (19.1) to the marginal product of capital $(\partial Y/\partial K)$.

16. To the model of page 316, Equation (19.2k) add the hypothesis of an output lag such that

$$Y(t) = D(t - 1)$$
$$D(t - 1) \equiv C(t - 1) + I(t - 1) + H(t - 1) + R(t - 1).$$

Construct a revised version of Table 19.1. Does it modify the general conclusions derived from Table 19.1? If so, how and why?

17. Figure 19.2 shows residential investment and nonresidential fixed investment. How does the behavior of these series differ? What explanations of this difference can you suggest?

SUGGESTED READING

R. C. O. Matthews, *The Trade Cycle* (Cambridge, England: Cambridge Univ. Press, 1959) particularly Chaps. 1–3.

A. H. Hansen, *Business Cycles and National Income* (New York: Norton, 1951) Chaps. 9–12.

M. Evans, *Macroeconomic Activity* (New York: Harper and Row, 1969) Pts. 2 and 3. *Advanced reference.*

A. Gordon, *Business Cycles* (Harper and Row, 1961).

Executive Office of the President, *Economic Report of the President* (various years).

20

Inflation

IN CHAPTER 15 we discussed the factors determining the price level. We now turn to a closely related problem, the *process* of rising prices—in other words, inflation.

Keynesian theory was developed in the 1930s essentially to explain why we had large-scale unemployment and what to do about it. To do so it provided an analysis of aggregate demand, and the same analysis can be used to look at the problem of inflation. When aggregate demand is deficient, involuntary unemployment occurs; when aggregate demand is excessive, there is inflation. We have here an asymmetry: excessive demand causes inflation, but deficient demand causes primarily unemployment rather than falling prices. The reason for this asymmetry is that wages and prices are flexible upward, but much less flexible downward.

However, although excessive demand results in inflation, it is not necessarily the case that every inflation is caused by excessive demand. Inflation could also result from shifts in the supply curve.

DEFINITION AND TYPES OF INFLATION

Open inflation is generally defined as a significant increase in the price level. It is convenient to reserve the term for price increases which are not trivial. If we were to call any price increase or decrease, however slight, inflation or deflation, then there would be no empirical counterpart to the notion of price stability. Exactly where to draw the line and start talking about inflation is rather arbitrary. The word "inflation" is not a technical term with a precisely defined meaning.

One can distinguish between inflations on the basis of their magnitude. On the one hand, we have an extreme inflation, called "hyperinflation." Hyperinflation is a dramatic event when the currency rapidly loses nearly all its value. Again there is no generally accepted cut-off point, but one line of demarcation which has been used is prices rising by more than 50 percent *per month*. It is these hyperinflations which produce the dramatic stories, such as people going shopping carrying their money in a suitcase. In Germany after World War I it was said that anyone going into a bar should order at least two drinks at the same time, because by the time he finished the first one, the price was likely to have gone up. Indeed some hyperinflations have been so rapid that the government's printing presses could not keep up, and old currency notes were simply stamped with an additional zero to raise their value. In one case, Hungary, even this process was not sufficient, and the government simply announced on the radio each day what the currency notes were worth that day. Perhaps the best known hyperinflation is that of Germany, when, in December 1923, the cost of living was more than a billion times what it had been a year earlier. Hyperinflations amount to the expropriation of those who hold their wealth in items with fixed money values such as bonds, and can cause the ruin of a large part of the middle class. Fortunately, such hyper-inflations are very rare events. They occur only if a government loses effective control over economic events, and finances itself by the printing of more and more money. They are phenomena associated with the loss of a disastrous war rather than with more normal circumstances.

The other extreme case is that of a moderate inflation, say 2–3 percent per year, called creeping inflation. (Again there is no hard and fast line of demarcation.) The reader should note that what is involved in a creeping inflation is a rise in actual prices rather than just in the price index. As will be shown later, a small rise in the price *index* is consistent with price stability because the price index has an upward bias due to its inability to take sufficient account of quality improvements and new products.

In between hyperinflation, at one extreme, and creeping inflation at the other, there is a very large area of what is usually referred to just as inflation, though the term "galloping inflation" is sometimes used for fairly sharp inflations.

Some related terms are deflation, reflation, and disinflation. Deflation simply means a decline in the price level. However, since sharp deflations are associated with substantial unemployment, and are characteristic of major depressions, the term "deflation" is sometimes used loosely to mean falling prices and substantial unemployment. Reflation, a term used only occasionally, means bringing prices which have previously fallen back to their "normal" level. Since the idea of a "normal" price level is vague, the term "reflation" is not a very clear one; in fact, one may rather cynically look upon this word as a polite term for "inflation." Similarly, a polite term for a small deflation to offset some previous inflation is "disinflation."

Finally, we distinguish between "open inflation" and "suppressed inflation." Open inflation is what is generally meant by inflation—i.e., rising prices—and therefore the word "open" is normally not used. Hence we will use the term "inflation" to mean open inflation. Suppressed inflation, on the other hand, is a condition which most people would probably not call inflation at all since prices are not rising. Instead, excessive demand is prevented from raising prices by price (and generally wage) controls. In most of this chapter we will be dealing with open inflation, but before doing so let us look briefly at suppressed inflation.

SUPPRESSED INFLATION

Until 1971 it was correct to say that general wage and price controls had been used in the United States only in wartime and in the immediate postwar years. However, in 1971 general wage and price controls were imposed on what was essentially a peacetime economy. It is too early to tell whether or not this is a temporary aberration.

The basic mechanism of suppressed inflation is very simple. Although demand exceeds supply at the prevailing price level, prices cannot—at least, in principle—rise. Since the economy is already operating essentially at capacity, supply cannot rise either. As a result, the market mechanism is frustrated, there is excess demand at the controlled prices, and price alone no longer rations the available supply. Instead, government rationing may be resorted to, or else the available supply may be rationed by an informal system of shopkeeper rationing (or favoritism) or by a "first come, first served, last come, not served" rule.

The reason controls are used, instead of letting the inflation proceed, is that in this way the government hopes to avoid the effects of open inflation on the distribution of income which are discussed below. But suppressing an inflation has a number of serious disadvantages. One of these is that it prevents prices from serving as an efficient allocator of resources. We generally rely on the price mechanism to provide producers with a signal telling them what they should produce. If prices are controlled, this signaling mechanism cannot function. If prices are fixed, and if everything that is produced can be sold, the producer has no incentive to produce more of those items for which consumer demand is greater, and less of others. To give a concrete example, after World War II there was a shortage of business shirts while stores had a large supply of sports shirts. Since they could not raise prices of white shirts, the manufacturers had no incentive to switch production to business shirts.

A second major disadvantage of suppressed inflation is that with demand being excessive, available goods are bought up rapidly and there are too few inventories in the pipelines. Hence, any disruption of production or distribution tends to create acute shortages right away. This condition is described very graphically by the phrase "the empty economy." A third major disadvantage is an obvious one. Controls require government supervision and hence a great deal of red tape, and there is evasion and corruption. Moreover, price and wage controls generally do not work perfectly, and despite the controls, some increase in prices and wages takes place, and quality deteriorates. In addition controls are obviously a very serious interference with economic freedom. Finally, it is worth noting that controls do not eliminate the basic cause of the inflation. Hence, when controls are finally eliminated, there is the danger that open inflation will occur. Hopefully, some exogenous factor will turn up and reduce the excess demand before controls are lifted, but a policy of just hoping that something will turn up is not always a wise policy.

THE CAUSES OF INFLATION I—DEMAND PULL THEORIES

The traditional way of explaining inflation has been to treat it as the result of excessive demand, i.e., of excess demand pulling prices up. The value of aggregate supply and demand must be equal. Hence, if aggregate demand increases at a time when the economy is operating at full capacity, the price of output must rise enough for supply to equal demand. But supply and demand interactions are much more complicated in the aggregate case than they are in microeconomics. This is so because an increase in prices, by raising incomes, raises demand. Hence a price increase, instead of bringing supply and demand into balance, *may* increase excess demand even more. We are dealing with a dynamic process which *may* be unstable.

In previous chapters we explained at length what determines the level of aggregate demand. Fortunately, this analysis can be used to explain the inflationary process as well, and we will therefore not have to build a new elaborate analytical structure. The variables which determine aggregate demand, and hence money income, operate regardless of whether we are at full employment. Only their effect is different. If we are at full employment, an increase in aggregate demand results in inflation rather than in an increase in output as well as prices. But in either case the level of aggregate demand is explained by the same variables.

Suppose, for example, that there is an increase in the quantity of money when the economy is already at full employment. Interest rates fall and investment and consumption both increase in money terms. But since output is at its limit, prices rise in proportion to the increased demand. Similarly, suppose there is a *de*crease in liquidity preference. Again the interest rate falls and, as a result, prices rise. Alternatively, assume that the marginal efficiency of investment or the propensity to consume increases. Again the result is inflation.

In Chapter 17 we described the monetarist approach to macroeconomics. In this theory inflation can be attributed primarily to one factor, an excessive growth of the money stock, rather than to the several other factors just discussed. While the monetarist admits that, in principle, a decline in liquidity preference (read a decrease in k) can bring about inflation, he considers an autonomous decrease in liquidity preference to be very unlikely. But while changes in k are not likely to initiate an inflation, this does not mean that k is constant during an inflation. Rather than being numerically stable, k is taken as a *stable function* of other variables. One of these variables is the cost of holding money, and one of the two components of this cost is the percentage rate of change of prices. Hence, during inflation, as the cost of holding money increases, k declines. It therefore follows from the Cambridge equation, $M = kPT$, that, holding T constant, prices initially rise proportionately *more* than the quantity of money. Only after k has fallen to its new equilibrium value corresponding to the higher cost of holding money will a, say, 10 percent rise in M and a 3 percent rise in T lead to a 7 percent rise in prices. Essentially, the quantity theory, like the Keynesian theory, explains inflation by the same set of factors it uses to explain money income under other conditions.

Returning to the Keynesian theory, the similarity between the explanation of inflation and of income in general can be illustrated by going back to the income determination diagram we used earlier except that we now use money values rather than real values on the axes. In Figure 20.1 we use the same diagram to illustrate both the familiar concept of underemployment equilibrium, denoted by the Y_1Y_0, and the so-called "inflationary gap" Y_0Y_2. The inflationary gap tells us by how much aggregate demand exceeds the value of full employment output at current prices. It is therefore a measure of the potential for inflation. This does not mean that if there is an inflationary gap of, say, 10 percent, a 10 percent price increase would restore equilibrium. This would be so only on the unwarranted assumption that the price increase does not itself, in turn, raise demand. The inflationary gap is a static concept and measures only the inflationary pressures we start out with. But one can use it as a measure of the amount by which demand would have to be decreased to keep prices stable.

The assumption just mentioned, that an increase in prices would not

Figure 20.1 / *The inflationary gap.*

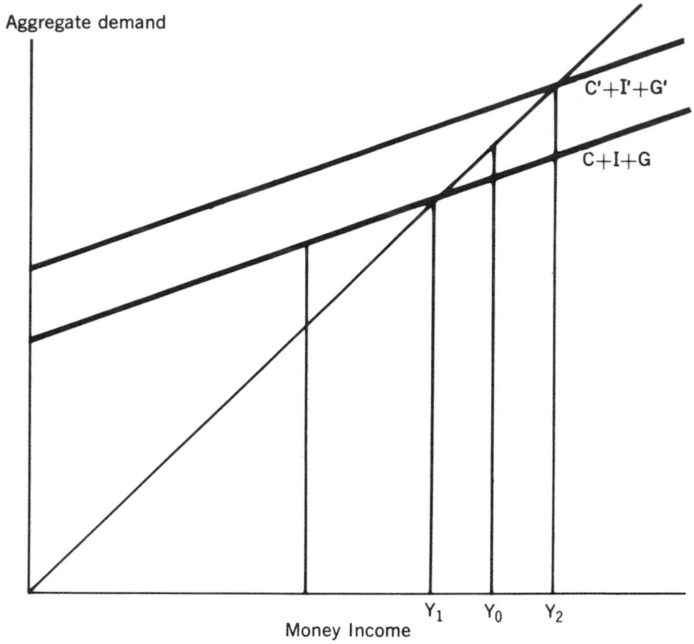

Note: Y_0 is the value of full employment income at present prices.

change aggregate demand is, of course, naïve. It is a very basic proposition of macroeconomics that one man's price is another man's income. If prices rise and output is constant, the seller's income obviously rises proportionately and, as a result, he will raise his demand. In fact, one can easily build up a simple-minded model in which inflation, once started, just continues with prices rising steadily each year. To do this we have to assume that inflation does not change the propensity to consume or to invest, that the nominal money supply increases in proportion to prices, that the real value of the government's deficit (or surplus) is constant, that there is no real balance effect, and foreign investment is constant. To see this, consider the following simple system of equations explaining real income:

$$C_p = f(Y_r) \tag{20.1}$$

$$I_p = f\left(\frac{dY_r}{dt}, r_r\right) \tag{20.2}$$

$$r_p = f(M_r) \tag{20.3}$$

$$M_p = \text{constant.} \tag{20.4}$$

In this system of equations real expenditures depend only on real magnitudes. Hence, if prices rise while real income is constant, expenditures are constant in real terms too. This implies that expenditures in money terms rise proportionately to prices. And if money expenditures rise in proportion to prices, there is nothing to prevent prices from rising continually.[1]

But such a simple model is hardly a good description of the behavior of our economy. As Figure 5.2 (p. 57) showed, while there have been periods of inflation, it would be more than slightly inaccurate to say that we have had continuous inflation. So now let us see what terminates inflations.

Before turning to the endogenous factors which stop an inflation, there is one thing we must admit. An inflation need not be ended by endogenous factors. Inflations can be—and presumably some have been—terminated by extraneous events. Suppose, for example, that in an economy described by the above system of equations the marginal efficiency of investment declines because of an exhaustion of investment opportunities or because of government policies. Such a decline in investment can cause a switch from inflation to a situation of deficient demand. But if inflation is not brought to a stop by such an outside factor, what endogenous factors are likely to terminate it?

The endogenous factors which stop inflation operate by reducing aggregate demand. We therefore have to see why the simple-minded model (20.1)–(20.4) is invalid, and just how rising prices reduce real demand. Looking first at investment, there are two such factors. One is that inflation is likely to reduce the value of a country's exports and to increase its imports so that its net foreign investment is reduced. While this effect is important in countries with a large foreign trade sector, it is much less important for the U. S. economy.

Of greater significance for the United States is what inflation does to the real money stock and to interest rates. Equation (20.4), above, assumed that the central bank keeps the real money stock constant by increasing the nominal money stock in proportion to price increases; in other words, that it is financing inflation. But the Federal Reserve has the duty, among other things, of preventing inflation. Hence it is unlikely to finance continual inflation, particularly if this inflation is accompanied by balance of payments deficits. If the Federal Reserve therefore reduces the growth rate of the money stock below the rate of price increase, the real money supply falls as inflation continues. And, as the real money stock declines, interest rates rise and credit becomes less available, so that investment

1. This is in some respects similar to a situation in which Say's Law (see p. 264 above) holds. But since supply is taken as fixed here, it is not really the same thing as saying that supply creates its own demand.

and consumption decline. Ideally aggregate demand declines by just enough to end the inflation without creating unemployment, though such a fortunate state of affairs is rather unlikely.

A number of factors which reduce aggregate demand as inflation continues work through the consumption function. One of these operates through the tax system. As inflation proceeds, the rise in money income shifts taxpayers into a higher tax bracket so that their disposable income becomes a smaller proportion of their personal income. Since consumption is a function of disposable income rather than personal income, this tax effect therefore reduces consumption. The second is the operation of real balance effect in the consumption market as discussed in Chapter 17. As prices rise the real value of wealth holdings declines and households react to this decline in wealth by reducing their consumption. Third, the reduced availability of credit (and *perhaps* the rise in the interest rate) reduces dis-saving by households and this too causes consumption to decline.

There are other possible effects of inflation on the consumption function, but these are only hypothetical effects which may, but need not, occur. One of these operates through a money illusion. Even if both prices and money incomes rise proportionately households may *think* that their real incomes have fallen, and hence may cut their consumption. But one can turn this argument around and say that when households feel poorer, they cut their saving rate, and thus unintentionally raise their real consumption. (Since there is a money *illusion,* either real consumption or real saving must in actuality differ from what households intended it to be.) Similarly, one can produce two other possibilities by arguing that with both prices and wages rising, households believe that their real incomes have increased. All in all, it would be unwise to rely on a money illusion to limit inflationary pressures.[2]

Another possibility is the occurrence of buyers' strike. As prices rise the public may indignantly refuse to buy "unnecessary" items at these high prices. But while this may happen, it is rather unlikely. Inflation may also reduce consumption by engendering a sense of pessimism.[3]

Inflation may be retarded by a redistribution of income. If inflation redistributed income from wage earners to firms, this would reduce the propensity to consume for two reasons. First, since profits are received initially by firms, an increase in profits raises corporate saving, and insofar as profits are distributed to stockholders this occurs with a lag. Second,

2. A recent empirical study found that price increases raise, rather than lower consumption, thus suggesting that a money illusion stimulates inflation. See W. H. Branson and A. K. Klevorick, "Money Illusion and the Aggregate Consumption Function," *American Economic Review,* Vol. LIX (December 1969), pp. 832–49.

3. One would expect that households who foresee inflation would decide to buy now rather than later. But many households seem to believe that if prices are likely to rise in the future, it is now a "bad time to buy." Presumably they are afraid that inflation will reduce their real incomes.

profit recipients, being essentially high-income households, have a lower propensity to consume than do wage earners. But this income redistribution effect does not provide a reliable brake on inflation for three reasons. First, there is considerable doubt that there actually is a significant wage lag, that inflation really redistributes income from wages to profits. (And while inflation does redistribute income from interest to profits, interest is a relatively small proportion of national income.) Second, while an increase in profits raises corporate saving, it may also raise corporate investment. Finally, to the extent that the permanent income theory discussed in Chapter 9 is correct, there is no difference in the propensities to consume of profit recipients and wage earners.

Thus, none of these four factors—money illusion, buyers' strike, increased pessimism, and income redistribution—can be relied upon to stop an inflation. If an inflation is to be terminated by endogenous rather than exogenous "accidental" factors, one has to rely on:

1) the decline in net foreign investment;
2) the effect of rising tax rates on consumption;
3) the real balance effect on consumption;
4) the liquidity effect of a decline in the real quantity of money.

The last of these, changes in the real quantity of money, is given much more attention in analyzing inflation than in analyzing periods of deficient demand. One reason for this is that money can operate without restriction as a limiting factor in inflation; there is no analogue to the possible operation of absolute liquidity preference. Absolute liquidity preference could, in principle, prevent an increase in the real quantity of money from reducing real interest rates. But there is nothing which prevents a decrease in real quantity of money from raising real interest rates in the short run.

Another reason why a decrease in the real quantity of money during an inflation receives more attention in the Keynesian model than does an increase in the real quantity of money during a depression is that this model takes prices to be flexible upward but not downward. Regardless of whether there is inflation or not, an increase in the quantity of money initially lowers the rate of interest. Since in a Keynesian model prices are stable in a period of deficient demand, the interest rate remains at this lower level, and so the public is induced to hold more money. In other words, part of the effect of an increase in the quantity of money is dissipated by a movement down the liquidity preference curve, and hence money income does not change to the full extent of the increase in the money stock. But, during an inflation, a process described in Chapter 17 takes place: the increase in the stock of money raises prices further, so that the real money stock increases less than the nominal money stock. This process continues until the real interest rate is back to where it was before. Once the real interest rate is back to its previous level, the public wants to hold the same real quantity of money as before. In other words, since the real rate of interest has not fallen, income must have risen enough to make the public want to hold all the additional money. This means that in an inflationary situation, if the quantity of money is increased by 10 percent above what it would otherwise be, the price level must rise by 10 percent too.

Thus the Keynesian theory of inflation is similar to the quantity theory discussed in Chapter 17. However, there are some differences. One is that in the quantity theory the factor which initiates the inflation is primarily a change in the quantity of money. In the Keynesian theory, on the other hand, changes in liquidity preference, the marginal efficiency of investment, and the propensity to consume can also initiate the inflation. Second, the Keynesian approach does not rely only on the decline in the real quantity of money and real balances to stop inflation; the fiscal effect discussed above and the decline in net foreign investment also counteract inflation. Third, in the Keynesian theory changes in the real quantity of money operate primarily through the interest rate, while, as we saw in Chapter 17, in the quantity theory they work more directly. Fourth, the Keynesian theory is much more hospitable to attempts to explain inflation through a cost push process—to which we turn next—than is the quantity theory.[4]

THE CAUSES OF INFLATION II—COST PUSH THEORIES

In the postwar period an alternative explanation of inflation has come to the fore. This explanation does not deny that many inflations are caused by excessive demand, but it claims that this is not true for all inflations. Some inflations can be attributed not to a shift in the demand curve but to a shift in the aggregate supply curve. Such "cost push inflation," sometimes called "seller's inflation," is the result of sellers of labor or of products raising their prices even though demand may be constant. One example of this would be oligopolistic firms deciding to raise profit margins and prices even though, with the demand curve being stable, this means a decline in their output. Another example is a labor union demanding, and obtaining, wage increases even though this results in substantial unemployment for its members. A seller's inflation can be illustrated by the Keynesian idealized aggregate supply curve discussed previously in Chapter 15 and redrawn as curve AA in Figure 20.2. You will recall that in Chapter 15 we called the elbow of this curve full employment. But need this really be the case? It is certainly conceivable that wages will start to rise rapidly well before we reach what may be called full employment. One can imagine a situation

---

4. In addition, the quantity theory is more ready than the Keynesian theory to allow for the fact that rising prices, by raising the cost of holding money, may reduce the demand for money.

Figure 20.2 / *Unemployment and wage increases.*

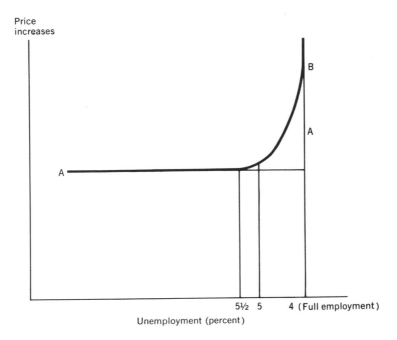

where if aggregate demand increases enough to reduce unemployment, say from 6 percent to 5 percent, unions decide to take the benefit of this increased demand in the form of substantial wage increases rather than as reduced unemployment. This is shown by curve *AB* in Figure 20.2. For example, from July 1957 to June 1958 the consumer price index rose by 2.4 percent despite an average unemployment rate of 5.7 percent. Similarly, in 1970, while unemployment averaged 4.9 percent, the consumer price index rose by more than 5 percent. Such inflations do not *seem* to be caused by excessive demand.

There is considerable dispute, not about the theoretical possiblity of cost push inflation in the abstract, but whether our economy actually behaves in this way. To see the reasons for this, consider first an economy in atomistic competition. In such an economy cost push inflation is impossible. Firms take the market determined price as given, and produce and sell at this price until marginal cost equals price. And the wage rate is determined by the marginal productivity of labor on the one hand and the marginal disutility of labor on the other. Admittedly, much of our economy does not operate in this way, so let us now introduce some monopolies, oligopolies, and labor unions. However, let us further assume that the *degree* of monopoly, oligopoly, and unionization is constant. If so, there would be no reason to expect cost push inflation. To be sure, monopolists and oligopolists will have raised their prices, and unions will have raised their wages. But note our phrasing; we said "will have," not "will." These prices and wages will have risen when these imperfections of competition originally occurred. Once monopolists and oligopolists have set a higher price, there is no reason to expect this price to rise further. While monopoly and oligopoly prices are *high,* there is no reason to think that they are *rising.* And the same is true for union wages.

It may seem to the reader that this sort of theorizing is not called for, that one could simply determine empirically whether we actually do experience cost push inflation. But the empirical data are hard to interpret, because the distinction between cost push and demand pull inflation is a distinction based on the initiating cause of inflation only. Once the process of inflation is in motion, cost push and demand pull elements interact. Since one man's price is another man's income, cost push inflation raises money incomes and aggregate demand, and hence looks like demand pull inflation. Similarly, demand pull inflation raises costs, and hence it looks like cost push inflation.

More specifically, some characteristics which at first glance seem to distinguish between demand pull and cost push inflation fail to do so. One of these is whether wages or prices rise first. It may seem that if prices rise first and wages rise only afterward, then the inflation cannot be attributed to unions pushing up wages. But this is not a usable test, because one can generally find one starting point which shows wages rising first and also another starting point which shows prices rising first. A similar observation applies when one asks the question which rose more. Another simple test might seem to be whether wages rose more than productivity. But wages rising more than productivity is a characteristic of both demand pull and cost push inflation and hence cannot help to distinguish between the two.

With this background let us look at one of the two variants of the cost push theory, the "administered price" explanation. This theory asserts that many prices in our economy do not respond freely to supply and demand conditions but are administered by firms with substantial market power. These firms may raise prices even if the underlying demand and cost conditions have not changed. In some industries, the argument runs, competition primarily takes the form of product differentiation and advertising, and firms therefore have some leeway in setting their prices. They can set prices to achieve a certain target rate of return. If wages rise in such industries, the wage increase is likely, due to pattern bargaining, to be similar for all firms, and hence they just pass this wage increase on to the public. Moreover, since a new union contract provided a convenient excuse for a price increase, firms in oligopolistic industries can raise their prices by more than wage increase.

Such an approach is, however, hard to reconcile with the traditional marginalist theory of the firms. If firms are already maximizing profits by setting marginal revenue equal to marginal cost, then they will not raise prices unless there are shifts in the marginal revenue or marginal cost curves. If you are already maximizing profits, the target rate of return has little significance. Thus, as pointed out above, while monopoly power leads to *high* prices, it does not explain *rising* prices. Insofar as one accepts the marginalistic theory of the firm, to use monopoly power as an explanation of inflation one would have to show that the degree of monopoly increased. Note, however, that the increase in monopoly power need not occur during the inflation but can precede it. If firms do not know the elasticity of their demand curves, they may experiment by raising prices in a stepwise fashion for many years.[5]

The problem of *high* vs. *rising* prices is much less serious if one rejects the marginalist theory of the firm, as many cost push theorists do, and argues instead that firms do not always maximize profits but, instead, often have a margin of unused monopoly power. Anything, such as an industry-wide wage increase, which causes firms to exploit this unused monopoly power then results in cost push inflation.

Now let us look at the second part of the cost push inflation theory. Cost push inflation need not be attributed to business market power; it can also result from the market power of labor unions and quasi-unions such as professional associations. One way in which unions may generate inflation is via a political route. Unions may have enough political power to force the government to adopt a strong full employment policy. As we discussed in Chapter 15 in connection with the Phillips curve, a policy of trying to force unemployment down to a very low level results in large wage increases, and is inflationary. If union strength is sufficient to force the Federal Reserve to keep on increasing the money supply enough to finance inflation, then one of the important limits of the inflationary process disappears. However, it is very questionable whether unions actually have such power in the United States.

Leaving this political route and looking at purely economic factors, we have to turn back to the Phillips curve discussed in Chapter 15 and reproduced in Figure 20.3. Consider first curve A. If the point at which wages start rising faster than productivity (x_o) is also the point of full employment, there is no cost push problem. Wages start to rise only when demand is excessive. But suppose that x_o represents a state of, say, 5 percent unemployment. In this case, once we get close to full employment, wages

5. Cf. M. A. Adelman, "Steel, Administered Prices and Inflation," *Quarterly Journal of Economics*, Vol. LXXV (February 1961), pp. 16–40.

Figure 20.3 / *Shifting Phillips curves.*

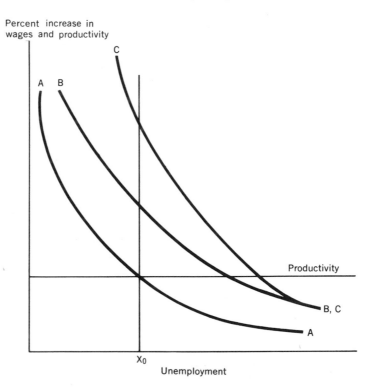

are being pushed up enough to raise prices. And such a situation is by no means implausible. A union may well bargain away some jobs for higher pay. There is nothing necessarily irrational about this, particularly if the union has a seniority clause in its contract so that the majority of its members know that they are not likely to be among the unemployed.

Moreover, there is no reason to assume that the Phillips curve necessarily has to stay put. Starting with curve *A* in Figure 20.3 we could, over time, move to curves *B* and *C*. Indeed, it has been argued that this is what happened during the 1960s, that the Phillips curve changed so that our trade-off worsened.

But when discussing wage push, one should always keep in mind that only about one quarter of the American labor force is unionized. If one looks upon inflation as being caused by unions pushing up wages, either union wages must rise very substantially relative to nonunion wages, or else there must be some mechanism by which wage increases won by unions spread to the nonunionized sector. Since we generally do not observe a substantial increase in the union-nonunionized wage differential during inflations, the wage push hypothesis implies that wage increases won by unions spread readily into the nonunionized sector of the economy. Is this reasonable? One factor suggests that the answer is "yes." This is the demonstration effect. We can see that large gains won by some unions cause other unions to demand the same, or an even larger, gain. A similar mechanism may operate in the nonunionized sector; as union wages rise, nonunionized firms, particularly those in the same industry or employing the same type of labor, may also raise their wages. They may do this to hold on to their labor force, to maintain the morale of their workers, or to stave off unionization. But there is also an offsetting effect. As wages rise in the unionized industries, some workers lose their jobs and then drift into other industries. And this increased supply of labor in the nonunionized industries exerts downward pressure on their wages. If this effect predominates, large union wage increases are offset by smaller increases in nonunion wages.

But, as discussed in Chapter 15, there is a Phillips curve in the nonunion sector as well as in the unionized one. At a certain point firms find it more profitable to raise wages than to undertake more recruiting effort. Moreover, as pointed out in Chapter 15, the way search unemployment operates can also generate a Phillips curve. And the Phillips curve in the nonunion sector *may* also be such that wages, and hence prices, rise well before we reach full employment. To be sure, in these cases the term cost *push* may give a misleading impression.

Let us now combine wage push and administered prices into a single process. Assume that prices are set by a simple mark-up over wage costs, so that

$$\frac{dP}{dt} = a + b\left(\frac{dW}{dt} - \frac{dR}{dt}\right) \qquad (20.5)$$

where R is labor productivity, W wages, and P prices.

Wage increases depend upon the unemployment rate (U) and previous prices

$$\frac{dW}{dt} = c - dU + eP_{-1}. \qquad (20.6)$$

Note that this wage equation includes a constant term. In most of our previous equations we have paid little attention to the constant term, but in this case let us give it a strategic role. Let us assume that it is positive and of significant magnitude. This means that wages have an upward trend; even if the unemployment rate and prices are constant, wages will be higher each year. Assuming that the increase in wages is greater than the rise in productivity, let us now see how the price level behaves in such a model.

Assuming that both U and P_{-1} have not changed, wages in year 1 rise because c is greater than zero. As a result, as (20.5) shows, prices rise. This rise in prices feeds back into next year's wage equation and raises the size of the wage increases of that year. What is now critical is the behavior of U. In the previous section we discussed how a demand pull inflation is terminated. It turned out that there are several ways in which an increase in price lowers *real* aggregate demand. This analysis is also applicable to cost push inflation. But this certainly does not mean that a cost push inflation necessarily comes to an end soon. Three things are critical. One is the actual strength of the factors discussed in the previous section. The second is the government's reaction as unemployment develops. If the government responds to the decline in *real* aggregate demand by expansionary monetary and fiscal policies, the inflation can continue. (Whether one wants to call such a situation a cost push or a demand pull inflation is essentially a terminological point.) But, suppose that the government does not support cost push inflation by increasing real aggregate demand. In this case there is a third critical factor, the coefficient d in (20.6). If it is low, i.e., if the Phillips curve is flat, wages will continue to rise and so will prices. To be sure, eventually there is a point at which unemployment is so great that wages rise by no more than the rise in productivity, and then the cost push inflation comes to a stop on its own. But this point *may* involve more unemployment than society is willing to tolerate.

A similar analysis applies to the case where firms are raising prices, i.e., where a in (20.5) is positive and significant. The increase in a raises prices which, through the price term in (20.6) raises wages and this in turn feeds back into prices. Again, whether or not such an inflation continues depends upon how much excess capacity it takes to prevent firms from raising prices, the coefficients of the wage equation, and on whether or not the government intervenes to support the inflation.

The process of cost inflation can therefore take two forms. One version is a situation where the coefficients b, d, and e are such that we experience inflation long before we reach full employment. This corresponds to a stable Phillips curve. The other case, an upward shifting Phillips curve, is one in which c is positive and large enough to more than offset the annual rise in productivity.

The model we have discussed is what is often called the "inflationary spiral." Popular discussions of this "inflationary spiral" tend to overdramatize it by oversimplifying it. They assert that as wages rise so do prices and that this price increase then, in turn, raises wages in a never-ending spiral. As we pointed out above, there are factors which tend to reduce this spiral. Moreover, the popular discussions ignore another limiting factor. This is that wages are not the only costs. Hence, as wages rise, prices rise by a smaller percentage than wages. This increase in prices then in turn raises wages, at least in the short run, less than proportionately. Hence the "spiral" is likely to be a damped one.

COMBINING COST PUSH AND
DEMAND PULL THEORIES

The two approaches to inflation theory we have so far presented need not necessarily be treated as rivals; instead we can combine them into a synthetic theory. Let us assume that a demand pull inflation which has been going on for a substantial period of time comes to an end. Sellers, of both commodities and labor, form their expectations on the basis of past events. Hence, they expect prices and wages to continue their upward course even when, in fact, the excess demand has actually been eliminated. They therefore continue to raise their prices and wage demands. Since there no longer is the excess demand which would justify these increases, they eventually find that they cannot sell all they thought they could at these higher prices and wages. But it takes some time until the rise in excess capacity and in unemployment teaches the sellers that conditions have changed and that their price and wage demands are excessive. In the meantime, while this learning process takes place, we have both rising prices and considerable unemployment plus excess capacity. This situation is a mixture of demand pull and cost push. On the one hand it is a demand pull situation since the wage and price increases are the result of excessive demand, albeit of excessive demand in the previous period. On the other hand, it is a cost push situation because, if sellers could not temporarily set their prices, but instead had to act, as in the pure atomistic competition model, as pure quantity adjusters, then wages and prices would stop rising as soon as the excess demand disappeared.

Another synthesis of the cost push and demand pull approaches is the so-called "sectorial shift" theory.[6] This theory focuses on shifts of demand between industries. Suppose that there is a strong shift in demand. The industries toward which demand is shifting respond in the traditional way by raising prices, so that we have demand pull inflation in some industries. But how about the industries which lost demand? According to classical theory, they should react by cutting prices so that price declines in some industries offset price increases in others. But now introduce a cost push element, namely that prices are inflexible downward. In this case there will no longer be price decreases in some industries to balance price increases in others. In fact, firms with declining demand may *raise* their prices to protect their profits from falling. Similarly, wages in the declining demand industries may rise substantially rather than fall as large wage increases won from the profitable industries to which demand has shifted now spread

6. See Charles Schultze, *Recent Inflation in the United States*, U. S. Congr. Joint Economic Committee, *Study Paper #1* (Washington, D.C. 1959), Chapter 3.

to the declining demand industries too. Thus the sectorial shift theory explains the coincidence of inflation and substantial unemployment by saying that it is the result of demand pull elements in growing industries and cost push elements in declining industries.

EFFECTS OF INFLATION

In looking at the effects of inflation it is useful to draw a sharp distinction between anticipated and unanticipated inflations. If an inflation is fully anticipated by everyone, then its effects on production, income distribution, and growth are very limited. An accurately anticipated inflation would have only two disadvantages. One is that there would be a need to recalculate prices and wages frequently, and hence some time would be lost in clerical tasks, such as printing price lists, etc. Second, if interest is not paid on all money balances, and prices are known to go up, the public will try to reduce its money holdings below what they would otherwise be. But while economizing on money balances reduces the loss of purchasing power as the value of money falls, it creates other costs and inconveniences for the public, such as having to spend more time in securities transactions. In this way too, anticipated inflation creates some real costs and welfare losses for the economy unless interest (which includes an allowance for inflation) is paid on all cash balances.

The more serious problems about inflation arise when an inflation is not anticipated accurately. We can look at them best by seeing how unanticipated inflation differs from an anticipated one. We will first discuss the effects on production, then on the distribution of income.

In an anticipated inflation, all prices can rise enough to maintain equilibrium, but in an unanticipated inflation this is not the case. Some prices, such as public utility charges, are controlled, and are allowed to rise only with a lag. Similarly, in some industries there are long-term contracts which were made at the old price level. In these industries unanticipated inflation sometimes causes losses and product deterioration. The price system is distorted and resources are misallocated. Moreover, businessmen who borrowed prior to the inflation at interest rates which do not take account of inflation tend to make excess profits because the real rate of interest is reduced. (If, as we shall discuss later, wages lag behind prices, then this tendency towards excess profits may be strongly reinforced.) As a result, investment which would otherwise be marginal now turns out to be profitable. Business expectations therefore become more sanguine, and some investment occurs which would not have been undertaken had it not been for the unanticipated inflation. Such investment is inefficient for the economy as a whole. If the unanticipated inflation now comes to an end, either because it becomes generally anticipated, or because prices stop rising, this investment, if it has to be refinanced at higher interest rates, is no longer profitable. As a result losses and bankruptcies occur. Some of the economy's effort has gone into relatively unproductive investment, and when the resulting losses show up this could possibly either bring about a recession or make worse a recession which would occur in any case.

However, apart from these unfavorable effects, an unanticipated inflation may have two favorable effects on production. One is that if the economy starts out with substantial unemployed resources, at least in the early stages of inflation, these resources will be absorbed into production. Second, in any economy with downward wage and price inflexibility, inflation provides a way of reducing real wages and *relative* prices. Inflation makes it possible for workers to accept real wage cuts with less psychological turmoil than would be the case if these real wage cuts had to be brought about by cutting money wages.

Before leaving the effects of unanticipated inflation on production let us briefly look at one aspect of its effect on real income. Many people appear to believe that inflation reduces real incomes because prices rise faster than incomes. This is very questionable. In the aggregate (including corporations) incomes are equal to output times prices. Hence, if an inflation does not reduce output, then prices cannot rise faster than money incomes (including corporate profits).[7] But even if it does not lower the level of income, what an unanticipated inflation does do is to redistribute income. Let us look at these distributional effects now.

A view accepted for a long time is that wages lag behind prices in an unanticipated inflation. To be sure, as prices rise, wages start to rise too, but they do so with a lag. Hence real wages fall and real profits rise. It is not clear why this should necessarily be the case. One can build models which show how the relatively disorganized state of the labor market causes wages to lag behind, but one can also build models which do not show this. And the empirical evidence from many inflations does not give strong support to this so-called "wage-lag" hypothesis.

However, there is another, much more certain way in which unanticipated inflation redistributes income. This is through its effects on the real value of debts. Consider, for example, a man who bought a $50,000 house with a $40,000 mortgage. If prices rise by 20 percent, his house is worth $60,000, but his mortgage is still only $40,000. Hence his equity in the house has doubled while the lender has had a 20 percent reduction in the

7. But, as discussed in Chapter 17, inflation does reduce the public's wealth through the Pigou effect.

real value of the mortgage he holds. Since there is a large volume of outstanding debts in our economy, even a moderate inflation can bring about
a substantial redistribution of wealth.

Given that the redistribution between creditors and debtors is so important, how can one identify these creditors and debtors with specific
income groups? Can one argue, for example, that the rich gain and the poor
lose by unanticipated inflation? It is tempting to argue that obviously the
poor are debtors and the rich creditors, so that unanticipated inflation
makes the distribution of income more equal. But it is not at all clear that
this is actually the case. What is involved in the creditor relationship are
not primarily personal IOUs but rather the ownership of claims fixed in
money terms, such as Savings and Loan shares, government securities, etc.
Since low-income groups tend to hold most of their (nonhuman) wealth in
assets fixed in money terms, while the upper income groups tend to hold
proportionately more equity investments, it is by no means clear that it is
the rich who lend to the poor and not the other way around. And the
empirical evidence is mixed.

One important aspect of this question is that the biggest debtor in the
economy is the federal government. Since World War II inflation has transferred very substantial amounts of purchasing power from government
security holders to the federal government. But which income groups gain
from this lowering of the real value of the federal debt? It is easy to say
that it is taxpayers and recipients of income from the government, and
then to jump to the conclusion that households have gained in proportion
to the share of their incomes they pay in taxes and receive from the government. But this is not really correct. The people who have gained are the
marginal taxpayers and *marginal* recipients—that is, those people whose
taxes would have been raised, or receipts lowered, if the real value of the
debt had not fallen. But there is no way of knowing whose taxes would
have been raised or whose receipts lowered if the real value of the debt
had been higher.

But the difficulty of identifying debtors and creditors with specific
income classes does not mean that one cannot make a firm judgment about
the inflation-induced income redistribution. Suppose, for example, it were
somehow shown that creditor and debtor relationships cancel out *within*
each income class so that no income class gains or loses from inflation. One
could still argue that an unanticipated inflation has deleterious effects on
the income distribution. Economic justice involves more than justice
between income classes; it also relates to the distribution *within* each
income class. Unless one were disposed to argue that the distribution of
income and wealth within each income class is completely arbitrary and
has no justification, then a redistribution between creditors and debtors
within each income class creates inequities. Consider, for example, a pro-

posal to redistribute income within each income class by taxing those whose names begin with the letters A–M for the benefit of those whose last names start with N–Z. Such a proposal would be hard to justify. But does its equity really differ from a redistribution between creditors and debtors in the same income class?

Before leaving this topic of debtors and creditors it may be useful to warn the reader about two things. First, he should interpret the term "creditor" broadly in this context. Anyone who holds claims fixed in money terms in excess of such debts is a net creditor. It is not only the holders of IOUs, bonds and mortgages, but also the holders of money, time deposits, Savings and Loan shares, etc., who are creditors. Moreover, people who hold an equity in insurance policies or in corporate pension funds are also creditors. And while in recent years social security benefits have been adjusted in response to rising prices, this may not always be the case. Insofar as this is not done, anyone who expects to receive social security benefits stands to lose from inflation in this way. Since the elderly often receive a substantial part of their income from assets fixed in money term such as life insurance endowment policies or pension funds, it is not surprising that inflation has hurt the elderly disproportionately.

The second thing to keep in mind is that this discussion has dealt only with *un*anticipated inflation. If the inflation, and its magnitude, are correctly anticipated, then there is no redistribution between creditors and debtors. Instead, as described in Chapter 17, the money rate of interest rises so that the real rate of interest is unaffected.

Creditors are not the only ones whose money incomes do not adjust quickly to unanticipated inflation. Certain wages and salaries are sticky. This is perhaps more likely to be the case for salaries in the public than in the private sector. To be sure, eventually even these salaries are raised, but in the meantime their recipients suffer from inflation for several years.

Finally, there is one more important redistributional effect of inflation connected with government. If we had strictly proportional taxes, government revenues would rise proportionately to prices. If the prices of goods and services bought by the government rose in proportion to the general price level, real government revenues would then be constant. But, with our progressive *federal* tax system, this is not the case. As prices rise taxpayers with a rising money income and constant real income move into higher income tax brackets since these brackets are, of course, fixed in money terms. And, being in a higher tax bracket, they pay a higher proportion of their incomes in taxes. Hence inflation brings about a redistribution of income from the public to the federal government.

State and local governments, on the other hand, usually are hurt by inflation. They rely to a substantial extent on revenue from property taxes, and property tax assessments tend to lag behind the inflation.

Finally, before leaving the effects of inflation, it is worthwhile to consider briefly its effects on the balance of payments. An increase in the domestic price level lowers the *relative* prices of imports, and hence leads to an increase in imports. At the same time, increasing export prices are likely to cause a decline in the value of exports. (This effect need not happen; it depends upon the elasticity of foreign demand, but it is likely to take place.) As a result, inflation causes a deterioration of the current account. But, by the mechanism described in Chapter 17, inflation tends to raise the nominal rate of interest, and in this way to improve the capital account. (However, this effect may be counteracted, at least in part, by foreign long-term investors fearing that the inflation may lead to a devaluation. And such a fear may also stimulate foreign investment by residents.) All in all, it is generally believed that inflation causes a deterioration of the U. S. balance of payments.

CONCLUSION

The theories we have discussed are not the only explanations of inflation which have been given. But even so, the reader may feel bewildered by the multiplicity of the ones we have presented, and may well ask which is the true one. On this there is, of course, still substantial disagreement. But hopefully one can expect that time will reduce this disagreement. If prices continue to rise when there is substantial unemployment, it will become harder to defend a demand pull explanation; one can rely on the expectational argument for only a limited length of time. On the other hand, if future inflations occur only at a time of excessive demand, or for a limited time thereafter, then the cost push explanation will become less and less plausible.

QUESTIONS AND EXERCISES

1. "An anticipated inflation of even 100 percent per year is relatively harmless; an unanticipated inflation of 1 percent is more harmful." Discuss.

2. Suppose inflation has continued at a steady 10 percent rate for the last 10 years. (1) Write a brief essay justifying a policy of letting the inflation continue. (2) Now write a brief essay justifying a policy of terminating it.

3. It has frequently been argued that the best way of defeating inflation is to increase output. Discuss this argument.

4. Do you think that in the period 1968–1971 the U.S. suffered demand pull or cost push inflation? Use the *Economic Report of the President* as a source of data to support your conclusion.

5. "Our price indexes make no allowance for improvements in the quality of goods. If proper allowances were made for this, the apparent rate of price increase might easily be halved." Discuss. If this proposition were correct, would it be important? If so, in what contexts?

6. "Full employment and union wage bargaining inevitably entail wage inflation. One must go. The real question is which one." Discuss.

7. "Ultimately, unless the money supply is consistently increased, inflation of whatever kind must come to a stop." Do you agree?

8. "The rate of price increase depends crucially upon the rate of increase in productivity. This is what we should be worrying about, not the rate of wage increase." Discuss.

9. "The effect of a wages increase on prices is far less important than the effect of a price increase on wages." Is it?

10. "Inflations inevitably accelerate." Use the price data for various countries published by the International Monetary Fund in *International Financial Statistics* to discuss this contention.

11. "If the rate of change of wages depends upon the past behavior of prices as well as the percentage of unemployment, then, since this is certainly a cost element, the demand pull theory is refuted." Do you agree? Show how a demand pull theory can be formulated to take account of this relationship.

12. "What goes up usually comes down—a proposition which holds even for prices." What does the historical behavior of U.S. prices show?

13. "The historical record shows that the U.S. is immune from significant peacetime inflation." To what extent do the historical data bear this statement out? Do you think that it gives us an adequate guide to the future?

14. "Inflation is the scarecrow of modern times." Discuss.

15. "It is not union officials who push wage rates up; it is the employers who in their greed compete for labor." Discuss.

16. "More output has been wasted in attempts to moderate inflation than in any other single way." Examine this contention in the light of postwar experience.

17. Examine alternative definitions of cost push and demand pull inflation. Does your examination lead you to think that the concepts are either necessary or useful in discussing the process of rising prices? Give your reasons.

18. "A dollar of government demand is more inflationary than a dollar of private demand." Do you agree?

19. "Inflation in the postwar U.S. has been due to excessive government expenditures." Discuss using data given in the *Economic Report of the President*.

20. What do you think will happen to the price level over the next year? How about the next ten years? Give reasons for your answers.

21. Explain as carefully as you can just how a limitation of the money growth rate operates to limit inflation.

22. A study found that 53 percent of the rise in the U.S. wholesale price index in the period 1953–58 was accounted for by the rise in steel prices both directly and indirectly in the form of steel users passing on steel price increases. Does this mean we had cost push inflation in these years?

23. "While the Keynesian theory can 'live with' cost push inflation, the quantity theory can admit only demand pull inflation." Discuss.

SUGGESTED READING

W. Thorp and R. Quandt, *The New Inflation* (New York: McGraw-Hill Book Co., 1959).

R. Ball, *Inflation and the Theory of Money* (Chicago: Aldine Publishing Co., 1964).

M. Bronfenbrenner and F. Holtzman, "Survey of Inflation Theory," *American Economic Review,* Vol. LIII (September 1963), pp. 593–661. *Advanced reference.*

H. Johnson, "A Survey of Theories of Inflation," in *Essays in Monetary Economics* (Cambridge: Harvard Univ. Press, 1969), pp. 104–42.

F. Machlup, "Another View of Cost-Push and Demand-Pull Inflation," *Review of Economics and Statistics,* Vol. XLII (May 1960), pp. 125–39.

G. Ackley, "Administered Prices and the Inflationary Process," American Economic Association, *Papers and Proceedings,* Vol. XLIX (May 1959), pp. 419–430.

G. Ackley, *Macroeconomic Theory* (New York: Macmillan, 1961) Chap. 16.

G. Bach, *Inflation: Economics, Ethics and Politics* (Providence, R.I.: Brown University Press, 1958)

P. Cagan, "The Monetary Dynamics of Hyperinflation," in M. Friedman, ed., *Studies in the Quantity Theory of Money* (Chicago: Univ. of Chicago Press, 1956) Chap. 2. *Advanced reference.*

R. Selden, "Cost-Push vs. Demand-Pull Inflation, 1955–57," *Journal of Political Economy,* Vol. XLVII (February 1959), pp. 1–20. *Advanced reference.*

21

Economic Analysis and Economic Policy

IN CHAPTERS 1–20 of this book we have tried to do two things. The first is to show *how* economists seek to develop—and test—theories which explain the way the economic system operates. The second is to set out those parts of macroeconomic theory which, as the result of the work of many economists, now command general support. In short we have tried to display the methods and some of the results of positive economics.

Positive economics is concerned with popositions of the form *"if X occurs in a specified context q, then Z occurs."* In this chapter and the next we discuss economic policy. Policy recommendations are, of course, propositions about what the authorities, or some other body, *ought* to do. They are *normative propositions*. Each *normative proposition* concerning policy consists of three parts: first, a *value judgment* which defines the objectives considered to be desirable; second, a *theory or model* of how the economic system behaves; and third, a *recommended act of policy* which, if the model is correct, will in specified circumstances attain the desired objective. It follows from this that, in examining any policy recommendation, we need to ask three questions:

1) What model or theory of positive economics does it assume and what reasons are there for thinking this model to be tenable?

2) What value judgments underlie the recommendation?

3) Is the recommendation consistent with both the model and the desired objective? That is if we take the recommended action *and* the

353

model correctly specifies the working of the economic system *will* the recommendation ensure the desired result?

Strictly speaking all policy proposals should be set out so as to distinguish clearly the objective and the model and the reasons for thinking that the recommended course of action is consistent with both. Unfortunately they usually are not. One is constantly meeting statements of the kind "A tax increase would be economic folly" in which the whole process of reasoning supporting the recommendation (if there is one) has been, deliberately or inadvertently, suppressed. Occasionally the statement is put in a form in which it is alleged that (positive) economics *proves* a particular policy to be wrong. This is particularly often the case where a policy is highly controversial. For example, "Economics makes it clear that quantitative import restrictions are unsound" or "To impose price control at this time would be economic retrogression of the worst type." This kind of statement implies something which is obviously erroneous, for, as we well know, *positive economics* is simply concerned with the way in which the economic system will respond to a given stimulus. This is ultimately an issue which can be decided only by appeal to observation. In contrast we cannot tell whether the results of applying a particular stimulus are "sound" or "unsound," "progressive" or "retrogressive" by observation alone. To do this we must know the value judgments defining these terms. It follows that statements of the type quoted are either made in ignorance or with a deliberate intention to mislead. Whichever explanation of their origin is correct, they are plainly potentially dangerous and, as such, should be viewed with the deepest suspicion. As a preliminary test, whenever you meet one of them, you should immediately ask questions (1), (2), and (3) above.

Suppose we are confronted with a particular policy recommendation— let us say that in a given context *S* the President should take some action we will call *A* in order to achieve some objective we call *B*. We then ask:

if *A* is done in context *S*, will *B* follow?

This is an issue in positive economics. Suppose our knowledge of the working of the economic system leads us to feel confident that if *A* is done in context *S*, then *B* will follow. This does not end the matter. We must also ask:

4) What other results, apart from *B*, will follow from action *A*?

5) Are these other results desirable or undesirable in terms of the value judgment on the basis of which policy *A* was recommended?

Almost invariably these two questions will show that though policy *A* will produce result *B*, which is (by assumption) desirable, it will also produce results B_1, B_2, B_3 which, in terms of the original value judgment, are *not* desirable. This raises two further questions.

6) Is result *B* sufficient, in terms of the value judgment scale, to compensate for the disadvantages B_1, B_2, B_3?

This, of course, is ultimately a question of value judgments—not of positive economics.

7) Is there some other conceivable policy (say *A'*) which, while producing the desired result *B*, produces less of the undesirable results B_1, B_2, B_3?

This latter question, as the reader will recognize, is again a question of *positive economics*. What we are asking is, given our knowledge of the workings of the economic system, is there a more *efficient policy* than *A* for producing the desired result *B*.

To sum up the argument thus far, confronted with a policy recommendation, we must ask, first, will this policy, if carried out, produce the desired result; and second, if it will, is there a more *efficient* way of producing the desired result? Looked at in this light, a further conclusion of great importance emerges. This is:

All policy recommendations ultimately involve *quantitative,* not merely *qualitative,* estimates of their consequences.

To see this we merely have to extend our earlier example. Suppose policy *A* produces desirable result *B* and undesirable results B_1, B_2, B_3 and that policy *A'* produces desirable result *B* and undesirable results B_1, B_2, B_3. Assume that *B* is *defined* quantitatively—say an increase in the "trend" rate of growth in capacity output from 3 percent to 3¼ percent. Then both policies are equally efficient in producing *B*. We cannot, however, begin to estimate their *relative overall efficiencies* until we know the *extent* to which they generate the undesirable results B_1, B_2, B_3. To choose effectively between *A* and *A'* the President must be given a full, which means a quantitative, description of the results of each. Given this, then on the basis of his value scale—which will, in some degree, reflect the value scale of the electorate—the President can make a reasoned choice between *A* and *A'*.

What then is the role of *positive economic analysis* in relation to the formation of economic policy?

Given the objective of policy, positive economic analysis is concerned to specify, in quantitative terms, the full consequences of the various courses of action which will attain the desired objective.

As we have seen, an informed choice between alternative policies requires, strictly speaking, a quantitative statement of their results derived from a quantitatively estimated economic model. This explains why it is so difficult for economists to agree on policy matters even when they are agreed as to the objective at which policy is to be aimed. For, in the present state of economic knowledge, we simply do not know enough about the workings of the economic system to make, with a high degree of confidence, precise quantitative predictions about economic behavior and thus about the consequences of different policies. This does not make it less necessary to strive after precision. On the contrary it makes it more necessary. Where there can, legitimately, be differences in opinion as to how the economic system works, it is plainly a matter of the first importance to analyze, as precisely as possible, the nature of such differences. Indeed, only by doing this can a test designed to resolve the disagreement be specified.

GOALS OF MACROECONOMIC POLICY

The major goals of macroeconomic policy are the following:
1) full employment;
2) price stability;
3) balance of payments equilibrium;
4) minimum interference with resource allocation;
5) economic growth.

Each of these goals needs explaining. Full employment is desirable not only for its effects on the level of output, but also because unemployment, in and of itself, is a situation in which most people feel unhappy. In a production-oriented society such as ours, to be unemployed often means, rightly or wrongly, to feel useless. Yet we do not try to operate the economy at close to zero percent unemployment. As discussed in Chapter 15, some unemployment results from people looking for better jobs; from new entrants to the labor force not taking the first job they can locate, but looking for the type of job they feel entitled to; and from the numerous shifts in the demand for labor which occur all the time. Such frictional unemployment is quite consistent with our definition of full employment. In quantitative terms we usually define full employment as existing when only 4 percent or so of the labor force is unemployed. This is only a rough and ready definition; there is little that is scientific about it. In fact, we seem to have defined full employment as 4 percent unemployment, at least in part, because of an extraneous factor: the belief that if unemployment falls below 4 percent, prices will rise at an unacceptable rate. We therefore appear to have smuggled a trade-off between full employment and price stability into our definition of full employment. (This is a good example of how value judgments can creep into a definition.) It is worth noting in this connection that many other countries define full employment more stringently than we do (quite apart from differences in the actual figures resulting from differences in the way unemployment is measured.) The definition of full employment, the way we actually use the term, is perhaps as much a matter of political views as it is of economic analysis.

To some extent a similar statement can be made regarding price stability. It is also a matter of degree and of determining what is an acceptable standard. Few people would object to a price increase of, say, one-half of one percent per year, and again it is not clear where to draw the line. It probably depends on the extent of inflation the country has experienced in recent years; after, say, five years of 5 percent inflation, a 2 or 3 percent inflation would look like an acceptable degree of price stability.

A complication in deciding on the acceptable degree of inflation is the difficulty of measuring what is really happening to prices. Our measures of inflation—the various price indexes—are biased in an upward direction. One reason for this bias is that the indexes do not take sufficient account of quality changes. Some quality improvements can readily be measured and the indexes can be adjusted for them. But others are much more difficult to measure. For example, consider professional services, such as physician's services. As knowledge accumulates these services become more efficient; that is, an hour's service provides more benefit than it did before. But the statistician has no way of measuring this improvement. He is therefore forced to include in the index not the output, but input; that is, the cost of an hour's service, regardless of how efficient it is. (This bias is *one* reason why the service component of the consumer price index rises so much faster than do other components.)

But this problem is not confined to services; it exists for commodities too. For example, a detailed study of the automobile market showed that during the period 1954–60, while the consumer price index for autos rose by 11 percent, an index adjusted for quality changes actually fell.[1] A bias in the consumer price indexes results from the way new goods are introduced into it. This takes place only when the commodity has already come into fairly common usage. But by this time the sharp price declines which often occur early in a product's life cycle have been passed by. It is hard to say just how important these biases are.[2] It may be the case that they are so large that a 2 or 3 percent rise in the consumer price index really

1. Zwi Grilliches, "Hedonistic Price Indexes for Automobiles: An Econometric Analysis of Quality Change," in *The Price Statistics of the Federal Government* (New York: National Bureau of Economic Research, 1961), p. 187.

2. A rather dramatic illustration of how big these biases *could* be is to ask the following question: Suppose you were given the choice of receiving a gift of $500 of products from either the current Sears Roebuck catalogue, paying current prices, or from the 1940 catalogue paying 1940 prices. Which would you choose? If you prefer the current goods at current prices, then this would seem to suggest that there has been no inflation since 1940! However, there are several qualifications to this argument. First, suppose you were confronted with such a choice in a grocery store; you would clearly choose the 1940 opportunity. Second, the example is unfair because tastes have changed. The fact that a lady gets more utility currently from this season's dress than from a 1940 dress is not all due to "quality" improvements; in 1940 a lady would probably not have been willing to buy a 1971 dress even at 1940 prices.

implies stable rather than rising prices. However, it is certainly possible that the bias is actually much less important than this. Unfortunately statisticians have not been able to measure it adequately.

The third goal, balance of payments equilibrium, also presents serious measurement problems. One problem is that there are several different ways of defining what we mean by a surplus or deficit on the balance of payments. Should we count as a deficit only the increase in claims on the United States held by foreign monetary authorities, thus assuming that private holders of dollar claims hold them voluntarily, or should we include the increases in these private holdings in our definition of the deficit? Moreover, the relation between a deficit and disequilibrium is not clear. It is quite possible that balance of payments equilibrium for the United States does not mean a zero deficit, but a deficit of a billion dollars or so.[3]

In any case, from August to December, 1971, the United States operated on a system of floating exchange rates. This meant there was really no balance of payments restraint on U. S. domestic policies. Under such conditions a (potential) balance of payments "deficit" takes one of two forms. Either other countries allow their exchange rates to appreciate relative to the dollar so that foreign exchange markets clear via the price mechanism and there is no deficit, or else foreign countries simply accumulate the unwanted dollars. By the time you read this the United States may be back on a fixed exchange rate. In this case it is possible, but by no means necessarily the case, that prevention of large balance of payments deficits works as a major policy goal and as a restraint on expansionary policies called for by domestic conditions. (Since we do not know whether or not this will actually be the case, we will deemphasize the balance of payments goal in our discussion.)

The next goal, minimum interference with resource allocation, is even less clear-cut than are the other goals, in part because there is no feasible way of quantifying such interference. However, the desire not to interfere with resource allocation does operate as a very important restraint on macroeconomic policy.

The final goal is a high rate of economic growth. There is, of course, nowadays a great deal of dispute about the desirability of rapid economic growth. However, since policy makers do desire a high rate of growth, it must be listed among the goals of macroeconomic policy. In any case, to a considerable extent, economic growth is not an independent goal, because the government has few ways of aiming at economic growth directly. To a large extent, a high rate of economic growth is a by-product of full employ-

---

3. For a discussion of these issues see Richard Cooper, "The Balance of Payments in Review," *Journal of Political Economy*, Vol. 74 (August 1966), pp. 379–95, and C. P. Kindelberger, "Measuring Equilibrium in the Balance of Payments," *Journal of Political Economy*, Vol. 77 (November/December 1969), pp. 873–91.

ment and efficient resource allocation. This does not mean, however, that there exist *no* policies aimed specifically at a high growth rate. For example, a policy which increases investment rather than consumption will tend to raise the rate of economic growth, at least in the short run.

We therefore have five rather vague goals we wish to meet, and there is a genuine question whether these goals are compatible or conflicting. In addition, there is the question of whether we have enough policy tools to aim at all five goals at the same time. In principle, one can, at the *most,* meet as many independent goals as one has policy tools available.

Looking first at price stability and full employment, we see a potential for conflict between them. It may be necessary to sacrifice one to gain the other. One potential conflict may arise through the Phillips curve discussed in Chapter 15. If wages rise by more than productivity once the economy approaches full employment, then a hard choice between price stability and full employment may have to be made. To be sure, as pointed out in Chapter 15, some economists believe that such a choice is spurious—that, in the long run, inflation raises only wage demand and not employment. However, this view is still controversial, and, even if there is no trade-off in the long run, there certainly is a trade-off in the short run.

One way in which this short-run trade-off appears is through the uncertainty of national income forecasts. Given uncertain forecasts and some delay until stabilization policies have their effects on the economy, the policy-makers are sometimes in a situation where they don't know whether to prescribe for inflation or for unemployment. If they are very much more opposed to unemployment than to inflation, they will, when in doubt, apply expansionary policies. In some cases this will turn out to be the policy called for, but in many other cases it will lead to inflation. Conversely, a policy of avoiding inflation at all costs leads sometimes to policies which create substantial unemployment. Another way the short-run conflict appears is in a situation such as 1970–71 when prices were rising despite considerable unemployment. Since unemployment calls for policies which raise aggregate demand and inflation *per se* calls for a policy which reduces it, there is, at least in the short run, a genuine conflict between the two goals. In the longer run, however, there may be much less, if any, conflict between price stability and full employment. One reason for this is that, in the long run, the Phillips curve *may* be fixed in real terms; that is, inflation may simply result in a corresponding rise in the wage increases which correspond to each level of unemployment. Yet the natural level of unemployment *may* be so high as to be socially unacceptable. In this case structural changes in the economy are needed. The second reason is that inflation creates distortions which may make the subsequent recession worse. Hence, an inflationary policy *may* increase unemployment when one considers the whole cycle rather than just the expansion phase.

Turning to balance of payments equilibrium, there is a great potential of conflict with full employment. Rising income in the United States raises imports and reduces exports. Hence, policies which raise money income tend to create balance of payments deficits.[4] Fear of balance of payments deficits may limit a government in adopting full-employment policies. The conflict of the balance of payments objective and the price stability goal is less pronounced; in fact, these two goals are often complementary. The lower our rate of inflation, the more competitive are our products in foreign markets, and the less competitive are foreign goods in our markets. Hence, by curbing inflation, we improve our balance of payments. But this does not mean that price stability and balance of payments equilibrium are always complementary. For example, if we should have a balance of payments surplus (which is also a disequilibrium situation, albeit a "nice" one) correct balance of payments policy would call for inflation.

Optimum resource allocation conflicts in many ways with stabilization policies. In general, we are reluctant to adopt stabilization policies which disrupt the smooth functioning of some markets or change the distribution of income significantly. For example, there is much objection to high interest rates because they disrupt the mortgage market, even if overall stabilization policy calls for high interest rates. Similarly, fiscal policy might disturb resource allocation. For example, in a depression a public works program might be a good macroeconomic policy, but it might create excessive fluctuations in the demand for certain construction materials.[5] But there is also substantial complementarity between the resource allocation goal and the stabilization goal. As discussed in Chapter 20, inflation distorts resource allocation. If we stress the points of conflict in Chapter 23, this is because it is the conflicts, and not the complementarities, which create problems for stabilization policy.

If there are conflicts between the goals, then it is important to decide how much of one objective one should sacrifice to obtain more of the other. Such decisions involve not only positive economics, but also value judgments, and it would be inappropriate for us to make such judgments in a book on positive economics. However, leaving aside our own value judgments, it may be useful to describe the way the government has reacted to these conflicts in recent years. Before doing so, three qualifications should be mentioned. One is that the choices actually made were circumscribed by the actual problems. For example, we cannot tell from recent experience how the government would have reacted to a combination of

4. But, on the other hand, it has sometimes been argued that a high rate of growth in the United States helps our balance of payments because it fosters innovations.
5. See Julius Margolis, "Public Works and Economic Stability," *Journal of Political Economy*, Vol. 57 (August 1949), pp. 293–303.

8 percent unemployment plus 5 percent inflation. Fortunately, this situation never arose. Second, all we can observe is the actual behavior (and statements) of the government. We cannot tell to what extent a particular action reflects a value judgment and to what extent a positive judgment. Suppose, for example, that we observe the government adopting a highly restrictive policy because of inflation despite the presence of substantial unemployment. This could mean that it has made the value judgment that inflation is the greater evil, or it could mean that it believes that allowing the inflation to continue will not reduce unemployment. Third, there is the fact that the actions of the government have differed from time to time, partly as a result of political changes, and probably partly as a result of a learning process.

In general, it appears that, since World War II, the government has been more concerned about unemployment than about inflation, though this statement admittedly reflects the authors' judgment rather than verifiable data.[6] The extent to which the employment goal has received preference has varied among different administrations, and has also varied within the government. In general, the Council of Economic Advisers has placed relatively more stress on employment while the Federal Reserve has stressed price level stability more than the Council of Economic Advisers.

Balance of payments equilibrium has been given much less emphasis than unemployment or inflation. While, at times, monetary policy has been influenced by balance of payments considerations, stabilization policy, on the whole, has paid relatively little attention to the chronic balance of payments deficits we have experienced. It is therefore not surprising that, as of 1971, there have been six financial crises in the last three years, and we had to let the dollar float.

The importance placed on the next goal, optimal resource allocation, is hard to measure, in part because its influence consists primarily in preventing the adoption of certain stabilization policies which would otherwise have been adopted. However, resource allocation considerations have prevented many economists from supporting wage and price controls in periods of inflation, and have probably moderated the strength of monetary policies used to combat both inflations and, to a lesser extent, recessions.

It is difficult to describe the importance placed on the final goal, economic growth. This is so because there are few potential policies which favor economic growth as opposed to full employment, price stability, and optimal resource allocation. In general, policies which increase the rate of

---

6. However, it is indicative that the "charter" of stabilization policies, the Employment Act, does not mention price stability explicitly as a goal. Various attempts to amend it by adding an explicit price stabilization goal to its high employment goal have failed. (However, price stability is often taken as implied by it.)

economic growth are policies which also further one or more of the other goals.[7] Hence, there has been little opportunity for a clear trade-off between economic growth and the other goals to show up. And, further, since the effect of various policies on the *actual* rate of economic growth has often not been very clear, there has been a tendency to treat economic growth as just one of the factors which should be considered in choosing between, say, price stability and full employment.

So much for the various goals of stabilization policy. In the next chapter we will discuss the tools of stabilization policy and the way these tools operate. And in the final chapter we will take up the difficulties and problems faced by these policies.

QUESTIONS AND EXERCISES

1. Suppose there actually is a trade-off between inflation and unemployment. How much inflation would you be willing to accept to reduce the rate of unemployment from 7 percent down to 5 percent? How about from 4 percent to 3 percent? How great a cost in terms of unemployment would you be willing to accept to keep prices stable?

2. Suppose the unemployment compensation system were strengthened to pay each unemployed worker 75 percent of previous earnings for a three-year period. Would this change your answer to the previous question? If so, how? If not, why not?

3. It is sometimes argued that what seems like a high rate of unemployment is not really so bad because the unemployment rate is actually low for heads of families, much of the unemployment affecting teenagers and secondary earners. What value judgments are involved in this statement? What is your reaction?

4. Some people have argued that the government should see that there is enough aggregate demand to provide full employment at stable prices. If unions then push up wages, aggregate demand will be insufficient for full employment. But the resulting unemployment is then the fault of workers, and the government should not support the inflation by restoring full employment. What is your position?

5. "Unemployment is clearly a lesser evil than inflation. Sooner or later unemployment disappears on its own, but once the prive level rises, it will never come down again. If we have to choose between a temporary evil and a permanent one, we should clearly choose the temporary one." Discuss.

7. It is sometimes argued that creeping inflation raises the rate of economic growth. But there is considerable doubt that this is actually so, particularly in developed countries.

6. "In the postwar period unemployment has been a more serious problem than inflation." Discuss.

7. "Price stability is not the correct goal of stabilization policy. If prices are stable, fixed income groups do not share in the economy's increasing productivity. Instead of price stability, we should therefore aim at reducing prices as productivity increases." Discuss.

8. Suppose you were given a choice of foregoing all quality improvements (including new goods) for the next ten years in exchange for an increase in your income. How great an annual percentage increase in income would you need to make this choice attractive to you? What does this tell us about the definition of price stability? (To reduce the problem of changing tastes, assume that other people would make the same choice you do, so that you would not have to witness their use of new goods.)

9. What policies would you suggest for increasing the rate of economic growth?

10. List some potential stabilization policies which have not been adopted because of their deleterious effects on resource allocation. Are there any which you think should have been adopted anyway?

11. "Any attempt to increase the equality of the income distribution would, by slowing the rate of economic growth, do more harm than good. Indeed, there is a stronger case, if growth is a major objective, for increasing inequality." Analyze this from the point of view of (1) positive economics and (2) value judgments.

12. Give some reasons for thinking that inflation is favorable for economic growth. Then provide some reasons for thinking the opposite is the case.

SUGGESTED READING

R. Gordon, *Business Fluctuations* (New York: Harper and Row, 1961) Chap. 18.

A. Hart, P. Kenen, and A. Entine, *Money, Debt and Economic Activity* (Englewood Cliffs, N.J.: Prentice-Hall, 1969) Chap. 19.

J. Clark, *Guideposts in Time of Change* (New York: Harper and Row, 1951).

T. Scitovsky and A. Scitovsky, "Inflation vs. Unemployment: An Examination of their Effects," in Commission on Money and Credit, *Inflation, Growth and Employment* (Englewood Cliffs, N.J.: Prentice-Hall, 1964), pp. 429–70.

Commission on Money and Credit, *Money and Credit* (Englewood Cliffs, N.J.: Prentice-Hall, 1961) Chap. 2.

R. Mundell, "The Appropriate Use of Monetary and Fiscal Policy for Internal and External Stability," in International Monetary Fund, *Staff Papers,* Vol. 9 (March 1962), pp. 70–77.

22

Stabilization Policy: The Means

IN THE PREVIOUS CHAPTER we discussed the goals of stabilization policy. In this chapter we will look at the policies which are available for reaching the domestic stabilization goals, and the way in which they operate. The problems and difficulties which arise in the use of these policies will be postponed until the next chapter.

There are two major tools of domestic stabilization policy, *monetary policy* and *fiscal policy;* in addition, we will also discuss *incomes policy.* Monetary policy refers to changes in the quantity of money and in the rate of interest, fiscal policy to changes in government expenditures and taxation, and incomes policy to attempts to control income shares directly. Although these policies can be distinguished analytically, actual policies often combine both monetary and fiscal elements. For example, as the Treasury borrows to finance additional expenditures, the Federal Reserve may increase bank reserves, to prevent interest rates from rising.

MONETARY POLICY

Monetary policy is primarily the province of the Federal Reserve System. It has several tools for affecting the quantity of money and interest rates. The most important tool of the Federal Reserve is "open market operations." In open market operations the Federal Reserve buys or sells government securities. By bidding the prices of government securities up or down, the Federal Reserve can induce banks and others to buy or sell securities to it. When a bank sells securities to the Federal Reserve, it obtains an increase in its reserves and can therefore expand its loans and security holdings. And if someone other than a bank sells securities to the Federal Reserve, a similar thing occurs. The seller receives a check drawn on the Federal Reserve, and he deposits this check in his bank. As his bank clears this check through the Federal Reserve, its reserve account is credited. Conversely, in the same way, if the Federal Reserve sells securities, the reserve accounts of banks are debited regardless of whether these securities are bought by banks or by others.

The next tool is changes in the legally required reserve ratio. Within broad limits the Federal Reserve can change the proportion of deposits which member banks—that is, banks accounting for about 80 percent of all deposits—have to keep as reserves.[1] When the Federal Reserve lowers reserve requirements, banks can make loans and buy securities with some of the reserves which they previously had to keep immobilized (primarily in the form of book entries at the Federal Reserve). Moreover, any additional reserves the banks obtain can now support a larger volume of deposits. On the other hand, if the Federal Reserve raises reserve requirements, banks may be forced to use their excess reserves to meet these requirements, to borrow from the Federal Reserve, or perhaps even to run off some of their loans and sell some of their securities. Relatively small changes in reserve requirements have a big effect on the money stock. This is not only a source of strength but also a weakness of this method of changing the money supply. The reason it is a weakness is that the resulting change in the money stock may be much larger than is required. Hence, the Federal Reserve has been rather reluctant to change reserve requirements frequently. Instead it has relied much more on open market operations. Open market operations are more flexible than reserve requirement changes; they can be undertaken in very large or very small steps, and hence give the Federal Reserve more precise control over bank reserves than do reserve requirement changes.

Another tool the Federal Reserve has available is changes in the discount rate. This is the rate which the Federal Reserve charges when it makes loans or discounts notes. By raising the rate on these loans (which are normally available only to member banks), the Federal Reserve reduces the amount which member banks borrow. Conversely, by lowering the discount rate the Federal Reserve encourages banks to borrow. When banks borrow, total bank reserves are increased, and when banks reduce their outstanding loans, bank reserves fall. In addition, changes in the dis-

---

1. For banks in so-called reserve cities (i.e., financial centers), the Federal Reserve can set reserve requirements against demand deposits anywhere between 10 and 22 percent. For other banks, the limits are 7 and 14 percent. The time deposit limits applicable to all other member banks are 3 and 10 percent.

count rate have an effect on business expectations. They are frequently interpreted as a signal that the Federal Reserve wants interest rates to change. Since the Federal Reserve can follow up discount rate changes with more powerful open market operations, the money market may anticipate that interest rates in general will rise when the Federal Reserve raises the discount rate, or fall if the Federal Reserve lowers the discount rate. Interest rates are like most other prices: if there is reason to expect a change in the future, a change will occur right away as speculators enter the market. However, frequently the discount rate is changed merely to keep it in line with other interest rates in the market rather than in an effort to change other interest rates or to affect bank borrowing.

At present, though perhaps not for much longer, the Federal Reserve uses an additional tool of control. This is the ceiling it imposes on the rate of interest which member banks can pay on time deposits. (Other government agencies, the Federal Deposit Insurance Corporation and the Federal Savings and Loan Insurance Corporation, impose similar controls on non-member banks and on insured mutual savings banks and Savings and Loan Associations.) By keeping these ceilings low relative to what investors can earn on the securities market, the Federal Reserve can reduce the volume of time deposits the public keeps in banks, and hence the funds which banks have available for loans or investments.[2]

In addition to the above tools, the Federal Reserve also disposes of some minor tools. One is moral sausion and publicity. For example, the Federal Reserve can urge banks and businessmen in general to be more cautious. Or, conversely, it can suggest that the time is ripe for expansion. Another tool is direct action; that is, to bring pressure to bear on some banks which are behaving in an undesirable fashion. Finally, the Federal Reserve limits stock market speculation by setting minimum downpayments on security transactions.

The major impact of these tools operates through bank reserves. It is important to note that the Federal Reserve does not directly change the quantity of money itself. Instead, it changes bank reserves and relies upon commercial banks to change the volume of demand deposits, and hence the money stock, as their available reserves change.[3] The Federal Reserve can rely on banks to make more loans and deposits as they obtain addi-

2. If the public withdraws funds out of bank time deposits to buy securities, these funds are redeposited as demand deposits by the sellers of securities. Total deposits are therefore unchanged. But since reserve requirements are much higher for demand deposits than for time deposits, such a shift from time deposits to demand deposits raises required reserves so that banks have to use their excess reserves and even cut back on deposits.

3. Changes in the quantity of money are engineered only by changing the volume of bank deposits. The government does not try to increase or decrease the money stock by purposely changing the outstanding stock of currency. Instead it sells to the banks all the currency demanded. Since the amount of currency demanded depends upon the volume of demand deposits the public holds, the government can control the money stock (currency and demand deposits) by controlling the stock of demand deposits.

tional excess reserves, because this is the way for banks to maximize their earnings. As they make loans they give borrowers demand deposits, and, by a process with which you are presumably familiar, the money stock increases by a multiple of the initial increase in reserves. The multiple expansion which occurs should not be looked upon in a mechanical way as just the reciprocal of the required reserve ratio. It is not as simple as this. Banks may not want to expand fully to the limit of reserves, but may want to keep some excess reserves, or they may want to use some of their excess reserves to repay borrowings from the Federal Reserve. Moreover, the public reduces the bank reserves which are available for the expansion of demand deposits by drawing currency out of banks and by shifting funds into time deposits. As a result of these factors, the Federal Reserve does not know exactly by how much the money stock will change when it changes bank reserves. However, since factors such as the public's demand for currency and time deposits and the bank's demand for excess reserves can be measured fairly well, the Federal Reserve can predict the effect on the money stock of a change in reserves fairly well over a relatively long period, such as a calendar quarter. But on a week to week, or even month to month, basis, this is not so. On a weekly basis, changes in the money stock depend more on unpredictable actions of the banks and the public than on what the Federal Reserve does to bank reserves. Hence, while the Federal Reserve has ultimate control over the money stock, it is a control which has some "play" on it.

As for interest rates, the Federal Reserve affects them both directly and indirectly. When the Federal Reserve buys securities in the open market, it bids up security prices. In addition, there is a powerful indirect effect. Banks use the reserves they obtain from an open market purchase to buy securities and make loans, thus driving the rate of interest down further. The discount rate, as well, has both a direct effect (since the discount rate is competitive with other short-term rates) and an indirect effect (since it affects bank borrowing and hence bank lending as well as expectations). But, although the Federal Reserve has therefore some control over the interest rate, it is by no means clear how much this control actually amounts to. One very major limitation is that any reduction in the interest rate achieved by increasing the quantity of money (or any increase in interest rates resulting from a reduction in the money stock) is not lasting. As was discussed in Chapter 17, an increase in the quantity of money reduces the interest rate only temporarily; after a lag the rate of interest returns to its previous level. To be sure, the Federal Reserve could offset, or delay, this rise in the interest rate by increasing the quantity of money even more, but such action would be inflationary.

A second limitation on the Federal Reserve's control over interest rates is that the Federal Reserve operates largely on the short-term interest rate because in its open market operations it deals primarily in short-term securities. However, investment is mainly influenced by the long-term rather than the short-term rate of interest. To be sure, arbitrage in the money market transmits changes in the short-term interest rates to the long-term rate, but this transmission may be rather weak and subject to long delays. In addition, there is the fact that, at times, the Federal Reserve may be reluctant to lower the short-term rate of interest even though a lower rate of interest may be desirable for the domestic economy, because it would worsen the balance of payments deficit. Finally, if we should ever be in a situation of absolute liquidity preference, then, as pointed out in Chapter 12, the increases in the quantity of money could not lower the interest rate.

How important are these limitations of the Federal Reserve's control over the rate of interest? Economists differ on this issue. Some, in particular quantity theorists, would say that it does not matter. They argue that what is important is the change in the quantity of money and not the change in the observed market rates of interest. Keynesian economists, on the other hand, usually attach more importance to the rate of interest, and are often concerned about the imperfect transmission of interest rate changes from the short-term to the long-term interest rate.

Once interest rates change, there will be a change in expenditures and therefore in national income. We have already discussed the way expenditures change when interest rates vary, and we will now review this material and fill in some gaps.

In Chapters 10 and 11 we discussed the reasons why investment increases as the interest rate falls and talked briefly about the magnitude of this effect. At this point of the analysis it might be useful, however, to introduce two additional effects. One operates through the effect of changes in wealth on consumption, and the other works through the effect of changes in the liquidity of portfolios.

The first of these effects occurs because of the effect of interest rates on the public's stock of wealth. As explained above (see page 180), when interest rates rise, the value of outstanding securities falls. As interest rates rise, the public therefore suffers reduction in its wealth. Since, as we discussed in Chapter 9, the stock of wealth is one of the determinants of consumption, a rise in the interest rate is likely to reduce consumption even though the direct effect of the interest rate on the choice between present and current consumption *may* be insignificant. Conversely, a reduction in the interest results in an increase in the value of wealth—that is, in capital gains—and consumption rises.

The second effect operates more on firms, and particularly on financial institutions, rather than on households. This is the so-called locking-in effect. As interest rates rise and security prices fall, lenders may be able to maximize their returns by making loans at the higher interest rate even though they may have to sell securities at a loss to do so. But some lenders may be reluctant to do so. Rather than show a loss on their books, and thus admit that they made a mistake, they may hold on to securities, though they are foregoing some income by doing so. If this occurs on a large scale, then firms wishing to invest may be unable to obtain the wherewithal, and thus a rise in the interest rate, by discouraging lenders from lending, reduces investment.

In conclusion, let us look briefly at one major type of investment, residential construction, which is clearly influenced in a powerful manner by monetary conditions. A considerable amount of mortgage financing is done by mutual savings banks and Savings and Loan Associations. The interest rates which these institutions pay to savers are quite sticky. Hence, at a time when interest rates on open market securities, such as bonds, are rising, these institutions receive fewer deposits and are therefore limited in the mortgage loans they can make. In addition, since housing is long-term investment, a rise in interest rates can have a powerful effect on the cost of, and hence the demand for, housing.

AN ECONOMETRIC MODEL

It would be useful if one could go beyond the general qualitative considerations which have been adduced above and measure the effect of monetary policy quantitatively. One way of doing so would be to take each of the equations which have been formulated in previous chapters and to estimate the values of their parameters statistically. This can certainly be done, but, quite apart from certain statistical problems, such a piecemeal treatment suffers from the weakness that it leaves interactions and feedback effects out of account. For example, one of the previous equations tells us that if the quantity of money is increased, the rate of interest declines. But the decline in the rate of interest results in an increase in income, and the rise in income feeds back on the rate of interest, raising it again. Similarly, the rise in income results, via the accelerator, in a rise in investment, and this, in turn, raises income and interest rates further. To get a reliable estimate of the impact of monetary policy on income, one should try to capture these interaction effects and feedbacks. This can be done by solving the various equations simultaneously, using a so-called "econometric model." In recent years many such models have been constructed, and we will look briefly at one which has been prepared specifically to describe the impact of monetary policy changes. However, we have to warn the reader that econometric models are still in the early stages of development and suffer from many weaknesses. Hence, the specific results shown by the model discussed below should be treated as suggestive evidence rather than as a set of firmly established conclusions. There exist other econometric models which give different results.

Economists at the Federal Reserve and academic economists mainly at MIT have collaborated in constructing a model which looks at monetary factors in considerable detail. Figure 22.1 shows the flow chart of this model. The story starts with a change in the Aaa corporate rate; that is, the interest rate paid on long-term bonds by the soundest borrowers. As a result of this change, stock prices change too. Stocks provide their owners with a right to future dividend income. As interest rates rise, the present value of this future income stream declines. Put differently, to make people willing to hold stock when the yield on bonds rises, the yield on stock must rise too. Since dividend payments do not change, stock prices must fall until stock yields are back in their previous relation to the bond yield. This change in stock values, in turn, affects consumption and saving, because, as we discussed in Chapter 9, the stock of wealth is one of the determinants of the propensity to consume. The effect on income of the change in consumption is obvious; it is explained by the theory of the multiplier. But there is also an effect which operates through saving. A significant proportion of household saving lands up as deposits in mutual savings banks and in Savings and Loan Associations. Since these institutions make primarily mortgage loans, the change in saving affects residential construction. (To be sure, household saving also goes into other assets, but its effects on these other markets is not as important.)

Changes in the Aaa corporate bond rate affect mortgage rates more directly too because mortgages and corporate bonds are substitutes in the portfolios of some lenders, such as insurance companies. And the change in mortgage rates induced by a change in the corporate bond rate, in turn, changes housing starts and residential construction.

Aaa bonds and other corporate bonds, obviously, are substitutes too. Thus, a change in the Aaa rate changes the cost of borrowing also for corporations whose bonds are rated less highly than Aaa. As a result of this general change in interest rates, the *net* profit (quasi-rent) which firms can earn if they buy structures and equipment with borrowed funds changes. This, in turn, changes their desired capital-output ratio and hence their orders for new equipment.

Finally, there is investment by state and local governments. One of the determinants of such investment is the interest rate on state and local bonds, and this rate fluctuates with the Aaa corporate bond rate. (Federal government investment is assumed to be unaffected by the interest rates.)

Figure 22.1 / *Flow chart of first round effects of monetary policy:
Federal Reserve—MIT model.*

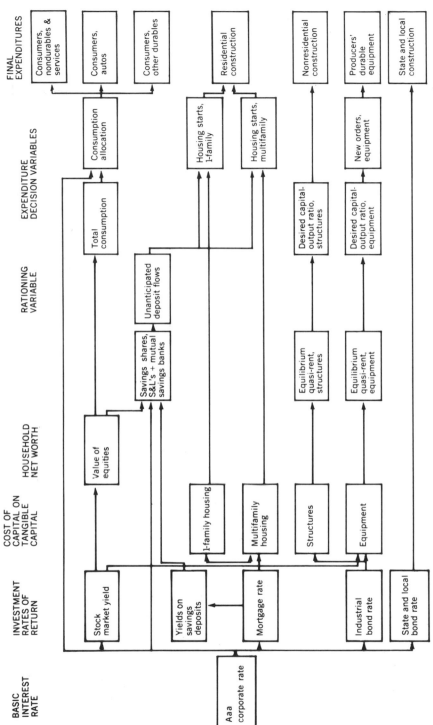

Source: F. de Leeuw and E. Gramlich, "The Channels of Monetary Policy," *Federal Reserve Bulletin*, Vol. 55 (June 1969), pp. 472–91.

The various equations of this model, and there are a large number, can be solved to measure the effects of a one billion dollar increase in "unborrowed reserves"—that is, bank reserves minus the amount which banks have borrowed from the Federal Reserve.[4] Since the economy is growing, the magnitude of the effect of a billion dollar unborrowed reserve injection will change over time. The figures which we will give here apply to conditions as of the first calendar quarter in 1964.

We will first look at the direct effects—that is, at the initial impact of a change in unborrowed reserves excluding multiplier effects, accelerator effects, etc. These direct effects operate through three channels: a cost of capital effect (an elaboration of the interest rate effect we discussed in earlier chapters), a wealth effect operating through the impact of changes in security values on consumption (discussed in the previous section), and an effect operating through credit rationing ("credit rating" effect).[5] Figure 22.2 and Table 22.1 show that the sum of these effects is fairly substantial. However, they take a long time to build up. Thus while the total effect after three calendar quarters is 3.5 billion, it is twice that after 16 quarters. (The implications of such a long lag will be discussed in the next chapter.) The lower part of Table 22.1 shows the percentage of the impact felt by each of the major sectors, as well as the relative importance of each channel. While the traditional cost of capital effect is the biggest one, the wealth effect is also very substantial.

Figure 22.2 and Table 22.1 show only the direct effects. Table 22.2, on the other hand, shows the full effects taking into account all the repercussions, such as accelerator effects, considered in the complete model. (In addition to monetary policy effects it also shows fiscal policy effects which will be discussed subsequently.) It shows monetary policy as having a substantial effect on various macroeconomic variables, real GNP, prices, interest rates, and unemployment. However, there are again long lags. While the peak impact on real GNP is reached in the tenth quarter, for prices the impact keeps rising for all the four years covered in the table. Monetary policy is, according to this model, a powerful but slow-acting tool. But once again we must warn the reader that other models give different results. For example, a monetarist model developed by the Federal Reserve Bank of St. Louis shows monetary policy to be much quicker-acting than this model does and fiscal policy to be virtually ineffective.

---

4. The version of the Federal Reserve-MIT model described here has 75 equations in addition to 35 identities. Seventy variables are assumed to be given exogenously.

5. The capital market is not a perfect one. Borrowers are limited in the amount they can borrow (if they can borrow at all) at the prevailing interest rate. As banks and other lenders pile up more loanable funds, they are willing to make loans they previously refused to make, so that there is less "rationing" of credit.

Figure 22.2 / *Direct effects on final demand of a billion-dollar step increase in unborrowed reserves (initial conditions of first quarter, 1964).*

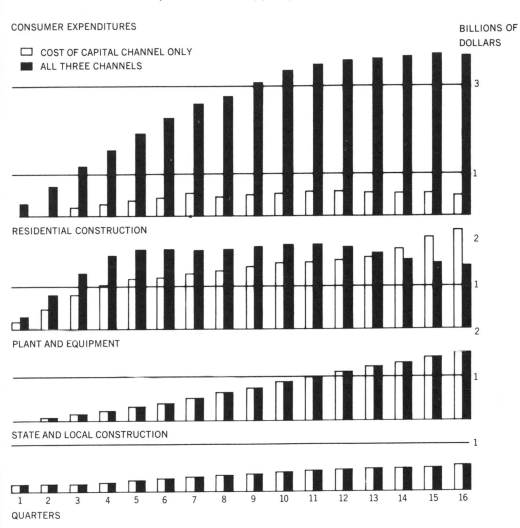

Source: Same as Fig. 22.1.

Table 22.1 / *Direct effects of a billion-dollar step increase in unborrowed reserves (initial conditions of first quarter 1964).*

a. Billions of Current Dollars

QUARTER	PERSONAL CONSUMPTION EXPENDITURES			RESIDENTIAL CONSTRUCTION EXPENDITURES			PLANT AND EQUIPMENT	STATE AND LOCAL CONSTRUCTION	TOTAL			
	COST OF CAPITAL	WEALTH	TOTAL	COST OF CAPITAL	CREDIT RATING	TOTAL	COST OF CAPITAL	COST OF CAPITAL	COST OF CAPITAL	WEALTH	CREDIT RATING	TOTAL
4	.3	1.2	1.5	1.0	.6	1.6	.2	.2	1.7	1.2	.6	3.5
8	.4	2.3	2.7	1.3	.5	1.8	.6	.3	2.6	2.3	.5	5.4
12	.5	3.0	3.5	1.5	.3	1.8	1.1	.4	3.5	3.0	.3	6.8
16	.4	3.2	3.6	2.2	-.8	1.4	1.5	.5	4.6	3.2	-.8	7.0

b. Percentages of Total Effect

QUARTER	RESIDENTIAL CONSTRUCTION	PLANT AND EQUIPMENT	STATE AND LOCAL	CHANNEL		
				COST OF CAPITAL	WEALTH	CREDIT RATIONING
4	45	6	6	49	34	17
8	33	11	6	48	43	9
12	26	16	7	51	44	5
16	20	21	8	66	45	-11

The results shown describe only the effect of unborrowed reserves in financial markets and, through financial markets, on final demand for goods and services. They do not include multiplier-accelerator interactions or feedbacks from goods markets to financial markets.

Source: Same as Fig. 22.1.

Table 22.2 / *Effects of three expansionary policies.*
Initial conditions of first quarter, 1964; in percentage points
unless otherwise indicated.

QUARTER	REAL GNP (BILLIONS OF 1958 DOLLARS)			GNP DEFLATOR			MONEY GNP (BILLIONS OF CURRENT DOLLARS)			CORPORATE Aaa BOND RATE			UNEMPLOYMENT RATE		
	A	B	C	A	B	C	A	B	C	A	B	C	A	B	C
1	.7	6.6	1.4	...	...	...	.8	7.3	1.6	−.27	.06	.03	...	−.2	...
2	2.0	8.3	2.9	...	...	...	2.3	9.4	3.4	−.14	.05	.02	−.1	−.5	−.2
3	3.6	8.7	3.6	.1	.2	.1	4.3	10.3	4.4	−.12	.05	.02	−.2	−.6	−.2
4	5.4	8.9	4.0	.1	.2	.1	6.6	11.2	5.2	−.16	.06	.03	−.3	−.6	−.3
5	7.0	9.0	4.5	.2	.4	.2	8.9	12.0	6.1	−.19	.08	.04	−.4	−.6	−.3
6	8.3	8.7	4.8	.3	.4	.2	11.1	12.4	6.8	−.22	.09	.05	−.5	−.6	−.3
7	9.3	8.0	5.0	.4	.6	.3	13.2	12.6	7.6	−.23	.10	.06	−.6	−.6	−.3
8	10.0	7.9	5.2	.6	.7	.4	15.1	13.5	8.5	−.24	.12	.07	−.6	−.6	−.3
9	10.4	7.6	5.3	.8	.9	.5	16.9	14.1	9.3	−.25	.14	.09	−.7	−.5	−.4
10	10.7	6.8	5.4	.9	1.0	.6	18.6	14.3	10.1	−.26	.16	.10	−.7	−.5	−.4
11	10.3	6.1	5.4	1.2	1.1	.7	19.9	14.5	10.9	−.24	.17	.12	−.7	−.4	−.4
12	9.4	5.6	5.2	1.4	1.3	.8	20.6	15.2	11.6	−.25	.19	.14	−.6	−.4	−.3
13	7.9	5.8	4.7	1.7	1.4	.9	20.6	16.5	11.8	−.25	.20	.14	−.6	−.4	−.3
14	6.1	6.2	3.9	1.9	1.6	1.1	20.1	18.2	11.7	−.23	.22	.15	−.5	−.4	−.3
15	3.9	5.7	2.8	2.1	1.8	1.2	19.0	18.8	11.3	−.23	.24	.16	−.3	−.4	−.2
16	1.4	5.0	1.6	2.2	1.9	1.2	17.2	19.2	10.6	−.23	.25	.18	−.2	−.3	−.2

A indicates step increase in unborrowed reserves of $1.0 billion; B indicates step increase in real Federal wage payments of $5.0 billion; and C indicates step decrease in personal tax rate of .02 (about $4.5 billion in revenue).
Source: Same as Fig. 22.2.

FISCAL POLICY

Our earlier discussion of fiscal action (Chapter 13) made it clear that there are four variables, with differing equilibrium multipliers, which the government may manipulate, namely:

$G \equiv$ government expenditure on goods and services;

$T \equiv$ receipts from direct taxes;

$R \equiv$ transfer payments;

$T_i \equiv$ receipts from indirect taxes.

We need, therefore, to discuss the consequences of adjusting each and to show how, given the properties of the dynamic multiplier, an appropriate adjustment of the chosen variable (or variables) will permit us to reach our target. Since, as we already know from Chapter 13, there are an infinite number of possible changes in *G*, *R*, *T*, and T_i which will enable us to reach our target, the example finally discussed is only an illustration; for the choices of variable to change must rest on criteria other than the manipulation of demand—and the systematic discussion of these would take us too far afield.

Fiscal policy has a reassuring *appearance* of precision. For most tax and expenditure programs the *direct* impact on income is easier to measure than it is for monetary policy. But it, too, is not obvious. Since what is legislated is a tax structure, *not* a quantity of tax receipts, the impact of, say, a reduction in the first bracket rate of income tax on tax receipts must depend on what happens to the level of national income and its distribution. Our problem, however, is to inquire into the consequence of a change in the tax structure *given* an unchanged level of income. In practice the government is usually able to make calculations of this kind with an acceptable degree of accuracy. Since much the same situation exists with regard to the main forms of transfer payments, we can assume that the government can calculate the consequences, given national income, for the variables *T* and *R*, of any proposed change in the legislation relating to tax rates or transfer rates. This is extremely important, for it means that if the government selects changes in *T* and *R* which are designed to influence consumption through changing personal disposable income, they are already freed from a form of uncertainty which afflicted monetary policy.

To see this consider an example. Suppose tax rates are lowered in such a way that, given the value of national income, the value of disposable personal income, at annual rates, will be raised by $1 billion (the amount that the direct tax bill falls). The consequences of this for demand now depend on two factors: (1) how quickly personal disposable income responds to the tax change which, with withholding, is very rapid; and (2) the dynamic multiplier process. In the alternative approach of monetary policy the government is unsure what response—and with what lags—the monetary variables would make to the instruments and what response, say, investment in fixed capital (and again what lags would be involved) would make to changes in the monetary variables. We may conclude that, provided direct tax and transfer changes are made with the object of influencing consumption through a function of the familiar form:

$$C_p = H + c(Y - D - T + R) + d \times r + e \times Q + f \times A,$$

the impact effect depends only on the marginal propensity to consume about which we know, or think we know, a good deal more than we do about the parameters involved in the monetary policy calculation.

Alternatively if the government decides to act through increasing government expenditure in real terms by a given amount, it can be reasonably confident (1) that its plans will be carried out (though the actual magnitude of the expenditure may well differ from the originally planned amount) and (2) of the directional impact of its additional expenditure. We may thus conclude that, insofar as the authorities choose to operate along these lines they have a greater measure of certainty about the outcome than in monetary policy cases. Moreover where the authorities choose to vary T and/or R they can make useful calculations of the social impact of their policies. Fiscal policy changes can then be used to bring about changes in income distribution which the government regards as desirable.

There are, however, two forms of fiscal action about which it is less easy to make quantitative calculations.

The first of this relates to official attempts to stimulate (or, more rarely, retard) private investment in fixed capital by improving depreciation rates. The income derived from any investment is subject to tax. However, the depreciation of the capital asset is an allowable tax deduction. Thus, given the interest rate, the present value of any capital asset is given by the sum of (1) the present value of the incomes expected over its lifetime *after tax,* and (2) the present value of the depreciation allowance tax offsets allowed over its life. Formally:

$$\text{Present value} + \frac{Q_1 + D_1}{1 + r} + \frac{Q_2 + D_2}{(1 + r)^2} + \cdots + \frac{Q_n + D_n}{(1 + r)^n}, \quad (22.1)$$

where $Q_1 \ldots Q_n$ are incomes *after* tax and $D_1 \ldots D_n$ are the depreciation tax concessions in year $1 \ldots n$.

For a given set of $Q_1 \ldots Q_n$ and a given interest rate, the present value of the capital asset can be increased (and hence its purchase made more attractive) in two ways. To see this we recall that if C is the cost of the asset then, in general, the rates of depreciation accepted for tax purposes satisfy the condition:

$$\sum_{i=1}^{i=n} D_i \equiv \text{sum of depreciation allowances} = C \quad (22.2)$$

To stimulate investment, therefore, the authorities, while maintaining this equality, can arrange for the bulk of the depreciation to be charged in the early years of life. The limiting case of this is when *all* depreciation is charged in the first year: that is, $D_1 = C$ and $D_2, D_3 \ldots Dn = 0$. The reader can easily satisfy himself, by a numerical example, that the earlier depreciation can be charged off, the higher, *ceteris paribus,* is the present value of the asset. Hence rapid amortization is a stimulus to investment—at least in principle.

Such a policy of rapid tax amortization has on several occasions been used in the United States. The effect upon private investment in fixed capital is believed by some to be considerable. However, the precise quantitative impact on investment of any given decrease in corporate tax revenue is hard to estimate. Moreover, because of the lags involved in the investment process, whatever response there is may take place slowly. This type of tax change has, therefore, many of the uncertainties of monetary policy.

The second form of tax change which is subject to uncertainties is the variation of rates of indirect taxes, such as excise taxes. Suppose that a federal sales tax of 10 percent is imposed. Then market prices are now 10 percent above factor cost from the identity:

$$\text{market price} \equiv \text{factor cost} + \text{indirect taxes}$$
$$\equiv \text{factor cost} + 10 \text{ percent factor cost}$$
$$\equiv \text{factor cost} \ [1 \times 10]$$

In money terms personal disposable income is unaltered. Hence real personal income has fallen by 10 percent. The consequence now depends, as before, on the marginal propensity to consume.

But we do not, at least at present, have a federal sales tax. Instead, we have excise taxes on just a few products. Hence an increase in excise tax rates raises the price of commodities which *are* taxed relative to those which are not. Insofar as the latter are substitutes for the former, consumers may avoid the tax by switching their purchases. The result could be simply to direct real expenditure from taxed to untaxed commodities without reducing the real demand for all commodities in the least. For example, if an excise tax is placed on silverplated flatware but not on stainless steel flatware, consumers might give up silverplated flatware in favor of the stainless steel. If they did so to a very large extent, the increase in tax revenue might be minuscule. Hence there would be no decrease in aggregate demand. Both for this reason and because of the relatively small role which indirect taxes play in the federal tax system, a countercyclical tax change is more likely to take the form of changes in personal and corporate income taxes.

When discussing monetary policy we had to look not only at its direct impact, but beyond that at its total impact. The same is true for fiscal policy. For example, a cut in personal income taxes raises consumption, and the rise in consumption, in turn, raises investment via the accelerator, and this induced increase in investment and in income then raises the rate of interest. This rise in the rate of interest reduces consumption and investment to some extent. When one includes these indirect effects in one's purview, then fiscal policy loses its simplicity and predictability. Nevertheless one can try to estimate the total effect of a given fiscal policy by use of econometric models such as the Federal Reserve-MIT model discussed in the previous section. Table 22.2 shows its estimate of the effects of two hypothetical fiscal policies. It shows that the two policies considered, a

$5 billion increase in federal wage payments (Policy B) and a decrease of 0.2 percent in the personal income tax rate (Policy C) have a substantial effect on real income, prices, interest rates, and employment.

Although the two policies involve roughly similar dollar amounts, the increase in expenditures has stronger effects than does the tax cut. This is not surprising; it is, in fact, what the balanced budget theorem discussed in Chapter 14 suggests. It is tempting to go on and to compare the strength of the two fiscal policies with that of the monetary policy (Policy A). But this temptation should be resisted because there is no simple way one can properly compare the size of monetary and fiscal policies. Is a $1 billion increase in unborrowed reserve a larger or a smaller policy than a $5 billion increase in Federal wage payments?

One thing which can be compared, however, is the lags of these policies. Table 22.2 shows that fiscal policy as well as monetary policy is subject to long lags. In the case of real GNP the expenditure policy has a much shorter lag than monetary policy while tax policy has a lag about equal to that of monetary policy. As far as money GNP is concerned, however, monetary policy and the tax cut have about equal lags, while the lag for our government expenditures is longer. In conclusion, we must repeat our earlier warning: the model described here, while an important model, is just one of several which have been constructed, and they do not all show the same results. For example, the monetarist model of the Federal Reserve Bank of St. Louis shows fiscal policy as having very little effect.

INCOMES POLICY

Monetary and fiscal policy are in a sense similar since they both operate by raising or lowering aggregate demand. On the whole, though, this is not true of some specific fiscal policies (such as excise taxes or particular public works projects); they concern themselves with national aggregates rather than with the behavior of specific industries. This approach of letting individual wage and price decisions be determined by market forces has obvious advantages. But these policies may fail because of a conflict among goals such as is illustrated by the Phillips curve on page 339 above. If an acceptable level of employment involves an unacceptable degree of inflation, then demand-oriented policies cannot succeed. Monetary and fiscal policies can raise demand, thus avoiding unemployment, or they can lower demand, thus sooner or later curbing inflation—but clearly they cannot both raise and lower demand at the same time.

The obvious solution for such a dilemma model is to introduce another policy, a policy which limits inflation as monetary and fiscal policies raise demand enough to provide full employment. One such policy is to change the way labor and product markets function. If inflation is due to cost push on the wage side, the answer would be to curb (eliminate?) unions; if the cost push results from uncompetitive pricing policies, the answer is to break up oligopolies and similar forms of market power.[6] These are not simple policies which a government can easily adopt and easily carry out without regard for their economic and social side effects! A less funda-mental policy therefore recommends itself. This is incomes policy.

Incomes policy consists of trying to limit wage and price increases as aggregate demand rises. It is really a broad label for a general type of policy rather than a specific policy. Thus incomes policy can take any of the following forms:

1) Moral suasion applied to wage and price decisions generally.

2) Moral suasion applied to specific wage and price actions.

3) Threats to punish specific industries or firms which are "out of line" such as freeing imports, shift in government purchases, release of materials from government stockpiles, antitrust investigations, etc.

4) The imposition of general guidelines which all firms and unions are supposed to follow. Such guidelines can be enforced by moral suasion or by threats as described in (3).

5) Requiring firms to notify the government, say, three months before raising prices. This allows time for moral suasion and, in addition, slows price increases.

6) Legally enforced wage and price controls. The rules may allow specified wage and price increases or may freeze nearly all prices.

Such policies have been used by many countries. In the United States we had price controls in World War I, World War II, the Korean War, and now (1971) we have them again. Moreover, from 1962–1968 we had a "guidelines" policy. This policy consisted of trying to limit wage increases to the average rate of increase in the economy's productivity. These wage guidelines were enforced by moral suasion; that is, by the President bring-ing unfavorable publicity to bear on wage settlements which exceeded the guideline. On the price side there was President Kennedy's angry confron-tation with the steel industry when, following a wage settlement reached under White House pressure, the steel industry raised prices by more than the President thought had been agreed to.

---

6. For reasons explained in Chapter 15, wages and prices may start to rise well before full employment is reached even if there is no *cost push* inflation. The organization of the labor market may make it profitable for firms to raise wages while there is still considerable unemployment. Such an interpretation of the coexistence of underemployment and inflation suggests policies for changing the organization of the labor market. They may range from such mild measures as keeping the U. S. Employment Service's offices open at night to much stronger policies such as requiring firms to list all their vacancies with the U. S. Employment Service.

This system of guidelines was eliminated in 1969, and from 1969 until August, 1971, the fight against inflation relied entirely on monetary and fiscal policies. But in August, 1971, prices and wages were frozen for three months, and at the end of these three months, a new system of price and wage controls was inaugurated.

The purpose of this system is to bring the inflation rate down to 2–3 percent at the same time as fiscal policy is eased to combat unemployment. Accordingly, wage increases are, with some specific exceptions, limited to 5½ percent per year.[7] Similarly, prices can be raised only if the firm's profit margin is below that of a base period. (This base period is two of the company's last three fiscal years prior to August, 1971.) And if prices are permitted to rise, they may do so only to the extent that predicted increases in productivity will not offset higher costs.

For prices the enforcement provisions are: firms with sales of over $100 million have generally to obtain prior approval before raising prices, companies with sales between $50–100 million must notify the Price Commission after they raise prices, and companies with sales of below $50 million are not required to notify the Price Commission, but their prices are spot checked.

In general, there are three steps in formulating incomes policy: (1) setting a target, (2) formulating specific rules to guide income growth in accordance with this target, and (3) establishing sanctions to enforce these rules.

The first of these, choosing the target, involves estimating (1) the growth in productivity and (2) the acceptable degree of inflation. Determining the acceptable degree of inflation involves many complex value judgments and is, in large part, a political problem.

Turning to the problem of estimating the increase in productivity, it is tempting to argue that one should calculate it for each industry separately, and allow wages to rise in accordance with productivity in each industry. But this is undesirable. Productivity as measured by our data refers to average productivity, but what should guide wages is marginal productivity. And there is little reason for thinking that average and marginal productivity always move together. An innovation which allows a firm to produce its output with only half its previous labor force raises average productivity but not necessarily marginal productivity. In such an industry, sometimes wages should fall rather than rise. If wages fall and the economy is reasonably competitive, prices will fall too, and hence the economy will now use more of the cheaper product. In addition, falling, or at least stable, wages give workers an incentive to move to other industries. On the other

---

7. However, this created a problem about catch-up raises and raises agreed to but not yet paid when wage controls were imposed. If such raises are allowed, the 5½ percent ceiling is breached significantly, and if they are denied there are obvious inequities.

hand, in industries with no productivity increases wages should, in many cases, rise as overall productivity increases in the economy. Otherwise those industries with no productivity increases would lose their labor force.

Thus wages should not necessarily change in accordance with productivity changes in each industry. A more acceptable rule, a rule which keeps the functional distribution of income stable, is that, on the average, wages should rise in accordance with the average increase in productivity for the whole economy. Under this rule nonwage incomes, profits plus interest and rent rise at the same rate.[8] Unfortunately, it is not easy to derive an operating rule from this general principle. One simple rule would seem to be to allow dividends to grow at the same rate as wages. But this is misleading. If corporate profits rise and dividend payments are limited, then the undistributed profits still belong to the corporation's stockholders. Instead of dividends, stockholders receive capital gains. Profits are the difference between costs and selling prices, and given the increase in wage costs, the two feasible ways of controlling after-tax profits are either to raise taxes or to control prices. The first of these alternatives means, in effect, either an excess profits tax (which is hard to administer and probably involves waste) or an across-the-board increase in corporate taxes which firms without abnormal profits consider to be inequitable. On the other hand, controlling prices involves many problems discussed above (see pp. 331–32).

The third component of incomes policy consists of sanctions used to enforce the income growth guidelines. There are several alternatives depending on the strength of the incomes policy as set out on page 380 above. One type of sanction consists of public exposure of the offending industry or union. The government can condemn a price increase or an excessive wage demand and, in this way, try to get the offender to change. Firms may be required to notify the government, say, three or six months in advance of a price increase; during this time the government may try to organize public opinion against the price increase. Obviously, "jawbone control" works better in a few highly visible industries such as the steel industry, for example, rather than in industries with widely diffused and less visible wage and price actions such as construction.

The government may go beyond jawbone control and use economic pressure on the offending industry. Thus the government may use its position as a major buyer of many products and as an important employer of

---

8. The fact that wages rise at the same rate as productivity does not mean that profits are constant and that all the benefit of increased productivity goes to labor. If prices are constant and wages (as well as rent and interest) rise by the same percent as productivity, then profits rise by this percentage too. For example, assume initially wages are 80 and profits 20. If output now increases from 100 to 110, and wages rise by 10 percent (i.e., from 80 to 88), profits rise from 20 to 22, that is, by 10 percent too.

labor. Moreover, the government has large strategic stockpiles of a number of products and can threaten to sell part of these stockpiles. In addition, an industry can be threatened with the loss of its protective tariff or import quota. Going beyond these measures, there is the possibility of price and wage controls discussed above (see pp. 331–32).

We will take up the disadvantages of incomes policy in the following chapter. But, even at this point, you will probably already realize that this policy is far from ideal. Unless actual controls over wages and prices are instituted, an incomes policy is rather weak. It *may* be strong enough to halt mild inflationary pressures or to terminate inflationary expectations which are not justified by the underlying events, but it is not likely to be effective in the face of strong inflationary pressures. As Professor Robert Solow wrote about the guidelines policy in 1966:

The wage-price guideposts, to the extent that they can be said to constitute a policy, are not the sort of policy you would invent if you were inventing policies from scratch. They are the type of policy you back into as you search for ways to protect an imperfect economy from the worst consequences of its imperfect behavior.[9]

QUESTIONS AND EXERCISES

1. "Everything we know suggests that the rate of interest is a pretty unimportant price." Do you agree? What are your reasons?

2. "Monetary policy works in subtle and mysterious ways." What are these ways?

3. "Very few businessmen say that their investment decisions are affected by the rate of interest. This shows that monetary policy is powerless." Discuss.

4. "An increase in the money supply raises the ratio of money to other assets in private portfolios. This makes the portfolios more liquid and so, even if wealth does not vary, raises spending." Discuss.

5. If the interest elasticity of U.S. investment is 0.2, what would be the approximate response (in dollar terms) of an increase in the interest rate from 4 to 5 percent? A fall from 10 to 9 percent?

6. Go back over this chapter and select two statements which seem to you the most dubious. Give your reasons.

9. "The Case against the Case against the Guideposts," in George P. Shultz and Robert Aliber (eds.), *Guidelines, Informal Controls and the Market Place* (Chicago: University of Chicago Press, 1966), p. 41.

7. Suppose you were offered a large grant to investigate the validity of the two propositions you selected in the previous question. How would you propose to set about it?

8. Use the data given in the *Economic Report of the President* to describe U. S. monetary policy in the last five years.

9. In the first half of 1970 interest rates were unusually high by historical standards, and, at the same time, the money stock was growing at an unusually fast rate. (1) How was this possible? (2) Would you refer to this period as one of tight money or easy money?

10. Consider the flow chart of the Federal Reserve-MIT model shown in Figure 22.1. Write out what you think three of the underlying equations look like. Can you think of some relationships which should be added? Write out equations for them. How would you decide whether these equations should be added?

11. How flexible is fiscal policy?

12. "To make fiscal policy effective we need to give the President authority to raise or lower taxes by 10 percent without congressional authorization." Do you think this is the case? Do you favor giving the President this authority? Why or why not?

13. Suppose it were shown conclusively that the income velocity of money is stable (and more predictable) than is the marginal propensity to consume. What would this imply about the relative effectiveness of monetary and fiscal policy?

14. Calculate the present value of the following two projects:

PROJECT 1		PROJECT 2	
INCOME BEFORE TAX	DEPRECIATION ALLOWANCE	INCOME BEFORE TAX	DEPRECIATION ALLOWANCE
500	100	500	300
400	100	400	100
300	100	300	75
300	100	300	20
300	100	300	5

Assume that the interest rate is 5 percent, the tax rate 50 percent.

15. How would you seek to estimate the effect on consumption of a 5 percent increase in taxes on cigarettes and tobacco?

16. Using the data to be found in the *Economic Report of the President,* describe U. S. fiscal policy in the last five years.

17. Do you think state and local governments should follow a countercyclical fiscal policy or should they try to balance their budgets every year?

18. "It is possible to develop incomes policies somewhere between the excessive rigidity of wage and price controls, on the one hand, and the rather feeble

Presidential exhortations on the other." Can you think of such schemes? Do you favor them?

19. Do you think wage and price guidelines are desirable at present? How about 1969–70?

SUGGESTED READING

See list at the end of the following chapter.

23

Stabilization Policy: Problems and Difficulties

READING IN THE previous chapter about the methods of economic stabilization, you may have wondered why we still suffer from fluctuations, since we have these methods available to us. Why don't we just use monetary and fiscal policy to eliminate fluctuations? The answer to this is twofold. First, these policies suffer from serious defects, which we will discuss in this chapter; and second, it is possible that we are, in fact, already eliminating much of the inherent instability of an uncontrolled economy by monetary and fiscal policy. It is possible that in the absence of stabilization policy we would experience considerably more severe fluctuations than we actually do. Whether or not this is the case is hard to say.

In this connection it is useful to distinguish between what, for want of better terms, we might call "active" and "passive" stabilization policies. Passive fiscal policy involves the change of neither tax *rates* nor government expenditure *programs*. Instead, it consists of relying on built-in *automatic stabilizers*. As pointed out in our discussion of inflation, the federal tax system is progressive. As a result, when income rises during the expansion phase of the cycle, tax revenues increase more than proportionately to the rise in income even with tax rates constant. Conversely, during a recession government revenues fall, and, in addition, certain government expenditures such as unemployment compensation payments rise automatically. As a result of these automatic stabilizers, the federal deficit increases (or surplus decreases) during a recession, while during the expansion the federal deficit decreases (or surplus increases). Since these automatic revenue and expenditure changes are very large, a substantial part of the original fluctuation in aggregate demand is absorbed by a change in the government's deficit or surplus and does not reduce the disposable income of the public.[1]

Monetary policy has something analogous to an automatic stabilizer. History suggests that if the Federal Deposit Insurance Corporation (FDIC) and the Federal Reserve did not exist, we would, from time to time, experience substantial bank failures and financial crises. Preventing these crises from happening—a sort of housekeeping function—already does much to stabilize the economy.

FISCAL AND MONETARY POLICIES

Although automatic stabilizers are an important part of stabilization policy in the broader sense of the term, let us now look at stabilization policy defined in a narrower way as *discretionary* policy—that is, changes in tax *rates* and expenditure *policies* (as distinct from changes in tax *yields* and expenditure levels resulting from income changes) and at changes in the quantity of money and interest rates. In the previous chapter, when discussing the methods of stabilization policies, it was these discretionary policies that we considered. To see what can go wrong with these policies, consider in general why someone may fail to do what he wants to. It may be because he wants to do two conflicting things at the same time, because he does not have the required means, or because he may not know how to use these means. Dividing the second of these two possibilities into two parts, we can set out the difficulties of stabilization policies under the following four headings:

1) Conflict of goals;

2) Inability to change the relevant variables sufficiently;

3) Inadequate strength of the variable;

4) Inability to determine the proper magnitude and timing of changes in the variable.

We have already discussed the first of these, the conflict of goals, in Chapter 21. If an income level high enough to insure full employment is

---

1. One estimate of the importance of automatic stabilizers for the period 1954–63 shows changes in federal tax collections and in unemployment compensation payments absorbing about one third of the swings in GNP (A. G. Hart, P. Kenen and A. Entine, *Money, Debt and Economic Activity* (Englewood Cliffs, N. J.: Prentice-Hall, 1969), p. 457. When one takes into account the lags in their indirect effects, it is possible that some automatic stabilizers actually destabilize rather than stabilize the economy. A recent study argued that this was the case for some Canadian automatic stabilizers. See John Helliwell and Fred Gorbet, "Assessing the Dynamic Efficiency of Automatic Stabilizers," *Journal of Political Economy*, Vol. 79 (July/August 1971), pp. 826–45.

also high enough to create inflation, then monetary and fiscal policy cannot insure both price level stability and full employment.

Next there is the inability to change the relevant variables sufficiently. In the previous chapter we described how the Federal Reserve can bring about a change in the money stock. One would think from this that the Federal Reserve would insure that it grows faster in a recession than it does in the expansion. But this is not the way the money stock has actually behaved. Just the opposite; it has tended to grow faster in the expansion phase than in the recession phase of the cycle.[2] One plausible way to explain this surprising fact is to argue that the Federal Reserve has been clumsy or that it has tried to stabilize the interest rate rather than the stock of money.[3] Another possible explanation—though a highly debatable one— is that it is not the fault of the Federal Reserve; that due to the wish of banks to hold varying amounts of excess reserves at different times, and due to leakages of demand deposits into currency and time deposits, the Federal Reserve is simply not able, in the short run, to make the money supply behave the way it wants to. A similar problem can arise with respect to interest rates. As pointed out above, if the Federal Reserve does engineer an increase in the money supply, this will reduce the rate of interest only temporarily, and even this temporary reduction will be primarily a reduction in the less important short-term rate rather than in the long-term rate.

One might think that this problem of inability to influence the strategic variables exists only for monetary policy and not for fiscal policy. But this is not quite the case. To be sure, in principle, the government can control government expenditures, to some extent at least. But it faces two difficulties. First, a large proportion of government expenditures are fixed in the sense of being payments which are unavoidable (e.g., interest on the national debt) or payments which could be reduced only by holding up ongoing construction programs or changing laws in a way which would offend powerful interests (e.g., veterans' benefits and agricultural subsidies). Second, sometimes government expenditures rise sharply because of some sudden need, such as a defense emergency. In other words, government

2. While this *pro*cyclical movement of the money growth rate seems shocking at first, it can be defended in several ways. One is to note that if commercial bank time deposits are included in the definition of money, the money stock no longer behaves procyclically. Second, insofar as there are long lags in the effects of monetary changes on income—a point discussed below—a fast growth rate of the money stock during the expansion, and a slower growth rate during the recession is not necessarily inconsistent with the changes in the money stock having a countercyclical effect on income. Third, there is the fact that correct stabilization policy does *not* necessarily call for reducing income during the expansion phase and increasing it during the recession phase, but rather for increasing income when it is too high and reducing it when it is too low—which is a different thing.

3. During the expansion phase interest rates tend to rise, and during the contraction phase of the cycle they tend to fall as business demands fewer funds for investment. A policy of stabilizing interest rates therefore requires increasing the money stock more during an expansion than during a recession.

expenditures are not a plastic tool in the hands of economic stabilizers; instead they have a life of their own.

To be sure, the difficulty of changing the level of government expenditures in accordance with stabilization needs does not, in principle, prevent a countercyclical fiscal policy. One could always vary tax rates sufficiently to create deficits or surpluses—whichever stabilization policy calls for. But, in actuality, changing tax rates, particularly increasing them, is frequently not possible for political reasons. And sneering references to politicians will not change matters, especially when one dwells upon the fact that a substantial majority of the public may be opposed to raising tax rates.

The next potential difficulty is that the policy tool used may not have a strong enough effect on aggregate demand. This was widely believed to be true for monetary policy until some years ago when the revival of the quantity theory and the emergence of new statistical results caused many American economists to reevaluate their views on the strength of monetary policy. In previous chapters we have already discussed the strength of monetary policy. However, one additional point should be made. This is the argument that, in principle, monetary policy *must* be strong enough to change income to the required extent. One can always subject the economy to such a large dose of monetary expansion or contraction that income changes by the desired amount, even though each dollar of additional bank reserves pumped into or out of the banking system has little effect on income. While this argument does make a useful point, there are two qualifications. First, there are limits to strength of a tight money policy set by public concern about rising interest rates, and about the severe impact of monetary policy on the construction industry. As Table 22.2 shows, the impact of monetary policy is not even. Some industries, such as construction, are hit much harder than others, and, rightly or wrongly, concern about the burden tight money creates for construction is likely to limit the magnitude of a tight money policy. This problem does not exist for an easy money policy, but here it is at least conceivable that absolute liquidity preference might make a very large easy money policy ineffective.

The problem of inadequate strength generally does not arise for fiscal policy. Very substantial changes in disposable income can be produced by changing tax rates. Similarly, with government expenditures being as large as they are, big changes in aggregate demand can be obtained by reasonable percentage changes in government expenditures. Admittedly, however, the will to bring about sufficiently big changes may not be there, particularly if it is a matter of raising taxes or cutting back expenditures. In fact, one might argue that the same thing applies to fiscal policy as applies to monetary policy; in principle, powerful effects can be obtained by taking very strong actions, but in both cases the undesired side effects of strong actions make the government unwilling to take them. To say that in the case of monetary policy the unwillingness to take strong (contractionary) actions is due to fear of hurting some sectors (such as construction) too hard, while in the case of fiscal policy it is due to "political" factors, may not really be fair, because the fear of hurting some sectors too much is also, in some sense, a "political" decision.

The next problem facing stabilization policy is to determine the proper magnitude and timing. To appreciate this problem it is necessary to keep in mind that there are lags in the effects of stabilization policy. One type of lag, the so-called "inside lag," arises because (1) it takes some time before the government realizes income has changed—the available data being a few months out of date—and (2) additional time may be required for the government to take action. (However, if the government uses an econometric model, or some other ways to forecast, this inside lag may be negative.)

Second, there is the "outside lag"—that is, the lag between the taking of action and the effect of this action on aggregate demand. For example, suppose taxes are cut. Disposable income is increased, and as a result consumption increases. But this increase does not occur right away. While consumption may increase to a small extent as soon as disposable income increases, much of the increase may come with a delay. Or suppose the quantity of money is increased. It takes time until investment plans are drawn up and acted upon, and until consumer credit is eased. Again, it may take a substantial amount of time until, say 50 percent of the effect of the new monetary policy are felt. A similar point applies in the case of government expenditures.

The existence of a significant lag means that stabilization policy is necessarily based on *some* sort of a forecast. Such a forecast may amount to no more than assuming that current conditions will continue, but this is a forecast too. Moreover, in addition to predicting the course of income in the absence of stabilization policy, it is also necessary to predict what a stabilization policy itself will do to income; that is, to predict the timing and the magnitude of its impact.

If we know (1) the future behavior of income in the absence of policy action, (2) the change in income per million dollars change in government expenditures, taxes, or the money stock, and (3) when this impact will occur, then we are in a position to operate an effective stabilization policy. We then simply select a desired level of national income and institute a stabilization policy which, when one includes its repercussions (such as the multiplier and accelerator), is just large enough to make up the difference between the desired level of income and the one predicted in the absence of this policy. But suppose we do not have the required knowledge or, more precisely, that our estimates of the above three magnitudes (the course of income in the absence of policy, the magnitude of the impact of the policy, and its timing) are subject to considerable error. In this case—which is unfortunately the realistic one—stabilization policy *may* destabilize, rather than stabilize, the economy. In stabilization policy, as elsewhere, good intentions are not enough. For example, assume that we forecast a recession when actually inflation is in the offing. If we then try to offset this predicted recession by adopting an expansionary policy, we make the inflation worse. Similarly, if we act on a prediction of inflation when the economy is actually going into a recession, stabilization policy will only make the recession worse. Moreover, if we err in predicting the strength of the impact of our stabilization policy, we may adopt a policy which is too weak or too strong, and in the latter case it may well destabilize, rather than stabilize, income.

Finally, suppose we predict accurately income in the absence of stabilization policy, as well as the strength of the stabilization policy; the policy may still be destabilizing if its timing is wrong. Suppose, for example, that during a recession expansionary monetary and fiscal policies are adopted, and that while these policies have a small proportion of their effect on income within a few months, most of the effect takes, say, a year to occur. By that time the economy may be facing inflation rather than unemployment. The expansionary policies then make this inflation worse. So now contractive policies are adopted and these policies too take a long time to have most of their impact, so that by the time they do the problem is again unemployment rather than inflation. Figure 23.1 below illustrates this "stabi-

Figure 23.1 / *Effects of badly timed stabilization policy.*

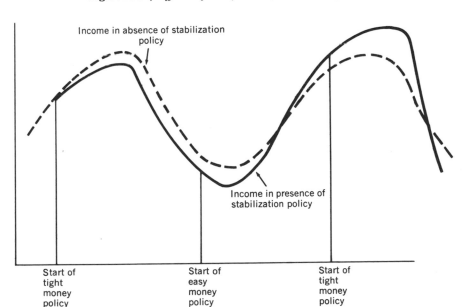

lizer's nightmare." The problem of inappropriate policies is serious enough to deserve more extensive treatment. However, since this requires some knowledge of statistical techniques, we have segregated it into an appendix to this chapter. This appendix shows how our degree of ignorance about the relevant variables limits the proportion of the fluctuation in income which stabilization policy should try to offset.

How serious is the danger that a stabilization policy actually destabilizes the economy? To get some understanding of this possibility, let us look at what we know about each of the strategic variables listed above. The first of these is our ability to forecast income. Here the picture is mixed. While some of our econometric models do forecast fairly well, the errors of these forecasts are by no means insignificant. Second, there is the magnitude of the income change resulting from a given monetary or fiscal policy. About this there is considerable dispute. Quantity theorists argue that we can predict the effect of a change in the money stock fairly well (and that it is large) while Keynesians would generally dispute this. Conversely, Keynesians argue that we predict the effect of fiscal policy accurately, (and that it is large) while quantity theorists are skeptical.

Third, there is the length of the lag. Here too, there is very substantial disagreement, though on this issue economists do not divide up along Keynesian and monetarist lines. In the previous chapter we showed the lags implied by the Federal Reserve-MIT model for three policies: (1) increasing unborrowed reserves, (2) raising federal wage payments, and (3) lowering taxes. For all three policies the lag was very long. And for a fourth type of policy, public works expenditure, the lag is presumably even longer since most construction projects are slow to get going. Moreover, the lags shown in Table 22.2 are only the outside lags, and one should add to them the inside lags. While, as pointed out above, the inside lag *may* be negative for monetary policy, for fiscal policy it may be very long. Congress sometimes—though by no means always—has been very slow to change fiscal policy. Once again, however, we must warn the reader that some other studies disagree with the results of the Federal Reserve-MIT model; some of them have found much shorter outside lags. But, in any case, quite apart from the average length of the lag, what is also important is its variability. It does little good to know that the *average* lag is, say, a year, when for any *particular* policy being considered the actual lag may vary from, say, three months to two years. Unfortunately, very little is known about the variability of the lag; while there are some data which suggest that, at least for monetary policy, it is substantial, we do not know what factors explain its variability.

Given these uncertainties, one cannot dismiss out of hand the possibility that stabilization policy *may* actually be destabilizing. What does this imply for policy? One possible answer is to say that while we cannot be certain that stabilization policy is actually stabilizing, we can presume (or hope?) that this is the case, and hence we should use stabilization policy. A second possible answer is to say that, given our present institutions and state of knowledge, we should not attempt to use countercyclical stabilization policy at all. Instead we should do the following: for fiscal policy we should set tax rates so that at high levels of employment the budget is balanced. If unemployment develops, the automatic stabilizers discussed above will insure that a deficit occurs on its own, while during periods of excessive demand there will be an automatic surplus. Such a policy of balancing the full employment budget, rather than the regular budget, ameliorates economic fluctuations, but it still leaves a substantial part of the fluctuation in the economy. For monetary policy the corresponding rule is to increase the money supply at a steady rate—say, 4 or 5 percent a year—regardless of economic conditions. While such a monetary policy does not offset business cycles, at least it does not make them worse.

A third policy is possible, one in between these two policies. This is to use countercyclical monetary and fiscal policy only on a moderate scale. One example would be to increase bank reserves somewhat more in a recession than in an expansion but to keep the growth rate of the money stock between, say, 3 and 6 percent.

APPENDIX: A METHOD OF JUDGING STABILIZATION EFFECTS[1]

One way of looking at the stabilization problem is to take the average income level as equal to the desired income level and then to treat deviations above and below this average income level as fluctuations which are to be minimized. Let us treat deviations of equal magnitude above and below the average income line as equally undesirable—in other words, we treat a dollar of above average demand as just as bad as a dollar of below average demand. Furthermore, let the disadvantage of a given deviation from the average income be proportional, not to the magnitude of the deviation, but to its square; for example, a twenty-billion-dollar deviation is four times as bad as a ten-billion-dollar deviation.

Keeping these assumptions in mind, one can measure the deviation of actual from average income by the variance.[2] We can treat the fluctuations in income in the absence of policy as one variance and can treat the changes

1. This discussion is a summary of Milton Friedman, "The Effects of a Full Employment Policy on Economic Stabilization: A Formal Analysis," reprinted in his *Essays in Positive Economics* (Chicago: University of Chicago Press, 1953), pp. 117–32. This is not the only existing formalization of the problem, but it is the simplest.
2. The variance is the square of the standard deviation.

in income induced by the stabilization policy as a second, we hope offsetting, variance. To find the fluctuation in income which persists if we use stabilization policy, we add the two variances.

The equation for the sum of two variances is

$$\sigma_{1+2}^2 = \sigma_1^2 + \sigma_2^2 + 2R_{1\,.\,2}\sigma_1\sigma_2.$$

Note that this equation has a term (R) for the correlation coefficient between the two variances. To see this in its present context, consider first the case where the stabilization policy is perfectly timed, filling in the valleys of below average demand and reducing the peaks of above average demand. In this case the correlation between σ_1, the original fluctuations of income, and σ_2, the fluctuation in income induced by the stabilization policy, is -1.0, and the fluctuation in income is completely eliminated. But if the correlation coefficient is positive—that is, if stabilization policy tends to raise income at a time when income is already high, and lower it when income is already low—then the stabilization policy increases the instability of the economy.

What is important to notice is that, as can be seen from the above equation, the stabilization policy can be destabilizing even if the correlation is not positive. For example, if it is zero, any stabilization policy greater than zero (that is, $\sigma_2 > 0$) is destabilizing. Similarly, suppose a strong stabilization policy is adopted, one which changes income by as much as the original variance, so that σ_2 is set equal to σ_1. In this case, if the correlation coefficient is (algebraically) less than -0.5, the policy will be destabilizing. As a general rule, the stronger the policy, the higher must be the negative correlation between the policy and the fluctuations in income if one is to avoid destabilizing the economy.

QUESTIONS AND EXERCISES

1. Suppose you wanted to measure the lag in the effects of monetary policy. Can you suggest some ways of doing so?

2. What factors account for the lag in fiscal policy?

3. Make a list of automatic stabilizers. Can you suggest some additional automatic stabilizers we could introduce? Can you think of measures to increase the degree of automatic stabilization in the economy?

4. In view of the problems discussed in this chapter, do you think discretionary stabilization policy can be effective? Explain.

5. Write a memorandum for the Federal Reserve Board of Governors setting forth the monetary policy they should follow for the next three months. Write a similar memorandum on fiscal policy.

6. "The trouble with monetary policy is not that it is too weak, but rather that it is too strong." Discuss.

7. "Fiscal policy has a great advantage over monetary policy. Fiscal policy allows us to aim changes in income directly to where they are needed while monetary policy changes aggregate demand across the board." Discuss.

8. Looking back over the last ten years, do you think fiscal policy has been stabilizing or destabilizing? How about monetary policy?

9. "There is great hostility toward incomes policy because this policy explicitly sets limits to income claims. Monetary and fiscal policy limit these claims implicitly. In a democracy policies should be explicit, and hence incomes policy is to be preferred to fiscal and monetary policies." Discuss.

10. Write an essay either defending or criticizing the use of incomes policy.

11. "Unemployment is the only really effective incomes policy we have." Discuss.

SUGGESTED READING

A. Hart, P. Kenen, and A. Entine, *Money, Debt and Economic Activity* (Englewood Cliffs, N.J.: Prentice-Hall, 1969) Chaps. 19, 22, 23.

M. Evans, *Macroeconomic Activity* (New York: Harper and Row, 1969) Part III. *Advanced reference.*

J. Tinbergen, *Economic Policy: Principles and Designs* (Amsterdam: North Holland Publishing Co., 1956) Chaps. 1–3.

D. Suits, "Forecasting with an Econometric Model," *American Economic Review,* Vol. LII (March 1962), pp. 104–132.

M. Friedman, *Essays in Positive Economics* (Chicago: Univ. of Chicago Press 1953) Chaps. 3–4.

M. Friedman, *A Program for Monetary Stability* (New York: Fordham University Press, 1959) Chap. 4.

D. Wrightsman, *Monetary Theory and Policy* (New York: The Free Press, 1971) Part 3.

T. Mayer, *Monetary Policy in the United States* (New York: Random House, 1968).

F. de Leeuw and E. Gramlich, "The Channels of Monetary Policy," *Federal Reserve Bulletin,* Vol. LV (June 1969), pp. 472–91.

F. de Leeuw and E. Gramlich, "The Channels of Monetary Policy: A Further Report on the Federal Reserve-MIT Model," *Journal of Finance,* Vol. XXIV (May 1969), pp. 265–90.

L. Anderson and J. Jordan, "Monetary and Fiscal Actions: A Test of Their Relative Importance in Economic Stabilization," Federal Reserve Bank of St. Louis, *Review,* November 1968, pp. 11–24. *Advanced reference.*

E. Gramlich, "The Usefulness of Monetary and Fiscal Policy as Discretionary Stabilization Tools," *Journal of Money, Banking and Credit,* Vol. III (May 1971) Pt. 2, pp. 506–32.

American Economic Association, *Readings in Fiscal Policy* (Homewood, Ill.: Irwin Publishing Company, 1955) Chaps. 17, 25, 27, 30, 31.

C. Shoup, "Debt Financing and Future Generations," *Economic Journal,* Vol. LXXII (December 1962), pp. 887–98.

C. Shoup, *Public Finance* (Chicago: Aldine, 1969) Chaps. 19, 22.

A. Packer, "The Two-Way Relationship between the Budget and Economic Variables," American Economic Association, *Papers and Proceedings,* Vol. LXI (May 1971), pp. 139–49.

G. Shultz and R. Aliber, eds., *Guidelines, Informal Controls and the Market Place* (Chicago: University of Chicago Press, 1966), pp. 1–78 and 97–141.

Index